Promoting Psychological Well-Being in Children and Families

Promoting Psychological Well-Being in Children and Families

Edited by

Bruce Kirkcaldy
Director, International Centre for the Study of Occupational and Mental Health, Düsseldorf, Germany

Editorial matter, introduction and selection © Bruce Kirkcaldy 2015
Individual chapters © Respective authors 2015

All rights reserved. No reproduction, copy or transmission of this publication may be made without written permission.

No portion of this publication may be reproduced, copied or transmitted save with written permission or in accordance with the provisions of the Copyright, Designs and Patents Act 1988, or under the terms of any licence permitting limited copying issued by the Copyright Licensing Agency, Saffron House, 6–10 Kirby Street, London EC1N 8TS.

Any person who does any unauthorized act in relation to this publication may be liable to criminal prosecution and civil claims for damages.

The authors have asserted their rights to be identified as the authors of this work in accordance with the Copyright, Designs and Patents Act 1988.

First published 2015 by
PALGRAVE MACMILLAN

Palgrave Macmillan in the UK is an imprint of Macmillan Publishers Limited, registered in England, company number 785998, of Houndmills, Basingstoke, Hampshire RG21 6XS.

Palgrave Macmillan in the US is a division of St Martin's Press LLC,
175 Fifth Avenue, New York, NY 10010.

Palgrave Macmillan is the global academic imprint of the above companies and has companies and representatives throughout the world.

Palgrave® and Macmillan® are registered trademarks in the United States, the United Kingdom, Europe and other countries.

ISBN 978–1–137–47995–2

This book is printed on paper suitable for recycling and made from fully managed and sustained forest sources. Logging, pulping and manufacturing processes are expected to conform to the environmental regulations of the country of origin.

A catalogue record for this book is available from the British Library.

A catalog record for this book is available from the Library of Congress.

Contents

List of Figures and Tables   vii

Notes on Contributors   viii

1. Introduction – Enhancing Mental Health and Psychological Well-Being   1
   Bruce Kirkcaldy

2. Lay People's Knowledge of Mental and Physical Illness   14
   Adrian Furnham and Bruce Kirkcaldy

3. A Paradigm Shift: Social Functioning Rather Than Symptom Reduction   33
   Ahmed Hankir and Dinesh Bhugra

4. Mental Health Promotion in School: An Integrated, School-Based, Whole School   52
   Carmel Cefai and Valeria Cavioni

5. Understanding and Overcoming Guilt, Shame, and Anxiety: Based on the Theory of Negative Legacy Emotions   68
   Peter R. Breggin

6. Understanding and Enhancing the Subjective Well-Being of Children   81
   Mark D. Holder and Robyn L. Weninger

7. Using Acceptance and Commitment Therapy to Help Young People Develop and Grow to Their Full Potential   102
   Louise Hayes and Joseph Ciarrochi

8. Child Well-Being: Indicators and Measurement   123
   Axel Schölmerich, Alexandru Agache, and Birgit Leyendecker

9. Child Mental Health and Risk Behaviour Over Time   135
   Kathleen Ares, Lisa M. Kuhns, Nisha Dogra, and Niranjan Karnik

10. Psychosocial Factors and Suicidal Behaviour in Adolescents   154
    Alexander-Stamatios Antoniou, Eftychia Mitsopoulou, and George P. Chrousos

11 It Takes a Global Village: Internet-Delivered Interventions
    Supporting Children and Their Families   172
    Nicole Pugh, Kathy Chan, and Christine Korol

12 Becoming Invisible: The Effect of Triangulation on Children's
    Well-Being   187
    Rudi Dallos

13 Special Education in the Complex Institutional Environment
    of Health Care and Social Work – Structural Frame and
    Empirical Reality   208
    Peter Nenniger and Mathias Mejeh

14 Parental Acceptance and Children's Psychological Adjustment   226
    Abdul Khaleque

15 Rehearsals! for Growth: Enhancing Family Well-Being Through
    Dramatic Play   244
    Daniel J. Wiener

16 Trauma and Development: Holistic/Systems-Developmental
    Theory and Practice   259
    Jack Demick

17 Relationships Between Grandparents and Their
    Grandchildren: An Applied Dyadic Perspective   279
    Bert Hayslip Jr., Robert J. Maiden, and Megan L. Dolbin-MacNab

18 The Psychology of Possibilities: Extending the Limits of
    Human Functioning   296
    Christelle Ngnoumen and Ellen Langer

Index   309

Figures and Tables

Figures

2.1	(Percentage) subjective perceived determinants of psychological disorder – example of an individual suffering from obsessive-compulsive disorder	18
7.1	The DNA-V model for adolescent psychological flexibility	112
8.1	A family biography showing transition from two-parent family to single motherhood to patchwork family	125
8.2	Theoretical model of measured variables, reflective and formative latent variables, and second-order latent variable. Not all variables and connections are shown	131
12.1	Triadic attachment relationships	189
12.2	Graph of average responses for SAT or triadic pictures across all dimensions (n = 8)	199

Tables

7.1	DNA-V high and low skills	113
12.1	Dyadic scenario picture prompts	194
12.2	Triadic scenario picture prompts	195
12.3	Scoring of dyadic and triadic pictures	197
12.4	Invisible children	201

Contributors

Alexandru Agache is Lecturer in the Faculty of Psychology at the Ruhr-University Bochum. His current thesis focuses on the effects of family economic well-being on adolescents' future orientation at the University of Konstanz. Further research interests include child well-being indicators and fathers' involvement. He is the co-author of a German diagnostic manual on sleep disorders in children and adolescents, and the author of several journal articles.

Alexander-Stamatios Antoniou is Lecturer in Psychology at the University of Athens, Greece. He holds a PhD in occupational health from the University of Manchester Institute of Science and Technology (UMIST) and a PhD in organizational psychology and behaviour from the University of Manchester. His publications include research papers and chapters in refereed academic journals, books, and edited volumes. His main research interests include occupational stress, work values and attitudes, transformational and charismatic leadership, individual power and organizational politics, and communication networks in organizations. He teaches occupational health and organizational behaviour in undergraduate and postgraduate programmes and delivers seminars to staff in public and private organizations on relevant issues. He has served as Director of the Institution 'Epanodos' of the Ministry of Justice, consultant psychologist for the National Council of Radio-Television (ESR) and several HRM projects, as well as being elected coordinator of the Division of Organisational Psychology, Hellenic Psychological Society.

Kathleen Ares is currently a doctoral candidate at The Chicago School of Professional Psychology, specializing in child and adolescent clinical psychology. Her wide range of training experiences includes administering neuropsychological assessment to children and adults, providing paediatric psychotherapy to infants and toddlers, and treating adolescent mood disorders. Kathleen is focusing her clinical and scholarly pursuits on the effects of disruption to neurodevelopment in children and adolescents. In addition, she is also conducting research examining neurological conditions and psychopathology in homeless youth in Chicago.

Dinesh Bhugra is Professor of Mental Health and Cultural Diversity at the Institute of Psychiatry, King's College London. He is also an honorary consultant at the Maudsley Hospital, where he runs the sexual and couple therapy clinic. Dinesh's research interests are in cultural psychiatry, sexual dysfunction, and service development. He has authored/co-authored over 300 scientific papers, chapters, and 20 books. His recent volumes include *Principles of Social Psychiatry*, *Textbook of Cultural Psychiatry* (awarded a recommendation in the BMA Book Awards in 2008), *Culture and Mental Health*, and *Management for Psychiatrists*. He is the editor of the *International Journal of Social Psychiatry*, *International Review of Psychiatry*, and *International Journal of Culture and Mental Health*. In 2008, he was elected President of the Royal College of Psychiatrists, and more recently elected President of the World Psychiatric Association.

Peter R. Breggin is Founder and Director of the Center for the Study of Empathic Therapy, and psychiatrist in private practice in New York. He has been called 'the Conscience of Psychiatry' for efforts to reform the mental health field, including his promotion of caring psychotherapeutic approaches and his opposition to the escalating overuse of psychiatric medications, the oppressive diagnosing and drugging of children, electroshock, lobotomy, involuntary treatment, and false biological theories. He is a Harvard-trained psychiatrist and former full-time consultant at the National Institute of Mental Health (NIMH). He is the author of dozens of scientific articles and more than 20 books, including *Toxic Psychiatry* (1991), *Talking Back to Prozac* (1994, with Ginger Breggin), and *Medication Madness: The Role of Psychiatric Drugs in Cases of Violence, Suicide and Crime* (2008). He was honoured with the biography *The Conscience of Psychiatry: The Reform Work of Peter R. Breggin, MD*.

Valeria Cavioni is an adjunct professor at the Department of Brain and Behavioural Sciences, University of Pavia, Italy, and Lecturer in Developmental Psychology and Psychometrics at Università Telematica e-Campus. She was a visiting researcher at the European Centre for Educational Resilience & Socio-Emotional Health, University of Malta, and at the Behavior Support Team in Leicester City Council, UK. She is an educational psychologist, an eligible candidate for the European Commission, a member of the Italian Association of Psychology, a member of ENSEC, the European Network for Social and Emotional Competence, and a member of the editorial board of the *International Journal of Emotional Education*. Her fields of research include social and emotional aspects of learning, training of teachers in managing behavioural problems in school and school readiness. She is the author of several national and international publications.

Carmel Cefai is Director of the EuroCentre for Educational Resilience and Socio-Emotional Health, and Head of the Department of Psychology at the University of Malta. He was a visiting fellow at the School of Education, University of Leicester, UK; a honorary visiting scholar at Flinders University, Australia; and a Fulbright scholar at the Prevention Research

Centre, Pennsylvania State University, USA. He is Joint Founding Honorary Chair of the European Network for Social and Emotional Competence (ENSEC), founding co-editor of the *International Journal of Emotional Education*, and associate editor of *Emotional Behavior Difficulties*. His research interests include educational resilience, and social and emotional health in children and young people. His recent books include *Building Resilience in School Children* (2011, with L. Camilleri), *Promoting Emotional Education* (2009, with P. Cooper), and *Promoting Resilience in the Classroom: A Guide to Developing Pupils' Emotional and Cognitive Skills* (2008).

Kathy Chan received her master's degree from the University of Regina and is completing her doctoral degree in clinical psychology at the University of Ottawa. She is passionate about her work with children and families, from both a research and clinical perspective, and has been studying and disseminating research on parenting for the past decade. Kathy is interested in helping families through the implementation of evidence-based practices, and currently, her doctoral work focuses on the Internet delivery of parenting interventions.

George P. Chrousos is Professor and Chairman of the First Department of Pediatrics at the University of Athens School of Medicine, Athens, Greece, and former chief of the Pediatric and Reproductive Endocrinology Branch of the National Institute of Child Health and Human Development (NICHD), National Institutes of Health (NIH), Bethesda, MD. He further holds the UNESCO Chair on Adolescent Health Care since 2010 and the Kluge Distinguished Chair on Technology and Society, Library of Congress, Washington, DC, since 2011. He has written over 600 original scientific papers. He is one of the most cited scientists in clinical medicine and in biology and biochemistry, and the highest cited clinical endocrinologist and paediatrician in the world. He was inducted as a master of both the American College of Endocrinology and the American College of Physicians and is former President of the European Society of Clinical Investigation.

Joseph Ciarrochi is a professor at the Institute for Positive Psychology and Education, Australian Catholic University. He has written over 90 scientific journal articles and many books, including the best selling *Get Out of Your Mind and Into Your Life Teens*, and the widely acclaimed *Mindfulness, Acceptance, and Positive Psychology: The Seven Foundations of Well-Being*. He has been honoured with over two million dollars in research funding. His work has been discussed on TV, and in magazines, newspaper articles, and radio.

Rudi Dallos is Professor and Clinical Director of Clinical Psychology Training at the University of Plymouth. His current clinical practice is with the

Family Matters family therapy service in Plymouth offering early interventions for families within a primary care context. He has worked in a variety of family therapy and clinical settings including couples therapy, eating disorders services, and adult mental. He has several research interests and is currently looking at children's experiences of triangulation, changes in attachments through the process of therapeutic foster care, and trans-generational patterns of attachments in families. In addition to journal publications, he has produced a number of books: *An Introduction to Family Therapy*, *Attachment Narrative Therapy*, and *Reflective Practice in Psychotherapy and Counselling*. He is the co-editor of the *Journal of Clinical Child Psychology and Psychiatry* with Arlene Vetere and together they have published extensively, including the book *Working Systemically with Attachment Narratives*.

Jack Demick a clinical and developmental psychologist, was trained at Yale University, Clark University, and the McLean Hospital/Harvard Medical School. He has held research, teaching, and/or clinical appointments at Brown University, Clark University, Harvard University, and the University of Massachusetts Medical School. His representative research interests include cognitive development (e.g., cognitive style, environmental cognition) and social development (e.g., adaptation of families to infant and child adoption, other life transitions) across the lifespan. He has authored numerous journal articles and book chapters, has co-edited eight volumes, and serves as the editor-in-chief of the *Journal of Adult Development*. This Spring (2015), he published a revision and extension of the classic *Group Embedded Figures Test Manual* and developed the first online version of this test that assesses the field dependence-independence cognitive style, the most widely researched construct in the field of psychology each year for some time.

Nisha Dogra is Professor of Psychiatry Education and an honorary consultant child and adolescent psychiatrist at the University of Leicester. She is a fellow of the Institute of Learning and Teaching and the Academy of Medical Educators. She developed innovative programmes to teach diversity and child psychiatry as well as leading national work on developing a core curriculum for undergraduate psychiatry. Her research interests include effective methods of training, diversity training for medical students and health care professionals, evaluation of training, and child mental health and diversity. Her major books include *Ten Teachers: Psychiatry* (2011, with S. Cooper and B. Lunn); *100 Cases in Psychiatry* (2010, with B. Wright and S. Dave); and *A Multi-Disciplinary Handbook of Child and Adolescent Mental Health for Front-Line Professionals*, 2nd edition (2009, with A. Parkin, F. Gale, and C. Frake).

Megan L. Dolbin-MacNab is an associate professor in the Department of Human Development at Virginia Tech and a licensed marriage and family therapist. Her programme of research focuses on families in which grandparents are raising grandchildren. She has examined how factors within the family environment (e.g., parenting stress, caregiver coping) and the larger socio-economic context (e.g., parental involvement) influence the experiences and well-being of children being raised by grandparents. Her research has also examined the delivery of effective community-based services for grandparent-headed families. She is the author of many journal articles and book chapters, as well as publications for practitioners. She also consults with numerous local and state support programmes on delivering services to custodial grandparents and their grandchildren, and is a member of the editorial boards of *Family Relations* and the *Journal of Marital and Family Therapy*.

Adrian Furnham was educated at the London School of Economics, where he obtained a distinction in MSc Econ., and at Oxford University, where he completed a doctorate (DPhil) in 1981. He subsequently earned a DSc (1991) and a DLitt (1995) degree. Previously he was Lecturer in Psychology at Pembroke College, Oxford, he is now Professor of Psychology at University College London. He has lectured widely abroad and held scholarships and visiting professorships at, amongst others, the University of New South Wales, the University of the West Indies, and the University of Hong Kong. He has written over 1,250 scientific papers and 85 books. He is on the editorial board of a number of international journals, as well as past elected President of the *International Society for the Study of Individual Differences*. He writes regularly for the *Sunday Times* and the *Daily Telegraph* and is a regular contributor to BBC radio and television.

Ahmed Hankir is a National Institute for Health Research Academic Clinical Fellow in Psychiatry with Manchester University and a research fellow with the Bedfordshire Centre for Mental Health Research in association with Cambridge University. He is also Global Health, Health Humanities, and Psychiatry lead of the medical education organization Doctors Academy and editor of the *World Journal of Medical Education and Research*. His research interests are wide ranging, including public understanding of psychiatry, recruitment into psychiatry, cultural psychiatry, mental health of refugees in conflict zones, stigma, and the mental health of health care practitioners. His articles have extensively appeared in journals including the *British Medical Journal* and he has presented at national and international conferences, and is a recipient of numerous awards, notably the First Prize in the Oral Presentation Competition of the Biennial International Conference on Mental Health in Cambridge University and the 2013 Royal College of Psychiatrists Foundation Doctor of the Year Award.

Louise Hayes is an academic, clinical psychologist, and peer-reviewed ACT trainer at Orygen Youth Health Research Centre, University of Melbourne. She is a world expert in ACT for young people and the co-author of *Get Out of Your Mind and Into Your Life for Teens: A Guide to Living an Extraordinary Life*, the first ACT book for adolescents. Louise completed one of the first research trials using ACT for adolescents; she has an active research programme in schools, therapy settings, and online: www.louisehayes.com.au.

Bert Hayslip Jr. is Regents Professor Emeritus of Psychology at the University of North Texas. He holds a doctorate in experimental/developmental psychology from the University of Akron (1975). His research focuses upon grandparenting, grandparents raising grandchildren, cognition and ageing, mental health and ageing, gerontological counselling, death and dying, and grief and bereavement adjustment. He is a fellow of the American Psychological Association, the Gerontological Society of America, and the Association for Gerontology in Higher Education, and has held grants from the National Institute on Aging, the National Institute of Nursing Research, the Hilgenfeld Foundation, and the National Endowment for the Humanities.

Mark D. Holder holds a PhD from the University of California, Berkeley, and completed his post-doctoral training at the Neuropsychiatric Institute at the University of California, Los Angeles. He is Associate Professor of Psychology at the University of British Columbia in Canada. He is an award-winning teacher and researcher, and has authored over 50 journal articles and chapters. He has recently written two books on happiness, including *Happiness in Children*. He leads a research team that is focused on understanding and promoting enduring improvements in subjective positive well-being.

Niranjan Karnik is a child/adolescent psychiatrist and sociologist at the University of Chicago. He has previously conducted research using psychiatric and psychometric instruments in the assessment of psychopathology in the California juvenile justice system, and in homeless shelters in San Francisco and Chicago. In addition, he has conducted qualitative and ethnographic research in the Illinois foster care system, in Mumbai among Indian street children, and also in refugee encampments in South Asia. He has a long-standing interest in the assessment and treatment of under-served youth. In addition, his academic research has included substantial work on minority mental health issues within the juvenile justice, foster care, and homeless youth populations. He is currently examining the social networks of homeless youth in Chicago with a goal of developing new interventions for homeless youth. He also examines the research ethics of working with vulnerable populations.

Abdul Khaleque holds a BA (Honors) in philosophy from the University of Dhaka, Bangladesh; an MSc in applied Psychology from the University of the Punjab, Lahore, Pakistan; an MA in human development and family studies from the University of Connecticut, USA; and a PhD in psychology from the Catholic University of Leuven, Belgium. He is working as a senior scientist at the Ronald and Nancy Rohner Center for the Study of Interpersonal Acceptance and Rejection, University of Connecticut, USA. He also works part-time in the Department of Human Development and Family Studies at the University of Connecticut. He has authored around 100 research articles, 30 book chapters, and 12 books on psychology and human development. He is President of the International Society for Interpersonal Acceptance and Rejection. He is a member of the editorial and review boards of several international journals.

Bruce Kirkcaldy has academic degrees in psychology from the Universities of Dundee and Giessen, as well as postgraduate professional training as a behavioural therapist and clinical psychologist. He is Director of the International Centre for the Study of Occupational and Mental Health, and runs his own psychotherapy practice specializing in the treatment of anxiety and depressive disorders. In addition, he has been a visiting professor of Psychology at the Jagiellonian University, Cracow, Poland. He has authored over 200 articles including some 25 book chapters and nine authored/edited books, most recently *The Art and Science of Health Care: Psychology and Human Factors for Practitioners*, with research and writing interests directed towards clinical and health issues and organizational and leisure psychology. He is/was on the editorial board of five international journals in the area of organizational and health care, and has served as reviewer for over 20 peer-reviewed scientific journals.

Christine Korol is the psychologist on the Concurrent Disorders Intervention Unit, Inpatient Psychiatry, Vancouver General Hospital, and Chair and Project Lead of the Kelty Online Therapy Service at Vancouver Coastal Health. She is currently creating therapeutic courses for an online therapy platform that will be used by therapists throughout Vancouver. She is also a cartoonist and columnist for *TILT Magazine*, a publication focused on integrating technology into a therapy practice, and a host of a series of online self-help podcasts on wiredtoworry.com. She holds a PhD in clinical psychology from the University of Ottawa, and was a postdoctoral fellow in the Department of Psychology, University of British Columbia.

Lisa M. Kuhns is a research assistant professor in the Department of Pediatrics at the Feinberg School of Medicine, Northwestern University, and Associate Director of the Center for Gender, Sexuality and HIV Prevention at

Ann & Robert H. Lurie Children's Hospital of Chicago. Her academic work has focused on health risks and disparate health outcomes among urban sexual and gender minority youth. She has been an investigator on several studies of sexual risk for HIV infection among young men who have sex with men and transgender women. Her most recent work focuses on the use of technology to promote medication adherence among youth infected with HIV.

Ellen Langer is Harvard Professor of Psychology, an artist, and recipient of a Guggenheim Fellowship, three Distinguished Scientist Awards, the APA Staats award for unifying psychology, among a host of other awards, has authored 11 books and over 200 research articles on topics such as perceived control, ageing, learning, and decision-making. Each of these is examined through the lens of her theory of mindfulness. Her research has demonstrated that by actively noticing new things – the essence of mindfulness – health, well-being, and competence will follow. Her best-selling books include *Mindfulness*; *The Power of Mindful Learning*; *On Becoming an Artist: Reinventing Yourself Through Mindful Creativity*; and her most recent book, *Counterclockwise: Mindful Health and the Power of Possibility*.

Birgit Leyendecker is Professor of Developmental Psychology at the Ruhr-University Bochum. Her research focus is on cultural perspectives on child development and parenting, cultural and psychosocial adaptation of immigrant children and their families, and resilience, particularly on the role of internal and external resources in children's developmental pathways. She is the principal investigator of an international study on the development of resilience among immigrant children and their families. In cooperation with Natasha Cabrera, Birgit is currently editing the *Handbook of Positive Development of Minority Children*.

Robert J. Maiden is Professor of Psychology and Director of the Gerontology Program at Alfred University. He is a licensed clinical psychologist with a private practice specializing in the diagnosis and treatment of adults and families, alcohol and substance abuse, psychological and neuropsychological assessment, and custody evaluation/expert testimony. Robert teaches a variety of undergraduate and graduate courses dealing with the clinical aspects of behaviour, clinical assessment and intervention, and the ageing process. He is a member of the State Society on Aging of New York and is a fellow of the Gerontological Society of America. Robert's published research deals with personality and cognitive functioning in later life, the use of mental health services among older adults, interventions with grandparents raising grandchildren, grandparenting, and accreditation and training issues as they apply to gerontology.

Mathias Mejeh is a scientific research associate at the University of Applied Sciences & Arts of Northwestern Switzerland in Brugg, Switzerland. He is a former junior project researcher at Sonderpädagogisches Zentrum für Verhalten und Sprache Bachtelen, Grenchen, Switzerland, and at the University of Koblenz-Landau, Germany. Mathias's main fields of research interests are neo-institutional theories focusing on systems of inclusion for children with special needs, teacher education with focus on the creation of learning environments, and methodological approaches based on topological aspects of network theory. Mathias is a member of the Junior Researcher Group (JURE) and the Special Interest Group for Special Needs Education of the European Association for Research in Learning and Instruction (EARLI), and junior fellow of the Humboldt-Association for Science, Art and Education. In 2012, he received a PhD-Award at the Biennial Meeting of the EARLI Special Interest Group for Special Needs Education at Utrecht.

Eftychia Mitsopoulou works as a religious subject teacher at the 2nd Model Experimental Junior High School of Athens. She holds a bachelor's degree in theology from the Aristotle University of Thessaloniki, a bachelor's degree in primary education from the National and Kapodistrian University of Athens, an MPhil in special didactics of the religious subject from the National and Kapodistrian University of Athens, and an MPhil in psychology and education from the University of Cambridge. She is a PhD student at the Faculty of Primary Education at the National and Kapodistrian University of Athens and specializes in the field of special education and gifted students. Her research interests include social aspects of special education, resilience of gifted and talented students, and the birth and development of stereotypes and prejudice in children.

Peter Nenniger is Professor Emeritus of Education at the University of Koblenz-Landau, Germany. He was a member of the directorial boards of the Centre for Educational Research and the Institute of Educational Sciences. He was/is a visiting professor at the University of Basle, Switzerland, and a lecturer at the Universities of Aachen, Berlin, Cordoba, Lisbon, Turku and Zagazig, and the Bulgarian Academy of Sciences. He served as the university's trustee of the German Research Foundation. His research interests are in motivation, learning and instruction, and research methodology. He has served as consultant in parliamentary, governmental, and scientific committees in Finland, France, Germany, the Netherlands, and Switzerland, and was the former president of Division 5 of the International Association of Applied Psychology, President of the Humboldt Society in Germany, and a member of the New York Academy of Sciences. He is author of monographs, and editor of the journal *Empirische Pädagogik* and several book series.

Christelle Ngnoumen is a doctoral student and researcher in the Department of Psychology, Harvard University. She completed her undergraduate studies at Brown University and holds two BAs in psychology and education studies. Her research seeks to understand the intersection of social cognition and visual perception, and began with an analysis of the relationship between people's attributional theories and their visual, proprioceptive, and social orientations to their external environments. Her early research was rooted in Ellen Langer's conceptualization of mindfulness and in Herman Witkin's concept of field-dependence and field-independence. Her current research examines the mindlessness of stereotyping, implicit social cognition, and person perception. She teaches a course on face-based trait inferences and their influences on social judgements, decision-making, and behaviour.

Nicole Pugh is a psychologist on the Brief Intervention Unit, Inpatient Psychiatry, Vancouver General Hospital. She is also the Chair of the Research Committee for the Kelty Online Therapy Service at Vancouver Coastal Health, where she is responsible for developing and evaluating a diverse library of online courses to be used by therapists working in local hospitals and the community. She holds a PhD from the University of Regina. Her clinical and research interests are in the areas of perinatal mental health and Internet therapy. She has been an active member of the Mother First provincial working group that has developed policy recommendations to address gaps related to maternal mental health in Saskatchewan. She has received research funding through the Canadian Institute of Health Research, Saskatchewan Health Research Foundation, and the University of Regina.

Axel Schölmerich has been Professor and Chair of Developmental Psychology at the Ruhr-University Bochum, since 1997. His research interests include contextual factors in child development, early life stress, emotional regulation, and migration. He was a Fogarty-Fellow at the National Institute of Child Health and Human Development in Bethesda, MD, USA, and the Chair of Human Development at the Martin-Luther-University in Halle-Wittenberg. He served as the editor of the *Zeitschrift für Entwicklungspsychologie und Pädagogische Psychologie*, the *Journal of Reproductive and Infant Psychology*, and the *European Journal of Developmental Science*.

Robyn L. Weninger is a graduate student in the Social Work Programme at the University of British Columbia. She recently authored a book chapter titled 'Extraversion and Subjective Well-Being' and she has contributed to an entry on Personality for the *Encyclopedia of Positive Psychology*.

Daniel J. Wiener, Professor of Counselor Education and Family Therapy at Central Connecticut State University, is an AAMFT-approved supervisor, a diplomate in family psychology of the American Psychological Association, a certified group therapist, and a registered drama therapist/board-certified trainer of the North American Drama Therapy Association. He has a private practice as a licensed psychologist in Massachusetts and is a licensed marriage and family therapist in Connecticut. His Rehearsals! for Growth (RfG), a drama therapy of relationships, was first developed in 1986. Daniel has written two books and edited/co-edited three others. His DVD, *Action Methods in Couple Therapy*, was released in 2011. He has received the Zerka Moreno Award from the American Society for Group Psychotherapy and Psychodrama and both a Gertrude Schattner Award and a Research Award from the National Association for Drama Therapy (now, the North American Drama Therapy Association).

1
Introduction – Enhancing Mental Health and Psychological Well-Being

Bruce Kirkcaldy

Over the last century (1900–2000), there have been significant improvements in medical health care. For the US and most European countries, the infant mortality rate has dropped from 140 deaths per 1000 to 5.8 deaths per 1000. Crude mortality rates have halved and people are living 30 years longer on average, for example, from 47 years in 1900 to 78 years in 2000 (Centers for Disease Control and Prevention (CDCP), 1999; Hicks & Allen, 1999). Several ailments no longer have potentially lethal consequences, for example, tuberculosis, gastroenteritis, and diphtheria. Looking back further, Blagosklonny (2010) reported that three centuries ago 'life expectancy was less than 16 years and 75% of people born in London in 1662 died before they reached the age of 26 (Graunt's life table)'. Causes of death among the young were less related to age diseases as they are today but rather occurred through starvation, violence, and epidemics (e.g., smallpox, cholera, tuberculosis).

What about psychological health? What are the rates of psychological disorders in the general population and what evidence, if any, is there that they have changed over the last decades? In a large cross-cultural survey of European nations (Alonso et al., 2004), the prevalence rate of a lifetime history of mood disorders was 14%, of anxiety disorders 13.6%, and alcohol disorders 5.2%. A meta-analysis a year later showed that 27% of adult Europeans are or will have been affected by at least one major mental disorder during the previous 12 months, with the most likely being anxiety, depressive, somatoform, and substance dependence disorders.

Christensen and coworkers (2012) estimated that one in ten children between the ages of 5 and 16 years has a clinically diagnosable mental health problem, one-half of which are conduct disorders, followed closely by anxiety, depression, and severe attention-deficit disorders. One-half of those with lifetime mental illness issues will display symptoms by the age of 14 years and three-quarters before their mid-20s. Moreover, self-harming behaviour among the young is fairly common (10–13% of 15–16-year-olds). Of children and adolescents between 11 and 16 years of age, those exhibiting an emotional disorder are more likely to smoke, drink, and use drugs. Young persons in prison are 18 times more likely to commit suicide.

Some researchers suggested that, over the last decades, a marked increase has been observed in the incidence of mental illnesses. For example, there has been a reported fourfold increase in suicides in the years after the economic crisis in 2007, with 10,000 more suicides being observed in North America and Europe. Others have argued that the observation of higher rates of mental ill-health in the population may simply be a product of better screening and identification methods.

A third intriguing explanation is that the construct of mental illness/health changes over time and, depending on its definition, more or fewer individuals will be 'inflicted'. Psychiatric diagnosis has been a 'guild monopoly' of the American Psychiatric Association, although psychiatrists constitute only 7% of all mental health clinicians and 'experts in clinical care, epidemiology, health economics, forensics and public health' (Frances, 2013, p. 219) have been ignored. Frances (2013) used the term diagnosis inflation to refer to the substantial increase in the number of children being diagnosed as suffering from attention-deficit disorder, bipolar disorder, and autism. He argued that the over-diagnosis coupled with overenthusiastic drug company marketing strategies implies that significant numbers of the population will be wrongly prescribed medications (e.g., antidepressants, anxiolytics, sleeping pills, analgesics), leading to 'a society of pill poppers'. He reported that expenditures on antipsychotics tripled and on antidepressants quadrupled from 1988 to 2008, with 80% prescribed by primary care physicians.

Contemporary research (e.g., Heitler, 2012) indicated that psychotherapy is effective and that the average effect sizes are larger than those of medication for ameliorating adverse negative affect such as anxiety, depression, and anger. Psychotherapy has also been found to reduce physical and emotional disability, death rates, and psychiatric hospitalizations, as well as to improve functioning at work. The American Psychological Association (Nordal, 2010) observed that the percentage of persons in outpatient mental health care had remained approximately the same over the last decade (3.2–3.4%) but the pattern of care had changed. Yet, there has been a decrease in the use of psychotherapy alone or indeed psychotherapy combined with medication, but a dramatic increase in medication alone. In 2008, 57.4% received solely medication. More particularly, there was a marked increase in the prescription of psychotropic medications (e.g., antipsychotics) among children and adolescents. Further, research has seriously questioned the appropriateness of widespread use of antidepressants for children and youth.

There has been a paradigm shift in mental illness treatment, with dramatic improvements with the application of cognitive behavioural therapy, and developments in acceptance and commitment therapy and mindfulness training. Added to this has been the recognition of emotional intelligence and social skills training in the educational context to promote psychological wellbeing. This edited volume is an attempt to address these issues. The constituent chapters of the book offer insightful and creative approaches to the treatment of families, children, and adolescents in promoting a culture of improved psychological wellbeing and mental health relying on the empirically demonstrable psychotherapeutic tools available. This collection of essays is an attempt to bridge theoretical and research concepts and findings with clinical practice, adopting interdisciplinary and cross-cultural perspectives. It reveals determinants and other factors that are implicated in the effectiveness of health promotion and therapeutic interventions as well as in the identification of reliable diagnostic and health programmes and/or the enhancement of learning and teaching programmes. Over the last few decades, we have witnessed advancement in psychological models of health – incorporating biological, psychological, and sociocultural factors – which stand in contrast to the traditional medical model of illness, which we address in this book.

The opening chapter (2) by Adrian Furnham and Bruce Kirkcaldy focuses on personal, lay ideas, models, and theories of health as opposed to formal scientific models. There is not necessarily any clear consensus with respect to the scientific model: A *biomedical* approach in medicine assumes that ill-health and disease are directly and exclusively caused by physical and biological diseases and their specific pathological processes. Wade and Halligan (2004) claim that biomedical models of illness that have dominated medicine for the last century seem deficient in explaining both psychological and physical disorders, as they stem 'partly from three assumptions: all illness has a single underlying cause, disease (pathology) is always the single cause, and removal or attenuation of the disease will result in a return to health' (p. 1398). Overall, the evidence for the medical model is sorely lacking. The *biopsychosocial* approach, on the other hand, suggests we best understand chronic conditions by also considering the patient, his or her physical condition, the social context of both, *and* the health care system.

The biomedical approach represents an essentially *reductionist* and sometimes *exclusionist concept*. It underlines a biological *rather* than a clinical approach, which is more inter-disciplinary and promotes wholeness. Such a biopsychosocial model emphasizes the indissoluble nature of the mind–body link in contrast to clinical practice, which is nearly always dualistic. We know that somato-psychic and psychosomatic illness calls for drugs and counselling. According to the biopsychosocial model, the healthy process occurs for three reasons: the *self-healing properties* of the body; the *patient–doctor relationships*; and the *medicines and treatments* prescribed. Subsequently, medical health professionals generally offer cognitive, emotional, and pharmaceutical care.

Consistent with the idea of elaborating on a paradigm shift in mental health, Ahmed Hankir and Dinesh Bhugra provide a brief introduction to the traditional medical model concept of symptom reduction as central to psychiatry and go on to explore disease versus illness and explanatory models. The authors suggest a broader focus than what traditional psychiatry has pursued, shifting from the focus of symptom removal (elimination of symptoms, diagnosis, and classification) towards concepts associated with improved social functioning. They emphasize the need for medical health professionals to familiarize themselves with sociology and anthropology to gain a better understanding of the social context from which our patients originate. This chapter offers succinct and creative openings for mental health care in the future and identifies challenges and possible solutions.

There then follows a contribution from Carmel Cefai and Valeria Cavioni, which underlines the value of educational psychology's contribution to emotional and social skill training within the school setting. The rapid global social, economic, and technological changes taking place in the adult world today are exposing children to unprecedented pressures and challenges at a young and vulnerable age. As many as 20% of schoolchildren experience mental health problems during the course of any given year and may need the use of mental health services; this may increase to 50% among children coming from socially disadvantaged areas such as urban regions (Adelman & Taylor, 2010). According to the 2001 US Surgeon General's Report on Mental Health, 11% of children have significant functional impairment and 5% have extreme impairment, constituting a significant economic burden on the country's resources, including health and social services.

The current interest in positive education and resilience education underlines the shift towards a broad-based, holistic conceptualization of child development and education, a proactive approach to the promotion of growth, health, and wellbeing. It is making us rethink the objectives of education and the role of schools as primary settings for health promotion. While one may argue that schools are not therapeutic centres and that teachers are not psychologists or mental health workers, Chapter 4 will describe the role schools may have in promoting the mental health and wellbeing of children and youth. It presents a mental health promotion framework for schools, depathologizing mental health and positioning the classroom teacher as an effective and caring educator in both academic and social and emotional learning. It focuses on prevention and universal interventions for all schoolchildren in mental health and wellbeing, while providing targeted interventions for children at risk of, or experiencing, mental health problems. This perspective is clearly different from interventions simply targeting students experiencing social, emotional, and behaviour difficulties, though the latter are not excluded. Besides promoting health and wellbeing, universal interventions often lead to a reduction in multiple problem areas in children, particularly at a time when their personality is still developing and serious behaviour problems are not yet manifest. At the same time, they are accompanied by complementary targeted interventions, thus having an additive, reinforcing effect.

A final contribution in this first section ('Understanding Mental Health. A Shift in Paradigm') of the book is Peter Breggin's personal contribution titled 'Shame, Guilt, and Anxiety' drawn on a long career in psychiatry. He removes the clouds that surround the origins of guilt, shame, and anxiety to show how these processes developed during our biological evolution as nature's way of inhibiting wilfulness and violence in close relationships. For millions of years, humans have evolved as both the most violent and the most sociable creatures on Earth. Human survival depended on its unique combination of ferocity and cooperation, enabling small bands to bring down and butcher creatures much larger than modern elephants.

However, if humans routinely unleashed violence when frustrated in their close personal relations, the human branch of evolution would have been short-lived. Natural selection came to the rescue by favouring the survival and propagation of individuals born with emotional inhibitions against unleashing violence in their closest relationships. This is the origin and function of our negative legacy emotions of guilt, shame, and anxiety, namely, to protect ourselves from each other within the family and also the clan or tribe. Negative legacy emotions are *primitive* in that they developed during biological evolution before the advent of culture and because they are triggered in early childhood before mature judgement or ethics. They are *prehistoric* in that they developed before recorded history and were triggered before we can remember in early childhood. Even if we can recall some of the early events associated with the development of our guilt, shame, and anxiety, it is but the tip of the iceberg of biological evolution and childhood.

Understanding the source of negative legacy emotions allows us to identify them and to reject them as guidelines for our conduct. It also helps us realize that, while we may feel guilty, ashamed or anxious, it has nothing to do with our real value or with the actual merit of our thoughts or actions. This realization enables us to let go of these self-defeating emotions while we learn to guide our adult lives with reason, sound principles, and love.

The second section of the volume ('Children and Adolescents') makes a transition to applying some of these ideas into work with children and adolescents. Mark Holder and Robyn Weninger, Canadian psychologists, examining many areas of research from psychology, education, and medicine, have emphasized identifying and treating deficits and dysfunction. Although this approach has proved valuable, it does not exhaust the range of the human experiences and behaviours that researchers should investigate. In addition to deficits and dysfunction, it is important to understand human strengths and what contributes to humans' thriving. The past two decades have witnessed the active development of a complementary approach to cataloguing and correcting illness. This approach, now referred to as positive psychology, is focused on wellbeing instead of on ill-being.

New studies are reporting the correlates of happiness, hope, and life satisfaction. This research has identified some of the factors associated with children's wellbeing (e.g., friends, spirituality, physical activity). This identification represents only the initial stage of understanding children's positive wellbeing, including their happiness. The next and critical stage of research is to use the recent research findings to develop and assess strategies and interventions to encourage enduring enhancements of children's positive wellbeing. The present chapter first reviews some of the relevant research on children's wellbeing. The authors then suggest several possible interventions based on these research findings, which investigators need to replicate in terms of their potential efficacy in enhancing children's positive wellbeing.

Over the last decade, the third wave of behavioural therapy, acceptance and commitment therapy (ACT), has stimulated much interest both in clinical practice and in research endeavours. Two of the pioneers in this area are the Australian psychologists, Louise Hayes and Joseph Ciarrochi, who use contextual behavioural processes to promote vitality among children and adolescents. They argue that young people are on a social and emotional journey of discovery, perhaps one of the most profound journeys of human life. ACT is a revolutionary approach that can promote wellbeing and fulfilment on this journey. Numerous published studies have shown that ACT is useful in treating clinical problems such as anxiety, depression, eating disorders, and addiction. As a broad science of human psychology, ACT is also effective for dealing with school-based teaching issues such as education, managing stress, promoting wellbeing, thriving, health, and performance. ACT is founded on a comprehensive model of human adaptation and change called contextual behavioural science. This model views the challenges of young people functionally, by seeing them as adaptations to context rather than deviations from the norm. ACT brings to light how the traps of language, culture, and social norms influence our suffering and, in this way, we approach these struggles from a paradigm of normality rather than deficit. ACT helps young people to overcome unhelpful mental habits and self-doubt, live more fully in the present moment, and make choices that help them to reach their potential. This chapter provides an overview of this practical theory using a flexible intervention model that can harness young people's energy in multiple settings. ACT can bring vitality into a young person's life, promote growth, compassion, and connection, and help young people develop resilience.

There then follows a German contribution (Chapter 8) from Axel Schölmerich and his colleagues Birgit Leyendecker and Alexandru Agache. Child wellbeing indicators as used in international comparisons (UNICEF, OECD) are highly aggregated measures. Typically, the proportions of cohorts with certain characteristics are reported (e.g., teenage pregnancies, smoking, children living in poverty). Much less attention is given to positive development, for example, the 5C model (competence, character, confidence, connection, and caring) measurable through the assessment of developmental achievements (e.g., language development, social–emotional maturity). With existing large-scale data sets (e.g., SOEP 'German Socioeconomic Panel', and FID 'Familien in Deutschland' in Germany), such indicators can be obtained, which offer a window on individual development. If relationships between such indicators are studied longitudinally and/or the influence of contextual variables is of interest, the measurement model is of particular relevance. Measurement equivalence of combined indicators at the configural, metric, and scalar levels needs to be estimated. This chapter summarizes research with existing indicators from international comparisons and reports age-appropriate indicators based on SOEP and FID data. The authors go on to suggest several important take-home messages for mental health professionals.

Kathleen Ares, Lisa Kuhns, Nisha Dogra, and Niranjan Karnik next examine child mental health and risk behaviour over time. The authors begin by exploring the normative role of risk-taking in the development of children establishing peer relationships. They then consider the ways that aetiological factors increase risk due to trauma, environment, and individual characteristics. In the course of examining aetiological patterns, they specifically explore family breakdown, substance misuse, and mental health, as well as community violence and risk, as components of this complex environmental influence. Next the authors explore the counter force of resiliency and the ways that special talents, family and peers, and early interventions may mitigate risk behaviours. They close by outlining specific pathways for risk development including substance use, self-harm/borderline personality, sexual risk, and criminality/anti-sociality.

Alexander Antoniou, Eftyhia Mitsopoulou, and George Chrousos, Greek psychologists, next provide a comprehensive examination of the research literature on psychosocial factors related to suicidal behaviour in adolescents. Suicide rates are the second most common cause of death in young people globally. Psychiatric, psychological, social, and cultural factors, as well as genetic vulnerability, play an important role in suicide and self-harm in general. The rates of suicidal ideation and suicide attempts increase dramatically during adolescence, making it a critical period when potential aetiological factors such as chronic stress should be investigated. Both life event stress and chronic stress significantly predict suicidal ideation and suicide attempts. Evidence exists linking high levels of stress and poor problem-solving skills with high levels of suicidal ideation among inpatient adolescents. Moreover, studies confirm an increased link between suicidal behaviours (thoughts, plans, acts) and posttraumatic stress disorder (PTSD). Psychological factors, particularly psychological distress, are among the most important factors in suicidal ideation. The higher the psychological distress, the greater the risk of suicidal ideation, especially among vulnerable groups such as homeless youth. The links between negative experiences, such as physical and psychological abuse and suicidal ideation, are significantly mediated by psychological distress. As far as family environmental variables are concerned, adolescents who have experienced suicide attempts or suicide deaths show high levels of at-risk behaviours in the family.

This section ends with Chapter 11 on online mental health and parenting interventions supporting children and their families. The Canadian psychologists Nicole Pugh, Kathy Chan, and Christine Korol claim that parents traditionally refer their children to primary care physicians when concerned about their mental health. However, parents are increasingly turning to online communities, smart phone applications, and Internet searches to help understand and even diagnose and treat their children's mental health concerns. According to the Pew Research Center, approximately 53% of Americans search for health-related information online. The challenge with searching for information in this way is that many rely on symptom lists to self-diagnose their children's physical and mental health concerns, while ignoring base rates or the probability that they might have a particular condition. While it is understandable to want to be a caring parent and informed consumer of health-related research, it can be difficult for parents critically and objectively to evaluate their children's needs, and the acquired online information may, in turn, exacerbate parental anxiety from erroneous self-diagnosis.

Timely access to the right support, which is easily accessible to children and their families, is critical and may even prevent more serious concerns from developing. Psychological interventions are particularly well suited to online presentation. In particular, therapist-assisted online cognitive behavioural therapy (TAI-CBT) is a growing model of service delivery. In this model, consumers of mental health information complete online courses that explore common mental health and family issues, such as postpartum depression, anxiety, child behaviour problems, and sleep. A therapist is assigned to the parent or child and provides support and guidance as he or she works through the course. The materials are often interactive, appealing to both adults and children, and are aimed at increasing the understanding of motivation as well as encouraging a strength-based approach to physical and mental health.

The third and final section of this volume focuses on family relationships including children, parents, and grandparents. The British psychologist Rudi Dallos suggests that one of the cornerstones of systemic family therapy is the concept of triangulation whereby children become entangled in the distress and conflict among key attachment figures in their lives. The chapter explores how such processes play an extremely powerful role in producing distress and mental health problems for children. It considers that often the child in the family who attempts to be loyal with both conflicted parents experiences the most severe difficulties. The chapter draws on clinical case examples as well as Dallos' contemporary research exploring children's reactions to photographic depictions of conflictual triadic scenarios, such as the parents arguing, separating, or reacting negatively to the child's actions. Both clinical and empirical evidence suggests that children experience considerable distress and attachment anxiety in reaction to these situations. The effects can be even more severe than to dyadic attachment threats, such as separations from one or the other parent and a sense of being powerlessly caught between the parents. Triadic conflict can also engender a sense that the whole family, the child's secure base, is disintegrating. Findings also suggest that, in cases for example where parents have separated but continue to be in conflict, the children feel themselves to be emotionally 'invisible'. At these times, the parents may be so preoccupied with their own needs, anger, and anxieties that they are less capable of understanding and responding to their children's needs. Clinical implications for therapy and intervention are addressed.

Peter Nenninger and Mathias Mejeh investigate the impact of special education in the complex institutional environment of health care. Recently, special education has become a highly discussed issue all over the world in debates about alternative inclusive education. Despite the fact that these discussions have been characterized by vague ideas and misunderstandings of countries' educational systems, it has become increasingly clear that issues of special education must be discussed in a broader framework encompassing the fields of social work and health care. Moreover, the diversity of arguments proposed relates to specific practices and difficulties encountered during adaptations and transformations of educational systems. On the basis of a framework embracing current theories in educational, social, and health psychology, education, and sociology, the authors provide an overview of existent institutional systems for special education and related fields, then elaborate a typology based on institutional characteristics and properties of effective execution of action, and finally reveal – on the basis of empirical research and examples of attempts at inclusive education – a number of factors related to the success or failure of special education implementations particularly as they, in turn, affect the fields of social work and health care.

Over several decades, the concepts of parental bonding, acceptance, and rejection have been influential not only in clinical research but also in psychological health practice. Abdul Khaleque explores the influence of parental acceptance on the psychological wellbeing of children and adolescents. The chapter includes a brief description of parental acceptance and rejection theory. The basic assumptions of this theory are discussed, especially those concerning parental acceptance and children's psychological adjustment and healthy development cross-culturally, and an evidence-based theory of socialization and lifespan development of children and adults universally is described. The theory aims to predict and explain major causes, consequences, and other correlates of parental acceptance and rejection worldwide. Parental acceptance refers to warmth, affection, love, care, comfort, support, or nurturance that parents can feel or express towards their children. Parental rejection refers to the absence or withdrawal of warmth, affection, or love by parents towards their children. Parental acceptance and rejection theory assumes that parental acceptance is likely to lead to the development of psychological adjustment and positive personality dispositions and parental rejection to the development of psychological maladjustment and negative personality dispositions in children. Parental acceptance and rejection personality theory postulates that children who perceive themselves to be accepted by their parents are likely to develop (1) low hostility and aggression, (2) independence, (3) positive self-esteem, (4) positive self-adequacy, (5) emotional stability, (6) emotional responsiveness, and (7) a positive worldview. About 500 studies, including nine meta-analyses conducted globally, support the postulates of this theory. Consistent with the other chapters, the author provides an array of practical tools for clinicians and educationalists working with family and children.

An innovative contribution by Daniel Wiener applies 'Rehearsals for Growth' (RfG), an application of theatre improvisation techniques to psychotherapy for relationships, principally family relationships. These methods promote attentiveness and mutual validation among family members and explore alternatives to unproductive recurrent patterns of family interaction and increases in emotional expressiveness. By establishing a playful atmosphere and fully including children in therapy sessions, families are empowered to explore alternative choices and to co-create solutions to their problems. Following a review of RfG conceptual foundations (family systems theory, social constructivism, embodied psychotherapy, dramatic enactment), a brief family case example is presented. Italicized commentary interspersed throughout this section offers the rationale for both generic principles in the practice of this therapy and specific choices made by the therapist working with the case family. A concluding section instructs clinicians seeking to practise RfG therapy.

Holistic/systems-developmental theory (HSDT), an extension of Werner's (1957) classic organismic-developmental theory, offers many innovative ideas for treating trauma in individuals and the family. One of the pioneers in HSDT and in its application to traumatic events is Jack Demick. Although much research strongly claims that stress, adversity, and trauma create negative and pathological experiences, a gap exists in the literature regarding the potential development that can occur following difficult life events. As a recent exception, the positive psychology movement attempts to shift the focus towards strengths at the personal, interpersonal, and systems levels. In line with this, Demick's chapter also addresses the possible development that can occur following traumatic life events, but is not based on a new theoretical movement but rather on a grand developmental theory with a long and distinguished history within the field of psychology. Based on Gestalt theory and its laws of perceptual organization (e.g., 'the whole is greater than the sum of its parts' and 'one can see the glass as half full or half empty'), HSDT – with its organismic aspect advocating holistic analysis of the thinking, feeling, striving individual and its developmental aspect suggesting changes towards differentiation and integration to analyse not only age changes but also any person–environment transaction – has employed the *person-in-environment system* (with the biological, psychological, and sociocultural levels of the person mutually defining the physical, inter-organismic, and sociocultural levels of the environment) as the unit of analysis in its paradigmatic study of critical transitions across the lifespan.

Within this framework, Demick and his associates have conducted empirical studies on the effects of traumatic life events, complementing quantitative (to establish cause–effect relationships) and qualitative (to describe human experience and action) methodologies. Towards demonstrating this approach, the chapter describes studies relevant to the experience of traumatic events (e.g., adolescent girls' adaptation to maternal loss, family adaptation to infant and child adoption, older adults' entry into the nursing home), which focus on positive aspects of these experiences. Additional studies have also conducted on the controversial nature of resilience, which aim to assess exactly what this construct entails and how it impacts one's experience of trauma. However, most importantly, the chapter concludes with a discussion of the ways in which HSDT informs clinical practice in terms of both existent techniques and the generation of newer ones.

A frequently underexplored topic in child and family studies is transgenerational family patterns, which include grandparents and occasionally great-grandparents. The American psychologist Bert Hayslip has invested his academic life researching the influence of grandparents on their grandchildren. His chapter begins by examining the nature of the grandparenting role and its evolving nature, emphasizing its developmental aspects and taking into consideration changes over time in a variety of aspects related to both grandparents and their grandchildren. Hayslip et al. then explores the intergenerational aspects of grandparenting, stressing its dyadic nature. As the family structure and the nature of parenting have changed significantly over the last few decades (e.g., highlighted by the growth in the ageing population and increased longevity), it is clear that cultural and historical changes have impacted both the meaning and style of grandparenting. In this regard, he discusses such issues as follows: The meaning an individual assigns to being a grandparent gives rise to the idiosyncratic style he or she assumes in carrying out the role. Further, both meaning and style are actively constructed by the grandparent and are likely subject to differences in communication content and style between grandmothers and grandfathers. He then examines spheres of grandparents' influence on their grandchildren in both positive and negative ways, as embodied in benefits for each generation versus adverse interactions between generations. He then reviews the literature on variations in grandparent–grandchild relationships (e.g., grandfathers, step-grandparenting, grandparents raising their own grandchildren). The chapter concludes with a discussion of grandparents' roles in the future and the implications for educational and health professionals working with multigenerational families.

Consistent with the themes of neglect of the aged population and cultural 'disinterest' in applying positive psychology to older adults, pioneering research has been conducted over the decades by the American psychologist Ellen Langer and her colleague Christelle Ngnoumen. Since older adult community members frequently feel ignored, the authors discuss the overwhelming power of labels, stereotypic beliefs about ageing, and environmental cues signalling ageing and priming diminished capacity. These are seen as modifiable factors that impede healthy ageing and that can be eradicated via reverse priming. According to the authors, the most stable factors underlying illness are our mindsets about them. These mindsets are influenced by social constructions of health whose labels (e.g., 'chronic', 'ageing') encourage others to overlook fluctuations in symptoms and to prime states of low personal control. They propose that ageing may be at least somewhat controllable and hypothesize that health can be directly influenced by an increase in mindfulness. This redirection of control over health from the medical world to the individual has great implications for wellbeing and accompanying interventions.

My own experience as a researcher and clinician is that, while outstanding articles can be traced to certain journals and while excellent academic textbooks exist, there is still a need to draw together specialists and pioneers in their disciplines to provide contemporary perspectives on psychological wellbeing among children and families. As Edwards (2012) has claimed, 'Edited collections provide the space for authoritative comparative perspectives' to bring together new lines of inquiry and 'break through the isolationism inherent in the sole-authored publishing'. Such a multi-authored, edited volume offers a unique avenue for generating novel concepts integrating divergent views together: 'New ideas propelled by the debate, dialogue or breadth of the edited volume impact the field more quickly than those in a sole authored book'. Such edited volumes meet a series 'of distinct intellectual and community needs'. My own motivation for drawing together these contributors was to assemble a volume aimed at presenting state-of-the-art research with practical take-home messages for health practitioners.

Finally, it remains for me to thank Jack Demick and Claire Dutton, who read an earlier version of this introduction and made useful suggestions, to Eleanor Christie, Editorial Assistant at Palgrave Macmillan, London, and Benedicta Priya, Integra Software Services in connection with the publication process, whose continued support helped inspire the appearance of this book.

References

Adelman, S., & Taylor, L. (2010). Creating successful school systems requires addressing barriers to learning and teaching. *The F. M. Duffy Reports*, July, *15* (3), 1–7.

Alonso, J., Angermeyer, M.C., Bernert, S., Bruffaerts, R., Brugha, T.S., Bryson, H., de Girolamo, G., ... Vollebergh, W.A.M. (2004). Prevalence of mental disorders in Europe: results from the European Study of the Epidemiology of Mental Disorders (ESEMeD) project. *Acta Psychiatrica Scandinavica, 109*, 21–27.

Blagosklonny, M.V. (2010). Why human lifespan is rapidly increasing: solving 'longevity riddle' with 'revealed-slow-aging' hypothesis. *Aging, 2* (4), 177–182.

Centers for Disease Control and Prevention. (1999). Achievements in public health, 1900–1999: control of infectious diseases. *Morbidity and Mortality Weekly Report*, July 30, *48* (29), 621–629. Downloaded at: http://www.cdc.gov/mmwr/preview/mmwrhtml/mm4829a1.htm

Christensen, L., Murphy, M., Allister, J., Atkinson, M., Bhargava, A., Brennan, S., ... Wolpert, M. (2012). Improving children and young people's mental health outcomes. *Report of the Children and Young People's Health Outcome Forum – Mental Health Sub-Group*. Downloaded at: https://www.gov.uk/government/uploads/system/uploads/attachment_data/file/216853/CYP-Mental-Health.pdf

Edwards, L. (2012). Editing academic books in the humanities and social sciences: maximising impact for effort. *Journal of Scholarly Publishing*, Oct., doi: 10.3130/jsp.44.1.61

Frances, A. (2013). *Saving Normal: An Insider's Revolt Against Out-of-Control Psychiatric Diagnosis, DSM-5, Big Pharma, and the Medicalization of Ordinary Life*. New York: W. Morrow.

Heitler, S. (2012). *Resolution, Not Conflict. The Guide to Problem-Solving*. Downloaded at http://www.psychologytoday.com/blog/resolution-not-conflict/201208/8-reasons-cheer-psychotherapy-and-broaden-its-avai

Hicks, J., & Allen, G. (1999). A century of change: Trends in UK statistics since 1900. *House of Commons Research Paper, 1999*. Available at: //www.parliament.uk/documents/commons/lib/research/rp99/rp99-111.pdf

Nordal, K. (2010). Where has all the psychotherapy gone? *Monitor on Psychology, 41* (10), 17.

Wade, D.T., & Halligan, P.W. (2004). Do biomedical models make for good healthcare? *British Medical Journal*, Dec 11; *329* (7479), 1398–1401.

Werner, H. (1957). *Comparative Psychology of Mental Development*. New York: International Universities Press.

2
Lay People's Knowledge of Mental and Physical Illness

Adrian Furnham and Bruce Kirkcaldy

> Our body is a machine for living. It is organized for that, it is its nature. Let life go on in it unhindered and let it defend itself, it will do more than if you paralyze it by encumbering it with remedies.
> Leo Tolstoy

Introduction

There is a great difference between studying mental and physical illness and further studying psychological and physical *health*. For a 100 years psychologists studied such things as anxiety, depression and suicide supposing that happiness and adaptation was in some way just 'not genuinely experiencing' these powerful negative emotions. However, the rise of positive psychology and the serious acknowledgement of the biopsychosocial model of mental and physical health have changed our perspective for the better. We are both social and biological beings with a unique makeup. To fully understand how we function, and why some survive and thrive while others succumb to pressures, we need to look at *all* factors that influence our health. This includes the individual's own perceptions of his or her health/disorder.

Subjective models of psychological and physical illness differ in terms of whether the person is a lay person or a health professional. Among families, parents will construe their children illnesses in their own idiosyncratic style, just as children and young adults will seek explanations to make sense of their own or their parents' personal health problems. Further, models of illnesses differ substantially between health professionals, especially in the mental health field (cf. Harland et al., 2009; Kirkcaldy & Siefen, 2012). There are significant discrepancies in the reliability of diagnoses among mental health professionals across cultures. Clearly, the impact of unreliability of treatment forms will compound these factors; that is, if there is a low level of consensus of the accuracy of a psychiatric diagnosis among professionals, there is even less likelihood of finding the right treatment.

Helman (2007) underlined that the clinician's value is not confined to searching for disease, but

> should try to discover how patients and those around them view the origin, significance and prognosis of the condition, and also how it affects other aspects of their lives – such as their income or social relationships. The patient's emotional reactions to ill health (such as guilt, fear, shame, anger and uncertainty) are all as relevant to the clinical encounter as physiological data, and sometimes more so. (p. 153)

Vallis and McHugh (2004) noted that the cognitive model highlights the fact that individuals are not passive recipients of information from their environments but are instead active in their processing of information. Knowledge is not received, as in a radio receiver, but is actively constructed (Merluzzi, Rudy, & Glass, 1981). Thus, illness behaviour should be viewed as more than simply one's concerns about a disease state; it is based on many other factors. Since the amount of information available to the senses quickly outstrips even the most astute individual's attentional abilities and since not all available information can be processed, we need some form of selective processing. Numerous factors influence this selective filtering and we have advanced our understanding of human behaviour by identifying these factors (e.g., attentional demands, influence of past memory, 'availability heuristics', and schematic processing).

There is a rich literature on the public perception of physical and mental health, particularly on how people understand the cause, manifestation, and treatment of illness. There are *three* different definable research traditions in mental health: *public attitudes, lay theories,* and *mental health literacy*. The first concerns studies of *attitudes towards people with mental disorders* (Nunnally, 1961), and may concern specific mental disorders, such as neurosis, schizophrenia, and depression. They are often concerned with the labelling of mental illness, and are generally based on large survey studies. These studies are important as they can offer an explanation for negative and stigmatizing attitudes towards mental disorders (Nunnally, 1961; Link et al., 1999), and partly explain why so few of those diagnosed seek help (Lin et al., 1996; Andrews et al., 1999), and why the compliance rate may not be high even when help is sought (e.g., Rogalski, 1984).

Secondly, studies relating to *lay theories* of mental illness have been conducted primarily by Furnham and colleagues (i.e., Furnham & Lowick, 1984; Furnham & Manning, 1997; Furnham & Haraldsen, 1998; Kirkcaldy et al., 2001), focusing specifically on the nature, causes, and treatments of disorders such as heroin addiction (Furnham & Thompson, 1996) and schizophrenia (Furnham & Rees, 1988). These studies are concerned with the structure of beliefs about the aetiology and cure of such disorders and the relationship between them. They have been recently reviewed (Furnham & Telford, 2011).

The third approach is the term 'mental health literacy' research introduced by Jorm and colleagues (Jorm et al., 1997b) and reviewed by Eysenck (2011) to refer to public knowledge and, more specifically, recognition of mental disorders. This encompasses theories of mental disorders, as well as other important issues, such as knowing how and where to seek help (i.e., pathways to professional help).

The lay perspective

One important distinction is between the personal, lay ideas and explanations, which are essentially subjective models and theories of health, as opposed to formal, scientific, and explicit models of health. The first is frequently taken from the patient's perspective and the latter from the doctor's or scientist's perspective. By subjective model, we mean the idiosyncratic, personal, ideas of non-professionals concerning the causes, manifestations, and cures for illness and the markers of good health.

Researchers have pointed out various metaphors and models used by people relating to health: *time running out* (wearing out the body), *mechanical faults* (broken, faulty parts), *imbalance* (lack of harmony), and *invasion* (penetration of foreign bodies) (Helman, 2007). Stainton Rogers (1991) found evidence of eight lay models or accounts:

1. The Body as a Machine Account: the 'modern' biomedical models.
2. The Body Under Siege Account: at threat from germs, disease, and the stress of life.
3. The Inequality of Stress Account: poor availability or access to modern medicine.
4. The Cultural Critique of Medicine Account: a sociological model of dominance, exploitation, and oppression.
5. The Health Promotion Account, which stresses the important of a healthy lifestyle.
6. The Robust Individualism Account, which stresses people's right to choose a life for them.
7. The God's Power Account, which stresses 'right living' and spiritual wellbeing.
8. The Willpower Account, where people have a moral responsibility to use their will to achieve good health.

Her work has attracted much attention (Furnham, 1994a, 1994b; Swami et al., 2009) because of the recognition that the personal, lay theories that people hold about their own and others' health inform their lifestyle, help-seeking, and advice-giving to others.

Lay theories in psychology and psychiatry are generally thought of as explanations and descriptions, which lay people give for various disorders. They may be ambiguous, inconsistent, and incoherent, when compared to academic theories (Furnham, 1988). Research exploring lay beliefs of psychological problems highlights the value of studying perceived causes and treatments, as this allows an insight into the cognitive strategies people use when experiencing a problem, or advising both friends and family. Pathways to seeking professional help appear to be strongly related to lay theories (Furnham, 2008). As a result, lay theories could help in enhancing the effectiveness of psychological therapies (cognitive behavioural therapy, interventions, and psychotherapy). Initially, research into lay theories focused on investigating lay beliefs of mental illness in general; yet, it seems unlikely that beliefs about diverse illnesses such as schizophrenia and depression are similar (Furnham & Bower, 1992). This has led researchers to investigate beliefs and attitudes concerning a single disorder. Past research into lay theories has focused on well-known psychological disorders reviewed comprehensively by Furnham and Telford (2011).

For subjective models, people take very different positions. Sometimes they apply *biological/genetic/physiological* theories to finding the cause of and cure for their problems. There is a chemical imbalance which can be rectified or a genetic abnormality that cannot. Many see this as the 'modern scientific' approach to medicine. Others adopt a *psychological/psychoanalytic* approach in an attempt to understand illness in terms of early social experiences or personality factors. Others employ *a sociological or environmental* approach, seeing the problem as essentially external to the individual and in the environment. Still others suggest *luck, chance or the will of God*. Some individuals are happy to explain both the cause and best treatment for almost all mental afflictions by one or other model, while others are quite happy to explain one problem (i.e., addiction or depression or psychosis) by one model/theory and yet another by another model. Inevitably people 'mix' their models, believing that most causes are multi-faceted. Kirkcaldy (2014) provides examples of subjective explanations of disorders among family members (cf. Figure 2.1).

One recent paper that examined psychiatrists' conceptions of mental illness suggested that eight different models could be identified: biological, cognitive, behavioural, psychodynamic, social realists, social constructionist, nihilist, and spiritual (Harland et al., 2009). However, the question remains: why do people adopt certain models and what are the consequences of those beliefs, for them and for others with whom they interact?

Cause

Recent studies into lay theories have focused specifically on beliefs concerning the causes and treatments of mental disorders and the relationship between them (Furnham & Thompson, 1996; Furnham & Buck, 2003) to

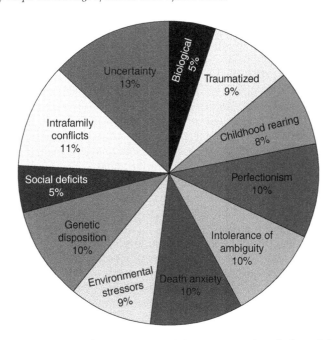

Figure 2.1 (Percentage) subjective perceived determinants of psychological disorder – example of an individual suffering from obsessive-compulsive disorder

find possible links between negative attitudes and erroneous beliefs. They have shown that lay theories are not arbitrary or incoherent: they can be classified into categories such as 'psychological' or 'social' in the same way as 'academic' theories (Furnham & Rees, 1988; Furnham & Thompson, 1996). This suggests that lay people have a basic, possibly implicit, understanding of the different levels of explanation for mental disorders. Studies have shown that the structure of the categories of lay and academic theories overlap to an extent, for example, 'biological' and 'psychological' models. Nevertheless, some lay conceptions may differ as regards, for example, 'external' influences, which include beliefs about the roles of luck and religion in the aetiology of mental illness (Furnham & Buck, 2003). Thus, if you ask people what causes addictions like alcoholism, they are inclined to stress social factors but include personal factors (traits and early life experiences), and are less likely to underline biological or physical factors.

Lay people place more emphasis on psychological, social, and familial causal factors (Sarbin & Mancuso, 1972; Angermeyer & Matschinger, 1996; Furnham & Thompson, 1996), which can be compared to primarily biological and genetic academic theories. Jorm and colleagues (1997a) found that schizophrenia was more likely to be attributed to genetic factors than depression, and lay theories of autism were more likely to be perceived as biological than theories of obsessive-compulsive disorder, which were more likely to be psychodynamic in orientation (Furnham & Buck, 2003). But, the finding that lay theories are generally psychosocial rather than biological has been frequently replicated. This appears to 'contradict' the perception of illness offered by the medical and psychiatric profession (Harland et al., 2009).

Treatment and cure

The general public (as potential clients) is increasingly faced with a bewildering array of available psychotherapeutic interventions, although some are similar in theory and practice. These may include seeing a therapist, attending training courses or focus groups, observation, and/or taking medication or getting hypnosis. Deciding whether to seek help is associated with a range of factors, including the availability of services, financial costs, and individual socio-demographic and psychological variables. It is also crucially associated with the perceived effort required in receiving treatment, and the possible psychological pain associated with it, which is the focus of this review. The term 'psychological pain' refers here to the distress associated with the treatment process.

Most members of the public believe that mental disorders are treatable; psychiatric treatments are considered generally rather unhelpful, whereas counselling is considered most helpful. Studies have shown that people have set ideas on counselling before taking up therapy: expectations appear important determinants of where people turn to for help and the effectiveness of their counselling.

People have very different beliefs about what occurs during psychotherapy (Furnham & Telford, 2011). Furnham and Wardley (1990) found respondents tended to believe that clients of psychotherapy feel better in therapy, and were more confident and hopeful. This study has been replicated by Wong (1994) and Heaven and Furnham (1994) using American college students and staff. Furnham and Wardley (1991) investigated lay theories of efficacy of therapies and prognosis for different problems. People who were more knowledgeable in psychology tend to be more sceptical. Knowledge about psychological cures led to a greater awareness of the limited benefits of therapy. This was confirmed when Furnham, Wardley, and Lillie (1992) compared the responses of lay adults, students, and clinical psychologists, and found the latter to be more cynical regarding the efficacy of therapy and prognosis of many disorders.

Lay theories on the *treatment*, as opposed to the cause, of mental disorders show marked differences from current practices in the mental health service. Lay people generally prefer psychotherapy to drug treatment (Angermeyer & Matschinger, 1996; Angermeyer & Dietrich, 2006), often due to less perceived side effects (Angermeyer, Daumer, & Matschinger, 1993; Priest et al.,

1996; Fischer et al., 1999). There is further a belief that 'will power' can facilitate recovery from mental disorders (Knapp & Delprato, 1980) such as agoraphobia and anorexia nervosa (Furnham & Henley, 1988). However, medication is believed to be the most effective treatment for disorders with a higher perceived severity (Furnham & Rees, 1988; Furnham & Bower, 1992), thus showing that lay and academic theories of treatment overlap to an extent.

The relationship between cause and cure

Studies have focused on assessing whether a *logical relationship* is found between lay theories of cause and treatment. It is expected that, if cause is attributed to biological factors, medication should be endorsed as treatment. This has been found in some studies which show a strong relationship between similar cause and treatment theories (Furnham & Buck, 2003), and those which are 'sensibly' linked (Furnham & Haraldsen, 1998, p. 696). These findings are not always replicated, for example, medication is often the *preferred* treatment for schizophrenia, despite participants attributing the cause to psychosocial factors (Furnham & Rees, 1988; Furnham & Bower, 1992). On the other hand, others are critical of using psychopharmacology, including in the most extreme psychiatric disorders (e.g. Breggin & Cohen 2007; Whitaker, 2010), in large part because of the potentially adverse effects of such medication.

Two general models of lay beliefs have been proposed. Lay theories can belong to the 'medical' model (Rabkin, 1974), which suggests that mental disorders are similar to other illness, with symptoms caused by an underlying biological pathology and a treatment which addresses this. The second model is the 'psychosocial' model (Sarbin & Mancuso, 1972), which shows that causes of mental disorder are psychological *and* environmental. This has positive implications for treatment, as it advocates social and community support rather than hospitalization. But it has been found that people with beliefs which correspond to this model are less trusting of ex-psychiatric patients than ex-medical patients (Sarbin & Mancuso, 1972). These models can, therefore, be used to classify lay theories and have wider implications for attitudes towards those with mental illnesses, causal beliefs, and treatment preferences.

Studies in this area have covered a wide range of specific illnesses, including alcoholism, anxiety, anorexia, autism, depression, gender identity disorder, heroin addiction, neurosis, paraphilia, phobia, schizophrenia, and suicide (Furnham & Telford, 2012). Many have looked at what lay people think *causes* these particular problems and how they are behaviourally manifested as well as the most effective treatment modality (Furnham & Telford, 2012). They show areas of ignorance about mental illnesses, particularly developments in isolating and describing biophysical and genetic processes relating to those illnesses.

Mental health literacy

The term 'mental health literacy' was introduced by Jorm and colleagues to mean '...knowledge and beliefs about mental disorders which aid recognition, management or prevention...' (Jorm et al., 1997a, p. 182). This includes the ability to recognize specific disorders, knowledge about the causes and risk factors, and knowledge of the help available. Mental health literacy is important as it can ensure that mental disorders are recognized early and that the appropriate help-seeking behaviour is promptly encouraged. This concept is thus linked to the concept of lay theories and is being used in this study to investigate the recognition of specific mental disorders.

Earlier studies relating to mental health literacy found that people have difficulty recognizing mental disorders when they are described in a vignette (Star, 1955; Hillert et al., 1999; Link et al., 1999), and many people hold common misconceptions, for example, that schizophrenia involves a 'split personality' (Furnham & Rees, 1988; Angermeyer & Matschinger, 1999; Furnham & Chan, 2004). Regarding specific disorders, the rates for people recognizing depression and schizophrenia correctly vary: they were 39% and 27%, respectively (Jorm et al., 1997a). More recently, studies have found that these rates have increased to around 50% for schizophrenia (Klimidis, Hsiao, & Minas, 2007) and 60–70% for depression (Jorm, Christensen, & Griffiths, 2005). The higher recognition rates for depression than for schizophrenia had not been explained in these studies, but may be due to the higher prevalence of depression in the population (Rippere, 1977, 1981), which increases the likelihood of contact with the disorder. This suggests that the recognition rate for bipolar disorder should be more similar to that for schizophrenia than that for depression (Kessler et al., 1994).

Much of this research regarding psychiatric literacy has focused on schizophrenia and depression. Results of studies investigating these disorders vary, but *lay people* appear to have difficulty understanding psychiatric terms and correctly labelling disorders (Jorm, 2000). However, a recent replication by Furnham, Daoud, and Swami (2009) asked participants to identify psychopathy (antisocial personality disorder). It was found that 97% of participants could accurately name depression, 61% recognized schizophrenia but only 39% identified psychopathy.

This literature is fast expanding. There have been a few studies on mental health literacy regarding the personality disorders, some concentrating exclusively on psychiatric literacy concerning a specific disorder, such as psychopathy (Furnham, Daoud, & Swami, 2009), borderline disorder (Furnham & Dadabehoy, 2011) or the conduct disorders (Furnham & Carter-Leno, 2012). Others have looked at several personality disorders, like the study of Furnham, Kirkby, and McClelland (2011), which looked at non-experts' knowledge of paranoid, narcissistic, and obsessive-compulsive disorders.

Two more recent studies examined the ability of lay people to identify all the disorders. Furnham, Abajian, and McClelland (2011), contrary to predictions, found that obsessive-compulsive disorder was perceived as a personality disorder by only 41% of the participants, whereas schizotypal was identified as a disorder by 65% of participants and as borderline by 86% of participants. They predicted that a high proportion of participants could recognize that a psychological problem existed, but that a much smaller number were able to label it correctly – which was also found to be the case. Paranoid personality disorder was correctly identified by 29% of participants, and obsessive-compulsive by 25%, but fewer than 10% could correctly identify the remaining disorders. They found that the likelihood of judging a problem would correlate negatively with how well-adjusted the individual in question appeared to be.

Furnham and Winceslaus (2011), using a similar vignette questionnaire, required 223 participants to respond to a questionnaire entitled 'Eccentric people', containing vignettes of ten personality disorders, which they rated and labelled. Participants recognized people with personality disorders as being unhappy, unsuccessful at work, and as having poor personal relationships, but did not associate these problems with psychological causes. Rates of 'correct' labelling were under 7% for seven out of ten personality disorders. Cluster A (apart from paranoid) was commonly labelled as depression or as an autism spectrum disorder. Clusters B and C (apart from obsessive-compulsive) were commonly labelled as 'low self-esteem'. The participants' history of psychological education and illness were positively correlated with the correct recognition of 70% and 60% of the personality disorders, respectively.

An important finding in this area is that the correct recognition of schizophrenia predicts endorsement of a biological or genetic aetiology (Jorm et al., 1997a). It is likely that those who correctly identify schizophrenia have formally studied the disorder and will have informed beliefs about the causes. However, the study suggests that higher levels of mental health literacy predict that lay theories will adhere to the 'medical' model as proposed by Rabkin (1974), which therefore leads to a more positive attitude towards mental disorders.

Again, some argue mental health literacy is a good indicator of the pathways to mental health services. People working in this area are very eager to educate people so that they can get help when they and their friends and relatives really need it (cf. Eysenck, 2011).

It has to be acknowledged, however, that the medical models continuously adapt to new scientific findings. Additionally, pathways to mental health depend on the available institutional networks and their professional orientation in a given area. When even professionals differ in diagnoses and treatment recommendations, lay persons will have problems finding the right explanations for symptoms and taking part in the right treatment decisions.

Some of the arguments against adopting clinical psychiatric diagnosis (frequently coming from clinical psychologists) relate to (un)reliability. Aboraya (2007) in reviewing the literature draw attention to the multitude of factors cited as problem areas, including psychiatric nomenclature and classifications, clinician's bias and prior training, and patient factors (anxiety, defence mechanisms, and poor memory). Hence, identification of such individual differences appears to be a rich source of data for exploring improved treatment plans.

Dickmann and colleagues (2008) could demonstrate a lack of diagnostic reliability for a group of medical doctors. Only one in four of general practitioners correctly diagnosed a depressive syndrome according to International Statistical Classification of Diseases and Related Health Problems (ICD)-10 criteria. In another study by Os and colleagues in the Netherlands and the UK (1999), involving some 700 psychotic patients classified according to one of three main psychiatric systems, including ICD-10, found amongst other observations that those suffering from mania formed 2.6% (using Research Diagnostic Criteria (RDC)) but up to five times more (12.3%) using DSM-III-R. In addition, schizoaffective bipolar had been used for 18.3% of RDC diagnostic criterion but only 3.3% of ICD-10 criterion; whilst major depression was used as a label for 2.7% using ICD-10, it was observed to be assigned to 10.1% of DSM-III-R diagnoses.

Psychiatric diagnoses are not always informative due in part to a lack of consensus among specialists. By implementing these 'descriptions' or labels as if they denote clear and easily defined disorders, this may only confuse the issue.

> By regarding a phenomenon as a psychiatric diagnosis – treating it, reifying it in psychiatric diagnostic manuals, developing instruments to measure it, inventing scales to rate its severity, establishing ways to reimburse the costs of its treatment, encouraging pharmaceutical companies to search for effective drugs, directing patients to support groups, writing about possible causes in journals – psychiatrists may be unwittingly colluding with broader cultural forces to contribute to the spread of a mental disorder.
>
> (Elliot, 2004, p. 230)

Why do people differ in their information about mental health? And why should they differ in their mental health literacy? (cf. Kirkcaldy, Trimpop, & Athanasou, 2001). There is now an extensive and growing literature on mental health literacy.

In a recent review, Eysenck (2011) comments 'Patients low in health literacy give significantly lower ratings than those high in health literacy to general clarity, explanation of care processes, and responsiveness to patient concerns. These findings suggest that communication difficulties impair the medical health care received by patients having low health literacy' (p. 264).

He goes on to link intelligence, working memory, and health in health literacy: it is the 'ability to read and make sense of information about health care, and then to use that information to make appropriate decisions'. He continues:

> Everyone can be regarded as a manager of his/her own health. That task is becoming progressively more complex. As a consequence of the ready availability of the Internet, most people have far more access than at any time in human history to information about the meanings of symptoms, how to diagnose disease, and so on. There has been a dramatic increase in the range of treatments available to many diseases. Which means it is more time consuming than before to work out what to do for the best.
> (Eysenck, 2011, p. 265)

Several studies have found that lay theories are predicted by demographic variables. Specifically, studies show that both younger and more educated people have more informed beliefs concerning mental disorders (Shurka, 1983; Hasin & Link, 1988; Yoder, Shute, & Tryban, 1990; Fisher & Goldney, 2003). Significant effects of gender (Furnham & Manning, 1997), political persuasion (Furnham & Thompson, 1996), and religiousness (Furnham & Haraldsen, 1998) have been found. This suggests that demographic variables may have value in predicting theories of, for example, bipolar disorder.

In relation to *familiarity with* and *knowledge about* mental disorders, participants with less knowledge of autism endorse external theories of cause, such as luck and religion, rather than academic theories (Furnham & Buck, 2003), whereas correct recognition of schizophrenia predicts more informed causal beliefs (Jorm et al., 1997a). Increased recognition of mental disorders has been found for mental health professionals compared to the general public (Jorm et al., 1997c). These studies suggest that informed beliefs about the nature, causes, and treatments of mental illness come from wide reading and academic study and/or extensive contact with people with mental disorders. Therefore, these variables should have predictive value for both recognition and theories of bipolar disorder.

Hamid and Furnham (2014) recently reviewed the Mental health literacy (MHL) studies. They noted three issues:

- The first is *terminology*; some researchers use the term mental health literacy, others psychiatric literacy. Some focus on identification and labelling, some on cause; others on the manifestation of symptoms, the incidence of the illness in the population, and on the treatment/cure of the illness.
- The second is the *theoretical basis* of most of these studies. Few are informed by grand or even mini-theories and this literature still has the feel of exploratory survey world. They could not readily be called surveys

in the technical sense because most are based on small unrepresentative, opportunistic samples. It would be helpful if researchers looked for patterns or types of understanding, as manifest by Siegler and Osmond (1966) or Furnham (1988), where understandings are essentially individualistic or psychological, psychoanalytical, biological or pharmacological, structural or sociological, or even spiritual or metaphysical. Further, an anthropological understanding of cultural issues in the conception and description of mental illness seems lacking.

- The third is *methodology*. Studies tend either to use vignettes for identification or attitude statements for beliefs. These may be administered verbally or in written form, by telephone or on the web, or for less literate people face-to-face in a standard interview. There appear to be no recognized and accepted sets of vignettes used by different researchers to study the same problem. Some have replicated others by 'borrowing' a particular vignette but others have tried to adapt them and still others devised their own. This may in part account for the confusion and lack of replication of results. In a recent study, Sai and Furnham (2013) used three different depression and three different schizophrenia vignettes from different sources. They showed how results differed as a function of the vignette. There seems a need for a library of well-constructed, agreed upon, but succinct vignettes to be used by researchers in this area.

Many groups are concerned with trying to educate lay people about mental health. This includes governments and educational authorities that see obvious benefits of having a psychiatrically literate population. It also includes health professions from psychiatrists to social workers. Furthermore, societies that are formed partly in keeping the public better informed about specific illnesses (i.e., schizophrenia, bipolar disorder) set up websites and conferences with the express aim of educating members of the public about the causes, manifestations, and best treatments for that particular problem.

Kirmayer and Young (1998) have explored the different ways that clinicians, psychiatrists, and anthropologists construe somatizations. Depending on the circumstances, these symptoms can be perceived as an index of disease or disorder, an indication of a specific psychopathology, a symbolic expression of intrapsychic conflict, a culturally coded, idiomatic expression of distress, a medium for expressing social discomfort, and a mechanism through which patients try to reposition themselves within their local worlds.

In an earlier report on treating problem behaviour in children (POST, 1997), several conclusions were reached including the need for: early detection and intervention; preventative measures; the distribution of resources; more information; an improvement in organizational issues ('straddle wide range of different agencies...social services, health, education, etc.'); and the gap between CAMHS (child and adolescent mental health services) and adult services to be closed.

Lessons for the practice

Psychotherapists and psychiatrists need to understand the perception that their clients (children and/or their parents) have of their illness. People have beliefs/ideas/theories concerning the causes, manifestations, and cures for their own and others' mental and physical illness. These ideas determine in part how people make sense of their symptoms, and how and when they seek help.

The literature on adherence suggests patients are more likely to adhere to their doctor's advice if:

> First, the patient wishes to undertake the treatment. Second, the patient is satisfied that the treatment offered is the right course of action. Third, the patient can understand, and is able to undertake, the behaviours required. Fourth, the patient is not impeded in any way during the course of action. Fifth, the patient can monitor progress to the final goal.

General practitioners, in particular, know the importance of the consultation. Pendleton et al. (2003) recommend the following steps, which have been widely adopted and found to be very significant in patient care.

1. Find out why the patient has come today, including: the nature and history of the problems, their causes, the patient's ideas, concerns and expectations, the effects of the problems on the patient and family.
2. Consider other problems such as continuing problems, other risk factors.
3. Choose with the patient an appropriate action for each problem.
4. Achieve a shared understanding of the problems with the patient.
5. Involve the patient in the management and encourage him/her to accept appropriate responsibility.
6. Use time and resources properly.
7. Establish or maintain a relationship with the patient that helps to achieve the other tasks.

If we can better understand the belief systems which our patients, whether children, parents or indeed grandparents, have regarding illnesses, we can better accommodate them and modify our medical treatment plan to take account of these idiosyncrasies. At the very least, in initial sessions with patients, we could include an open-ended question about their subjective models (reasons) for feeling they have that specific ailment; in all likelihood, there is no singular reason expressed, but several frequently conflicting explanations.

Understanding our 'clients' inevitably means gaining more insight into the personal issues that impact on their daily lives, in dealing with an illness. Helman (1981) listed several questions that we ask ourselves when we are taken ill or experience misfortune of any kind. (1) What has happened (labelling the condition)? (2) Why has it happened? (3) Why to me? (4) Why now? (These last three questions embody lay theories of aetiology, and may not relate to medical theories of origin of illnesses.) (5) What would happen if nothing was done about it (addressing lay theories of significance, prognosis, and probable natural history of an ailment)? (6) What should I do about it (strategy or health behaviour)? He argues that the manner in which we answer these queries, and the subsequent behaviour, represents the folk model of disorders. In understanding this level of conceptualization and grasping it, health professionals can address these questions and help resolve them. He concludes that 'For medical care to be most effective and acceptable to patients, general practitioners should treat both illness and disease in their patients at the same time. They should also be aware how the perspectives of the lay and medical models of ill-health differ and should recognize the clinical implications of these differences' (p. 551). Overall, this will facilitate the adherence of patients to medical treatment, and encourage physicians to use multidisciplinary team members, including clinical psychologists, family members, peer groups, educators, legal instructors, nutritional experts, physical and remedial therapists, occupational therapists, etc., to achieve target goals of therapy.

Note: Portions of this chapter have appeared in other publications by us.

References

Aakster, C. (1986). Concepts in alternative medicine. *Social Science and Medicine, 22*, 265–273.

Aborayam, C. (2007). Clinicians' opinions on the reliability of psychiatric diagnosis in clinical settings. *Psychiatry, 4*, 31–33.

Andrews, G., Hall, W., Teesson, M., & Henderson, S. (1999). *The Mental Health of Australians*. Canberra: Commonwealth Department of Health and Aged Care.

Angermeyer, M.C., Daumer, R., & Matschinger, H. (1993). Benefits and risks of psychotropic medication in the eyes of the general public: results of a survey in the Federal Republic of Germany. *Pharmacopsychiatry, 26*, 114–120.

Angermeyer, M.C., & Dietrich, S. (2006). Public beliefs about and attitudes towards people with mental illness: a review of population studies. *Acta Psychiatrica Scandinavica, 113* (3), 163–179.

Angermeyer, M.C., & Matschinger, H. (1996). Public attitude towards psychiatric treatment. *Acta Psychiatrica Scandinavica, 94*, 326–336.

Angermeyer, M.C., & Matschinger, H. (1999). Social representations of mental illness among the public. In: J. Guimon, W. Fischer & N. Sartorius (eds), *The Image of Madness: The Public Facing Mental Illness and Psychiatric Treatment*. Basel: Karger.

Arden, J.B. (2010). *Rewire Your Brain: Think Your Way to a Better Life*. New Jersey: John Wiley & Sons.

Breggin, P.R., & Cohen, D. (2007). *Your Drug May Be Your Problem. How and Why to Stop Taking Psychiatric Medications*. Philadelphia: Da Capro Press.

Dickmann, C., Dickmann, J., & Broocks, A. (2008). How reliably can general practitioners diagnose depression using ICD-10 criteria. *German Journal of Psychiatry, 11*, 148–148.

Elliott, C. (2004). *Better Than Well. American Medicine Meets the American Dream*. New York and London: Norton and Co.

Eysenck, M. (2011). Medical health care: Cognitive psychologist's contribution. In: B.D. Kirkcaldy (ed.), *The Art and Science of Health Care: Psychology and Human Factors for Practitioners*. Cambridge, MA and Göttingen: Hogrefe.

Fischer, L.J., & Goldney, R.D. (2003). Differences in community mental health literacy in older and younger Australians. *International Journal of Geriatric Psychiatry, 18*, 33–40.

Fischer, W., Goerg, D., Zbinden, E., & Guimon, J. (1999). Determining factors and the effects of attitudes towards psychotropic medication. In: J. Guimon, W. Fischer & N. Sartorius (eds), *The Image of Madness: The Public Facing Mental Illness and Psychiatric Treatment*, 162–186. Basel: Karger.

Furnham, A. (1994a). Explaining health and illness. *Social Science and Illness, 39*, 715–725.

Furnham, A. (1994b). Explaining health and illness. *Personality and Individual Differences, 17*, 455–466.

Furnham, A. (2009). Psychiatric and psychotherapeutic literacy: attitudes to, and knowledge of, psychotherapy. *International Journal of Social Psychiatry, 55*, 525–537.

Furnham, A., Abajian, N., & McClelland, A. (2011). Psychiatric literacy and the personality disorders. *Psychiatry Research, 189*, 110–114.

Furnham, A., & Bower, P. (1992). A comparison of academic and lay theories of schizophrenia. *British Journal of Psychiatry, 161*, 201–210.

Furnham, A., & Buck, C. (2003). A comparison of lay-beliefs about autism and obsessive-compulsive disorder. *International Journal of Social Psychiatry, 49*, 287–307.

Furnham, A., & Carter-Leno, V. (2012). Psychiatric literacy and the conduct disorders. *Research in Developmental Disabilities, 33*, 24–31.

Furnham, A., & Chan, E. (2004). Lay theories of schizophrenia. A cross cultural comparison of British and Hong Kong Chinese attitudes, attributions and beliefs. *Social Psychiatry and Psychiatric Epidemiology, 39*, 543–552.

Furnham, A., Cook, R., Martin, N., & Batey, M. (2011). Mental health literacy among university students. *Journal of Public Mental Health, 10*, 198–210.

Furnham, A., & Dadabehoy, J. (2012). Beliefs about causes, behavioural manifestations a treatment of borderline personality disorder. *Psychiatry Research, 197*(3), 307–313.

Furnham, A., Daoud, J., & Swami, V. (2009). 'How to spot a psychopath'. Lay theories of psychopathy. *Social Psychiatry and Psychiatric Epidemiology, 44*, 464–472.

Furnham, A., & Haraldson, E. (1998). Lay theories of etiology and 'cure' for four types of paraphilia: fetishism, paedophilia, sexual sadism, and voyeurism. *Journal of Clinical Psychology, 54* (5), 689–700.

Furnham, A., & Henley, S. (1988). Lay beliefs about overcoming psychological problems. *Journal of Social and Clinical Psychology, 26*, 423–438.

Furnham, A., Kirkby, V., & McClelland, A. (2011). Non-expert's theories of three major personality disorders. *Personality and Mental Health, 5*, 43–56.

Furnham, A., & Lowick, V. (1984). Lay theories of the causes of alcoholism. *British Journal of Medical Psychology*, 57, 319–322.
Furnham, A., & Manning, R. (1997). Young people's theories of anorexia nervosa and obesity. *Counseling Psychology Quarterly*, 10 (4), 389–415.
Furnham, A., & McDermott, M. (1994). Lay beliefs about the efficacy of self reliance, seeking help and estimated control as strategies for overcoming obesity, drug addiction, marital problems, stuttering and insomnia. *Psychology and Health*, 9, 397–406.
Furnham, A., Pereira, E., & Rawles, R. (2001). Lay theories of psychotherapy: perceptions of the efficacy of different 'cures' for specific disorders. *Psychology, Medicine and Health*, 6, 77–84.
Furnham, A., & Rees, J. (1988). Lay theories of schizophrenia. *International Journal of Social Psychiatry*, 34, 212–220.
Furnham, A., & Telford, K. (2011). Public attitudes, lay theories and mental health literacy: The understanding of mental health. In: L. L'Abate (ed.), *Mental Illness – Understanding, Prediction and Control*, 3–22. Croatia: Intech.
Furnham, A., & Telford, K. (2012). Public attitudes, lay theories and mental health literacy: The understanding of mental health. In: L. L'Abate (ed.), *Mental Illnesses: Understanding, Prediction and Control*. Croatia: Intech.
Furnham, A., & Thomson, L. (1996). Lay theories of heroin addiction. *Social Science and Medicine*, 43, 29–40.
Furnham, A., & Wardley, Z. (1990). Lay theories of psychotherapy I: Attitudes to and beliefs about psychotherapy and psychotherapists. *Journal of Clinical Psychology*, 46, 878–890.
Furnham, A., & Wardley, Z. (1991). Lay theories of psychotherapy II: The efficacy of different therapies and prognosis for different problems. *Human Relations*, 44, 1197–2010.
Furnham, A., & Wardley, Z. (1990). Lay theories of psychotherapy I: Attitudes toward, and beliefs about, psychotherapy and therapists. *Journal of Clinical Psychology*, 50, 624–632.
Furnham, A., Wardley, Z., & Lillie, F. (1992). Lay theories of psychotherapy III: Comparing the ratings of lay persons and clinical psychologists. *Human Relations*, 45, 839–858.
Furnham, A., & Winceslaus, J. (2011). Psychiatric literacy and the personality disorders. *Psychopathology*, 45, 29–41.
Gray, R. (1998). Four perspectives on unconventional therapy. *Health*, 2, 55–74.
Hamid, A., & Furnham, A. (2014). Mental health literacy and attitudes to mental illness: a review of the recent literature. *Mental Health Review Journal*, 19 (2), 84–98.
Harland, R., Antonova, E., Owen, G., Broome, M., Landau, S., Deeley, Q., & Murray, R. (2009). A study of psychiatrists' concepts of mental illness. *Psychological Medicine*, 39, 967–976.
Hasin, D., & Link, B. (1988). Age and recognition of depression. *Psychological Medicine*, 18, 683–688.
Helman, C.A. (1981). Disease versus illness in a general practice. *Journal of the Royal College of General Practitioners*, 31, 548–552.
Helman, C.A. (2007/1990). *Culture, Health and Illness*. London: Hodder/Arnold.
Hillert, A., Sandmann, J., Ehmig, S.C., Weisbecker, H., Kepplinger, H.M., & Benkert, O. (1999). The general public's cognitive and emotional perception of mental illnesses: An alternative to attitude-research. In: J. Guimon, W. Fischer & N.

Sartorius (eds), *The Image of Madness. The Public Facing Mental Illness and Psychiatric Treatment*. Basel: Karger.

Jorm, A.F. (2000). Mental health literacy. Public knowledge and beliefs about mental disorders. *British Journal of Psychiatry, 177*, 396–401.

Jorm, A.F., Christensen, H., & Griffiths, K.M. (2005). The public's ability to recognize mental disorders and their beliefs about treatment: changes in Australia over 8 years. *Australia & New Zealand Journal of Psychiatry, 39*, 248–254.

Jorm, A., Korten, A., Jacomb, P., Christensen, H., Rodgers, B., & Pollitt, P. (1997a). Public beliefs about causes and risk factors for depression and schizophrenia. *Social Psychiatry and Psychiatric Epidemiology, 32*, 1143–1145.

Jorm, A., Korten, A., Jacomb, P., Christensen, H., Rodgers, B., & Pollitt, P. (1997b). 'Mental health literacy': a survey of the public's ability to recognize mental disorders and their beliefs about the effectiveness of treatment. *Medical Journal of Australia, 166*, 182–186.

Jorm, A., Korten, A., Rodgers, B., Pollitt, H., Christensen, H., & Henderson, A. (1997c). Helpfulness of interventions for mental disorders: beliefs of health professionals compared to the general public. *British Journal of Psychiatry, 171*, 233–237.

Kessler, R.C., McGonagle, K.A., Zhao, S., Nelson, C.B., Hughes, M., & Eshleman, S. (1994). Lifetime and 12-month prevalence of DSM-III-R psychiatric disorders in the United States: results from the National Comorbidity Survey. *Archives of General Psychiatry, 51*, 8–19.

Kirkcaldy, B.D. (2014). *Descriptions of Clinical Psychotherapeutic Work* (in preparation), ICSOMH.

Kirkcaldy, B.D., Furnham, A., Trimpop, R., & Knobloch, J. (2001). Akzeptanz und Skepsis: Einstellungen und Verhalten von Nutzern der Alternativ- und Schulmedizin. (Acceptance and scepticism: attitudes and behaviour of users of complementary and traditional medicine.) *Zeitschrift für Gesundheitspsychologie, 9* (2), 57–66.

Kirkcaldy, B.D., & Siefen, R.G. (2012). Subjective models of psychological disorders: Mental health professionals' perspectives. *Asian Journal of Psychiatry, 5* (4), 319–326.

Kirkcaldy, B.D., Trimpop, R., & Athanasou, J. (2001). An evaluation of occupational health and safety information for professionals. *Evaluation Journal of Australasia, 1* (1), 73–74.

Kirmayer, L.J., & Young, A. (1998). Culture and summarization. *Psychological Medicine, 60*, 420–443.

Kirsch, I., Deacon, B.J., Huedo-Medina, T.B., Scoboria, A., Moore, T.A., & Johnson, B.T. (2012). Initial Severity and Antidepressant Benefits: A Meta-Analysis of Data Submitted to the Food and Drug Administration. http://www.plosmedicine.org/article/info:doi/10.1371/journal.pmed.0050045.

Klapheck, K., Nordmeyer, S., Cronjäger H., Naber, D., & Bock, T. (2012). Subjective experience and meaning of psychoses: the German Subjective Sense in Psychosis Questionnaire (SUSE). *Psychological Medicine, 42*, 61–71.

Klimidis, S., Hsiao, F-H., & Minas, H. (2007). Chinese-Australians' knowledge of depression and schizophrenia in the context of their under-utilization of mental health care: an analysis of labeling. *International Journal of Social Psychiatry, 53* (5), 464–479.

Knapp, J., & Delprato, D. (1980). Willpower, behavior therapy, and the public. *Psychological Record, 30*, 477–482.

Lin, E., Goering, P., Offord, D.R., Campbell, D., & Boyle, M.H. (1996). The use of mental health services in Ontario: epidemiologic findings. *Canadian Journal of Psychiatry, 41*, 572–577.
Link, B.G., Phelan, J.C., Bresnahan, M., Stueve, A., & Pescosolido, B.A. (1999). Public conceptions of mental illness: labels, causes, dangerousness, and social distance. *American Journal of Public Health, 89*, 1328–1333.
Merluzzi, T., Rudy, T., & Glass, C. (1981). The information-processing paradigm: Implications for clinical science. In: T. Merluzzi, C. Glass & M. Genest (eds), *Cognitive Assessment.* New York: Guilford Press.
Nunnally, J. (1961). *Popular Conceptions of Mental Health.* New York: Holt, Rinehart & Winston.
Pendleton, D., Schofield, T., Tate, P., & Havelock, P. (2003). *The New Consultation.* Oxford: Oxford University Press.
Petermann, F., & Wiedebusch, S. (2001). Patientenschulung mit Kindern: Wie lassen sich subjektive Krankheits- und Behandlungskonzepte berücksichtigen? *Kindheit und Entwicklung, 10* (1), 13–27.
POST (1997). *Treating Problem Behavior in Children.* London: The Parliamentary Office of Science and Technology.
Priest, R.G., Vize, C., Roberts, A., Roberts, M., & Tylee, A. (1996). Lay people's attitudes to treatment of depression: results of opinion poll for Defeat Depression Campaign just before its launch. *British Medical Journal, 313*, 858–859.
Rabkin, J.G. (1974). Public attitudes toward mental illness: a review of the literature. *Psychological Bulletin, 10*, 9–33.
Rasmussen, H.N., Scheier, M.F., & Greenhouse, J.B. (2009). Optimism and physical health: a meta-analytic review. *Annals of Behavioral Medicine, 37*, 239–256.
Rippere, V. (1977). Commonsense beliefs about depression and antidepressive behaviour. A study of social consensus. *Behaviour Research and Therapy, 17*, 465–473.
Rippere, V. (1981). How depressing: another cognitive dimension of commonsense knowledge. *Behaviour Research and Therapy, 19*, 169–181.
Rogalski, C.J. (1984). Professional psychotherapy and its relationship to compliance in treatment. *International Journal of the Addictions*, Aug, *19* (5), 521–539.
Sai, G., & Furnham, A. (2013). Identifying depression and schizophrenia using vignettes: a methodological note. *Psychiatry Research*, pii: S0165-1781(13)00261.
Sarbin, T.R., & Mancuso, J.C. (1970). Failure of a moral enterprise: attitudes of the public toward mental illness. *Journal of Consulting and Clinical Psychology, 35* (46), 66–74.
Sarbin, T.R., & Mancuso, J.C. (1972). Paradigms and moral judgments: improper conduct is not disease. *Journal of Consulting and Clinical Psychology, 13*, 6–8.
Shurka, E. (1983). Attitudes of Israeli Arabs towards the mentally ill. *International Journal of Social Psychiatry, 29*, 101–110.
Siegler, M., & Osmond, H. (1966). Models of madness. *British Journal of Psychiatry, 112*, 1193–1203.
Stainton Rogers, W. (1991). *Explaining Health and Illness: An Exploration of Diversity.* London: Wheatsheaf.
Star, S. (1955). *The public's ideas about mental illness.* Paper presented at the Annual Meeting of the National Association for Mental Health; November 5, Indianapolis, IN.
Swami, V., Arteche, A., Chamorro-Premuzic, T., Maakip, I., Stanistreet, D., & Furnham, A. (2009). Lay perceptions of current and future heath, the causes of illness, and the nature of recovery. *British Journal of Health Psychology, 14*, 519–540.

Tolstoy, L. (1869, 2009). *War and Peace*. Book 10: 1812. Chapter XXIX. http://www.gutenberg.org/files/2600/2600-h/2600-h.htm.

Vallis, T.N., & McHugh, S. (2004). Illness behaviour. Challenging the medical model. *Humane Medicine: Health Care, 3* (1), http://www.humanehealthcare.com/Article.asp?art_id=173.

van Os J., Verdoux H., Maurice Tison S., Gay B., et al. (1999). Self-reported psychosis-like symptoms and the continuum of psychosis. *Social Psychiatry and Psychiatric Epidemiology, 34*(9), 459–463.

Wade, S., & Halligan, S. (2004). Do biomedical models of illness make for good health care systems. *British Medical Journal, 329*, 1398–1401.

Whitaker, R. (2010). *Anatomy of an Epidemic. Magic Bullets, Psychiatric Drugs, and the Astonishing Rise of Mental Illness in America*. New York: Broadway.

Wilkinson, R., & Pickett, K. (2010). *The Spirit Level. Why Equality Is Better for Everyone*. London and New York: Penguin.

Wong, J. (1994). Lay theories of psychotherapy and perceptions of therapists: a replication and extension of Furnham and Wardley. *Journal of Clinical Psychology, 50* (4), 624–632.

Yoder, C.Y., Shute, G.E., & Tryban, G.M. (1990). Community recognition of objective and subjective characteristics of depression. *American Journal of Community Psychology, 18*, 547–566.

3
A Paradigm Shift: Social Functioning Rather Than Symptom Reduction

Ahmed Hankir and Dinesh Bhugra

Introduction

> All happy families resemble one another and each unhappy family is unhappy in its own way...
>
> Leo Tolstoy, *Anna Karenina*

The family unit, in any given time or place, can constantly shift between cohesion and fragmentation and can be influenced by political, psychosocial, economic, and cultural currents. Each member of a family can occupy a position on the continuum of the human lifespan and has a role to play, including children and adolescents, who are also expected to talk, behave, and function accordingly (not only by their families but also by society). In clinical care, too, such distinctions are applied, where neonatology, paediatrics, adolescence, and geriatric medicine are seen as sub-specialities of medicine; similarly, this is reflected by the variety of sub-specialities in psychiatric practice (i.e., child and adolescent psychiatry, general adult psychiatry, and later life psychiatry).

Psychopathology in any of its many forms will affect the dynamic between the different members of a family. Families create psychopathology but also have to deal with it. For example, in a patriarchal family unit, the father is expected to be the breadwinner. If, however, the father succumbs to a major depressive disorder, he may consequently no longer be able to function socially and occupationally, and the eldest son is then expected to be the 'man of the family' and work to provide for himself, his siblings and his parents, and maybe even his extended family. Modern medicine, which has become synonymous in many peoples' minds with 'Western' medicine, may not take into consideration the cultural context of *illness* and *disease* and their psychosocial consequences on the family unit and the community at large in an increasingly globalized world.

There is a growing perception that science alone provides overall insufficient foundation for the holistic understanding of the interaction between health, *illness*, and *disease*. Notwithstanding the aforementioned, other myriad issues have also been identified in modern medicine, such as the fact that 5–15% of schizophrenia sufferers experience psychotic symptoms despite medication. Over recent years, the health humanities have emerged as a distinct entity in attempts to ameliorate the limitations in the provision of health care services.

In this chapter we discuss and describe the merits of the health humanities and how it can be utilized as an effective form of adjunctive therapy as well as an educational tool for service users and their families, carers, and the general public. We highlight the role that culture plays, particularly with regard to the advent of globalization and the subject of migration, and consider the effects that these factors can have on the functioning of the family unit. We also provide a brief overview on the inception of a relatively new branch of psychiatry, namely cultural psychiatry, and its relevance and application to modern health care. We start off by defining and discussing two important concepts in health care, *illness* and *disease*, and what these two concepts mean to practitioners and patients. We then describe how *illness* and *disease* influence the dialectic between service provider and service user.

Disease vs. illness

Eisenberg (1977) and Kleinman (1980) argue that in psychiatry, as in the rest of medicine, a line of demarcation must be made between disease and illness. Disease, succinctly put, is about pathology. Illness, however, is something that a person develops when their disease starts to have effects on their lives and on the lives of the people who encompass them. Disease literally means 'dis-ease', a malfunctioning of biological or psychological processes, whereas illness refers to the psychosocial aspects of disease. Illness, thus, includes the subjective perception of the disease and its social and interpersonal dimensions and implications. With respect to the assessment, diagnosis, and management of individuals presenting with physical or psychological symptoms, the culture can be such that doctors, including psychiatrists, are solely trained and interested in recognizing and addressing disease. Patients, however, are by and large interested on the effects that disease has on their functioning, that is, the implications that illness might have on their social and occupational functioning (e.g., the so-called 'illness' role and sick leave from work), and indeed on their existence in general.

Thus, doctors are primarily preoccupied with formulating a differential diagnosis and, although patients are often concerned and interested in what the diagnosis may be, they are more concerned about what the mechanism of the disease is as well as how the disease might impact on their lives. There exists, therefore, a clash between the patient's views and explanatory models and those of his or her doctor. Consequently, the space and discord between the patient and the doctor can lead to tension and poor outcomes. A perceptive and culturally competent clinician must be able to detect this issue and act accordingly to ameliorate it (i.e., ensure that the provision of health care services are service-user centred).

The health humanities: A succinct definition

The health humanities are broadly described as including medical ethics, medical sociology, social history of medicine, and the application of arts and literature in general to medicine. It has been argued that the health humanities can complement medical science and technology through contrasting perspectives of the arts and humanities by shaping the nature, goals, and knowledge base of medicine. What is implicit in these arguments is that there is something about the scientific stance that detaches the medical practitioner from the subjective experience of patients and, this view proposes, the arts or the humanities can facilitate the re-engagement of the practitioner with the subjective world of the patient (Oyebode, 2009).

The wide-ranging remit of the health humanities: The indisputable power of the written word – narrative and illness

> When I was first aware that I had been laid low by the disease, I felt the need, among other things, to register a strong protest against the word 'depression'. Depression, most people know, used to be termed 'melancholia' a word which...crops up more than once in Chaucer, who in his usage seemed to be more aware of its pathological nuances. 'Melancholia' would still appear to be a far more apt and evocative word for the blacker forms of the disorder, but instead was usurped by a noun with blank tonality and lacking any magisterial presence, used indifferently to describe an economic decline or a rut in the ground, a true wimp of a word for such a major illness. It may be that the scientist generally held responsible for its currency in modern times, a John Hopkins Medical School faculty member justly venerated – the Swiss born Psychiatrist Adolf Meyer – had a tin ear for the finer rhythms of English...As one who has suffered from the malady in extremis yet returned to tell the tale, I would lobby for a truly arresting designation...Told that someone has evolved a storm – a veritable howling tempest of the brain, which is indeed what clinical depression resembles like nothing else – even the uniformed layman might display sympathy rather than the standard reaction that 'depression' evokes, something akin to 'so what' or 'you'll pull out of it' or 'we have all had bad days'...
> (Styron, 1990, p. 19)

In the above excerpt, Styron effectively and evocatively describes the perils of reductionism in his own autobiographical narrative in reference to the usage of the term depression (which he experienced in later life) and how it came to replace the more apt term, certainly in his opinion, melancholia. Styron's account commands the attention of all those who stake a claim in wanting to fathom the subjective experience of a major depressive disorder in older people.

The 2013 chief medical officer's Annual Report on Public Mental Health stated that depressive disorder (and not dementia) is the commonest mental illness in older people (Copeland et al., 2003). The above account may have relevance and resonance with older people (either because they may be at the throes of a major psychiatric disorder or they are the carer of someone who is) and is certainly recommended reading, as far as the authors are concerned, for mental health care providers since they may be in contact and have to treat older people (or indeed have a grandparent) who have first-hand experience of clinical depression.

It is with the immediacy and authenticity of the first-person narrative that the 'mental illness memoir' creates a vivid account of human existence in the 'Kingdom of the Sick' (Sontag, 1978). The eminent 20th-century British neurologist Oliver Sacks emphatically argues in the preface of his best-selling book *The Man Who Mistook His Wife for a Hat* that, '...in order to restore the human subject at the centre, the suffering, afflicted, fighting human subject we must deepen a case history into a narrative or tale...' (Sacks, 1985, p. iii).

As mentioned above, autobiographical narratives from people who have first-hand experience of a mental health challenge fall under the wide-ranging remit of the health humanities. Autobiographical narratives of psychopathology sufferers are gaining popularity as an effective form of adjunctive therapy and also as a means to campaign against the stigma associated with mental illness (Hankir & Zaman, 2013).

The health humanities are beneficial for both service providers and service users (although the two are not necessarily dichotomous as will be expanded upon and explained further below). Indeed, reading autobiographical narratives of psychopathology sufferers can 'augment' and 'embellish' service providers' and the general public's humanity by offering precious qualitative insights into minds that are afflicted with mental illness (Hankir & Zaman, 2013). This might actually help to reduce the public stigma associated with mental illness. Moreover, a service user, as a human being, can derive solace from shared experience, and 'survivors' of mental illness have reported the therapeutic and even cathartic effects of composing and reading autobiographical narratives from fellow *'passengers'* (the metaphor 'journey' is often used by those who have first-hand experience of psychopathology) who have experienced mental illness (Kirkcaldy, 2013; Hankir et al., 2014).

Cutting Edge Psychiatry in Practice (CEPiP) is a peer-reviewed psychiatry journal that includes in each issue an autobiographical narrative from a person who suffers from that issue's particular theme. In the inaugural issue of CEPiP entitled *The Management of Schizophrenia: An Update*, the poet David Holloway authors an article entitled 'My colourful life with schizophrenia'. Tom Inskip, a general practitioner who was invited to comment on the article, stated that David's publication was, '...a very moving account from a highly articulate individual with schizophrenia and illustrates that the condition [schizophrenia] can occur in wonderfully sensitive, creative and caring individuals...' (Holloway, 2011).

Inskip's comment is important for multifarious reasons. Firstly, it gives credence to the notion that those who have an 'enduring' mental illness (schizophrenia and bipolar disorder in particular) can make meaningful and valuable contributions to the arts and society. It also helps to debunk the perception and myth that all those who have psychopathology have a preoccupation with committing violent acts.

John Perceval, the progeny of Spencer Perceval (who was murdered in the House of Commons and who remains the only British prime minister ever to be assassinated), composed a poignant autobiographical narrative about his own experiences with schizophrenia and the painstaking lengths that he would go to in order to be a law-abiding, peace-promoting citizen of society:

> ...If anyone knew how painful the task of self-examination and self-control was, to which I devoted myself to at the time, every minute, without respite, except when I was asleep, in order that I might behave, and with the sincere desire of behaving becomingly; they would understand how cruel I felt it afterwards, when I required my liberty for the further pursuit of health and strength of mind, to have it denied to me for fear of my doing any person any bodily harm....
>
> (Bateson, 1962)

Indeed, Holloway eloquently states in his own autobiographical narrative that, '...I pray that the perception of schizophrenia can be altered to that of a renewed awareness which evokes notions of love, peace and harmony...instead of the crude depictions [of schizophrenia] that are perpetuated by negative crime films in Hollywood productions...' (Holloway, 2011).

The point that we are trying to make is the following: we encourage mental health practitioners to deconstruct and reformulate their views on psychiatry and 'madness' not based on impulse, sensationalism, anecdote, or myths but on their sense of reason, morality, and evidence. (A recent study in collaboration with researchers based in the Karolinski Institute in Stockholm, Sweden, that was spearheaded by Seena Fazel, University of

Oxford, revealed that those who have a severe mental illness are no more likely to be violent than those who don't have one – unless they abuse alcohol or substances (Fazel et al., 2010).)

The wounded healer and autobiographical narratives

Each individual is capable of developing some form of mental or physical illness. This includes health care professionals who also have the capacity to 'transform' into treatment-seeking patients. Indeed, despite the perception that doctors should be 'invincible', mental health challenges are actually over-represented in this population (Henderson et al., 2012). Carl Jung used the term the 'wounded healer' as an archetypal dynamic to describe a phenomenon that may take place, both positively and negatively, in the relationship between the analyst and analysand (Jackson, 2001). The 'wounded healer' remains a powerful archetype in the healing arts. Carl Jung discovered this archetype in relation to himself; for Jung, 'A good half of every treatment that probes at all deeply consists in the doctor's examining himself... it is his own hurt that gives a measure of his power to heal. This, and nothing else, is the meaning of the Greek myth of the wounded physician' (Stevens, 1994).

Jung traced the origins of the concept of the 'wounded healer' to the epoch of the ancient myths of Chiron and the wounded centaur and his student Asclepius, who later became the God of medicine and healing. The 'wounded healer' archetype probably precedes this, however. For example, in Shamanism, traditions have held that the healers must first be wounded themselves before they can be truly effective in helping another to heal.

Autobiographical narratives of the 'wounded healer' are gaining popularity among doctors with mental health challenges as an effective form of adjunctive therapy (Hankir et al., 2014). A notable example is Kay Redfield Jamison, Professor of Psychiatry at the Johns Hopkins School of Medicine, whose magnum opus on bipolar disorder was chosen in 1990 as the most outstanding book in the biomedical sciences by the American Association of Publishers.

Kay Jamison is a world authority on bipolar disorder; she also has firsthand experience of it. *An Unquiet Mind* is the title of Jamison's autobiographical narrative and in it she eloquently describes the subjective experience of profound oscillations in mood and the effects that this had on her cognitive schema, behaviour, and functioning. She is able to adopt the dual perspectives of objectivity and subjectivity, and thus repudiates the unfounded perception that service provider and service user are ostensibly dichotomous. She reconciles the healer with the healed, and her mastery of the English language gives a voice to the voiceless and serves as an efficacious adjunct to psychotherapy and pharmacotherapy, especially for those who derive solace from shared experience.

The 2012 Morris Markowe Award-winning article, 'Doctors go mad too'

Morris Markowe was Registrar for the Royal College of Psychiatrists (RCPsych). Funds were donated in his memory to found the Morris Markowe Award, which falls under the auspices of the Public Education Committee of the RCPsych, and is considered by many to be highly prestigious. It is given yearly to the most outstanding article that improves the public understanding of psychiatry. The 2012 winner was Claire Polkinghorn for her article entitled 'Doctors go mad too'.

Polkinghorn begins her award-winning article by alluding to Atticus Finch in Harper Lee's Pulitzer Prize-winning novel *To Kill a Mocking Bird*. According to Atticus Finch, 'You never really understand a person until you consider things from his point of view... until you climb into his skin and walk around in it.' Polkinghorn candidly and, indeed, courageously describes her own feelings about her experiences as a doctor with mental health challenges:

> ...As a psychiatrist, I had hoped that I was pretty good at empathising with my patients. However the last nine months of my life has taught me more about mental illness than years of clinics, ward-rounds, home visits or reading psychiatric literature. I have been signed off sick with a depressive illness, was detained under the Mental Health Act and spent six weeks in an NHS psychiatric hospital...
> (http://www.rcpsych.ac.uk/pdf/Doctors%20Go%20Mad%20Too.pdf)

It would appear that Polkinghorn is intimating that, as a doctor, having first-hand experience of mental health challenges made her more empathetic towards mental health care service users. Indeed, a motif or recurrent theme of narratives from doctors who have experienced mental illness is that they have, without a doubt, become more empathetic as a result. Laurence Kirmayer, Professor of Cultural Psychiatry at McGill University in Montreal, Canada, argues in an interview that '...as a physician, coming to terms with one's own vulnerability and using it to help understand the predicaments of our patients can provide an important path to empathy and a way to mobilize their own capacities to heal...' (Hankir, 2014).

If the parents of a family were aware that doctors who experience mental health challenges can make a full recovery and develop what Prince Charles has described as a 'healing empathy' as a result, perhaps there would be less public stigma associated with mental illness, particularly in health care professionals. We also know that there are physicians who have had first-hand experience of psychopathology and have become highly successful leaders and experts in their respective fields (as in the cases of Kay Redfield Jamison, and the 2013 Royal College of Psychiatrists Foundation Doctor of the Year, who also has first-hand experience of profound oscillations in his mood (Hankir & Zaman, 2013)). These are but a few of the many examples that should sound the death knell of associating mental health challenges with poor performance and under-achievement. After all, wouldn't you rather that you, your child or a family member be treated by a compassionate and competent clinician than a competent but 'cold' one?

Psychiatry and film

The study of the portrayal of mental illness in film also falls under the wide-ranging remit of the health humanities. Film wields colossal power: through the journey of a single film, we can take a roller-coaster ride across the spectrum of human emotion. Film can enthral an entire auditorium heaving with people, or it can silence and even reduce them to tears.

Films are extremely popular across different cultures. India is the country that produces the largest number of films every year. In 2009 alone, the Hindi film industry, Bollywood, contributed a staggering 1,288 Indian feature films. The US, Hong Kong, and Nigeria are examples of other countries where film industries are booming.

One could argue that for as long as human beings continue to seek entertainment and escapism – in the words of T.S. Eliot, *'mankind cannot bear very much reality'* – cinema will remain deeply embedded in our society. Thus, the storylines of films are influenced by the society in which we live. Given that one in four of us has a mental illness at some point in our lives (World Health Organization, 2001), mental illness and the psychiatrists who treat these illnesses play huge roles in our society and on our screens. Movies can provide an insight into what it is like to have a psychiatric illness, they can portray the role of a psychiatrist, and they can reveal how society reacts to either or both. In view of this, Bhugra has examined the Bollywood films produced since the early 1960s as a means of analysing the changes in Indian society's attitudes towards mental health issues (Deakin & Bhugra, 2012).

Bhugra's (Deakin et al., 2012) analyses reveal how, in post-colonial India in the 1950s and 1960s, there were many films featuring people with mental illness that were subject to ridicule, but also that there were some films that had sympathetic portrayals of sufferers of mental illness. In the 1970s and 1980s, when the country was going through major economic, social, and political upheavals, the portrayal of mental illness in film was very much of psychopaths who couldn't rely on the system to provide for the vulnerable, so they were vigilantes taking the law into their own hands. This image of mental illness sufferers transformed in the 1990s, when many motion pictures portrayed the theme of morbid jealousy. These films typically involved men who were trying to control women and who viewed women as a kind of commodity. This period overlapped with the economic liberalization that was taking place in India, which gave people the power and freedom to have possessions. Many men extended this to include women and viewed them as property that they could and should own.

Inaccurate portrayals of mental illness can perpetuate stigma and propagate myths, but when correctly presented they can educate the public, inform employers, and empower service users. Film, therefore, can be used for educational purposes and the RCPsych is not oblivious to this. Indeed, an example of an initiative that the College supports is a monthly blog on their website entitled *Minds on Film*. According to the website, *Minds on Film* '...*explores psychiatric conditions and mental health issues as portrayed in a selection of readily available films...*' http://www.rcpsych.ac.uk/discoverpsychiatry/mindsonfilmblog.aspx

The stigma associated with mental health challenges

> Both experiences were horrible but with breast cancer people ran towards me with open arms and hugged me, with depression people ran away... When I was diagnosed with breast cancer I was inundated with get well soon cards. When news leaked out that I was in a psychiatric hospital following a mental breakdown, not a peep and certainly no cards...
>
> Trisha Goddard, British Television Personality
> (http://www.timetochangeleeds.co.uk/wp-content
> uploads2012/11/Trisha-Goddard-talks-about-her-
> own-experience-with2.pdf)

In Ancient Greece, 'stigma' referred to as a scar on the skin of criminals. It was a sign to all that these people were unsafe, unclean, and unwanted (Sartorius et al., 2010). Such stigma is found to persist today in the attitudes towards those who have a mental illness (Evans-Lacko et al., 2013). Nowhere is this more apparent than in the medical profession; indeed, the results of the 2008 Stigma Shout Survey of almost 4,000 mental health service users and their carers, conducted by a UK mental health charity, revealed that health care professionals are a common source of discrimination towards people with mental illness (http://www.time-to-change.org.uk/news/stigma-shout-survey-shows-real-impact-stigma-and-discrimination-peoples-lives). This would also be consistent with the results of recent research on health care professionals, which has identified them as a source of discrimination (Henderson et al., in press).

Stigma: A contemporary definition

Although the term 'stigma' has ancient origins, it was only in the 20th century that the term was introduced into the psychological and sociological literatures. Evans-Lacko and co-workers conducted a systematic mapping of the literature on the state of the art in European research on reducing social exclusion and stigma related to mental health. As part of their study, they examined whether published studies included a formal definition of the social issue being studied in order to better understand the theoretical underpinnings of the studies (Evans-Lacko et al., 2014). Goffman's seminal definition of stigma as 'an attribute that is deeply discrediting and that reduces the bearer from a whole and usual person to a tainted, discounted one' (Goffman, 1963, p. 3) was often quoted, when an explicit definition was provided. However, in recent years, Link, Phelan, and colleagues have revisited this definition to reflect advances in stigma research. Their definition distinguishes between five main components of stigma – labelling, stereotyping, separation, status loss, and discrimination (Link et al., 2001, 2004) – and this was used in the majority of the studies that included a definition.

Sadow and Ryder (2008) have demonstrated that social contact with someone who has mental health challenges is an effective way of reducing public stigma. In fact, the results of a meta-analysis of outcome studies on challenging the public stigma of mental illness revealed that social contact was actually better than education in reducing stigma for adults (Corrigan et al., 2012).

Certain programmes have been set up that are specifically designed to reduce mental health stigma among professionals and professional trainees. The Education Not Discrimination (END) intervention is an example of such a programme that is targeted at medical students. Friedrich et al. (2013) investigated the impact of the END anti-stigma programme, at the time it was introduced and 6 months later, with regard to knowledge, attitudes, behaviour, and empathy. Their results revealed that, although END produced a short-term improvement, there was little evidence of its persistent effect in reducing stigma. They concluded that their findings suggested there was a need for greater integration of ongoing measures to reduce stigma into medical school curricula; they also discussed the potential merits of 'booster' sessions.

Stigma and discrimination are pervasive phenomena which exert a negative influence, in a multitude of ways, on the lives of many individuals affected by mental illness. Anti-stigma work targeting specific groups, such as health care staff, or strategies which empower individuals facing discrimination, are likely to play a key role in reducing the impact of stigma. Interventions building on the principle of contact frequently show promise in reducing the stigma associated with mental health challenges and we need to continue to incorporate personal stories and narratives into interventions in order to build awareness at local and national levels.

The role of culture in the provision of mental health care services

> We human beings are, after all, cultural beings...
> Professor Laurence Kirmayer, James McGill Professor
> and Director of the Division of Social and Transcultural
> Psychiatry at McGill University, Montreal, Canada

Culture has been defined as the *'Learned, shared and transmitted values, beliefs, norms and life ways of a particular group [of people] that guides their thinking, decision-making, and actions in patterned [stereotypical] ways'* (Leininger & McFarland, 2002). We know that culture is integrated; people acquire and assimilate culture. Although culture can change (gradually or abruptly), culture also ensures generational continuity. It is society and culture – through the proxy of policymakers – that determines the provision of physical and mental health care services (and the parity or *dis*parity of esteem between the two), and those who may receive and use them.

A given culture can also determine what is considered to be mental illness. For example, Muslims have been known to attribute mental and psychological phenomena to Jinn possession and/or the 'evil eye'. The explanatory models that a cultural group formulates can influence why they may, for instance, consult a faith healer as opposed to a general practitioner and hence not receive the benefits of early intervention.

There are some cultures that are more stigmatizing than others towards psychiatry and psychiatric illnesses, and this can have an effect on recruitment into the specialty and the number of psychiatrists there are in a given place. For example, in an interview with a British consultant psychiatrist who rendered voluntary mental health humanitarian services to civilians in post-Arab Spring Libya, he reported that there was not a single psychiatrist in the entire city of Misrata (Hankir & Sadiq, 2013). A contributory factor to this statistic is the perception, certainly in the Arab world but not confined to it, that psychiatrists are not 'real' doctors and that the specialty does not have a robust scientific basis or 'is not scientific enough'. Medical graduates may thus be reluctant to specialize in this area of medicine, since they may gravitate to what they perceive (and certainly what the media portrays) to be the more 'glamorous' and 'legitimate' specialities such as plastic surgery.

Culture can also determine the amount of resources that a government allocates to certain health care services. From a mental health care policy and provision point of view, this can result in the closure of psychiatric inpatient beds, which has been happening in the UK, resulting in some service users in a crisis having to travel hundreds of miles from where they live in order to receive emergency inpatient care.

Cultural factors in the context suicidal behaviour

Self-harm and suicidal behaviour have existed for millennia across different cultures, although each specific culture may attach its own unique meaning to these acts. Thakur (1963) discusses two types of suicide: religious suicide and general suicide. Religious suicide has been observed in both the Hindu and Jain religions (Embree, 1994). General suicide encompasses social, economic, and political factors. Politically motivated suicides tend to be dramatic and carried out in public (Bhugra, 1991).

Both the person's cultural background and the destination culture that the individual is migrating to can influence his or her proclivity towards suicidal behaviours. The term 'self-harm' evidently incorporates the word 'self' and the concept of 'the self' has great variation across cultural groups. A culture that has a socio-centric concept of the self would mean that a member of that culture who engages in self-harming behaviour can unintentionally 'harm' those who may encompass him or her, since the socio-centric concept of self transcends the plane of the egocentric self. This can be a protective factor, since the person contemplating suicidal behaviour may not want to harm those who have his or her best interests at heart and hence this would preclude them from carrying out the act.

Conversely, the concept of the self as being socio-centric can also be a risk factor since acts of self-harm can be aimed towards certain individuals in order to antagonize them and/or to communicate a message to them. For example, a young Asian female in an arranged marriage, who has migrated to a British culture and left her family behind her in India, may feel isolated, trapped, and 'voiceless'. She may feel that the only way of getting her voice heard is by killing herself as has tragically been noted in case studies. Indeed, the results of a prospective study revealed that females of Asian origin, who migrated to England and later attempted suicide, reported arranged marriages to be a contributory factor for their behaviour (Bhugra & Desai, 2002).

Cultural bereavement

As discussed and described above, an immigrant often has to come to terms with loss and this is often heralded by bereavement. Psychoanalytic explanations of the loss of all that is important for an individual may lead to melancholia and depression, and have been termed 'cultural bereavement' (Eisenbruch, 1990, 1991). The stress of migration may also produce physical illnesses, and clinicians must be aware of the interaction between physical and mental illness (i.e., an individual with schizophrenia who also has hypercholesterolemia may lack the ability to comply with pharmacotherapy). Since hypercholesterolemia is a risk factor for ischaemic heart disease, this patient may develop acute coronary syndrome as a result, which could be fatal without life-saving intervention.

'Culture conflict' and 'culture shock'

> The term 'culture conflict' describes tensions between individuals or even the struggle that an individual has with oneself when they attempt to resolve and integrate perceived or real irreconcilable values.
>
> (Bhugra & Becker, 2005)

Individuals may sometimes find themselves in conflict concerning their own 'soul'. Take, for example, a single Muslim Algerian man who has migrated to a Western destination culture where prostitution and alcohol are both rife and legal (e.g., Belgium). That very man must, if he wishes to practise his religion, attempt to resist these temptations which are seemingly ubiquitous. Despite the fact that he may be a pious person, he is a human being after all, and as such it is only natural for him to have a desire to fornicate, for instance. He may not be able to resist this powerful impulse and, by surrendering to it, may be consumed by remorse for not being steadfast to his religious beliefs (in his perception). A possible consequence of this is the development of a severe depressive illness and, in extremis, suicidal ideation (Hankir & Zaman, 2013).

Regarding tensions between individuals, we can use the example of a younger member of a migrant family being attracted to the destination culture he or she is thrust into. This young immigrant may individuate and deviate from the culture of origin, and imitate the prevailing culture. The family may then attempt to reel the perceived maverick youth back into the fold and inculcate him or her with traditional cultural values. Here we have a clash between the ostensibly dichotomous orthodox values of the origin culture and the less traditional values of the destination culture. This can cause the renegade individual to feel melancholic, isolated, ostracized and, in extreme cases, suicidal. This would be consistent with the findings of research into intergenerational conflict in young people of Asian origin in the US, which showed that intergenerational conflict increased the risk of suicide by 30-fold, especially in less educated young people (Bursztein & Makinen, 2010).

'Culture conflict' should be distinguished from 'culture shock', which is what individuals may experience after migration, as their adjustment to the destination culture may occur over a prolonged and protracted period. There is, however, a degree of overlap between the two. Culture shock has been defined as the 'Sudden unpleasant feelings that violate an individual's expectations of the new culture [they have migrated to] and cause them to value their own culture negatively' (Bhugra & Ayonrinde, 2004). Oberg (1960) identified six aspects of culture shock: strain; a sense of loss or feelings of deprivation; rejection by members of the new culture; role expectation and role confusion; surprise, anxiety and indignation; and feelings of impotence.

Migration and mental health

Setting the scene: A narrative offering a qualitative insight into suicidal behaviour in a refugee family:

Imagine that you are an Afghani refugee. You are a single mother with two children who has fled an abusive marriage, and survived two rapes, including one in a refugee detention centre that resulted in pregnancy. You have endured separation from your supportive parents, who die in Afghanistan while you are still awaiting asylum. While attempting to cope with all this, together with unemployment, isolation and ostracism from your ethnic community, you hear that your refugee claim has been denied. In despair, you threaten to kill yourself and your children.
Lost in Translation: Mental Health of Newcomers. Written for New Canadian Media by Aparna Sanyal

Birthplace is an index of migration and can form part of the definition of a migrant ethnic population. Immigrants, particularly refugees, have long been treated as a marginalized, stigmatized, and socially excluded people from their destination culture. This and other issues that immigrants can encounter (i.e., acculturation stress, poverty, unemployment, and the inability to speak the dominant language to name but a few) can have profound effects on their mental wellbeing, so much so that they may resort to tragically ending their lives by their own hands.

It is important to differentiate between groups who have migrated voluntarily and those who have migrated through compulsion, for example, the exodus of Syrians into Turkey due to the conflict in their country of origin. Refugees are perhaps the most vulnerable group of all immigrants. According to the Geneva Convention (1951), a refugee is a person who has a 'well-founded fear of being persecuted for reasons of race, religion, nationality, membership of a particular social group or a particular political opinion, is outside the country of their nationality and cannot, or will not, because of fear, benefit from the protection of that country'.

Conflict in the refugee's country of origin may result in the development of severe psychopathology, such as posttraumatic stress disorder and major depressive disorder. Severe psychiatric illnesses in refugees may be a prelude to suicidal ideation. This and the way in which they are received by the destination country, dilapidated living conditions, and lack of social support and isolation all contribute and conspire to rendering this immigrant group particularly vulnerable to suicidal behaviour (Bhugra et al., 2011).

Cultural psychiatry

Cultural psychiatry has developed as an entity in its own right over the last seven decades, with the term 'transcultural psychiatry' being introduced into the psychiatric lexicon by Wittkower in Montreal (dubbed 'the birthplace of cultural psychiatry') in the 1950s. An array of researchers were also central in a renewed engagement between medical anthropology and psychiatry initiated by the work of the psychiatrist/anthropologist Arthur Kleinman (Hankir, 2014).

Cultural psychiatry has focused on health disparities – both globally and locally – in terms of the needs of immigrants, refugees, and ethnocultural minorities. At the same time, it has continued to advocate for an integrative caring approach challenging mainstream psychiatry. In recent decades, there has been a striking biologization of psychiatry, especially in the US, with the assumption that neuroscience provides the core understanding of the aetiology and treatment of illness and disease. To a large extent this has become the dominant view, and the perspectives of social science and psychology have been played down (Hankir, 2014).

It has been argued, however, that human biology is cultural biology. The brain is the organ of culture – and we use our brains to acquire and adapt through cultural inventions like reading, mathematics, and other complex social practices. Many of the problems that are seen in psychiatry may reflect not structural abnormalities in the brain but the consequences of learning – programming the brain – and the unhealthy environments and social relationships people must negotiate (Hankir, 2014).

A major step in recent years has been the effort to clarify how to collect and organize information about culture and context in mental health. The DSM-5 (the recent revision of the diagnostic system of the American Psychiatric Association) introduces a Cultural Formulation Interview. This is a basic approach to exploring the social and cultural context and meaning of illness. It should be part of the toolkit of every physician (Hanker, 2014).

A personalized approach to managing mental illness

> To the world you may be just one person but to one person you may be the world.
>
> Bill Wilson

We encourage mental health care service providers to take a holistic and personalized approach in the assessment and treatment of people who present with psychopathology, to deploy the 'soft skills' of listening and empathy in order to allow narratives to flow and, consequently, a rapport and therapeutic alliance to become established. Sometimes, just being made to feel that someone is genuinely listening to you with all earnestness and compassion and that someone actually cares can be the antidote that a lonely and forlorn human needs with which to nourish their soul. In this scenario, non-verbal (and non-judgmental) communication and tranquil silence can be more efficacious than any drug, and can offer a safe sanctuary where deep and seemingly indelible wounds can heal.

Take home messages for the practitioner

- There is a growing perception that science alone provides overall insufficient foundation for the holistic understanding of the interaction between health, illness, and disease. The health humanities have emerged as a distinct entity in attempts to ameliorate the limitations in the provision of health care and can be broadly described as the application of arts and literature to medicine.
- Autobiographical narrative, which falls under the wide-ranging remit of the health humanities, is gaining popularity among service users, both as an effective form of adjunctive therapy and as a means to campaign against stigma. Autobiographical narrative is also of benefit to health care providers and the general public as they provide precious qualitative insights into the subjective experience of mental distress.
- Mental health care providers and practitioners, as well as the general public, are encouraged to deconstruct and reformulate their views on psychiatry and 'madness', not based on impulse, sensationalism, anecdote or myths but on their sense of reason, morality and evidence.
- Culture is dynamic and affects all aspects of illness and behaviour across the human lifespan and familial generations. Although culture is being homogenized by globalization, the 'idioms of distress' that people (particularly immigrants) use may not necessarily match diagnostic criteria, and there are no universal models of psychotherapy or pharmacotherapy for the treatment of mental illness. To summarize succinctly: one size does *not* fit all.
- The lack of culturally competent health care practitioners and personalized mental health services can present as major barriers for people, particularly immigrants, to accessing and engaging with the relevant services.
- Disease primarily centres around pathology, whereas illness is something that a person develops when their disease starts to have effects on their lives and on the lives of the people who encompass them. Health care providers and practitioners tend to focus on disease, whereas patients are by and large interested on the consequences of illness in their psychosocial functioning. There thus exists a clash between service provider and service user. A perceptive and culturally competent practitioner must be able to detect this issue and act accordingly to ameliorate it (i.e., ensure that the provision of health care services are service-user centred).
- Assessing the mental health needs of families across the generations includes openness to exploring personal and individualized formulations to elicit the meaning of symptoms. A presenting complaint has to be explored facilitating an understanding of the suffering behind the symptom.

- As in other areas of medicine, education is key, and training in cultural competency should be part of the curriculum for all mental health professionals, including teachers, nurses, and medical students, in attempts to detect the early warning signs of psychopathology and to offer timely intervention to prevent the illness from worsening and spiralling out of control.

References

Bhugra, D. (1991). Politically motivated suicides. *British Journal of Psychiatry, 159*, 594–595.
Bhugra, D., & Ayonrinde, O. (2004). Depression in migrants and ethnic minorities. *Advances in Psychiatric Treatment, 10* (1), 13–17.
Bhugra, D., & Becker, M. (2005). Migration, cultural bereavement and cultural identity. *World Psychiatry, 4* (1), 18–24.
Bhugra, D., & Desai, M. (2002). Attempted suicide in South Asian women. *Advances in Psychiatric Treatment, 8*, 418–423.
Bhugra, D., Gupta, S., & Bhui, K. (2011). WPA guidance on mental health and mental health Care in migrants. *World Psychiatry, 10* (1), 2–10.
Bursztein, L.C., & Makinen, I.H. (2010). Immigration and suicidality in the young. *Canadian Journal of Psychiatry, 55* (5), 274–281.
Copeland, J.R.M., Beekman, A.T.F., Braam, A.W., Dewey, M.E., Delespaul, P., Fuhrer, R., Hooijer, C., ... Wilson, K.C.M. (2003). Depression among older people in Europe: the EURODEP studies. *World Psychiatry, 3*, 45–49.
Corrigan, P.W., Morris, S.B., Michaels, P.J., Rafacz, J.D., & Rüsch, N. (2012). Challenging the public stigma of mental illness: a meta-analysis of outcome studies. *Psychiatric Services, 63* (10), 963–973. doi: 10.1176/appi.ps.201100529.
Deakin, N., & Bhugra, D. (2012). Families in Bollywood cinema: changes and context. *International Review of Psychiatry, 24* (2), 166–172. doi: 10.3109/09540261.2012.656307.
Eisenberg, L. (1977). Disease and illness: distinction between professional and popular ideas of sickness. *Culture Medicine and Psychiatry, 1*, 9–23.
Eisenbruch, M. (1990). The cultural bereavement interview: a new clinical research approach for refugees. *Psychiatric Clinics of North America, 13*, 715–735.
Eisenbruch, M. (1991). From post-traumatic stress disorder to cultural bereavement: diagnosis of Southeast Asian refugees. *Social Science and Medicine, 33*, 673–680.
Embree, L. (1994). *Phenomenology of the Cultural Disciplines.* New York: Springer.
Evans-Lacko, S., Courtin, E., & Fiorillo, A. (2014). The state of the art in European research on reducing social exclusion and stigma related to mental health: a systematic mapping of the literature. *European Psychiatry, 29*(6), 381–389. doi:10.1016/j.eurpsy.2014.02.007.
Evans-Lacko, S., Henderson, C., & Thornicroft, G. (2013). Public knowledge, attitudes and behaviour regarding people with mental illness in England 2009–2012. *British Journal of Psychiatry – Supplement, 55*, 51–57.
Fazel, S., Lichtenstein, P., Frisell, T., Grann, M., Goodwin, G., & Långström, N. (2010). Bipolar disorder and violent crime: time at risk reanalysis. *Archives of General Psychiatry, 67* (12), 1325–1326.
Friedrich, B., Evans-Lacko, S., London, J., Rhydderch, D., Henderson, C., & Thornicroft, G. (2013). Anti-stigma training for medical students: the Education Not Discrimination project. *British Journal of Psychiatry, 202*, 89–94.

Goffman, E. (1963). *Stigma: Notes on the Management of Spoiled Identity*. Englewood Cliffs, NJ: Prentice-Hall.
Hankir, A. (2014). Interview with Professor Laurence Kirmayer: Director of Cultural Psychiatry, McGill University, Montreal, Canada. *World Journal of Medical Education and Research,* 5 (1), DAUIN 20140039.
Hankir, A., & Sadiq, A. (2013). Lessons from psychiatry in the Arab world – a Lebanese trainee psychiatrist's qualitative views on the provision of mental healthcare services for Palestinian refugees in Lebanon and an interview with a consultant psychiatrist on the effects of the Arab spring on the mental health of Libyans. *Psychiatria Danubina 2 Sep, 25* Suppl 2, 345–349.
Hankir, A., & Zaman, R. (2013). Jung's archetype, 'The Wounded Healer', mental illness in the medical profession and the role of the health humanities in psychiatry. *BMJ Case Reports 2*, pii: bcr2013009990.
Hankir, A.K., Northall, A., & Zaman, R. (2014). Stigma and mental health challenges in medical students. *BMJ Case Reports* 2 Sep; pii: bcr2014205226. doi: 10.1136/bcr-2014-205226.
Henderson, M., Brooks, S.K., & Del Busso, L. (2012). Shame! Self-stigmatisation as an obstacle to sick doctors returning to work: a qualitative study. *BMJ Open*, 2; pii: e001776.
Henderson, C., Corker, E., Hamilton, S., Williams, P., Pinfold, V., Rose, D., Webber, M., Evans-Lacko, S., & Thornicroft, G. (2014). Viewpoint survey of mental health service users' experiences of discrimination in England 2008–12. *Social Psychiatry and Psychiatric Epidemiology*, 49, 1599–1608.
Holloway, D. (2011). My 'colourful' life with schizophrenia. *CEPiP, 1*, 111–114.
Jackson, S.W. (2001). The wounded healer. *Bulletin of the History of Medicine, 75*, 1–36.
Kirkcaldy, B.D. (2013). *Chimes of Time: Wounded Health Professionals*. Sidestone, Leiden: Essays on Recovery.
Kleinman, A. (1980). *Patients and Healers in the Context of Culture*. University of California Press, Berkley, CA, 259–286.
Leininger, M., & McFarland, M. (2002). *Transcultural Nursing: Concepts, Theories, Research, and Practice*. 3rd edition. New York: McGraw-Hill.
Link, B.G., Struening, E.L., Neese-Todd, S., Asmussen, S., & Phelan, J.C. (2001). Stigma as a barrier to recovery: the consequences of stigma for the self-esteem of people with mental illnesses. *Psychiatric Services 52* (12), 1621–1626.
Link, B.G., Yang, L.H., Phelan, J.C., & Collins, P.Y. (2004). Measuring mental illness stigma. *Schizophrenia Bulletin, 30* (3), 511–541.
Oberg, K. (1960). Culture shock: adjustment to new cultural environments. *Practical Anthropology, 7*, 177–182.
Oyebode, F. (2009). Preface. In: F. Oyebode (ed.), *Mindreadings, Literature and Psychiatry*, pp. vii–ix. London: RCPsych Publications.
Perceval, J.A. (1962). *Narrative of the Experience of a Gentleman During a State of Mental Derangement to Explain the Causes and the Nature of Insanity and to Expose the Injudicious Conduct Pursued Towards Many Sufferers Under That Calamity*; 1838. In: G. Bateson (ed.), *Perceval's Narrative*, 271p. London: Hogarth Press. Reprinted 1962.
Sacks, O. (1985). Preface to *The Man Who Mistook His Wife for a Hat*. London: Picador.
Sadow, D., & Ryder, M. (2008). Reducing stigmatizing attitudes held by future health professionals: the person is the message. *Psychology Services, 5*, 362.
Sartorius, N., Gaebel, W., & Cleveland, H.R. (2010). WPA guidance on how to combat stigmatization of psychiatry and psychiatrists. *World Psychiatry, 9*, 131–44.

Sontag, S. (1978). *Illness as Metaphor.* Preface by Susan Sontag. New York: Farrar, Straurs and Giroux.
Stevens, A. (1994). *Jung: A Very Short Introduction,* 110p. Quoted by Anthony Stevens. Oxford: Oxford University Press.
Styron, W. (1990). *Darkness Visible: A Memoir of Madness.* New York: Random House.
Thakur, U. (1963). *The History of Suicides in India.* Delhi: Munshiram Manohar Lal Publications.
World Health Organization. (2001). *The World Health Report 2001 – Mental Health: New Understanding, New Hope.* http://www.who.int/whr/2001/en/ (accessed 01/11/2008).

4
Mental Health Promotion in School: An Integrated, School-Based, Whole School

Carmel Cefai and Valeria Cavioni

Introduction

About 20% of schoolchildren across different cultures experience mental health problems, such as conduct problems, anxiety, and depression, during the course of any given year and may need the use of mental health services (WHO, 2013). The most recent report by the Centers for Disease Control and Prevention (2013) shows that the prevalence of mental health difficulties amongst children and young people in the US has been increasing in the last 25 years, and related services are costing the country about US$247 billion per year. A report on adolescent health just published by WHO (WHO, 2014) portrays depression as the top global cause of illness and disability amongst adolescents, with suicide being the third biggest cause of death. The report mentions that half of mental health difficulties begin before the age of 14, underlining the need for early intervention and mental health promotion from an early age.

Mental health and well-being are the result of the biological, psychological, and social systems in the child's world, and the interaction of these influences shapes the developmental trajectory of the child (Cooper, Bilton, & Kakos, 2011). Within such a biopsychosocial approach, systems such as the family, community, and school have a crucial role in providing contexts and tools which actively prevent or minimize the development of mental health problems on one hand, and promote the healthy social and emotional development of children and young people on the other (Guerra & Bradshaw, 2008; Furlong et al., 2011). The onset of social, emotional, and behaviour difficulties at an early age is a predictor of mental health difficulties in adolescence (Fergusson, Horwood, & Ridder, 2005; WHO, 2013), underlining the need for early identification and consequent early intervention at a time when children's personality is still developing and before difficulties become more serious and entrenched (Domitrovich,

Cortes, & Greenberg, 2007; McLaughlin & Clarke, 2010). Schools are thus ideally placed to operate as health-promoting contexts for children, having access to all children, from an early age and over an extended period of time, and possessing expertise and resources in health promotion (Greenberg, Domitrovich, & Bumbarger, 2001).

This chapter will first discuss the role of schools as contexts for mental health promotion, arguing that schools need to broaden their agenda to focus on both the cognitive and affective development of children and young people. It will then propose an evidence-based, multilevel, and school-based approach to mental health promotion, focusing on health promotion, prevention, and targeted interventions involving the whole school community in collaboration with the parents, the local community, and external support services. The final section presents a number of recommendations for the application of the model in actual practice.

Schools as contexts for mental health promotion

The WHO has been actively engaged in various health promotion initiatives in schools, such as the health promoting schools amongst others (Stewart-Brown, 2006). The erstwhile focus on exercise, nutrition, and drugs education of such initiatives has been shifting to a more holistic approach, with more focus in the past decades on mental health promotion (WHO, 2013). The main thrust of the mental health approach in school has been a whole school approach, integrating the development of individual social and emotional competencies such as self-awareness and management, building healthy relationships, and effective problem-solving, with the creation of healthy communities at classroom and whole school levels (Weare & Nind, 2011; CASEL, 2012; Cefai & Cavioni, 2014). Within such an approach, the whole school community collaborates to promote the health and well-being of all its members, with culture, policies, practices, curriculum, pedagogy, and relationships contributing to a climate conducive to the development of mental health and well-being (Adi et al., 2007; Weare & Nind, 2011; Bywater & Sharples, 2012; Cefai & Cavioni, 2014). Universal interventions are accompanied by targeted interventions for students experiencing difficulties in their social and emotional development, with schools providing in-house support where appropriate, and referring students at risk for mental health difficulties to mental health and psychosocial services. Early and multidisciplinary referral and interventions is the hallmark of effective targeted interventions (Greenberg et al., 2003; Weare & Nind, 2011).

The movement for mental health promotion in schools, particularly at the preventive, universal level, has been particularly driven by strength-based approaches to human development, such as social and emotional learning, positive psychology, educational resilience, and positive youth development. These underline the need for proactive strategies which strengthen and promote children's healthy development, and thereby prevent difficulties from developing in the first place, making use of children's strengths and assets while providing enabling and protective contexts (Masten, 2001; Youngblade et al., 2007; Guerra & Bradshaw, 2008; Seligman et al., 2009; Furlong et al., 2011). Mental health promotion in schools is now establishing itself as 'a permanent fixture rather than a transitory blip on the radar screen of education... schools are increasingly being held responsible for putting in place plans, programs and practices that promote student social and emotional health and to prevent problems of poor mental health' (Bernard, Stephanou, & Urbach, 2007, p. 2). Initiatives and programmes such as the Collaborative for Academic, Social and Emotional Learning in the US (CASEL, 2011), Social and Emotional Aspects of Learning (SEAL) programme in the UK (DCSF, 2009), KidsMatter (KidsMatter, 2012), Mind Matters (Mind Matters, 2005) frameworks in Australia, and the Network for Social and Emotional Competence in Europe (ENSEC, 2014) have been pushing the agenda of mental health promotion in school and underlining the benefits of broadening the educational agenda to include the social and emotional needs of children and young people.

One of the issues with the increasing salience of mental health promotion in school has been the concern about the 'the rise of therapeutic education' (Ecclestone & Hayes, 2009). The introduction of social and emotional education in schools, particularly programmes targeting specific groups of children, may lead to potential labelling and stigmatizing of vulnerable children (Ecclestone & Hayes, 2009; Watson, Emery, & Bayliss, 2012). Education is not about mental health and well-being, and teachers are educators and not surrogate psychologists or mental health workers (Craig, 2009). Such arguments, however, reflect the traditional deficit discourse of mental illness, equating mental health with mental illness and psychopathology. In line with the de-medicalization and depathologizing of mental health in education, mental health promotion in school is about the health, well-being and growth of all children and young people, including those facing risks in their development. It seeks to prepare children and young people for the tests of life, providing a relevant and meaningful education leading to the formation of academically, socially and emotionally literate young people who have the skills, abilities and emotional resilience necessary to thrive in a challenging world. It is about children and young people being creative and effective in problem-solving and decision-making, building and maintaining healthy relationships, and mobilizing their personal resources in times of difficulty (Cooper & Cefai, 2009; Cefai & Cavioni, 2014). Within this perspective, the goals of education become both cognitive and affective, with teachers teaching the skills of both academic and social and emotional learning. The compartmentalization of education and well-being does not only lead to deskilling of teachers and short-changing of pupils, but has been found to be fraught with difficulties in terms of implementation, service delivery, multidisciplinary collaboration, and particularly effectiveness (Greenberg et al., 2003; Spratt et al., 2006).

The idea of broadening the educational agenda to address both the academic and social and emotional needs of the students has also been meeting resistance from the movement for increasing academic standards in education. International academic standards, such as PISA, TIMSS and PIRLS, underline a culture of competition, examinations, and performance indicators, pressuring governments, educational authorities, and school heads to 'deliver' and raise academic standards in an effort to climb the rankings of the international league of countries (Pring, 2012). Mental health promotion may have little currency in a system focused on a narrow range of measurable aspects of education, and may even be seen as a waste of time and resources as countries engage frantically in the 'race to the top' international competition. School staff and parents themselves may have doubts about the relevance of mental health promotion to education and see it as taking precious time away from academic learning, which may lead to lower academic achievement (Benninga, Berkowitz, Kuehn, & Smith, 2006).

The evidence shows, however, that rather than weakening academic achievement, a focus on social and emotional processes in education provides a foundation upon which effective learning and success can be built and socio-emotional competence developed. It enables students to regulate their emotions and deal with emotional distress, cope better with classroom demands and frustration, solve problems more effectively, and relate better and work more collaboratively with others (Greenberg & Rhoades, 2008; Durlak, Weissberg, Dymnicki, Taylor, & Schellinger, 2011). In their meta-analysis of over 200 studies, Durlack et al. (2011) reported that students who participated in universal social and emotional learning programmes scored significantly higher on standardized achievement tests when compared to peers not participating in such programmes. Mental health promotion may thus serve as 'meta-ability' for academic learning (Goleman, 1996). Clearly, those seeking to raise academic standards and those striving to promote mental health and well-being in school are 'on the same side', rather than on diametrically opposite sides (Diamond, 2010). It is thus ironic that in their efforts to raise academic standards and move higher up the academic league of tables (alias PISA), educational authorities and schools choose to move mental health promotion to the margin instead of using it as a medium to enhance academic learning and achievement. Besides killing the joy and fun of learning, international competitions for higher scores may also become a health hazard for children and young people, raising stress to unhealthy levels at a young and vulnerable age.

What works in mental health promotion in school: An evidence-based approach

The WHO framework for health promotion in schools recommends a whole school approach to mental health, addressing social and emotional issues in the curriculum and in the organization of teaching and learning, the development of a supportive school ethos and environment, and partnership with the wider school community (WHO, 2007, 2013). Long-term effectiveness for mental health and well-being in school requires an integrated whole school approach, making use of interpersonal, instructional, and contextual supports, sustained over time (Elias & Synder, 2008; Weare & Nind, 2011; Bywater & Sharples, 2012). Such an approach underlines multilevel and multi-component interventions, including classroom curricula, school environment, universal and targeted interventions, and collaboration with parents and the community (Adi et al., 2007; National Institute for Health and Clinical Excellence, 2008; Durlak et al., 2011; Weare & Nind, 2011).

The following section presents a multilevel, comprehensive, and school-based approach to mental health in school, focusing on health promotion, prevention, and targeted interventions involving the whole school community in collaboration with the parents, the local community, and external support services (Cefai & Cavioni, 2014). The framework is grounded in theory and research, and informed by approaches which have been found to be effective in bringing about long-term targeted outcomes in mental health in children and young people. It consists of five components, namely multidimensional, multi-stage, multi-target, multi-intervention, and well-planned, well-implemented and well-evaluated. These are explained in the following sections.

Multidimensional. Mental health promotion may be organized as a comprehensive, universal approach at individual, classroom, and whole school levels. Explicit and regular teaching of social and emotional learning as a core competence by the classroom/subject teachers is one of the key components of the framework. Direct teaching of evidence-based and developmentally and culturally appropriate social and emotional competencies with application to real life situations is at the heart of mental health promotion in school. This necessitates a set curriculum and available resources to support consistency of delivery, one of the key criteria of program effectiveness (CASEL, 2008; Durlak et al., 2011). One-off, pull-out, add-on programmes are unlikely to have any long-term effect on students' behaviour.

Role of classroom teachers. Within a school-based, non-medical approach, school staff are at the centre of mental health promotion initiatives. One of the benefits of having classroom and subject teachers delivering the social and emotional curriculum is that they are more likely to integrate and infuse the skills into the general curriculum and daily classroom activities; such an approach is more likely to have greater long-term impact (Adi et al., 2007; Hoagwood et al., 2007; Diekstra, 2008). In their review of evaluations of the SEAL programme in the UK, Cooper and Jacobs (2011) attribute the lack of success of the programme to its not being embedded directly in the formal curriculum, and the teaching staff not being involved in its delivery. Sklad et al.'s (2012) review of studies found that the majority of the social and emotional learning programmes in their review of studies were conducted by classroom teachers, and that teachers could deliver such programmes without compromising their effectiveness. In their meta-analysis of over 200 studies, Durlak et al. (2011) found that when classroom programmes were conducted by the school staff they were found to be effective in both academic and social and emotional learning, and that only when school staff conducted the programmes did students' academic performance improve.

Specialists and professionals still have a key role to play in the promotion of mental health at school but more at targeted interventions. Even here, however, interventions need to be school-based and carried out by school-based personnel or by professionals with as much close contact with the children and the school as possible. As Zins (Zins, 2001, p. 445) put it 'now that we know more about SEL interventions, the shift must be done towards school-based personnel'.

Teacher education. School staff themselves believe that they should be involved in mental health promotion initiatives, particularly in teaching social and emotional competencies at universal level (Reinke et al., 2011; Askell-Williams & Cefai, 2014). One of the implications of such an approach, however, is that staff need to be adequately trained in exercising this role, at both initial and continuing professional education. Various studies showed that many classroom teachers' perceived sense of competence and confidence in promoting mental health in school is relatively poor, particularly if initial teacher education in the area was limited or inadequate (Askell-Williams et al., 2010; Reinke et al., 2011; Vostanis et al., 2013; Askell-Williams & Cefai, 2014). Teacher education thus needs to include such areas as building health relationships with students, developing students' social and emotional learning, increasing students' knowledge about mental health, recognizing and responding to early signs of mental health difficulties, and working collaboratively with colleagues, professionals, and parents in supporting students with mental health difficulties (Askell-Williams et al., 2010). Teacher education also needs to address issues related to programme implementation, such as fidelity and programme adaptation (Greenberg, 2010; Humphrey, Lendrum, & Wigelsworth, 2010; Weare & Nind, 2011).

Infusion into the curriculum. One of the most powerful ways in which to promote social and emotional well-being and mental health in school is by infusing it into the other areas of the curriculum in a structured way (Elias, 2003; Elias & Synder, 2008; Greenberg, 2010). By referring to and making use of social and emotional learning in the other areas of the curriculum, the teacher enables students to generalize and apply the skills across the curriculum, and to integrate social and emotional learning into their daily learning and social behaviours.

Positive classroom climate. Mental health promotion has a greater impact when it is integrated into the curriculum at both taught and caught levels, with teachers teaching and reinforcing the curriculum in their interactions with the students and providing opportunities for students to observe and practise the skills learned during day-to-day life in the classroom (National Institute for Health and Clinical Excellence, 2008; Greenberg, 2010; Weare & Nind, 2011; Durlak et al., 2011). Learning and working in a classroom climate characterized by caring and supportive relationships and engagement in meaningful learning activities adapted to students' needs and strengths provides an ideal context, where the promotion of mental health becomes embedded in the daily life of the classroom (Pianta & Stuhlman, 2004; Battistich, Schaps, & Wilson, 2004; Cefai, 2008; Osher et al., 2008). In such an environment, students have regular opportunities to 'catch' social and emotional competencies through observing them enacted by the classroom teacher/s and their peers, and through continuous opportunity to practise them in their daily classroom activities. Watson et al. (2012, p. 223) argue that in such 'a relational ethics of care', with students engaged in meaningful dialogic encounters based on caring relationships, choices and rights, play and learning experiences, mental health and well-being become integrated in 'positive experiences of being, becoming and belonging'.

Whole school ecology. A curriculum, classroom-based approach needs to be accompanied and supported by a whole school approach, with the school community in collaboration with parents and the local community supporting and reinforcing a climate conducive to mental health (Adi et al., 2007; Greenberg, 2010; Weare & Nind, 2011). A positive school climate has a complementary, value-added effect, reinforcing the work undertaken in the classrooms, and consequently influencing the relationships and behaviours of the school members (Wells, Barlow, & Stewart-Brown, 2003; Adi et al., 2007; Payton et al., 2008; Weare & Nind, 2011). A health-promoting school climate is characterized by caring and supportive relationships, meaningful and influential engagement, staff collaboration and continuing professional learning, empowering administration, staff and student peer education and mentoring, active parental involvement and education, and community participation, amongst others (Solomon, Battistich, Watson, Schaps, & Lewis, 2000; Bond et al., 2007; Askell-Williams et al., 2010; Weare & Nind, 2011).

Multi-Stage. Social and emotional education involves a similar process to that of other academic skills, with increasing complexity of behaviour, and social contexts requiring particular skills at the students' respective developmental level. A structured and developmental approach would thus develop basic to more complex social and emotional competencies from one year to the next, building on what students have already learned and equipping them with skills needed for different stages in their development. A spiral curriculum, straddling the early years, primary school, and secondary school, revisits each of the main topics at developmentally appropriate levels, which are also adapted according to the individual needs of the students. The curriculum usually focuses on self-awareness and self-management, social awareness, relationship-building, and decision-making (CASEL, 2005; DCSF, 2009), and more recently positive education and resilience skills such as positive emotions, hope, optimism, persistence, confidence and self-efficacy, autonomy/agency, and sense of leadership (Seligman, Gillham, Reivich, Linkins, & Ernst, 2009; Gilman, Scott Huebner, & Furlong, 2009). Some programmes may be focused on particular areas of mental health and well-being, such as bullying, restorative justice, resilience, depression and anxiety, or anger management.

The teaching of social and emotional competencies follows the SAFE approach; that is, it is sequenced, active, focused, and explicit. Effective programs adopt a sequenced step-by-step approach, make use of experiential and participative learning, focus on skills development, and have explicit learning goals (CASEL, 2005; Durlak et al., 2011). Assessment is a crucial part of the learning process, but the assessment of social and emotional learning needs to avoid the trappings of outcome-based and performance-driven academic assessment. Moreover there is a danger of exposing children and young people to labelling and pathologizing through such assessment (Watson et al., 2012). Formative and continuous assessment, making use of teacher/self and individual/group assessment, with a range of assessment modes and strategies, will ensure that assessment will become an integral part of the learning process (Cefai & Cavioni, 2014).

The curriculum and its delivery needs to be adapted to the diversity of backgrounds and characteristics of the students, making use of a variety of activities, instructional designs, resources, assessment modes and products according to the developmental level, learning styles, and the sociocultural context of the students. Adaptation of programmes, however, needs to be carried out without compromising programme integrity. Lack of adherence to implementation guidelines may lead to ineffectiveness in terms of expected student outcomes (Greenberg, 2010; Weare, 2010; Durlack et al., 2011; Bywater & Sharples, 2012). The limited effectiveness of the SEAL programme in the UK, for instance, is attributed to lack of structure and consistency in programme implementation (Humphrey et al., 2008, 2010).

Multi-Target. Although students are at the centre of mental health promotion in school, the health and well-being of school staff and parents themselves is a key part of a whole school approach to mental health (Jennings & Greenberg, 2009; Weare & Nind, 2011). Adults are more likely to be successful and effective in their efforts to teach, facilitate, and promote mental health if they take care of and nurture their own health and well-being as well. When teachers' own interpersonal needs are addressed, they are more likely to pay attention to the personal needs of their students (Kidger et al., 2010). Teaching today is considered a highly stressful career, with increasing levels of burnout, turnover, and attrition (Moon, 2007; Bricheno, Brown, & Lubansky, 2009). Teacher stress and anxiety lead to lower morale, lack of commitment, sense of vulnerability and helplessness, and poor self-efficacy (Dworkin, 2009; Kelchtermans, 2011), setting off a 'burnout cascade' resulting in emotional exhaustion (Jennings & Greenberg, 2009).

A whole school approach to mental health makes provision for information, education, and support to staff and parents in developing and maintaining their own health and well-being. School staff are provided with opportunities to develop their own social and emotional competence within a caring and supportive school context. A health-promoting context combined with the development of one's social and emotional resources serves to actively promote the staff's mental health while reducing the risk of burnout and psychological difficulties (Jennings & Greenberg, 2009; New Economics Foundation, 2009). This interactive individual-context approach ensures that school staffs are able to respond effectively to the cognitive and emotional challenges of working in difficult conditions, to strengthen their relationships with colleagues, students, and parents, and sustain their own motivation, sense of efficacy, and personal agency.

Parents' dynamic relationship with the school has long been recognized as a key factor in their children's education (Fan & Chen, 2001; El Nokali, Bachman, & Votruba-Drzal, 2010). Home–school collaboration does not only ensure parents' collaboration in facilitating the school's goals in mental health promotion, but it also addresses parents' own education and well-being, which in turn impact their children's health and well-being (Humphrey et al., 2010; Downey & Williams, 2010). Such collaboration would help parents to develop positive attitudes towards mental health promotion in school and reduce potential fears and resistance, to support the school's efforts by reinforcing the competencies being taught in school, and to develop and sustain their own psychological and social resources to take care of their own mental health. The provision of accessible and culture-sensitive information and resources, support, links to community services and facilities, and family learning, and parenting and personal development programmes would enable schools to operate as centres for parental collaboration, education, and well-being (Cefai & Cavioni, 2014).

Multi-intervention. Schools are more likely to be effective in mental health promotion if there is an emphasis on universal interventions for all children, supported by additional targeted interventions for children at risk or with additional needs (Adi et al., 2007; Diekstra, 2008; Weare & Nind, 2011). Some students may thus receive simultaneous universal and targeted interventions, benefiting from a complementary, additive effect (Merrell & Gueldner, 2010). While universal interventions are highly beneficial for students experiencing social, emotional, and behavioural difficulties (Cooper & Jacobs, 2011), targeted interventions are necessary for students who need extra support in view of the risks or difficulties they are experiencing (National Institute for Health and Clinical Excellence, 2008; Payton et al., 2008). The greater conceptual precision, intensity, and focus of targeted interventions may be particularly effective in this regard (Greenberg, 2010). Targeted interventions are also particularly essential in the early school years, to reduce the development of more severe difficulties at a later stage, when it is more difficult to change behaviour (Domitrovich, Cortes, & Greenberg, 2007).

A staged, school-based approach puts the onus on the school, in partnership with professionals, parents, services, and the community, to provide the necessary support for students experiencing difficulties in their social and emotional development. This requires integrated, inter-agency working, with professionals and services working collaboratively together and with parents, school staff, and the students themselves, where possible at the school, to support the social and emotional needs of children and young people. Students experiencing mental health difficulties will thus go through a school-based staged approach, with more intensive and transdisciplinary interventions as difficulties become more serious. A school-based team, including representatives of staff, students, and parents, will coordinate the targeted interventions in an efficient and effective way and integrate them with the universal interventions and other whole school approaches in mental health promotion. In universal and selective interventions, teachers and mental health professionals are likely to be found as partners in delivery of implementations, with more intensive interventions provided by mental health professionals (Franklin, Kim, Ryan, Kelly, & Montgomery, 2012).

Well planned, well implemented, and well evaluated

Any mental health promotion initiative needs to be well planned, well implemented and monitored, and well evaluated. Planning involves a needs assessment to match the intervention to the needs of the school, identifying and incorporating existing good practices, resources, and expertise at the school. The absence of such an assessment is likely to lead to underutilization of the school's strengths, and to barriers and resistance along the way (Askell-Williams, Lawson, & Slee, 2010). Organizational supports and policies to safeguard the success and sustainability of the initiative include supportive management, involvement of the school community, including parents and local community, in planning and implementation, education and mentoring of staff, provision of adequate resources, and alignment with regional and school policies (CASEL, 2005, 2008). Finally any initiative is monitored, evaluated, and improved regularly. Pre- and post-student outcomes help to determine the effectiveness of the intervention in terms of students' mental health and well-being. Initiatives that are not adequately coordinated, monitored, and evaluated are unlikely to work in the long term (CASEL, 2008; Greenberg, 2010).

Lessons for practice

The main thrust of this chapter has been that schools are not only about academic achievement and performance, but about the holistic development of the child and young person, with a particular focus on social and emotional development. It has argued that schools are ideal places for the promotion of mental health, well-being, and resilience, as they have access to all the population at a young, developing age, thus having a key window of opportunity to promote children's and young people's healthy development. This chapter has also taken a de-medicalized, depathologizing stance to mental health, positioning school staff and classroom teachers as key players in the promotion of children's mental health and well-being. Classroom teachers can not only teach specific social and emotional competencies in their classroom, but, through their relationships, pedagogy, and classroom management, they can create a classroom climate conducive to mental health and well-being.

Mental health in this chapter has been construed as a continuum ranging from universal interventions in health promotion to targeted interventions for children and young people exhibiting social, emotional, and behavioural difficulties. While school staff will need more support from professionals in supporting students with mental health difficulties, they still have a key role to play in targeted interventions as well. A school-based, whole school, transdisciplinary approach seeks to utilize the services and expertise of classroom teachers, school support staff, and other professionals, collaborating with the students and their parents, in providing support for mental health difficulties within non-medical contexts where possible. This would also reduce the risks of labelling and stigmatization. Parents are a key stakeholder in this collaborative effort, and their close collaboration and engagement with the school is critical for the success of the school's efforts in this area. Clearly, mental health is a multi-faceted and complex issue and requires the intervention of all the various stakeholders involved, rather than being the remit of one discipline, one agency, one institution, or one professional.

Another lesson for practice is that any mental health initiative needs to be well planned, monitored and evaluated. This calls for a self-reflexive stance amongst practitioners, striving to improve their practice on the basis of their reflective observations, discussions with, and feedback from, colleagues, and other forms of assessment. Finally, the mental health and well-being of children and young people is symbiotic with that of the significant adults in their lives, particularly parents and teachers. Parents and teachers are more likely to be effective in supporting the mental health needs of their children and students if they take care of their own health and well-being as well. Healthy parents and healthy teachers make for healthy children and healthy students. Schools would thus need to have in place structures which provide adequate education and support to staff and parents in developing and maintaining their own health and well-being, not only for their own sake, but for that of their children and students as well.

References

Adi, Y., Killoran, A., Janmohamed, K., & Stewart-Brown, S. (2007). *Systematic Review of the Effectiveness of Interventions to Promote Mental Well-Being in Primary Schools: Universal Approaches*. London, UK: National Institute for Clinical Excellence.

Askell-Williams, H., Lawson, M.J., & Slee, P.T. (2010). Venturing into schools: locating mental health initiatives in complex environments. *International Journal of Emotional Education, 1* (2), 14–33.

Askell-Williams, H., & Cefai, C. (2014). Australian and Maltese teachers' perspectives about their capabilities for mental health promotion on school settings. *Teaching and Teacher Education, 40*, 1–12.

Battistich, V., Schaps, E., & Wilson, N. (2004). Effects of an elementary school intervention on students' 'connectedness' to school and social adjustment during middle school. *Journal of Primary Prevention, 24*, 243–262.

Benninga, J.S., Berkowitz, M.W., Kuehn, P., & Smith, K. (2006). Character and academics: What good schools do. *Phi Delta Kappan, 87* (6), 448–452.

Bernard, M.E., Stephanou, A., & Urbach, D. (2007). *ASG Student Social and Emotional Health Report*. Australia: Australian Scholarships Group.

Bond, L., Butler, H., Thomas, L., Carlin, J., Glover, S., Bowes, G., et al. (2007). Social and school connectedness in early secondary school as predictors of late teenage substance use, mental health, and academic outcomes. *Journal of Adolescent Health, 40* (4), e9–e18.

Bricheno, P., Brown, S., & Lubansky, R. (2009). *Teacher Wellbeing: A Review of the Evidence*. London, UK: Teacher Support Network.

Bywater, T., & Sharples, J. (2012). Effective evidence-based interventions for emotional well-being lessons for policy and practice. *Research Papers in Education, 27* (4), 398–408.

CASEL Collaborative for Academic, Social, and Emotional Learning. (2005). *Safe and Sound: An Educational Leader's Guide to Evidence-Based Social and Emotional SEL Programs*. Retrieved 30 June 2014 from: http://static.squarespace.com/static/513f79f9e4b05ce7b70e9673/t/5331c141e4b0fba62007694a/1395769665836/safe-and-sound-il-edition.pdf.

CASEL Collaborative for Academic, Social, and Emotional Learning. (2008). *Social and Emotional Learning (SEL) Programs Illinois Edition*. Chicago, IL: CASEL.

CASEL Collaborative for Academic, Social, and Emotional Learning. (2011). *What Is SEL: Skills & Competencies*. Retrieved 30 June 2014 from: http://casel.org/why-it-matters/what-is-sel/.

CASEL Collaborative for Academic, Social, and Emotional Learning. (2012). *2013 CASEL Guide Effective Social and Emotional Learning Programs Preschool and Elementary School Edition*. Retrieved 30 June 2014 from: http://www.casel.org/guide.

Cefai, C. (2008). *Promoting Resilience in the Classroom. A Guide to Developing Pupils' Emotional and Cognitive Skills*. London, UK: Jessica Kingsley Publishers.

Cefai, C., & Cavioni, V. (2014). *Social and Emotional Education in Primary School. Integrating Theory and Research into Practice.* New York, NY: Springer Publications.

Center for Disease Control and Prevention. (2013). Mental Health Surveillance Among Children – United States 2005–2011. *Morbidity and Mortality Weekly Report Supplements, 62* (2), 1–35.

Cooper, P., & Cefai, C. (2009). Contemporary values and social context: implications for the emotional well-being of children. *Journal of Emotional and Behaviour Difficulties, 14* (2), 91–100.

Cooper, P., & Jacobs, B. (2011). *From Inclusion to Engagement: Helping Students Engage with Schooling through Policy and Practice.* Chichester, UK: Wiley-Blackwell.

Cooper, P., Bilton, C., & Kakos, M. (2011). The importance of a biopsychosocial approach to interventions for SEBD. In: T.H. Cole, H. Daniels & J. Visser (eds), *The Routledge International Companion to Emotional and Behavioural Difficulties.* London: UK: Routledge.

Craig, C. (2009). *Well-Being in Schools: The Curious Case of the Tail Wagging the Dog.* Glasgow, UK: Centre for Confidence and Well-Being.

DCSF. (2009). *Promoting and Supporting Positive Behaviour in Primary Schools. Developing Social and Emotional Aspects of Learning (SEAL).* Nottingham, UK: Department for Children, Schools and Families.

Diamond, A. (2010). The evidence base for improving school outcomes by addressing the whole child and by addressing skills and attitudes, not just content. *Early Education & Development, 21* (5), 780–793.

Diekstra, R. (2008). Effectiveness of school-based social and emotional education programmes worldwide – Part one, a review of meta-analytic literature. In: F.M. Botin (ed.), *Social and Emotional Education: An International Analysis*, pp. 255–284. Santander, Spain: Fundacion Marcelino Botin.

Domitrovich, C.E., Cortes, R., & Greenberg, M.T. (2007). Improving young children's social and emotional competence: a randomized trial of the Preschool PATHS program. *Journal of Primary Prevention, 28* (2), 67–91.

Downey, C., & Williams, C. (2010). Family SEAL – a home-school collaborative programme focusing on the development of children's social and emotional skills. *Advances in School Mental Health Promotion, 3*, 30–41.

Durlak, J.A. (2008). Implementation matters: A review of research on the influence of implementation on program outcomes and the factors affecting implementation. *American Journal of Community Psychology, 41*, 327–350.

Durlak, J.A., Weissberg, R.P., Dymnicki, A.B., Taylor, R.D., & Schellinger, K. (2011). The impact of enhancing students' social and emotional learning: a meta-analysis of school-based universal interventions. *Child Development, 82*, 474–501.

Dworkin, G.A. (2009). Teacher burnout and teacher resilience: assessing the impacts of the school accountability movement. In: L.J. Saha & A.G. Dworkin (eds), *International Handbook of Research on Teachers and Teaching*, Vol. 21, pp. 491–502. New York, NY: Springer.

Ecclestone, K., & Hayes, D. (2009). Changing the subject: the educational implications of emotional well-being. *Oxford Review of Education, 35* (3), 371–389.

El Nokali, N.E., Bachman, H.J., & Votruba-Drzal, E. (2010). Parent involvement and children's academic and social development in elementary school. *Child Development, 81* (3), 988–1005.

Elias, M.J. (2003). *Academic and Social-Emotional Learning.* Brussels: Belgium, International Bureau of Education.

Elias, M., & Synder, D. (2008). *Developing Safe and Civil Schools: A Coordinated Approach to Social-Emotional and Character Development*. Retrieved 30 June 2014 from www.njasp.org/notes/confarc/DSACS_handout_12_09.doc.

ENSEC (2014). European Network for Social and Emotional Competence. Retrieved 30 June 2014 from www.enseceurope.org.

Fan, X., & Chen, M. (2001). Parental involvement and students' academic achievement: a meta analysis. *Educational Psychology Review, 13* (1), 1–22.

Fergusson, D.M., Horwood, J.L., & Ridder, E.M. (2005). Show me the child at seven: the consequences of conduct problems in childhood for psychosocial functioning in adulthood. *Journal of Child Psychology and Psychiatry, 46,* 837–49.

Franklin, C., Kim, J.S., Ryan, T., Kelly, M., & Montgomery, K. (2012). Teacher involvement in school mental health interventions: a systematic review. *Children and Youth Services Review, 34,* 973–982.

Furlong, M.J., Sharkey, J.D., Quirk, M., & Dowdy, E. (2011). Exploring the protective and promotive effects of school connectedness on the relation between psychological health risk and problem behaviors/experiences. *Journal of Educational and Developmental Psychology, 1,* 18–34.

Gilman, R., Scott Huebner, E., & Furlong, M.J. (2009). *Handbook of Positive Psychology in Schools*. London: UK: Routledge.

Goleman, D. (1996). *Emotional Intelligence*. London, UK: Bloomsbury.

Greenberg, M.T. (2010). School-based prevention: current status and future challenges. *Effective Education, 2,* 27–52.

Greenberg, M.T., Weissberg, R.P., O'Brien, M.U., Zins, J.E., Fredericks, L., Resnik, H., et al. (2003). Enhancing school-based prevention and youth development through coordinated social, emotional, and academic learning. *American Psychologist, 58,* 466–474.

Greenberg, M.T., & Rhoades, B.L. (2008). *State-of-Science Review: Self Regulation and Executive Function – What Can Teachers and Schools Do?* London, UK: Office of Science and Innovation Foresight Project: Mental Capital and Mental Well-Being.

Greenberg, M., Domitrovich, C., & Bumbarger, B. (2001). The prevention of mental disorders in school-aged children: current state of the field. *Prevention and Treatment, 4* (1), 1–59.

Guerra, N., & Bradshaw, C.P. (2008). Linking the prevention of problem behaviors and positive youth development: core competencies for positive youth development and risk prevention. *New Directions for Child and Adolescent Development, 122,* 1–17.

Hoagwood, K.E., Olin, S.S., Kerker, B.D., Kratochwill, T.R., Crowe, M., & Saka, N. (2007). Empirically based school interventions target at academic and mental health functioning. *Journal of Emotional and Behavioral Disorders, 15,* 66–94.

Humphrey, N., Kalambouka, A., Bolton, J., Lendrum, A., Wigelsworth, M., Lennie, C., et al. (2008). *Primary Social and Emotional Aspects of Learning (SEAL) Evaluation of Small Group Work*. Nottingham, UK: Department for Children, Schools and Families.

Humphrey, N., Lendrum, N., & Wigelsworth, M. (2010). *Social and Emotional Aspects of Learning (SEAL) Programme in Secondary Schools: National Evaluation*. London, UK: Department for Education.

Jennings, P.A., & Greenberg, M.T. (2009). The prosocial classroom: teacher social and emotional competence in relation to child and classroom outcomes. *Review of Educational Research, 79,* 491–525.

Kelchtermans, G. (2011). Vulnerability in teaching: The moral and political roots of a structural condition. In: C. Day & J.C. Lee (eds), *New Understandings of Teacher's Work*, pp. 65–83. New York, NY: Springer.

Kidger, J.L., Gunnell, D., Biddle, J., Campbell, L.R., & Donova, J.L. (2010). Part and parcel of teaching? Secondary school staff's views on supporting student emotional health and well-being. *British Educational Research Journal, 36*, 919–935.

KidsMatter. (2012). *KidsMatter: Growing Healthy Minds*. Retrieved on 30th June 2014 from: http://www.kidsmatter.edu.au.

Masten, A.S. (2001). Ordinary magic: resilience processes in development. *American Psychologist, 56*, 227–238.

McLaughlin, C., & Clarke, B. (2010). Relational matters: a review of the impact of school experience on mental health in early adolescence. *Educational & Child Psychology, 27*, 91–103.

Merrell, K.W., & Gueldner, B.A. (2010). *Social and Emotional Learning. Promoting Mental Health and Academic Success*. New York: The Guilford Press.

Mind Matters. (2005). *The Mentoring Journal* (Commonwealth of Australia). Retrieved on 30 June 2014 from: http://www.mindmatters.edu.au/verve/_resources/interpersonal_journal_mentoring.pdf.

Moon, B. (2007). *Research Analysis: Attracting, Developing and Retaining Effective Teachers – A Global Overview of Current Policies and Practices*. Paris, France: UNESCO.

National Institute for Health and Clinical Excellence. (2008). *Promoting Children's Social and Emotional Wellbeing in Primary Education*. London: UK: National Health Service.

New Economics Foundation. (2009). *National Accounts of Well-Being: Bringing Real Wealth onto the Balance Sheet*. London: UK: New Economics Foundation.

Osher, D., Sprague, J., Weissberg, R.P., Axelrod, J., Keena, S., Kendziora, K., et al. (2008). A comprehensive approach to promoting social, emotional, and academic growth in contemporary schools. In A. Thomas & J. Grimes (eds), *Best Practices in School Psychology, 5th Edition*, Vol. 5, pp. 1263–1278. Bethesda, MD: National Association of School Psychologists.

Payton, J., Weissberg, R.P., Durlak, J.A., Dymnicki, A.B., Taylor, R.D., Schellinger, K.B., et al. (2008). *The Positive Impact of Social and Emotional Learning for Kindergarten to Eighth-Grade Students. Findings from Three Scientific Reviews*. Chicago: NY: CASEL.

Pianta, R.C., & Stuhlman, M.W. (2004). Teacher-child relationships and children's success in the first years of school. *School Psychology Review, 33* (3), 444–458.

Pring, R. (2012). Putting persons back into education. *Oxford Review of Education, 38* (6), 747–760.

Reinke, W.M., Stormont, M., Herman, K.C., Puri, R., & Goel, N. (2011). Supporting children's mental health in schools: teacher perceptions of needs, roles, and barriers. *School Psychology Quarterly, 26*, 1–13.

Seligman, M.E., Gillham, J., Reivich, K., Linkins, M., & Ernst, R. (2009). Positive education. *Oxford Review of Education, 35* (3), 293–311.

Sklad, M., Diekstra, R., De Ritter, M., & Ben, J. (2012). Effectiveness of school-based universal social, emotional, and behavioral programs: do they enhance students' development in the area of skill, behavior, and adjustment? *Psychology in the Schools, 49* (9), 892–909.

Solomon, D., Battistisch, V., Watson, M., Schaps, E., & Lewis, C. (2000). A six district study of educational change: direct and mediated effects of the child development project. *Social Psychology of Education, 4*, 3–51.

Spratt, J., Shucksmith, J., Philip, K., & Watson, C. (2006). Part of who we are as a school should include responsibility for well-being: links between the school environment, mental health and behaviour. *Pastoral Care in Education, 24* (3), 14–21.

Stewart-Brown, S. (2006). *What Is the Evidence on School Health Promotion in Improving Health or Preventing Disease and, Specifically What Is the Effectiveness of the Health Promoting Schools Approach.* Copenhagen, Denmark: WHO Regional Office for Europe Health Evidence Network report.

Vostanis, P., Humphrey, N., Fitzgerald, N., Deighton, J., & Wolpert, M. (2013). How do schools promote emotional well-being among their pupils? Findings from a national scoping survey of mental health provision in English schools. *Journal of Child and Adolescent Health, 18* (3), 151–157.

Watson, D., Emery, C., & Bayliss, P. (2012). *Children's Social and Emotional Well-Being in Schools: A Critical Perspective.* Bristol, UK: The Policy Press.

Weare, K. (2010). Mental health and social and emotional learning: evidence, principles, tensions, balances. *Advances in School Mental Health Promotion, 3* (1), 5–17.

Weare, K., & Nind, M. (2011). Mental health promotion and problem prevention in schools: what does the evidence say? *Health Promotion International, 26* (S1), i29–i69.

Wells, J., Barlow, J., & Stewart-Brown, S. (2003). A systematic review of universal approaches to mental health promotion in schools. *Health Education, 103* (4), 197–220.

WHO. (2007). *What Is a Health Promoting School?* Retrieved 30 June 2014, from World Health Organisation: http://www.who.int/chool_youth_health/gshi/hps/en/index.html.

WHO. (2013). *Mental Health: A State of Well-Being. 10 FACTS ON MENTAL HEALTH.* Retrieved on 30 June 2014 from http://www.who.int/features/factfiles/mental_health/mental_health_facts/en/.

WHO. (2014). *Health for the World's Adolescents. A Second Chance in the Second Decade.* Retrieved on 30 June 2014 from: http://apps.who.int/adolescent/second-decade/files/1612_MNCAH_HWA_Executive_Summary.pdf.

Youngblade, L.M., Theokas, J., Schulenberg, L., Curry, I.C., Huang, C., & Novak, M. (2007). Risk and promotive factors in families, schools, and communities: a contextual model of positive youth development in adolescence. *Pediatrics, 119*, SS47–SS53.

Zembylas, M., & Schutz, P.A. (2009). Research on teachers' emotions in education: Findings practical implications and future agenda. In: P.A. Schutz & M. Zembylas (eds), *Advances in Teacher Emotion Research. The Impact on Teachers' Lives*, pp. 367–377. New York: NY: Springer.

Zins, J.E. (2001). Examining opportunities and challenges for school-based prevention and promotion: social and emotional learning as an exemplar. *Journal of Primary Prevention, 21* (4), 441–446.

5
Understanding and Overcoming Guilt, Shame, and Anxiety: Based on the Theory of Negative Legacy Emotions

Peter R. Breggin

I have spent more than half a century as a psychiatrist and psychotherapist trying to understand human suffering. Why does every single one of us come out of childhood suffering from guilt and shame? Where does anxiety fit in? How much influence does bad parenting have in causing these emotions? How can we limit their painful impact on ourselves, our children, and those we seek to help?

In recent years, too little attention has been given to these critical issues about human suffering and psychology. The dominant medical model completely ignores underlying psychological or emotional issues and leaps to irrational, unproven, and unfounded conclusions about biological and genetic causes (Breggin, 1991, 2008; Moncrieff, 2008; Lacasse & Leo, 2012).

Ronald Pies (2011), Professor of Psychiatry and Editor-in-Chief Emeritus of *Psychiatric Times*, recently ridiculed the biochemical imbalance theory:

> And, yes – the 'chemical imbalance' image has been vigorously promoted by some pharmaceutical companies, often to the detriment of our patients' understanding. In truth, the 'chemical imbalance' notion was always a kind of urban legend – never a theory seriously propounded by well-informed psychiatrists. (p. 1)

Although Pies claims the biochemical imbalance theory was *never* 'seriously propounded by well-informed psychiatrists', nearly all psychiatrists are still telling this lie to patients to push them into taking psychiatric drugs. He is right, however, in his implication that the theory is fakery driven by drug company money.

Non-medical frameworks, such as positive psychology, emphasize living by better principles and attitudes, and this can be very valuable.

Unfortunately, positive psychology largely tends to ignore the emotional impediments that interfere with self-improvement or therapy (e.g., Seligman, 1995). Meanwhile, important sociological insights into negative emotions have not sufficiently influenced clinical thinking or training (e.g., Scheff & Retzinger, 1991). Because they ignore guilt, shame, and anxiety, superficiality reigns in many contemporary psychological approaches.

A scientifically valid model for understanding and overcoming negative emotions, although rooted in part in biology and genetics, cannot be used to justify psychiatric diagnoses such as found in the American Psychiatric Association's (2013) *Diagnostic and Statistical Manual of Mental Disorders*. These categories for human suffering lack a genuine biological basis and instead impose a 'medical model' that does more harm than good (Breggin, 2008). A useful model should recognize that our emotional strengths and vulnerabilities are partly given to us by genetics and biology, that suffering is inevitable, but that mind, spirit, and choice can triumph over and transcend towards an ideal of emotional freedom.

Human emotional suffering is universal. It occurs in every culture and every individual. Although in part rooted in human nature and hence biology and genetics, there is nothing 'medical' or abnormal about emotional suffering, even when it is self-destructive. Despite relative degrees of suffering and despite inevitable variability, all human beings suffer from essentially the same conflicts and emotional struggles. The degree of the suffering usually depends upon the severity of traumatic events, usually abuse and neglect in childhood, as well as misfortune and mistaken decisions (Breggin, 2014).

The development of a theory

Several decades ago I began to think about the common elements in guilt, shame, and anxiety. I began to explore their similarities and differences with my patients and in my articles and books (e.g., Breggin, 1991). I began to notice that whenever someone feels one of these emotions, it comes with underlying feelings of helplessness and difficulties making healthy choices (Breggin, 1991). Guilt, shame, and anxiety discourage rational thought about how we want to carry on with our lives. They are emotional warning lights to cease and desist assertive behaviours. When they grow stronger, any one of these emotions can become paralysing, in the extreme rendering us unable to manage ordinary life challenges. Guilt can drive us in overwhelming depression, shame can make us withdraw into ourselves and even into psychosis, and anxiety can keep us immobilized.

After the breakthrough in discovering that feelings of helplessness are always associated with our negative emotions, the next step was to analyse the differences in how these emotions assign blame and direct anger. When feeling guilt, we typically blame ourselves and direct our anger at ourselves.

When feeling shame, we feel that others are doing something to us, and we tend to shift our blame and anger outward.

Anxiety was more difficult to understand until I realized that anxiety tends to obliterate blaming and to disperse anger. In an anxious state, we may feel incompetent and we may blame 'life' for our feelings of helplessness; but our feelings remain vague and effective. Although philosophy has argued that anxiety is existential in nature and although the behavioural sciences are researching anxiety as derived from our awareness of death and mortality (e.g., Klackl et al., 2013), in therapy this rarely seems to be the cause of severe anxiety. The roots of overwhelming anxiety can usually be traced back to primitive emotions that were amplified in childhood through conflict and the breakdown of the security of early relationships (e.g., Breggin, 1991; Bowlby, 1998).

Taking a moment to summarize, I had developed a concept easily applicable in life and therapy, that guilt, shame, and anxiety are always associated with feelings of helplessness, and that each has a different method of directing blame and anger. I still did not have a good explanation for why childhood generates so much guilt, shame, and anxiety in every person. It was also unclear why these emotions become most overwhelming when the child is abused or neglected. In short, the *function* of these painful and often dreadful emotions remained elusive.

From an unexpected direction

Over the past few years, I have been dismayed by the junk science being published in the name of evolutionary biology and neuroscience. Neuroscience in particular has been making outlandish claims for understanding the connection between brain and behaviour. Funded largely by the pharmaceutical industry, researchers were making absurd claims about connecting aberrant brain functions to 'mental illness'. The drug companies aimed at encouraging people to view their brains as their problem so they would more readily accept drugs as their solution (Breggin, 1991, 2013a). I was in the process of writing a book about 'neuromania' when I discovered that many others were already soundly dismissing the false application of biological sciences to human conduct (e.g., Legrenzi & Umilta, 2011; Tallis, 2011). Ironically and unexpectedly, thinking about the limitations of evolutionary biology and neuroscience was leading me to ponder how these sciences, if conducted properly, might contribute to our understanding ourselves as human beings.

Whilst considering the spectrum of human behavior and emotions, ranging from extremes of tenderness and compassion through to torment and violence, I was surprised to find that even the most seemingly shy and 'harmless' people often harboured the deepest resentments and violent feelings. Biological evolution and human history, as well as contemporary times, confirm that human beings are and have always been the most violent creatures on Earth and yet the most social and most loving. Fossil evidence shows that several hundred thousands of years ago our ancestors were hunting and butchering animals larger than modern elephants and doing so with little more than pointed sticks as weapons (Wenban-Smith et al., 2006; 'Giant Prehistoric Elephant Slaughtered by Early Humans,' 2013; also see Stiner et al., 2009). Bringing down these huge creatures while armed with puny spears must have required enormous ferocity combined with courage and social cooperation. I came to describe these conflicting inborn capacities as wilfulness and violence versus empathy and sociability.

Our nearest relative, the chimpanzee, was thought to be social and relatively peaceful, never making war on its own kind. Then the disheartening truth came out – even chimps at times slaughter each other in warlike encounters (Goodall, 1999; de Waal, 2005). Nonetheless, we are far ahead of all other creatures in having this unique combination of craving for social life and propensity for violence. These conflicting human impulses towards socialization and wilful aggression are perpetually in conflict everywhere on Earth not only in the political arena but in our personal and domestic lives, and in the raising of our children.

Given that violence is so deeply embedded in human nature and life, it seemed inevitable that people would be in constant conflict with each other and at risk of hurting not only strangers but also those with whom they live in close proximity. The survival of humanity required an innate set of emotional responses that would help us to manage our wilfulness and aggression in close personal relationships, especially in the family. Not only is our violence most dangerous in close personal relationships, it is most likely to be provoked by the inevitable conflicts and frustrations that characterized these relationships. I began to ask, 'How did such a violent and yet social creature manage to survive without destroying its own family life and bringing its evolutionary line to an inglorious violent end?'

The birth of a new theory

Guilt, shame, and anxiety are natural selection's answer to the problem of our enormously conflicting tendencies towards both violence and sociability in our closest relationships. These inhibitory emotions help to prevent the unleashing of wilfulness and aggression between parents and children, husbands and wives, friends, and perhaps members of the extended family or clan. Natural selection favoured human beings with a strong capacity for wilfulness and violence *against strangers and wild beasts*, while also maintaining built-in inhibitions against expressing these disruptive and dangerous emotions *in close relationships* (Breggin, 2014). The inhibiting effects of guilt, shame, and anxiety in close family relationships would promote individual survival and the capacity to reproduce in a creature otherwise primed to react with wilfulness and violence especially when frustrated or threatened by one's mates or children.

Individuals with the innate capacity for guilt, shame, and anxiety, and the groups within which they lived, developed a survival and reproductive advantage in competition with other humans or human-like creatures (hominins). They would be favoured through natural selection. Since humans and hominins have been both violent and social for probably a few million years, nature has had time to ensure that every human being is born with the capacity to feel guilt, shame, and anxiety in close relationships (Breggin, 2014). These emotions would inevitably be elicited or triggered early enough in childhood to help control the extraordinary wilfulness and potential for violence that even children display, especially when thwarted or frustrated in their relationships with siblings, parents, and caregivers.

To designate their origins in evolution and in early childhood, and to emphasize their function, I have given the name *negative legacy emotions* to guilt, shame, and anxiety (Breggin, 2014). Understanding guilt, shame, and anxiety as negative legacy emotions has many implications and applications in therapy and in everyday life.

How negative legacy emotions work

It is easiest to understand how guilt inhibits our wilfulness and violence. When in conflict with other people, and tempted to be angry with them, guilt instead makes us blame ourselves and direct our anger inward. When in conflict, shame makes us feel too impotent, worthless, or inconsequential to assert ourselves aggressively. Instead, we act shyly or withdraw. Anxiety, when we are in conflict, makes us feel so incompetent, baffled, and emotionally stupid that we can do nothing effectively. If we assign blame, it may be vaguely at our supposed incompetence or at 'how the world keeps coming at me'. This too keeps us from unleashing violence.

Each negative legacy emotion in its own way makes us feel so helpless that we cannot assert ourselves. When taken over by anxiety, we most openly feel the raw emotion of helplessness, but it is associated with all three negative emotions. By rendering us helpless at critical moments of personal conflict, these emotions help to rein in our wilfulness and violence.

Guilt, shame, and anxiety aim at stopping us dead in our tracks, preventing us from asserting ourselves against the people closest to us. Developed by natural selection, they are neither fine-tuned nor very effective. They can backfire destructively, leading to destructive reactions that harm us or the people closest to us. When guilt feels intolerable, we can become suicidal. When shame seems intolerable, we can break through our feelings of impotence and worthlessness, and strike back violently. From school and workplace shootings to domestic violence, nearly all personal violence is driven by shame and humiliation (Breggin, 2014).

Although guilt is the primary driver of self-destructive impulses, shame and anxiety can also fuel suicide in an effort to end the intolerable feelings. Conversely, although shame is the primary driver of violence, guilt can lead to resentment and anger, and anxiety can make people irritable and ultimately aggressive. These complicated responses reflect upon and influence the complexity of human relationships. Sorting them out requires separating their survival and reproductive value (preventing violence in close relationships) from their unintended consequences (suppressing self-assertiveness to such an extreme that it breaks out violently towards oneself and others).

Their prehistoric quality

The origins of guilt, shame, and anxiety in biological evolution and natural selection are deeply buried within our prehistoric existence. Embedded in the fabric of our brains and bodies, they are ready for triggering by environmental events in childhood. Later in life, we may feel we 'deserve' to feel guilty or ashamed or that we are justified in feeling anxious; but in reality we were programmed by biological evolution and natural selection to feel this way.

They are also prehistoric in the sense that they first surfaced in our individual lives in childhood before we can recall or grasp much of what was going on, so their stimulation in our lifetime remains buried in our childhood. 'Self-understanding' or 'self-analysis' can only go so far before it runs smack into biological reality – we were built to experience guilt, shame, and anxiety, and how we respond depends upon events that lie beyond self-understanding and self-analysis in the ancient annals of human evolution and the lost recesses of childhood. While it is true that we can often recall some of the stimulating events for guilt, shame, and anxiety in our childhood – and this can be very helpful in our emotional growth – we are looking at the tip of an iceberg that is submerged beneath consciousness and buried in the prehistory of childhood amnesia and biological evolution.

Their simplistic quality

Because guilt, shame, and anxiety evolved before human beings had sophisticated cultures and because they were built into our biology, these negative legacy emotions are rather simple emotional reactions that vary little from individual to individual. This makes them relatively easy to identify in ourselves and other people but also makes them very difficult to modify. After a therapist becomes attuned to identify these emotions, it will often become apparent in the first few minutes of therapy that an individual is dominated, at least at this moment, by one or another of the three emotions. Sometimes the individual's carriage and mannerisms will be characteristic of one of these emotions. Identifying these emotions can begin the work of therapy, but learning to apply this knowledge to everyday living can require a great deal of work on the part of client and therapist alike.

Their primitive quality

Guilt, shame, and anxiety are primitive emotions. Built into us throughout millions of years of evolution, we were struggling with them long before we evolved into *Homo sapiens* approximately 150,000 years ago (Breggin, 2014). They are Stone Age emotional reactions. They are also primitive in how they were triggered and moulded when we were infants and small children incapable of making rational ethical judgements. It is therefore unlikely that guilt, shame, and anxiety reactions would turn out to be consistent or reliable guidelines for mature adult reasoning, ethics, and choices. For this reason, guilt, shame, and anxiety can be seen as primitive, prehistoric, simplistic emotional reactions that do not accurately reflect on either our real value as persons or on how we should live our lives. A mature life can be lived with reliance on reason and love as its guidelines.

Emotional freedom

The realization that Stone Age negative legacy emotions too often rule over us provides the foundation of my theory in *Guilt, Shame and Anxiety: Understanding and Overcoming Negative Emotions*. The book provides the scientific basis and research basis for my concept of negative legacy emotions. It shows how they easily become the weapons of perpetrators in the form of child neglect and abuse, bullying, and domestic violence, offering several approaches to identifying these emotions in ourselves and in those who wish to receive our help. It describes the three steps to emotional freedom: identifying, rejecting, and triumphing over and transcending guilt, shame, and anxiety, as well as its derivative of chronic anger and emotional numbing.

Why guilt, shame, and anxiety have no redeeming features

The revelation that guilt, shame, and anxiety are prehistoric and primitive in origin leads to the conclusion that they are unlikely to correspond to sound values or rational ethics that can be used to guide a successful mature life. They are the combined product of natural selection and the influence of mostly early childhood triggering events. They are results of biological evolution selecting for rudimentary controls over our wilfulness and violence in close personal relationships.

If in adulthood, for example, we feel guilty about rejecting someone close to us, the guilt will not necessarily have any correspondence to what is good for us or even for the person we are rejecting. Or, if we feel ashamed about wanting to express ourselves in a new and creative way, shame is likely to inhibit us without any regard for how other mature people will in fact react to our innovative efforts. Similarly, if we become anxious about being abandoned, that emotional reaction will have no necessary connection to whether or not we are in reality facing abandonment or whether being abandoned by the particular person is good or bad for us in the long run.

In my clinical and forensic work, it is obvious that most people feel guilt, shame, and anxiety without regard for any realistic assessments of their behaviour or situation. Often the emotions remain overwhelming even though the individual has little or nothing in present time to feel guilty, anxious, or ashamed about. Much of the therapeutic process centres on helping people see that these emotions are self-defeating, causing inhibitions and feelings of helplessness that interfere with successful living, including the development and maintenance of loving relationships.

Many people commit crimes including murder without feeling any negative legacy emotions, but they may feel overcome with guilt, shame, and anxiety about doing something good for themselves and others, such as daring to find and build a loving relationship. In fact the two often go together in the same person – lack of negative emotions about real offences and an over-abundance of them about having a good life.

These conclusions shed enormous light on how to conduct therapy and how to run our own lives. If we wish to help other people prosper and if we want to succeed in our own lives, it helps enormously to decide that guilt, shame, and anxiety have no place in a mature, adult life. They need to be replaced with reason, sound principles, and love.

Do children need to feel guilt, shame, and anxiety?

Except in a most speculative fashion, it is impossible to determine whether children raised in modern families need to feel guilt, shame, and anxiety to control their wilful aggressiveness. Since all children under normal or average circumstances will develop some degree of guilt, shame, and anxiety in their closest relationships, there is no way to tell if they need these feelings in order to behave themselves and to grow up successfully. Only a child deprived of normal nurturing is likely to grow up lacking either guilt or shame, and probably no one grows up without anxiety.

Well-meaning parents often try hard to avoid instilling guilt, shame, and anxiety in their children; but they can never approach success. Because negative legacy emotions are so thoroughly embedded by nature in our brains and bodies, as parents we will unavoidably trigger some degree of guilt, shame, and anxiety in our children. In addition, we cannot completely control the negative impact of their siblings, peers, and other caregivers.

Meanwhile, psychologists and social scientists have become increasingly aware that from birth onward infants and children can respond positively to the people around them. Researchers speak of infants showing empathy anywhere from the nursery when they cry at the sounds of other infants crying (called contagion as if it were a disease) to when as toddlers they will offer comfort to other children and adults who seem unhappy.

A few years ago, I was happily reminded about the loving responsiveness of a few months old infant. My new grandson and I fell asleep while I held him in my arms, and on awakening we beamed into each other's faces with such joy that we seemed to glow with inner spiritual light in the photo that captured the moment. Undoubtedly, these very early experiences are eliciting the infant's innate capacity for empathy and bonding that positively influences both infant and caretakers.

I believe that only good can come from avoiding triggering guilt, shame, and anxiety in children while encouraging empathy and love from the earliest possible age. This same is true in our adult relationships with each other. Emotional freedom is achieved in part by refusing to inflict and refusing to accept communications corrupted by guilt, shame, and anxiety (Breggin, 2014).

A theory of all emotional suffering?

Do guilt, shame, and anxiety account for all or nearly all human psychological suffering? I think so, but I have not yet reached the point of applying this understanding in detail to all of what we call 'mental illness' or emotional suffering. Here is a brief sketch of how the theory can be used in clinical practice in helping deeply disturbed persons. When people are overwhelmed by depression, most clinicians would agree that it is probably driven by guilt, along with varying measures of shame and anxiety. When people withdraw into psychotic states, including what gets called schizophrenia, they are typically feeling overwhelmed by extreme shame and humiliation (Breggin, 1991). When people feel overwhelmed with panic or anxiety, the negative legacy emotion of anxiety is likely to be driving it. Obsessions and compulsions can be driven by guilt, shame, or anxiety. Child abuse and neglect and trauma can also produce varying degrees of all three emotions.

When recovery from traumatic loss or bereavement seems impeded, guilt, shame, and anxiety are usually interfering with healing. Child abuse and neglect gets its traumatizing power from the guilt, shame, and anxiety inflicted on the individual. From child abuse and neglect to traumatic losses and events in adulthood, negative legacy emotions play a major role in causation and/or in preventing emotional and spiritual recovery (Breggin, 2014).

Since feelings of helplessness are at the root of all negative legacy emotions, it follows that most emotional suffering and personal failure is rooted in these subjective feelings of helplessness. A key challenge in empowering ourselves and in helping other people is to address and to overcome feelings of helplessness.

As a clinician, I have found that emotional freedom from almost any expression of psychological suffering and personal failure, including the most extreme, can be largely understood and healed with the use of this model of negative legacy emotions in a caring, empathic relationship. It can be enormously liberating when clients learn to identify and reject their negative legacy emotions, and to replace them with positive values and attitudes such as personal responsibility and love (Breggin, 2013b; Breggin, 2014). The most important factor is a therapeutic relationship free of guilt, shame, and anxiety, and filled with empathic caring and love, expressed within professional boundaries (Breggin, 1997).

Guidelines for empathic therapy

With the help of Advisory Council members of the Center for the Study of Empathic Therapy, I developed the following Guidelines for Empathic Therapy (Breggin, 2011):
As Empathic Therapists –

(1) We treasure those who seek our help and we view therapy as a sacred and inviolable trust. With humility and gratitude, we honour the privilege of being therapists.
(2) We rely upon relationships built on trust, honesty, caring, genuine engagement, and mutual respect.
(3) We bring out the best in ourselves in order to bring out the best in others.
(4) We create a safe space for self-exploration and honest communication by holding ourselves to the highest ethical standards, including honesty, informed consent, confidentiality, professional boundaries, and respect for personal freedom, autonomy, and individuality.
(5) We encourage overcoming psychological helplessness and taking responsibility for emotions, thoughts and actions – and ultimately for living a self-determined life.
(6) We offer empathic understanding and, when useful, we build on that understanding to offer new perspectives and guidance for the further fulfilment of personal goals and freely chosen values.
(7) When useful, we help to identify self-defeating patterns learned in childhood and adulthood in order to promote the development of more effective choice-making and conduct.
(8) We do not treat people against their will or in any way use coercion, threats, manipulation, or authoritarianism.
(9) We do not reduce others to diagnostic categories or labels – a process that diminishes personal identity, oversimplifies life, instils dependency on authority, and impedes post-traumatic growth. Instead, we encourage people to understand and to embrace the depth, richness, and complexity of their unique emotional and intellectual lives.
(10) We do not falsely attribute emotional suffering and personal difficulties to genetics and biochemistry. Instead, we focus on each person's capacity to take responsibility and to determine the course of his or her own life.

(11) We recognize that a drug-free mind is best suited to personal growth and to facing critical life issues. Psychiatric drugs frequently cloud the mind, impair judgement and insight, suppress emotions and spirituality, inhibit relationships and love, and reduce will power and autonomy. They are often anti-therapeutic.
(12) We apply the Guidelines for Empathic Therapy to all therapeutic relationships, including persons who suffer from brain injuries or from the most profound emotional disturbances. Individuals who are mentally, emotionally, and physically fragile are especially vulnerable to injury from psychiatric drugs and authoritarian therapies, and are in need of the best we have to offer as empathic therapists.
(13) Because children are among our most vulnerable and treasured citizens, we especially need to protect them from psychiatric diagnoses and drugs. We need to offer them the family life, education, and moral and spiritual guidance that will help them to fulfil their potential as children and adults.
(14) Because personal failure and suffering cannot be separated from the ethics and values that guide our conduct, we promote basic human values including personal responsibility, freedom, gratitude, love, and the courage to honestly self-evaluate and to grow.
(15) Because human beings thrive when living by their highest ideals, individuals may wish to explore their most important personal values, including spiritual beliefs or religious faith, and to integrate them into their therapy and their personal growth.

The application of the theory of negative legacy emotions is represented in the fifth guideline: *We encourage overcoming psychological helplessness and taking responsibility for emotions, thoughts, and actions – and ultimately for living a self-determined life.*

Becoming the person you always wanted to be

As I describe in my new book *Guilt, Shame and Anxiety*, emotional liberation can take place in three overlapping steps. First, we identify our negative legacy emotions. Second, we reject them as having no worth or redeeming features in our lives. Third, we replace them with reason, ethics, and love as our guidelines. Is it easy? No. Does it take time and effort? Yes. Is it worth it? It is a giant key to living a happy life and to being as useful as possible to other people.

Instead of suppressing our painful emotions with psychoactive drugs, including psychiatric medications (Breggin, 1991, 2013a), we can liberate ourselves from guilt, shame, and anxiety, learning to require mutually respectful relationships in which love can thrive. As we leave these negative legacy emotions behind, life becomes much easier and richer. We become infinitely more able to love.

After leaving guilt, shame, and anxiety behind, we will never 'burn out' in our work or our relationships (Breggin, 2013b, 2014). Age will not seem daunting but instead increasingly filled with happiness now we understand how to sweep out negative legacy emotions in favour of life-enhancing and inspiring values and attitudes, especially love for others and for something or Someone greater than ourselves. Armed with knowledge about our conflicted human nature, we can triumph over and transcend the negativity within us in favour of our infinitely greater resources to live a rational and loving life.

Final thoughts

The medical approach to emotional problems often does more harm than good and should be replaced by theories and therapies that recognize the universal nature of human suffering and the universal ways of emotional, psychological, and spiritual healing. An understanding of negative legacy emotions – their imposition on us by biological evolution and childhood experiences – can help us to see the origins of emotional suffering. It can help us and our clients to see that emotional suffering is natural, that it does not reflect on our value as persons, and that it can be overcome. The identification of guilt, shame, and anxiety as the primary negative emotions, and the underlying helplessness that they bring along with them, can provide the theoretical foundation for emotional freedom. Regardless of whatever theoretical constructs may be brought to therapy, the process will be most effective when it is based on a caring, empathic relationship that is free of guilt, shame, and anxiety.

References

American Psychiatric Association. (2013). *Diagnostic and Statistical Manual of Mental Disorder, Fifth Edition*. Washington, DC: American Psychiatric Association.

Bowlby, J. (1998). *A Secure Base: Parent-Child Attachment and Healthy Human Development*. New York: Basic Books.

Breggin, P.R. (1991). *Toxic Psychiatry: Why Empathy, Therapy and Love Must Replace the Drugs, Electroshock and Biochemical Theories of the 'New Psychiatry.'* New York: St Martin's Press.

Breggin, P.R. (1997). *The Heart of Being Helpful: Empathy and the Creation of a Healing Presence*. New York: Springer Publishing Company.

Breggin, P.R. (2008). *Brain-Disabling Treatments in Psychiatry: Drugs, Electroshock and the Psychopharmaceutical Complex, Second Edition*. New York: Springer Publishing Company.

Breggin, P.R. (2011). Guidelines for Empathic Therapy. From the Center for the Study of Empathic Therapy (a nonprofit 501c3). http://www.empathictherapy.org/Founding-Guidelines.html.Retrieved 14 June 2014.

Breggin, P.R. (2013a). *Psychiatric Drug Withdrawal: A Guide for Prescribers, Therapists, Patients and Their Families*. New York: Springer Publishing Company.

Breggin, P.R. (2013b). Empathy, woundedness, burn out, and how to love being a therapist. In: Kirkcaldy, B.D. (ed.), *Chimes of Time: Wounded Health Professionals; Essays on Recovery*, Chapter 16, pp. 261–271. Leiden: Sidestone Press.

Breggin, P.R. (2014). *Guilt, Shame and Anxiety: Understanding and Overcoming Our Negative Emotions.* Amherst, New York: Prometheus Books.

'Giant Prehistoric Elephant Slaughtered by Early Humans.' *Science Daily* (2013, 19 September). http://www.sciencedaily.com/releases/2013/09/130919085710.htm?utm_source=feedburner&utm_medium=email&utm_campaign=Feed:+sciencedaily/plants_animals/animals+%28ScienceDaily:+Plants+%26+Animals+News+-+Animals%29. Accessed 22 September 2013.

Goodall, J. (1999). *Jane Goodall: 40 Years at Gombe.* New York: Stewart, Tabori & Chang.

Klackl, J., Jonas, E., & Kronbichler, M. (2013). Existential neuroscience: neurophysiological correlates of proximal defenses against death-related thoughts. *Social Cognitive and Affective Neuroscience*, 8 (3): 333–340. doi: 10.1093/scan/nss003.

Lacasse, J.R., & Leo, J. (2005). Serotonin and depression: a disconnect between the advertisements and the scientific literature. *PLoS Med.*, 2 (12): e392. doi: 10.1371/journal.pmed.0020392 – See more at: http://www.psychiatrictimes.com/blogs/couch-crisis/psychiatry-new-brain-mind-and-legend-chemical-imbalance#sthash.ouYlryjh.dpuf.

Legrenzi, P., & Umilta, C. (2011). *Neuromania: On the Limits of Brain Science.* Oxford: Oxford University Press.

Moncrieff, J. (2008). *Myth of the Chemical Cure: A Critique of Psychiatric Drug Treatment.* New York: Palgrave Macmillan.

Pies, R. (2011). Psychiatry's new brain-mind and the legend of the 'Chemical Imbalance.' *Psychiatric Times*, 11 June, p. 1.

Scheff, T.J., & Retzinger, S.M. (1991). *Emotions and Violence: Shame and Rage in Destructive Conflict.* Lanham, MD: Lexington Press.

Seligman, M. (1995). *The Optimistic Child.* New York: Houghton Mifflin Company.

Stiner, M.C., Barkai, R., & Gopher, A. (2009). Cooperative Hunting and Meat Sharing 400–200 kya at Qesem Cave, Israel. *Proceedings of the National Academy of Science*, 106 (32): 13207–13212. Published online 28 July 2009. doi: kn10.1073/pnas.0900564106.http://www.ncbi.nlm.nih.gov/pmc/articles/PMC2726383/(accessed 22 September 2013).

Tallis, R. (2011). *Aping Mankind: Neuromania, Darwinitis and the Misrepresentation of Humanity.* Durham, UK: Acumen.

de Waal, F.B.M. (2005). A century of getting to know the chimpanzee. *Nature*, 437, 56–59 (1 September 2005). doi: 10.1038/nature03999.

Wenban-Smith, F.F., Allen, P., Bates, M.R., Parfitt, S.A., Preece, R.C., Stewart, J.R., Turner, C., & Whittaker, J.E. (2006). The Clactonian elephant butchery site at Southfleet Road, Ebbsfleet, UK. *Journal of Quaternary Science*, 21, 471–483.

6
Understanding and Enhancing the Subjective Well-Being of Children

Mark D. Holder and Robyn L. Weninger

Health-oriented research, including psychology, education, and medicine, has emphasized identifying and treating deficits and dysfunction. Though this approach has proved valuable, it does not exhaust the range of the human experience that researchers should investigate. In addition to deficits and dysfunction, it is important to understand strengths and thriving. The past two decades have witnessed the active development of a complementary approach to cataloguing and correcting illness. This approach, now referred to as positive psychology, is focused on well-being instead of ill-being. New studies are identifying the correlates of happiness, gratitude, hope, and life satisfaction including factors associated with children's well-being (e.g., friends, spirituality, and physical activity). This identification represents only the initial stage of understanding children's well-being. The next and critical stage of research is to use the recent research findings to develop and assess strategies and interventions to encourage enduring enhancements of children's well-being. The present chapter first reviews some of the relevant research on children's well-being. We then suggest several possible intercessions, based on these research findings, which clinicians and practitioners might employ to enhance children's well-being.

Introduction

Research in health-related fields such as psychology, education, and medicine has traditionally emphasized identifying and treating deficits and dysfunction. Though this approach has proven valuable, it is also important to understand the factors, including the strengths, which allow humans to flourish. The past two decades have witnessed the active development of a complementary approach to cataloguing and correcting illness. This approach, now referred to as positive psychology, is focused on subjective well-being (SWB) as opposed to ill-being, and aims to understand the causes and correlates of human thriving (Park, Peterson, & Seligman, 2004;

Kim-Prieto, Diener, Tamir, Scollon, & Diener, 2005). To this end, new studies are investigating the components of SWB, including happiness, hope, gratitude, and life satisfaction. This research has identified factors associated with children's well-being; however, this identification represents only the initial stage of understanding. The next and critical stage of research is to develop and empirically assess the efficacy of strategies and interventions aimed at enhancing children's SWB.

The growing literature on SWB has led to a more nuanced understanding of the concept itself, but further positive psychology research is needed. For example, though the field has identified six broad virtues (e.g., Courage and Humanity), and 24 character strengths (e.g., creativity and gratitude) related to them through the Values in Action (VIA) Classification of Strengths (Peterson & Seligman, 2004), the underlying mechanism of the relationship between SWB and character strengths is not yet fully understood. Peterson and Seligman (2004) postulated that well-being is not directly produced by virtue but rather that well-being is an inherent component of virtue, and so utilizing character strengths is in itself fulfilling. Conceptualizing SWB and character strengths this way suggests that an effective way of enhancing SWB would be through interventions which target character strengths.

Importance of subjective well-being

Effectively enhancing SWB is important because high levels of SWB are related to important benefits including improved health, increased longevity, career success, enhanced quality of social relationships, and heightened cognitive functioning (see Weninger & Holder, 2014). Some of the benefits of SWB that have been identified through research with adults may apply to children. However, many of the factors that are important to adults' well-being (e.g., romantic relationships and job satisfaction) have little applicability to children (Holder, 2012). Furthermore, children's SWB may be related to factors that are not relevant to adults (e.g., school and imaginary friends). Thus, conducting research with children is necessary because the causes and correlates of SWB and its components may change across the lifespan.

Health. Research demonstrates a link between higher levels of SWB and lower blood pressure (Ostir, Berges, Markides, & Ottenbacher, 2006), lower rates of suicide (Koivumaa-Honkanen et al., 2001) and improved immune functioning (Lyubomirsky, King, & Diener, 2005). Evidence also suggests that psychological states such as reduced stress and positive feelings play a direct role in improving health (Argyle, 1997). For example, more optimistic older adults had significantly stronger cytokine immune responses to viruses and vaccines than individuals experiencing higher levels of negative emotions such as anger (Costanzo et al., 2004).

In contrast to health measures based on self-report, more objective health measures have not always found a robust link between health and SWB (Diener, Suh, Lucas, & Smith, 1999). As medical technology improves, this may improve our understanding of the mind–body link. One topic of recent research applicable to this involves telomeres. Telomeres are the small caps that prevent DNA deterioration and replication errors from occurring in new cells by protecting the ends of chromosomes. Not all research has supported the idea that SWB can influence telomeres (e.g., Ruis-Ottenheim et al., 2012), but there is growing evidence suggesting well-being may measurably impact their length. For example, individuals who practised Loving-Kindness Meditation to increase SWB-related traits such as unselfish kindness and warmth towards others had greater telomere length than controls matched for age, gender, education level, and depression history (Hoge et al., 2013).

Health research has primarily sampled from adult populations, but some studies conducted with younger populations reach similar conclusions. For example, in youths aged 12–14 years, health status is strongly associated both directly and indirectly with overall happiness (van de Wetering, van Exel, & Brouwer, 2010), and there is a strong, positive correlation between happiness and clinical health, perceived health status, and wellness in early adolescents (Mahon, Yarcheski, & Yarcheski, 2005). This suggests that promoting happiness in childhood could result in healthier children, and lead to a healthier population over time (Holder, 2012).

Longevity. Increased longevity and reduced mortality rates are predicted by happiness and life satisfaction in both healthy and diseased populations (Chida & Steptoe, 2008; Diener & Chan, 2011). The well-known Nun Study by Danner, Snowdon, and Friesen (2001) analysed autobiographies written in the 1930s and 1940s by Catholic nuns. These autobiographies were coded for positive, negative, and neutral emotion words. The nuns were then separated into quartiles based on how much positive emotional content was reflected in their writing. The least happy quartile had a mortality risk 2.5-fold greater than the happiest quartile. Similarly, a 28-year longitudinal study assessed SWB through measures of global life satisfaction, domain life satisfaction, and positive feelings, and found that SWB significantly predicted longevity in the general population (Xu & Roberts, 2010). Additionally, a twin study reported that SWB predicted increased longevity beyond what could be explained by genetics and shared environments (Sadler, Miller, Christensen, & McGue, 2011). However, although this relationship has been observed cross-culturally in healthy populations, it may be restricted to a preventative (i.e., not curative) role (Diener & Chan, 2011).

Career Success. Although the directionality and causality of the relationship may still require elucidation (Harter, Schmidt, & Keyes, 2003), happy individuals tend to experience greater career success than unhappy individuals (Lyubomirsky, King, & Diener, 2005). In fact, job and life satisfaction are strongly correlated (Tait, Padgett, & Baldwin, 1989). It makes sense that succeeding at work may contribute to SWB, but high levels of SWB also *precede* work-related success (Boehm & Lyubomirsky, 2008). More favourable work performance, increased work achievement, more positive supervisor evaluations, greater support from supervisors and co-workers, and higher salaries have all been linked to higher levels of well-being (Staw, Sutton, & Pelled, 1994; Cote, 1999; Boehm & Lyubomirsky, 2008). Encouraging high levels of SWB in employees can be beneficial for employers as well, as individuals who are higher in both job and life satisfaction are less frequently tardy and absent, work more efficiently, stay longer at a job, and engage in more helpful and cooperative behaviours towards co-workers than individuals who are dissatisfied (Spector, 1997; Avey, Patera, & West, 2006).

Although children are not part of the workforce, the relationship between career-related variables and SWB in adults may be similar to the relationship between school-related variables and SWB in children. High levels of SWB in children may be related to increased productivity and creativity at school as well as reduced absence from school (see Holder, 2012). School success has also been identified as a key happiness-increasing factor by 12-year-old students (Uusitalo-Malmivaara, 2012). Better academic performance in older students has been linked to hope (Gilman, Dooley, & Florell, 2006), optimism, and self-efficacy (Pintrich, 2000). A similar relationship between self-efficacy and academic arithmetic performance has been observed in younger children as well (Throndsen, 2011), suggesting that enhancing SWB-related traits such as optimism and self-efficacy might improve children's academic performance. However, though a five-week hope intervention with middle school students appeared to increase hope, self-worth, and life satisfaction, it did not improve academic performance (Marques, Lopez, & Pais-Ribeiro, 2011).

Quality of Social Relationships. Strong interpersonal relationships are associated with greater SWB. Many studies report that married individuals tend to be happier than those who are not married (Stack & Eshleman, 1998; Proulx, Helms, & Buehler, 2007; Dush, Taylor, & Kroeger, 2008). Similarly, happier students are more likely to rate their romantic relationships as higher quality (Berry & Willingham, 1997), individuals higher in positive affect tend to be more satisfied with their relationships (Lyubomirsky, King, & Diener, 2005), and very happy people tend to have stronger romantic and other social relationships (Diener & Seligman, 2002).

The role SWB plays in social relationships extends beyond romantic pairings to influence close friendships and familial relationships as well (Lyubomirksy, King, & Diener, 2005). Components of SWB including happiness are positively linked to many social variables, including the strength of social support, the quality of social interactions, and the size of social networks (Lyubomirsky, Sheldon, & Schkade, 2005). The relationship between

SWB and social connections is bidirectional: high levels of SWB may both result from and lead to better relationships (see Holder & Coleman, 2015).

Social relationships are also important to children's SWB. Children who visited friends more frequently were happier than children who visited them less frequently, as were children who felt that they were an important member of their family (Holder & Coleman, 2009). School-related happiness and global happiness in 12-year-old children are strongly related to social relationships (Uusitalo-Malmivaara, 2012). Furthermore, the least happy children in this study identified a desire for more friends more often than the happiest students. Even relationships with imaginary companions are associated with higher levels of SWB in children (see Holder & Coleman, 2015).

Cognitive Functioning. An individual's cognitive functioning can be influenced by their SWB. Positive emotions may broaden thinking by promoting more holistic processing (Fredrickson & Branigan, 2005) and more inclusive social categorization (Isen, Niedenthal, & Cantor, 1992; Dovidio, Isen, Guerra, Gaertner, & Rust, 1998). Positive moods appear to heighten all aspects of creativity (i.e., fluency, flexibility, originality, and insight), which are important in generating solutions for problems (Baas, De Dreu, & Nijstad, 2008).

There is little research on the links between cognition and SWB in children. However, relating the Broaden and Build Theory to children suggests that happier children will experience cognitive benefits associated with a broadened scope of attention (for a description of this theory see Fredrickson, 2013). This has implications for promoting learning and creativity in children.

Subjective well-being sources

Three domains have been proposed to explain variations in happiness levels: genetic set point, life circumstances, and intentional activity (Lyubomirsky, Sheldon, & Schkade, 2005; Lyubomirksy, 2007). These categories account for a variety of factors that influence SWB, including personality, living environment, and skills and hobbies.

Genetic Set Point. Approximately 50% of the variance in SWB has been attributed to an individual's genetic set point (Lyubomirsky, Sheldon, & Schkade, 2005; Lyubomirksy, 2007), which refers to the predisposition towards either happiness or unhappiness. Genes may be responsible for as much as 80% of the long-term stability in SWB, according to results from adoption and twin studies (Lykken & Tellegen, 1996; Nes, Røysamb, Tambs, Harris, & Reichborn-Kjennerud, 2006; Weiss, Bates, & Luciano, 2008). Genetics may play a significant role in well-being, primarily through influencing personality (Steel, Schmidt, & Shultz, 2008).

Despite disagreement as to precisely which traits comprise personality and which facets comprise each trait, there is wide acceptance of the Big Five model of personality (McCrae & Costa, 1987; Goldberg, 1993; John, Naumann, & Soto, 2008). This model identifies five higher-order personality traits, each comprising six facets: Neuroticism, Extraversion, Openness to Experience, Agreeableness, and Conscientiousness. Of these five traits, extraversion and neuroticism are most strongly linked to SWB (Steel et al., 2008). One conceptualization suggests extraversion is related to well-being through positive affect, and neuroticism is related to ill-being through negative affect (Costa & McCrae, 1980). A comprehensive meta-analysis supported this relationship, indicating there is a high degree of construct similarity between extraversion and positive affect as well as neuroticism and negative affect (Steel et al., 2008). However, extraversion and neuroticism are not the only personality traits related to SWB. For instance, positive affect may stem from connections with others, which would relate to extraversion through the quantity of social relationships an individual possesses and to agreeableness through the quality of those relationships (DeNeve & Cooper, 1998).

The SWB-related traits of hope and optimism may also be partly genetically derived, with heritability estimates of 53% (Chaturvedi, Arvey, Zhang, & Christoforou, 2011) and 36% (Mosing, Zietsch, Shekar, Wright, & Martin, 2009) respectively. Both hope and optimism have been conceptualized as relatively stable personality traits describing different aspects of the tendency to hold positive and favourable expectations regarding one's future (Gallagher & Lopez, 2009; Alarcon, Bowling, & Khazon, 2013).

The role of genetics in the SWB of children may be expressed through temperament. It is widely accepted that the temperament characteristics of children are the precursors to personality in adults (Buss & Plomin, 1984). According to the Emotionality, Activity, and Sociability theory of temperament (Buss & Plomin, 1984), the adult personality trait of extraversion may be represented in children by the temperament characteristics of high sociability (i.e., preferring social interaction to solitary settings) and low shyness, while neuroticism may be represented in children by emotionality (i.e., the tendency to become distressed easily). The relationship between SWB and temperament in children parallels the relationship between SWB and personality in adults in that the happiness of children has a positive association with high sociability and low shyness and a negative association with high emotionality (Holder & Klassen, 2010).

Life Circumstances. Only 10% of the variance in levels of happiness has been attributed to life circumstances such as geographic location, cultural setting, and demographics (Lyubomirsky, Sheldon, & Schkade, 2005; Lyubomirksy, 2007). This has been reflected by mostly modest or insignificant findings regarding SWB and demographic variables (e.g., age, gender, or employment) in general (Diener et al., 1999; Cheng & Furnham, 2003).

For example, one study with adult twins found that none of the variables of educational attainment, socio-economic status, family income, or even marital status could explain more than 1–3% of the variance in SWB (Lykken & Tellegen, 1996).

Research with children also supports a minimal relationship between SWB and life circumstances. Gender does not appear to influence SWB in children; boys and girls report similar levels of happiness (Nima, Archer, & Garcia, 2012; Uusitalo-Malmivaara, 2012). Children between the ages of 8 and 12 in Western Canada (Holder & Coleman, 2008, 2009) and children between the ages of 7 and 14 in New Delhi, India (Holder, Coleman, & Singh, 2012) report similar happiness levels despite very different life circumstances. Additionally, parental income and marital status are not significantly related to children's SWB. While one study found that children were aware of their own household income, only 2–4% of children's self-reported happiness could be attributed to family income (Holder & Coleman, 2008). Furthermore, some studies suggest that parental marital status does not relate to children's happiness (Holder & Coleman, 2008) or life satisfaction (Huebner, 1991). Similarly, adolescents' happiness was not related to their parents' marital status (Cheng & Furnham, 2003), even though parental divorce has been linked to greater psychological distress (Rodgers, Power, & Hope, 1997) and lower self-reported well-being (Grossman & Rowat, 1995) in adolescents. Perhaps the quality of the parental relationship is more important than the status of the relationship (Holder, 2012).

Intentional Activity. If genetics, including genetically determined personality traits, explains 50% of the variance in SWB, and life circumstances account for a further 10%, then the remaining 40% of the variance in happiness may be attributable to intentional activity (Lyubomirsky, Sheldon, & Schkade, 2005; Lyubomirksy, 2007). 'Intentional activity' refers to a discrete action which an individual engages in with conscious choice and active effort (Lyubomirsky, Sheldon, & Schkade, 2005). This definition is important, as self-determination (e.g., knowingly choosing to carry out an action) and personal agency (e.g., investing time and energy into an action) may influence the impact an activity has on well-being (Lyubomirsky, Dickerhoof, Boehm, & Sheldon, 2011). Although genes and many life circumstances are difficult to change, intentional activities represent a contributor to SWB that is possible to directly influence through the way one thinks and behaves (Lyubomirsky, 2007). Increases in SWB due to intentional activity may also be more resistant to hedonic adaptation (i.e., the tendency to adjust to changes in happiness levels instead of maintaining gains long-term) than increases in SWB due to changes to life circumstances (Sheldon & Lyubomirsky, 2006a).

Many different types of intentional activities are associated with SWB in children. For example, higher levels of children's well-being have been linked to participating in physical exercise (Parfitt & Eston, 2005) and active but not passive leisure activities (Holder, Coleman, & Sehn, 2009). Given that self-selection may influence the impact of various activities on well-being (Lyubomirsky et al., 2011), the relationship between leisure and SWB in children (whose activities are often selected for them) may not mirror that of adults (Holder, 2012).

Interventions for adults

To realize the positive psychology goal of understanding and promoting human flourishing, attention has turned to developing and testing interventions aimed at enhancing SWB. These interventions can be classified into one or more of four general categories (Timoney & Holder, 2013): behavioural, cognitive, volitional (Lyubomirsky, Sheldon, & Schkade, 2005), and observational (Algoe & Haidt, 2009). Behavioural interventions refer to actions or practices intended to increase SWB, including physical exercise programmes and leisure activities. This category also includes expressing gratitude and visualizing one's best possible self (Sheldon & Lyubomirsky, 2006b), as well as experiencing 'flow', a state of deep involvement and absorption when engaged in activities that have been chosen for their inherent value to the individual (Csikszentmihalyi, 1990). Cognitive interventions focus on developing more positive thoughts and perspectives, such as through cultivating optimism or savouring life's joys (Lyubomirsky, 2007). Volitional interventions involve encouraging goal pursuit, and tend to promote authenticity and commitment in goal-directed behaviours (Lyubomirsky, Sheldon, & Schkade, 2005; Lyubomirsky, 2007). Observational interventions consider the positive impact of witnessing excellence in others, perhaps by fostering emotions such as admiration and elevation (Algoe & Haidt, 2009). Many of these interventions are based on increasing SWB through utilizing the character strengths and virtues identified by the VIA Classification of Strengths (Peterson & Seligman, 2004). Though character is thought to be relatively stable, individual differences are 'also shaped by the individual's setting and thus capable of change' (Peterson & Seligman, 2004, p. 10). Thus, interventions tend to focus on intentional activities aimed at building hope, optimism, gratitude, social relationships, stress management skills, goal attainment, spirituality, physical health, and flow experiences (Csikszentmihalyi, 1990; Emmons & McCullough, 2004; Gander; Lyubomirsky, Sheldon, & Schkade, 2005; Seligman et al., 2005; Lyubomirsky, 2007; Diener & Ryan, 2009; Gander, Proyer, Ruch, & Wyss, 2013).

Although experimental research on happiness interventions is still relatively young, early findings suggest that interventions can efficiently and effectively increase well-being and decrease ill-being (Duckworth, Steen, & Seligman, 2005; Lyubomirsky, Sheldon, & Schkade, 2005). For example, having adults use their signature strengths in a novel way each day for one week and writing down three good things and their causes each day for one week both significantly increased happiness and reduced depression for six months, while writing and personally delivering a letter of gratitude increased well-being for one month (Seligman et al., 2005). A recent replication of these positive results supported the efficacy of these positive interventions (i.e., the gratitude visit, three good things, and using signature strengths) to increase well-being, and also found that all but one of the variant exercises they tested increased happiness in their participants (Gander et al., 2013). Another intervention involving writing about one's best possible self, leading to increase of positive affect (Sheldon & Lyubomirsky, 2006b), flow, and even (although to a lesser degree) feelings of relatedness (Layous, Nelson, & Lyubomirsky, 2013). For a review of existing SWB interventions, see Lyubomirsky (2007).

Interventions for children

Some of the factors associated with children's well-being include friends (Holder & Coleman, 2009; Holder & Coleman, 2015), physical activity (Parfitt & Eston, 2005), and spirituality (Holder, Coleman, & Wallace, 2010; Marques, Lopez, & Mitchell, 2013). Though the links that social relationships and physical activity have with SWB are similar in children and adults, this is not the case with spirituality. Spirituality can be conceptualized as encompassing four domains: the *personal domain* (i.e., relating with oneself), the *communal domain* (i.e., relating interpersonally), the *environmental domain* (i.e., relating with nature), and the *transcendent domain* (i.e., relating with the sense of mystery in life) (Fisher, Francis, & Johnson, 2000). While some research suggests spirituality may explain 4–5% of the variance in the happiness of adults, it may explain up to 26% of the variance in the well-being of children (Holder et al., 2010). However, this disparity may have been exaggerated by methodological limitations within the research conducted with adults (Holder, 2012), as some studies have found adult spirituality to be strongly related to aspects of SWB (e.g., Cohen, 2002).

The identification of the correlates of children's SWB represents only the initial stage of understanding children's well-being, including their happiness. Next, recent research findings must be used to develop and assess strategies and interventions that encourage enduring enhancements of children's well-being.

Strength-Specific Interventions. As with adults, many of the existing positive psychology interventions aimed at children are strengths-based, and target the characteristics identified by the VIA Classification of Strengths (Peterson & Seligman, 2004), such as kindness, forgiveness, self-regulation, gratitude, and hope. Interventions targeting gratitude (e.g., writing a gratitude letter, or identifying three good things in life) can enhance children's

SWB, and may also provide long-term benefits through improving emotional competence (McCabe, Bray, Kehle, Theodore, & Gelbar, 2011). This may be partially attributable to the role emotional competence (i.e., self-efficacy in social settings) plays in the formation of healthy relationships. Another gratitude intervention found that young adolescents in a 'counting blessings' condition self-reported increased gratitude, optimism, and life satisfaction and decreased negative affect relative to those in a neutral control condition and those who recorded their daily hassles (Froh, Sefick, & Emmons, 2008). This study also found a robust relationship between gratitude and school satisfaction.

Hope has received relatively more attention with children than many other SWB-related traits. Hope has been conceptualized as a strength involving the ability to generate goals, develop plans to achieve said goals, and maintain the motivation to both begin and continue goal-directed behaviours (Snyder, 1994). Hope-promoting interventions for children in school are beneficial (Marques, Lopez, Rose, & Robinson, 2014). A five-week hope intervention significantly increased hope, self-worth, and life satisfaction in middle school students, and these improvements were maintained at both six months and 18 months following the intervention (Marques, Lopez, & Pais-Ribeiro, 2011). A meta-analysis of 27 hope-enhancing interventions, which included child, adolescent, and adult populations, found small but significant effect sizes for hopefulness and life satisfaction (Weis & Speridakos, 2011).

One example of a broad strength-based initiative is the Penn Resiliency Program, a cognitive-behavioural programme designed to help 10–14 year olds identify their own character strengths and utilize them daily. This programme may modestly decrease depressive symptoms (Brunwasser, Gillham, & Kim, 2009), reduce or prevent anxiety, hopelessness, and behavioural problems (Seligman, Ernst, Gillham, Reivich, & Linkins, 2009), and improve well-being, social skills, and academic performance (though the latter effect was stronger in average students than in students from honours classes) (Gillham & Bernard, 2011).

Interventions Applied in Therapeutic Settings. Although a primary goal of therapy is often to reduce negative affect and ill-being, some therapeutic tactics have also been developed to increase well-being. Two examples of this approach are (1) well-being therapy (WBT), designed to improve well-being through the six dimensions of autonomy, personal growth, environmental mastery, purpose in life, positive relations, and self-acceptance (Fava & Ruini, 2003), and (2) positive psychotherapy (PPT), designed to increase positive emotions, engagement, and meaning (Seligman, Rashid, & Parks, 2006). Four children with mood, anxiety, and conduct disorders were treated with WBT, and showed improvements in clinical status and global functioning (Albieri, Visani, Offidani, Ottolini, & Ruini, 2009). Additionally, WBT was used with middle school students separated into two groups: one received

WBT and the other received anxiety management treatment (Tomba et al., 2010). The WBT group showed greater improvements in friendliness and the anxiety management group showing greater improvements in anxiety symptoms, but there were no significant between-group differences in SWB. Additionally, a randomized controlled trial assessing the efficacy of group PPT with middle school students found that the intervention group experienced increased happiness compared with the control group (Rashid & Anjum, 2008). These findings suggest therapy-based interventions administered within individual and group settings are able to reduce ill-being and increase well-being in children.

Interventions Applied in Educational Settings. Education and positive psychology share the goal of encouraging human flourishing and growth. Many programmes designed to increase children's SWB have been implemented within educational settings, including some of the strengths-based interventions described above. Recently, a ten-session positive psychology intervention aimed at increasing children's SWB was tested with middle school students (Suldo, Savage, & Mercer, 2014). The programme included many exercises based on existing interventions, and they targeted a variety of character strengths, including hope (e.g., 'you at your best'), gratitude (e.g. 'gratitude journal' and 'gratitude visit'), and kindness (e.g., 'performing acts of kindness'). These exercises addressed past-focused positive feelings (gratitude and savouring), present-focused positive feelings (engagement, which is an aspect of happiness according to the pleasure, engagement, positive relationships, meaning, and accomplishments (PERMA) conceptualization of well-being; Seligman, 2011), and future-focused positive feelings (hope and optimism). Although there were no significant between-group differences in life satisfaction, the control group reported slightly decreased life satisfaction while the experimental group reported significant increases that were maintained at follow-up. Also relevant is that student feedback about the programme following its conclusion indicated considerable interest, enjoyment, and general endorsement (Suldo et al., 2014).

The Strengths Gym is another intervention designed to build upon existing character strengths, foster new strengths, and encourage the identification of strengths in others (Proctor et al., 2011). When tested with adolescents within school curricula, participation in the Strengths Gym was associated with increases in life satisfaction. Similarly, the Positive Action programme, which integrates daily lessons, school-wide climate programmes, and components that address family and community involvement into K-6 curricula (Flay & Allred, 2003), appeared to show a dose-response relationship between participation in Positive Action and student behaviour (as measured by declining incidence of violence, suspension, and truancy), school involvement, and academic achievement. The long-term benefits spanned the elementary, middle, and high school levels (Flay & Allred, 2003).

Optimal Implementation of Interventions. It may be advantageous for programmes designed to prevent the development of ill-being and psychopathology to begin early in childhood, and no later than adolescence, to capitalize on the prolific cognitive, emotional, personality, and social development that occurs during this time (Park, 2003). Preventative programmes may have the greatest short- and long-term impact on wellness if they are broadly implemented for *all* children, as opposed to only targeting those with specific risk factors (Park, 2003). One avenue to offer happiness-enhancing interventions to children on such a large scale is through formal education. Given the considerable time children spend at school, schools may provide a realistic, cost-effective opportunity to deliver such programmes because activities could be integrated into classroom instruction or assigned as homework (McCabe et al., 2011). Despite benefits of high levels of SWB, the efficacy of interventions to increase SWB in children, and the practicality of using educational institutions to deliver these interventions, few schools have integrated evidence-based curricula of this nature (Bird & Markle, 2012).

Take home messages for clinicians and practitioners

As in other fields of applied psychology, compliance with treatment programmes in positive psychology is less than ideal. Improving this may require innovative, intrinsically rewarding activities. The ubiquitous, self-motivated use of gaming that children engage in suggests that prosocial gaming may represent a unique opportunity to encourage the flourishing of children. Although most research on video gaming considers the negative effects of violent video game content, emerging research on the positive potential of a wide range of video games suggests that gaming may also have positive outcomes. For example, prosocial gaming was related to enhanced self-reported prosocial behaviours (e.g., sharing, helping, and empathic attitudes) and reduced self-reported antisocial behaviours (e.g., aggressive thoughts and approval of aggression) in children in Singapore (Gentile et al., 2009). Furthermore, children who played a prosocial game, compared to those who played neutral or violent games, engaged in more helping behaviour (Saleem, Anderson, & Gentile, 2012). A recent review of the prosocial gaming literature suggests that content, context, and cooperation are all important in determining the impact that video games have on youth (Passmore & Holder, 2014). For the greatest intervention efficacy, each of these aspects should be considered in developing video games designed to enhance SWB through exercising character strengths and in embedding aspects of these interventions into recreational video games. The prosocial effects related to prosocial games suggest that strengths-based games may be able to encourage the flourishing of children through an activity that is self-motivating, enjoyable, and readily available to many children.

At present, interventions to enhance well-being appear to target the behaviours, moods, and cognitive functions of individuals. However, new interventions could be developed to influence the services (e.g., types of support structures available and ease of access), environment (e.g., atmosphere, accessibility, and appearance), and opportunities (e.g., recreational programming, social events, and access to nature) of a community. Such interventions may influence SWB through the role they play in community satisfaction. Community satisfaction is a multidimensional construct involving a process of cognitive evaluation regarding factual beliefs about the community that are relevant to the individual (Deseran, 1978). Thus, the services, environment, and opportunities available within a community may influence the well-being of its inhabitants by influencing community satisfaction, which appears to be strongly related to life satisfaction (Crawford & Holder, 2013).

Though physical safety and accessibility in the community may be a primary concern for older adults (Crawford & Holder, 2013), variables relating to education, recreation, and social connectedness may be more important for children. The Positive Action programme discussed earlier could be conceptualized as an example of this type of programming. Although the Positive Action programme was designed to directly influence children at an individual level, its relatively widespread integration into multiple school curricula could also be considered a service offered at the community level. Additionally, in the longitudinal assessment of this programme already reported (Flay & Allred, 2003), analysis was conducted at the community-level. The impact of participating in the programme was assessed by considering to what degree this elementary school programming was adopted in each school, and what percentage of students in the middle and high schools assessed had been exposed to the programme in the past. Thus the researchers determined the dose-response relationship between participation in the Positive Action programme and both improved academic performance (based on mean scores from student report card data) as well as reduced behavioural problems (based on incidence of violence and suspension per 100 students). This suggests that adapting positive psychology interventions for community-level implementation may be successful, and that it may be effective to measure impacts of these interventions using between-group as opposed to within-group differences.

Our own current research explores interventions that combine prosocial video gaming and community-level interventions. We are assessing the potential role for technology in enhancing the SWB of 748 children through engaging in nature (Crawford & Holder, 2014a, 2014b). We used a mobile nature application that children accessed through a tablet to navigate three different city parks. Using this application enhanced knowledge of and connection to nature, which is relevant because of the robust relationship between connectedness to nature and the well-being of children (se

Keniger, Gaston, Irvine, & Fuller, 2013). A second study from our research programme is titled the Wall of Well-being (WOW), which involves children completing the phrase 'I feel happy when...' where it is stencilled hundreds of times onto large walls. The children's SWB is assessed before and after the WOW's installation. Although results are not yet available, data could provide insight as to the impact of community-level SWB interventions on children who opted to participate as well as on children who did not, and thus were only indirectly affected by the presence of the intervention in their community.

Conclusion

Understanding is growing regarding the causes and correlates of children's well-being, and methods for reliably and effectively improving well-being are beginning to emerge. Continued research is needed, particularly with respect to testing new interventions designed to enhance children's SWB. To be effective, new interventions should be intrinsically rewarding and readily available (e.g., affordable and accessible) to a wide range of youth. Additionally, individual differences should be considered in choosing and administering interventions. For example, personality could influence the efficacy and enjoyment of an intervention owing to person–activity fit (Lyubomirsky, 2007). The relationship between temperament and children's SWB has clinical implications beyond tailoring interventions for individual children; it may also be possible to implement interventions which increase the happiness of children through enhancing the temperament traits related to extraversion (Weninger & Holder, 2014).

Despite strong theoretical support that such SWB interventions will work as intended, the efficacy of any new intervention still needs to be empirically investigated. This represents a significant but worthwhile undertaking, as it may uncover uniquely effective methods of increasing well-being and reducing ill-being in children.

Acknowledgements

The authors wish to thank Carmela White for her suggestions on an earlier version of this manuscript, as well as Holli-Anne Passmore and Maxine Crawford for contributions regarding their research.

References

Alarcon, G.M., Bowling, N.A., & Khazon, S. (2013). Great expectations: a meta-analytic examination of optimism and hope. *Personality and Individual Differences, 54*(7), 821–827. doi: 10.1016/j.paid.2012.12.004.

Albieri, E., Visani, D., Offidani, E., Ottolini, F., & Ruini, C. (2009). Well-being therapy in children with emotional and behavioral disturbances: a pilot investigation. *Psychotherapy and Psychosomatics, 78*(6), 387–390. doi: 10.1159/000235983.

Algoe, S.B., & Haidt, J. (2009). Witnessing excellence in action: the other-praising emotions of elevation, admiration, and gratitude. *Journal of Positive Psychology, 4*(2), 105–127. doi: 10.1080/17439760802650519.
Argyle, M. (1997). Is happiness a cause of health? *Psychology & Health, 12*(6), 769–781. doi: 10.1080/08870449708406738.
Avey, J.B., Patera, J.L., & West, B.J. (2006). The implications of positive psychological capital on employee absenteeism. *Journal of Leadership and Organization Studies, 13*(2), 42–60. doi: 10.1177/10717919070130020401.
Baas, M., De Dreu, C.K.W., & Nijstad, B.A. (2008). A meta-analysis of 25 years of mood-creativity research: hedonic tone, activation, or regulatory focus? *Psychological Bulletin, 134*(6), 779–806. doi: 10.1037/a0012815.
Berry, D.S., & Willingham, J.K. (1997). Affective traits, responses to conflict, and satisfaction in romantic relationships. *Journal of Research in Personality, 31*(4), 564–576. doi: 10.1006/jrpe.1997.2198.
Bird, J.M., & Markle, R.S. (2012). Subjective well-being in school environments: promoting positive youth development through evidence-based assessment and intervention. *American Journal of Orthopsychiatry, 82*(1), 61–66. doi: 10.1111/j.1939-0025.2011.01127.x.
Boehm, J.K., & Lyubomirsky, S. (2008). Does happiness promote career success? *Journal of Career Assessment, 16*(1), 101–116. doi: 10.1177/1069072707308140.
Brunwasser, S.M., Gillham, J.E., & Kim, E.S. (2009). A meta-analytic review of the Penn Resiliency Program's effect on depressive symptoms. *Journal of Consulting and Clinical Psychology, 77*(6), 1042–1054. doi: 10.1037/a0017671.
Buss, A.H., & Plomin, R. (1984). *Temperament: Early Developing Personality Traits.* Hillsdale, NJ: Lawrence Erlbaum Associates.
Chaturvedi, S., Arvey, R.D., Zhang, Z., & Christoforou, P.T. (2011). Genetic underpinnings of transformational leadership: the mediating role of dispositional hope. *Journal of Leadership and Organizational Studies, 18*(4), 469–479. doi: 10.1177/1548051811404891.
Cheng, H., & Furnham, A. (2003). Personality, self-esteem, and demographic predictions of happiness and depression. *Personality and Individual Differences, 34*(6), 921–942. doi: 10.1016/S0191-8869(02)00078-8.
Chida, Y., & Steptoe, A. (2008). Positive psychological well-being and mortality: a quantitative review of prospective observational studies. *Psychosomatic Medicine, 70*(7), 741–756. doi: 10.1097/PSY.0b013e31818105ba.
Cohen, A.B. (2002). The importance of spirituality in well-being for Jews and Christians. *Journal of Happiness Studies, 3*(3), 287–310. doi: 10.1023/A:1020656823365.
Costa, P.T., & McCrae, R.R. (1980). Influence of extraversion and neuroticism on subjective well-being: happy and unhappy people. *Journal of Personality and Social Psychology, 38*(4), 668–678. doi: 10.1037/0022-3514.38.4.668.
Costanzo, E.S., Lutgendorf, S.K., Kohut, M.L., Nisly, N., Rozeboom, K., Spooner, S., Brenda, J., & McElhaney, J.E. (2004). Mood and cytokine response to influenza virus in older adults. *Journals of Gerontology, 59*(12), 1328–1333. doi: 10.1093/gerona/59.12.1328.
Cote, S. (1999). Affect and performance in organizational settings. *Current directions in Psychological Science, 8*(2), 65–68. doi: 10.1111/1467-8721.00016.
Crawford, M.R., & Holder, M.D. (2013). Promoting happiness through urban design. In: F. Sarrancino (ed.), *The Happiness Compass: Theories, Actions and Perspectives for Well-Being*, pp. 177–202. Hauppauge, NY: Nova Publishing.

Crawford, M.R., & Holder, M.D. (2014a, July). Improving children's emotional wellbeing. In: *Insights for Well-Being*. Symposium conducted at the 2nd Canadian Conference on Positive Psychology, Ottawa, Canada.

Crawford, M.R., & Holder, M.D. (2014b, July). Technology and nature: unlikely allies. In: M.R. Crawford (Chair), *Promoting Pro-Environmental Behaviour and Connectedness to Nature*. Symposium conducted at the 28th International Congress of Applied Psychology, Paris, France.

Csikszentmihalyi, M. (1990). *Flow: The Psychology of Optimal Experience*. New York, NY: Harper and Row.

Danner, D.D., Snowdon, D.A., & Friesen, W.V. (2001). Positive emotions in early life and longevity: findings from the Nun Study. *Journal of Personality and Social Psychology, 80*(5), 804–813. doi: 10.1037/0022-3514.80.5.804.

DeNeve, K.M., & Cooper, H. (1998). The happy personality: A meta-analysis of 137 personality traits and subjective well-being. *Psychological Bulletin, 124*, 197–229. doi: 10.1037/0033-2909.124.2.197.

Deseran, F.A. (1978). Community satisfaction as definition of the situation: some conceptual issues. *Rural Sociology, 43*(2), 235–249.

Diener, E., & Chan, M.Y. (2011). Happy people live longer: subjective well-being contributes to health and longevity. *Applied Psychology: Health and Well-Being, 5*(1), 1–43. doi: 10.1111/j.1758-0854.2010.01045.x.

Diener, E., & Ryan, K. (2009). Subjective well-being: a general overview. *South African Journal of Psychology, 39*(4), 391–406. doi: 10.1177/008124630903900402.

Diener, E., & Seligman, M.E.P. (2002). Very happy people. *Psychological Science, 13*(1), 81–84. doi: 10.1111/1467-9280.00415.

Diener, E., Suh, E.M., Lucas, R.E., & Smith, H.L. (1999). Subjective well-being: three decades of progress. *Psychological Bulletin, 125*(2), 276–302. doi: 10.1037/0033-2909.125.2.276.

Dovidio, J.F., Isen, A.M., Guerra, P., Gaertner, S.L., & Rust, M. (1998). Positive affect, cognition, and the reduction of intergroup bias. In: C. Sedikides (ed.), *Intergroup cognition and intergroup behavior*, pp. 337–366. Mahwah, NJ: Erlbaum.

Duckworth, A.L., Steen, T.A., & Seligman, M.E.P. (2005). Positive psychology in clinical practice. *Annual Review of Clinical Psychology, 1*(1), 629–651. doi: 10.1146/annurev.clinpsy.1.102803.144154.

Dush, C.M.K., Taylor, M.G., & Kroeger, R.A. (2008). Marital happiness and psychological well-being across the life course. *Family Relations, 57*(2), 211–226. doi: 10.1111/j.1741-3729.2008.00495.x.

Emmons, R.A., & McCullough, M.E. (2004). *The Psychology of Gratitude*. New York, NY: Oxford University Press.

Fava, G.A., & Ruini, C. (2003). Development and characteristics of a well-being enhancing psychotherapeutic strategy: well-being therapy. *Journal of Behavior Therapy and Experimental Psychiatry, 34*(1), 45–63. doi: 10.1016/S0005-7916(03)00019-3.

Fisher, J.W., Francis, L.J., Johnson, P. (2000). Assessing spiritual health via four domains of spiritual wellbeing: the SH4DI. *Pastoral Psychology, 49*(2), 133–145. doi: 10.1023/A:1004609227002.

Flay, B.R., & Allred, C.G. (2003). Long-term effects of the Positive Action program. *American Journal of Health Behavior, 27*(Supplement 1), S6-S21. Retrieved from http://www.ingentaconnect.com/content/png/ajhb.

Fredrickson, B.L. (2013). Positive emotions broaden and build. In: P. Devine & A. Plant (eds), *Advances in Experimental Social Psychology*, Vol. 47, pp. 1–53. San Diego, CA: Elsevier Academic Press Inc.

Fredrickson, B.L., & Branigan, C. (2005). Positive emotions broaden the scope of attention and thought-action repertoires. *Cognition and Emotions, 19*(3), 313–332. doi: 10.1080/02699930441000238.

Froh, J.J., Sefick, W.J., & Emmons, R.A. (2008). Counting blessings in early adolescence: an experimental study of gratitude and subjective well-being. *Journal of School Psychology, 46*(2), 213–233. doi: 10.1016/j.jsp.2007.03.005.

Gallagher, M.W., & Lopez, S.J. (2009). Positive expectancies and mental health: identifying the unique contributions of hope and optimism. *Journal of Positive Psychology, 4*(6), 548–556. doi: 10.1080/17439760903157166.

Gander, F., Proyer, R.T., Ruch, W., & Wyss, T. (2013). Strength-based positive interventions: further evidence for their potential in enhancing well-being and alleviating depression. *Journal of Happiness Studies, 14*(4), 1241–1249. doi: 10.1007/s10902-012-9380-0.

Gentile, D.A., Anderson, C.A., Yukawa, S., Ihori, N., Saleem, M., Ming, L. K.,...Sakamoto, A. (2009). The effects of prosocial video games on prosocial behaviors: international evidence from correlational, longitudinal, and experimental studies. *Personality and Social Psychology Bulletin, 35*(6), 752–763. doi: 10.1177/0146167209333045.

Gillham, J., & Bernard, M. (2011, July). Teaching positive psychology to adolescents: 3 year follow-up. Symposium conducted at the 2nd World Congress on Positive Psychology, Philadelphia, United States of America.

Gilman, R., Dooley, J., & Florell, D. (2006). Relative levels of hope and their relationship with academic and psychological indicators among adolescents. *Journal of Social and Clinical Psychology, 25*(2), 166–178. doi: 10.1521/jscp.2006.25.2.166.

Goldberg, L.R. (1993). The structure of phenotypic personality traits. *American Psychologist, 48*(1), 26–34. doi: 10.1037/0003-066X.48.1.26.

Grossman, M., & Rowat, K.M. (1995). Parental relationships, coping strategies, received support, and well-being in adolescents of separated or divorced and married parents. *Research in Nursing and Health, 18*(3), 249–261. doi: 10.1002/nur.4770180308.

Harter, J.K., Schmidt, F.L., & Keyes, C.L.M. (2003). Well-being in the workplace and its relationship to business outcomes: a review of the Gallup studies. In: C.L.M. Keyes & J. Haidt (eds), *Flourishing: Positive Psychology and the Life Well-Lived*, pp. 205–224. Washington, DC: American Psychological Association. doi: 10.1037/10594-009.

Hoge, E.A., Chen, M.M., Orr, E., Metcalf, C.A., Fischer, L.E., Pollack, M.H., De Vivo, I., & Simon, N.M. (2013). Loving-Kindness Meditation practice associated with longer telomeres in women. *Brain, Behaviour, and Immunity, 32*, 159–163. doi: 10.1016/j.bbi.2013.04.005.

Holder, M.D. (2012). *Happiness in Children: Measurement, Correlates and Enhancement of Positive Subjective Well-Being*. Dordrecht, The Netherlands: Springer. doi: 10.1007/978-94-007-4414-1.

Holder, M.D., & Coleman, B. (2008). The contribution of temperament, popularity, and physical appearance to children's happiness. *Journal of Happiness Studies, 9*(2), 279–302. doi: 10.1007/s10902-007-9052-7.

Holder, M.D., & Coleman, B. (2009). The contribution of social relationships to children's happiness. *Journal of Happiness Studies, 10*(3), 329–349. doi: 10.1007/s10902-007-9083-0.

Holder, M.D., & Coleman, B. (2015). Children's friendships and well-being. In: M. Demir (ed.), *Friendship and Happiness*. Netherlands: Springer Publishing.

Holder, M.D., Coleman, B., & Sengh, Z.L. (2009). The contribution of active and passive leisure to children's well-being. *Journal of Health Psychology, 14*(3), 378–386. doi: 10.1177/1359105308101676.

Holder, M.D., Coleman, B., & Singh, K. (2012). Temperament and happiness in children in India. *Journal of Happiness Studies, 13*(2), 261–274. doi: 10.1007/s10902-011-9262-x.

Holder, M.D., Coleman, B., & Wallace, J.M. (2010). Spirituality, religiousness, and happiness in children aged 8–12 years. *Journal of Happiness Studies, 11*(2), 131–150. doi: 10.1007/s10902-008-9126-1.

Holder, M.D., & Klassen, A. (2010). Temperament and happiness in children. *Journal of Happiness Studies, 11*(4), 419–439. doi: 10.1007/s10902-009-9149-2.

Huebner, E.S. (1991). Correlates of life satisfaction in children. *School Psychology Quarterly, 6*(2), 103–111. doi: 10.1037/h0088805.

Isen, A.M., Niedenthal, P., & Cantor, N. (1992). An influence of positive affect on social categorization. *Motivation and Emotion, 16*(1), 65–78. doi: 10.1007/BF00996487.

John, O.P., Naumann, L.P., & Soto, C.J. (2008). Paradigm shift to the integrative Big Five trait taxonomy: History, measurement, and conceptual issues. In: O.P. John, R.W. Robins & L.A. Pervin (eds), *Handbook of Personality: Theory and Research*, pp. 114–158. New York, NY: The Guildford Press.

Keniger, L.E., Gaston, K.J., Irvine, K.N., & Fuller, R.A. (2013). What are the benefits of interacting with nature? *International Journal of Environmental Research and Public Health, 10*(3), 913–935. doi: 10.1016/j.jenvp.2004.10.001.

Kim-Prieto, C., Diener, E., Tamir, M., Scollon, C., & Diener, M. (2005). Integrating the diverse definitions of happiness: a time-sequential framework of subjective well-being. *Journal of Happiness Studies, 6*(3), 261–300. doi: 10.1007/s10902-005-7226-8.

Koivumaa-Honkanen, H., Honkanen, R., Viinamäki, H., Heikkilä, K., Kaprio, J., & Koskenvuo, M. (2001). Life satisfaction and suicide: a 20 year follow-up study. *American Journal of Psychiatry, 158*(3), 433–439. doi: 10.1176/appi.ajp.158.3.433.

Layous, K., Nelson, S.K., & Lyubomirsky, S. (2013). What is the optimal way to deliver a positive activity intervention? The case of writing about one's best possible selves. *Journal Of Happiness Studies, 14*(2), 635–654. doi: 10.1007/s10902-012-9346-2.

Lykken, D., & Tellegen, A. (1996). Happiness is a stochastic phenomenon. *Psychological Science, 7*(3), 186–189. doi: 10.1111/j.1467-9280.1996.tb00355.x.

Lyubomirsky, S. (2007). *The How of Happiness: A Scientific Approach to Getting the Life You Want*. New York, NY: The Penguin Press.

Lyubomirsky, S., Dickerhoof, R., Boehm, J.K., & Sheldon, K.M. (2011). Becoming happier takes both a will and a proper way: an experimental longitudinal intervention to boost well-being. *Emotion, 11*(2), 391–402. doi: 10.1037/a0022575.

Lyubomirsky, S., King, L., & Diener, E. (2005). The benefits of frequent positive affect: does happiness lead to success? *Psychological Bulletin, 131*(6), 803–855. doi: 10.1037/0033-2909.131.6.803.

Lyubomirsky, S., Sheldon, K.M., & Schkade, D. (2005). Pursuing happiness: the architecture of sustainable change. *Review of General Psychology, 9*(2), 111–131. doi: 10.1037/1089-2680.9.2.111.

Mahon, N.E., Yarcheski, A., & Yarcheski, T.J. (2005). Happiness as related to gender and health in early adolescents. *Clinical Nursing Research, 14*(2), 175–190. doi: 10.1177/1054773804271936.

Marques, S.C., Lopez, S.J., & Mitchell, J. (2013). The role of hope, spirituality, and religious practice in adolescents' life satisfaction: longitudinal findings. *Journal of Happiness Studies, 14*(1), 251–561. doi: 10.1007/s10902-012-9329-3.

Marques, S.C., Lopez, S.J., & Pais-Ribeiro, J.L. (2011). 'Building hope for the future': a program to foster Strengths in middle-school students. *Journal of Happiness Studies*, *12*(1), 139–152. doi: 10.1007/s10902-009-9180-3.

Marques, S.C., Lopez, S.J., Rose, S., & Robinson, C. (2014). Measuring and promoting hope in schoolchildren. In: R. Gilman, E.S. Huebner & M.J. Furlong (eds), *A handbook of positive psychology in the schools*, 2nd edition. Mahwah, NJ: Lawrence Erlbaum.

McCabe, K., Bray, M.A., Kehle, T.J., Theodore, L.A., & Gelbar, N.W. (2011). Promoting happiness and life satisfaction in school children. *Canadian Journal of School Psychology*, *26*(3), 177–192. doi: 10.1177/0829573511419089.

McCrae, R.R., & Costa, P.T. (1987). Validation of the Five-Factor Model of Personality across instruments and observers. *Journal of Personality and Social Psychology*, *52*(1), 81–90. doi: 10.1037/0022-3514.52.1.81.

Mosing, M.A., Zietsch, B.P., Shekar, S.N., Wright, M.J., & Martin, N. G. (2009). Genetic and environmental influences on optimism and its relationship to mental and self-rated health: a study of aging twins. *Behavior Genetics*, *39*(6), 597–604. doi: 10.1007/s10519-009-9287-7.

Nes, R.B., Røysamb, E., Tambs, K., Harris, J.R., & Reichborn-Kjennerud, T. (2006). Subjective well-being: genetic and environmental contributions to stability and change. *Psychological Medicine*, *36*(7), 1033–1042. doi: 10.1017/S0033291706007409.

Nima, A.A., Archer, T., & Garcia, D. (2012). Adolescents' happiness-increasing strategies, temperament, and character: mediation models on subjective well-being. *Health*, *4*(10), 802–810. doi: 10.4236/health.2012.410124.

Ostir, G.V., Berges, I.M., Markides, K.S., & Ottenbacher, K.J. (2006). Hypertension in older adults and the role of positive emotions. *Psychosomatic Medicine*, *68*(5), 727–733. doi: 10.1097/01.psy.0000234028.93346.38.

Parfitt, G., & Eston, R.G. (2005). The relationship between children's habitual activity level and psychological well-being. *Acta Paediatrica*, *94*(12), 1791–1797. doi: 10.1080/08035250500268266.

Park, N. (2003). Building wellness to prevent depression. *Prevention and Treatment*, *6*(1), Article 16, No Pagination Specified. doi: 10.1037/1522-3736.6.1.616c.

Park, N., Peterson, C., & Seligman, M.E.P. (2004). Strengths of character and well-being. *Journal of Social and Clinical Psychology*, *23*(5), 603–619. doi: 10.1521/jscp.23.5.603.50748.

Passmore, H.-A., & Holder, M.D. (2014). Gaming for good: video games and enhancing prosocial behaviour. In: J. Graham (ed.), *Video Games: Parents' Perceptions, Role of Social Media and Effects on Behavior*, pp. 141–166. Hauppauge, NY: Nova Science Publishers.

Peterson, C., & Seligman, M.E.P. (2004). *Character Strengths and Virtues: A Handbook of Classification*. Washington, DC: American Psychological Association.

Pintrich, P.R. (2000). The role of goal orientation in self-regulated learning. In: M. Boekaerts, P.R. Pintrich & M. Zeidner (eds), *Handbook of Self-Regulation*, pp. 451–502. Burlington, MA: Elsevier Academic Press.

Proctor, C., Tsukayama, E., Wood, A.M., Maltby, J., Eades, J.F., & Linley, P.A. (2011). Strengths Gym: the impact of a character strengths-based intervention on the life satisfaction and well-being of adolescents. *Journal of Positive Psychology*, *6*(5), 377–388. doi: 10.1080/17439760.2011.594079.

Proulx, C.M., Helms, H.M., & Buehler, C. (2007). Marital quality and personal well-being: a meta-analysis. *Journal of Marriage and Family*, *69*(3), 576–593. doi: 10.1111/j.1741-3737.2007.00393.x.

Rashid, T., & Anjum, A. (2008). Positive psychotherapy for young adults and children. In: J.R.Z. Abela & B.L. Hankin (eds), *Handbook of Depression in Children and Adolescents*, pp. 250–287. New York, NY: Guilford Press.

Rodgers, B., Power, C., & Hope, S. (1997). Parental divorce and adult psychological distress: Evidence from a national birth cohort: a research note. *Journal of Child Psychology and Psychiatry, 38*(7), 867–872. doi: 10.1111/j.1469-7610.1997.tb01605.x.

Ruis-Ottenheim, N., Houben, J.M., Kromhout, D., Kafatos, A., van der Mast, R.C., Zitman, F.G., Geleijnse, J.M., Hageman, G.J., & Giltay, E.J. (2012). Telomere length and well-being in elderly men from the Netherlands and Greece. *Behaviour Genetics, 42*(2), 278–286. doi: 10.1007/s10519-011-9498-6.

Sadler, M.E., Miller, C.J., Christensen, K., & McGue, M. (2011). Subjective well-being and longevity: a cotwin control study. *Twin Research and Human Genetics: The Official Journal of the International Society for Twin Studies, 14*(3), 249–256. doi: 10.1375/twin.14.3.249.

Saleem, M., Anderson, C.A., & Gentile, D.A. (2012). Effects of prosocial, neutral, and violent video games on children's helpful and hurtful behaviors. *Aggressive Behavior, 38*(4), 281–287. doi: 10.1002/ab.21428.

Seligman, M.E.P. (2011). *Flourish: A Visionary New Understanding of Happiness and Well-Being*. New York, NY: Free Press.

Seligman, M.E.P., Steen, T.A., Park, N., & Peterson, C. (2005). Positive psychology progress: empirical validation of interventions. *The American Psychologist, 60*(5), 410–421. doi: 10.1037/0003-066X.60.5.410.

Seligman, M.E.P., Ernst, R.M., Gillham, J.E., Reivich, K., & Linkins, M. (2009). Positive education: positive psychology and classroom interventions. *Oxford Review of Education, 35*(3), 293–311. doi: 10.1080/03054980902934563.

Seligman, M.E.P., Rashid, T., & Parks, A.C. (2006). Positive psychotherapy. *The American Psychologist, 61*(8), 774–788. doi: 10.1037/0003-066X.61.8.774.

Sheldon, K.M., & Lyubomirsky, S. (2006a). Achieving sustainable gains in happiness: change your actions, not your circumstances. *Journal of Happiness Studies, 7*(1), 55–86. doi: 10.1007/s10902-005-0868-8.

Sheldon, K.M., & Lyubomirsky, S. (2006b). How to increase and sustain positive emotion: the effects of expressing gratitude and visualizing best possible selves. *Journal of Positive Psychology, 1*(2), 73–82. doi: 10.1080/17439760500510676.

Snyder, C.R. (1994). *The Psychology of Hope: You Can Get There From Here*. New York, NY: Free Press.

Spector, P.E. (1997). *Job Satisfaction: Application, Assessment, Cause, and Consequences*. Thousand Oaks, CA: Sage.

Stack, S., & Eshleman, J.R. (1998). Marital status and happiness: a 17-nation study. *Journal of Marriage and the Family, 60*(2), 527–536. doi: 10.2307/353867.

Staw, B.M., Sutton, R.I., & Pelled, L.H. (1994). Employee positive emotion and favorable outcomes at the workplace. *Organization Science, 5*(1) 51–71. doi: 10.1287/orsc.5.1.51.

Steel, P., Schmidt, J., & Shultz, J. (2008). Refining the relationship between personality and subjective well-being. *Psychological Bulletin, 134*(1), 138–161. doi: 10.1037/0033-2909.134.1.138.

Suldo, S.M., Savage, J.A., & Mercer, S.H. (2014). Increasing middle school students' life satisfaction: efficacy of a positive psychology group intervention. *Journal of Happiness Studies, 15*(1), 19–42. doi: 10.1007/s10902-013-9414-2.

Tait, M., Padgett, M.Y., & Baldwin, T. (1989). Job and life satisfaction: a reevaluation of the strength of the relationship and gender effects as a function of the date of the study. *Journal of Applied Psychology, 74*(3), 502–507. doi: 10.1037/0021-9010.74.3.502.

Throndsen, I. (2011). Self-regulated learning of basic arithmetic skills: a longitudinal study. *British Journal of Educational Psychology, 81*(4), 558–578. doi: 10.1348/2044-8279.002008.

Timoney, L.R., & Holder, M.D. (2013). "https://www.novapublishers.com/catalog/product_info.php?products_id=44892" The Happiness Compass: Theories, Actions and Perspectives for Well-Being. pp. 203–222 Chapter 13. In: *Happiness Interventions and the Efficacy of Affective Priming*. (F. Sarracino, Ed.). Nova Science Publishers, New York.

Tomba, E., Belaise, C., Ottolini, F., Ruini, C., Bravi, A., Albieri, E., Rafanelli, C., Caffo, E., & Fava, G.A. (2010). Differential effects of well-being promoting and anxiety-management strategies in a non-clinical school setting. *Journal of Anxiety Disorders, 24*(3), 326–333. doi: 10.1016/j.janxdis.2010.01.005.

Uusitalo-Malmivaara, L. (2012). Global and school-related happiness in Finish children. *Journal of Happiness Studies, 13*(4), 601–619. doi: 10.1007/s10902-011-9282-6.

van de Wetering, E.J., van Exel, N.J.A., & Brouwer, W.B.F. (2010). Piecing the jigsaw puzzle of adolescent happiness. *Journal of Economic Psychology, 31*(6), 923–935. doi: 10.1016/j.joep.2010.08.004.

Weis, R., & Speridakos, E.C. (2011). A meta-analysis of hope enhancement strategies in clinical and community settings. *Psychology of Well-Being, 1*(1), 1–16. doi: 10.1186/2211-1522-1-5.

Weiss, A., Bates, T.C., & Luciano, M. (2008). Happiness is a personal(ity) thing: the genetics of personality and well-being in a representative sample. *Psychological Science, 19*(3), 205–210. doi: 10.1111/j.1467-9280.2008.02068.x.

Weninger, R.L., & Holder, M.D. (2014). Extraversion and subjective well-being. In: A.D. Haddock & A.P. Rutkowski (eds), *Psychology of Extraversion*, pp. 1–26. Hauppauge, NY: Nova Science Publishers.

Xu, J., & Roberts, R.E. (2010). The power of positive emotions: it's a matter of life or death – subjective well-being and longevity over 28 years in a general population. *Health Psychology, 29*(1), 9–19. doi: 10.1037/a0016767.

7
Using Acceptance and Commitment Therapy to Help Young People Develop and Grow to Their Full Potential

Louise Hayes and Joseph Ciarrochi

Young people are on a social and emotional journey of discovery, perhaps one of the most profound journeys of human life. They are moving beyond family, building new relationships, and exploring sexuality, independence, and careers. The experiences they have during this journey are likely to be the ones they remember and return to for the rest of their life. Our task as professionals is to facilitate their journey, using the best empirical evidence available.

This chapter will describe a pragmatic framework for intervention, called Contextual Behavioural Science (CBS) (S.C. Hayes, Barnes-Holmes, & Wilson, 2012) and a concrete expression of that framework through Acceptance and Commitment Therapy/Training (ACT) for young people. ACT, along with other mindfulness-based therapies, has been finding application in all corners of human endeavour (S.C. Hayes, Strosahl, & Wilson, 1999, 2012). It is now being used with good effect in therapy, organizations, classrooms, homes, and community groups.

There has as yet been little work translating ACT for young people (cf., Ciarrochi, Hayes, & Bailey, 2012). Up to now, people have applied an adult model to adolescents (L.L. Hayes, Boyd, & Sewell, 2011; Livheim et al., 2012). We think the time has come for a developmental model, one that specifies the skills and contextual factors that are needed for young people to grow and thrive.

This chapter provides a brief review of our model for young people, called the DNA-V model (L.L. Hayes & Ciarrochi, 2015). This model views young people's behaviour as adaptations to context rather than deviations from an adult norm. DNA-V is a flexible model that can be used across settings, from learning in classes through to therapy. It aims to show how we might bring vitality into a young person's life, promote growth, compassion, and connection. We see this as a model that all young people can be exposed to so that as they grow, they also grow in their understanding of what it means to be human, how to have a peaceful relationship with their thoughts and feelings, and how to live mindfully, in this increasingly busy modern world.

This chapter will provide the reader with an overview of the key aspects of CBS to give a sense of the model's underpinnings. In the next section, we will show how the model extends from evolutionary theory, to functional contextualist worldviews, to operant learning, relational frame theory, and ACT. We will then provide a conceptual overview of the DNA-V model and show how it integrates all the above into a practical, easily understood approach for working with young people.

Contextual behavioural foundations

Evolution science

CBS is a principal-focused strategy for improving the human condition. Beginning broadly and working towards the specific, it utilizes the core evolutionary ideas of variation, selection, and retention. We will present a simple explanation of this idea here, but the interested reader should see S. Hayes and colleagues (2012) for a detailed explanation. ACT can be seen as encouraging young people to flexibly try different things (variation) to discover what works, or what is consistent with values (selection). Once they discover something that works, they are reinforced for persisting in that behaviour (retention). However, they need to be sensitive to ever-changing context; that is, they need to be psychologically flexible. If the environment changes and a previously retained behaviour ceases to work well, then they need to be willing to go back to variation and selection; that is, try something new and see if it serves valued ends. Our DNA-V model shows how this can be done.

Functional contextualism

Functional contextualism is a philosophical position which has the defined goal of considering how behaviour functions within the context in which it is expressed (S.C. Hayes, 1993). The subject matter therefore is always the 'behaviour-in-context'. Behaviour here means anything a person does – this includes the overt behaviour we see, as well as covert behaviour such as thoughts, feelings, sensations, and memories. Context means everything other than the behaviour of interest – it includes the physical space as well as interpersonal, intrapersonal, time, historical factors. The 'behaviour-in-context' is examined as a whole unit (Ciarrochi, Robb, & Godsell, 2005). Our underlying premise is that there is no 'right' behaviour, and no 'right' solution to a problem behaviour, only behaviour that has been adapted to a context, and solutions that work for a purpose (S.C. Hayes, Luoma, Bond, Masuda, & Lillis, 2006).

With behaviour-in-context as the view in which one sees a young person, all behaviour is then seen as purposeful – an adaptation to a specific context. Our goal then is to consider their need and how their behaviour meets this, irrespective of whether it is 'good' or 'bad' behaviour. We can then consider how alternative behaviour might be trained to meet this same need. Without a contextual view, it is easy to see 'problem' behaviour as inside a young person, and ignore how contextual factors such as their personal history, family, school, and community might be setting events, antecedents, or consequential factors in this behaviour.

Operant behaviour principles

Operant principles are analytical tools that are widely used to study behaviour of humans and animals (Skinner, 1969). Like evolutionary principles, operant principles involve selection by consequences – behaviour that is reinforced gets selected (or is more likely to be repeated), and behaviour that is not reinforced or is punished gets selected against (is less likely to be repeated). When it comes to child development, there can be little doubt that operant principles have helped us understand how a child's behaviour is shaped contingently, and how we might shape new behaviour in a child through reinforcement, punishment, imitation, and modelling (Patterson, 1982, 2002). In terms of psychological interventions, behaviour modification in classrooms and parent training stand out amongst very few 'well established' treatments for children (Brestan & Eyberg, 1998; Ollendick & King, 2004).

On the surface, traditional operant principles seemed to focus on shaping behaviour, without dealing with how the young person thinks, feels, or their attachment needs. The caricature of behavioural psychology went something like this. If you want to control a young person, you reinforce them with a treat for behaving well, and you withhold the treat if he or she behaves poorly. This might be how you train a rat or a dog, but it would not work with young people, who would be as likely to throw the treat in the psychologist's face as to eat it. Unlike the rat, young people would think about the treat symbolically, as an act of coercion.

Consequently, many practitioners abandoned operant psychology, or made it peripheral to their interventions, because it seemed to have no way of dealing with complex symbolic processes (such as equating a treat with coercion). However, in abandoning operant principles, the practitioners also abandoned one of the most reliable and powerful interventions available to them. Decades of research show that operant principles have a reliable influence on behaviour, across just about every situation imaginable. Far from being peripheral, we argue that operant principles should be the very foundation upon which youth interventions are built. All that was needed was a theory that could extend operant principles from overt behaviour to the covert behaviour called 'symbolic thinking'. Relational frame theory fills this gap.

Relational frame theory

The theory of human language and symbolic thinking upon which ACT was founded is called Relational Frame Theory (RFT) (S.C. Hayes, Barnes-Holmes, & Roche, 2001; S.C. Hayes, Strosahl, Bunting, Twohig, & Wilson, 2004). A thorough explanation of RFT is beyond the scope of this chapter (for a detailed theoretical discussion of RFT the reader should refer to S.C. Hayes et al., 2001; Blackledge, 2003). However, it is important to be clear that ACT as a therapeutic model arose from this theory of verbal behaviour, and it fits within the paradigm of CBS. RFT shows how symbolic thoughts, such as judging and believing, are under the control of contextual factors (reinforcement and punishment) and are therefore subject to the same operant laws that have proven so useful in shaping non-verbal behaviour.

RFT has added two key ideas to our understanding of symbolic behaviour: 'arbitrarily applicable derived relational responding' and 'transformation of stimulus functions' (S.C. Hayes et al., 2001). These phrases sound rather difficult to translate, so let's consider them in the context of a simple example. Arbitrarily applicable derived relational responding means that stimuli are *related* based on social convention or verbal history, rather than on their physical properties or 'thingness'. Derived refers to our capacity to infer relations without ever needing direct contact with an experience (Bach & Moran, 2008). Transformation of stimulus function refers to how language changes our responses to things.

For instance, an adolescent might overhear that 'geeks are unpopular' and also have a learning history that 'being unpopular is bad' – therefore, she derives that unpopular 'geek' and her own sense of popularity are related. Having a learning history of avoiding other 'bad' things, she may now avoid certain people based on her perceptions of their 'geekiness' for fear she will lose her 'popularity' if seen talking to them – in other words, I will become unpopular if I talk to them (transformation of stimulus function). Note that in all this verbal relating, the adolescent has developed an avoidant response to geeks, despite having had no experience with them. So far as we know, this ability to develop responses to the world without any direct experience with it is unique to humans. A dog will never respond with avoidance to the word 'geek', unless that word signals the onset of something aversive in physical experience (e.g., an electric shock).

The key insight from RFT is this: both deriving and transformation of stimulus functions can be influenced by reinforcement. For example, we can find a way to reinforce the girl for talking to many different kinds of people, and we can teach her to defuse from thoughts that her popularity is a 'thing' she must guard to have self-worth.

The above discussion of contextual behavioural science is included to provide the reader with an orientation to our DNA-V model and to illustrate how it arises from sound scientific reasoning and behavioural principles. We now turn to a review of ACT and its foundation for our model for young people.

Acceptance and commitment therapy

ACT aims to increase psychological flexibility, which is 'the ability to contact the present moment more fully as a conscious human being, and to change or persist in behavior when doing so serves valued ends' (S.C. Hayes et al., 2006). The model was built on adult psychological processes and therefore needs some special consideration for use with young people (we will attend to this shortly with the DNA-V model). The ACT model is commonly conceptualized as six *core* processes that together bring psychological flexibility, and six opposing rigid behavioural repertoires, which are conceptualized as contributors to psychopathology. Case conceptualization requires examination of an individual's behaviour in these dimensions: (1) *values guided behaviour-versus-weak values*, (2) *committed to action-versus-inactive/impulsive/avoidant action*, (3) *acceptance-versus-avoidance*, (4) *defusion-versus-fusion*, (5) *contact with the present moment-versus-ruminating about past or future*, and finally (6) *engaging in self as content-versus-self as context*. ACT is often taught with a model called the hexaflex (S.C. Hayes et al., 2006) showing the above six processes; however, it should be noted that there are other important elements of ACT that are not shown in the hexaflex such as behaviour-in-context, workability, flexible relating to verbal content, and self-as-process. Nonetheless the hexaflex model has helped thousands of practitioners to learn ACT with ease (the interested reader new to ACT is encouraged to view the many practical texts for adult treatment (Bach & Moran, 2008; S.C. Hayes et al., 2012).

The ACT core processes are outlined below, with a brief account of their applicability to development.

Values work is the heart of ACT (Bach & Moran, 2008). Eliciting deep-seated values can provide the motivation needed for behaviour change and build willingness to experience unwanted thoughts and feelings that might accompany valued action. The model purports that lack of valued living, unclear values, excessive pliancy, or avoidant tracking are all evidence of psychological inflexibility. These behaviours share a commonality in that they all pull us away from behaviour that is personally fulfilling. For example, an individual who shows excessive pliance would behave in socially expected ways in order to please the peer group, rather than behaving in ways that are personally meaningful. For adolescents, who are just beginning the journey into independence, it is unlikely that they will have 'clear' and well-identified values. There is still too much to learn – they have yet to choose careers, choose education, explore sexuality or orientation, and try out independence. Thus assuming that 'valuing' is fully developed in their behavioural repertoire neglects opportunities to 'build' this repertoire.

The core process of *committed action-versus-inaction/impulsivity/avoidant behaviour* includes teaching common goal-setting and behavioural activation skills for the purposes of leading a valued life. ACT purports that individuals who are psychologically inflexible behave impulsively, or have difficulty taking goal-directed action that might lead them to valued living. There are important developmental considerations in terms of measuring impulsivity or inaction for young people, particularly as sensation-seeking, risk-taking, and love of novelty are hallmarks of adolescence. These behavioural patterns hold true for humans and non-verbal species, suggesting they have adaptive value for this period (Schlegel & Barry, 1991; Hawley, 2011). Although it was never the intent in ACT to assume that all behaviour ought to be values directed for optimal development, too often we see practitioners labour with the idea of making all behaviour deliberate and devoted to values. That is, they labour to make young people act like an idealized version of an adult. We assume instead that some open exploration and risk-taking is needed for trial-and-error learning.

With regard to *avoidance-versus-acceptance*, ACT assumes that avoidance is a key factor in psychological problems. Avoidance is empirically established as a major factor in psychopathology (Foa, McNally, Steketee, & McCarthy, 1991; Zinbarg, Barlow, Brown, & Hertz, 1992) and is evident when an individual is unwilling to remain in contact with difficult private experiences and takes steps to avoid the contexts in which they occur (S. C. Hayes et al., 1999). ACT teaches *acceptance* as the alternative to avoidance. Thus a young boy who has trouble with anger would be helped to understand the feelings in his body and label them, knowing that anger is a feeling, and as humans we are destined to have the full range of feelings. In other words, no feeling is bad. This concept fits quite well with adults and young people, given that humans have a propensity to avoid discomfort across the lifespan.

With regard to *cognitive fusion-versus-defusion*, ACT takes the approach that thoughts and feeling are contextually controlled (S. C. Hayes et al., 2006). For example, a young girl with an abuse history has the thought 'I am a bad person' in many contexts. ACT does not attempt to stop, dispute, or override this negative thought with positive thinking. Instead defusion is used to 'unhook' from the thought. For instance, a therapist might use experiential exercises to demonstrate that trying to avoid or control the thought 'I am bad' has the paradoxical effect of making it stronger; in other words, 'I must think I am a good person whenever I think I am bad'. Defusion means we can have a distressing thought and still take valued action.

It is worth noting that ACT defusion focuses on releasing from unhelpful verbal content. However, there is no guidance in the six core ACT processes on how to develop helpful verbal content, a developmental task that is critical for young people. Fortunately, RFT does provide guidance, as we illustrate in our DNA-V model below.

ACT also contrasts the suffering that arises when an individual spends more time *thinking about the past or fearing the future* – living in their heads – rather than living in the present moment. This is evident with anxious presentations where worrying dominates, or in depressed presentations where rumination over old stories is common. ACT attempts to help individuals stay in the present so they can experience 'now' as a place that is richer and more value-consistent than ideas of the past or future. A range of mindfulness techniques would be used, many adapted from other mindfulness work (for examples see, S.C. Hayes, 2004; Segal, Teasdale, & Williams, 2004; Kabat-Zinn, 2005; Wilson & with Du Frene, 2009). Developmentally, children might be considered to be naturally 'mindful', and the process of acculturation into our modern society might facilitate mindlessness as they grow into adolescents.

There are three senses of self in ACT: *self-as-content, self-as-process, and self-as-context* (Foody, Barnes-Holmes, & Barnes-Holmes, 2012). Self-as-content describes the labelled self, which is evident in the descriptors, labels, and images that an individual constructs; for example, 'I am good' or 'I am worthless'. The ACT model suggests that when one is too attached to these verbal constructions, they can dominate other sources of information, reducing flexibility and effectiveness (S.C. Hayes et al., 2006). Self-as-context aims to help individuals experience their 'self' as the space in which all thoughts and behaviours arise. In other words, thoughts come and go, but people are not equivalent to their thoughts. Rather, they 'hold' the thoughts.

Self-as-process is poorly depicted in the hexaflex processes, but is essential to ACT, and also working with young people and our DNA-V model. Self-as process interventions aim to bring people into awareness of their thoughts and feelings as they arise – in the moment – noticing the ongoing flow of experiences and how they change like the ebb and flow of tides. Examples of self-as-process include noticing feelings ('I am angry', 'I am sad'), thoughts ('I am having the thought that....'), and sensations ('I am experiencing tension in my stomach'). Self-as-process is a critical developmental skill. For example, adolescents who struggle to notice and label their feelings are less likely to develop social support and well-being (Ciarrochi, Heaven, & Supavadeeprasit, 2008; Ciarrochi, Kashdan, Leeson, Heaven, & Jordon, 2011).

While ACT processes are commonly described in the literature separately, they are not discrete, and in practice there is much overlap during treatment. In addition to the processes shown above, there is importance placed in showing that human suffering is normal, that it is normal to worry about futures that may never occur, dwell on past suffering that may never reoccur, criticise and find fault with ourselves, and, in general, lose contact with the reinforcers in the present moment. This normalization piece is very important to young people who often feel as if they are unique in their suffering. Additionally, ACT sets about creating a context for change by revealing unworkable past attempts to change. This is a central consideration here for young people as their history of unworkable behavioural repertoires is shorter, and their opportunities to try new behaviours are greater.

Altogether, while ACT is an incredibly powerful model, we argue it can be strengthened for young people by bringing together all CBS and by considering developmental process rather than by forcing an adult model into a young person's world.

Empirical evidence supporting ACT – Why the lag for young people?

There are now over 100 randomized controlled trials using ACT across a variety of conditions. The list of conditions and contexts is impressive. For psychopathology they include: depression, anxiety, OCD, psychosis, polysubstance abuse, methamphetamine use, methadone detox, borderline personality disorder, self-harm, and trichotillomania. For health they include: epilepsy, chronic pain, smoking cessation, diabetes management, cancer patients, obesity, weight loss, promoting physical activity, bariatric surgery, tinnitus, body dissatisfaction, disordered eating, tinnitus, and headache sufferers. And for general psychological well-being (where ACT is repackaged as acceptance and commitment *training*), ACT has been shown to be useful for work stress, stigma, shame, for unemployed on sick leave, and teachers' well-being. For a meta-analysis and review, see the following F. Ruiz (2010); F J. Ruiz (2012); and Smout, Hayes, Atkins, Klausen, and Duguid (2012).

Despite this impressive list, we can count on one hand the number of randomized controlled trials using ACT with young people. There is one published study for each of the following: HIV knowledge (Luciano, Valdivia, Gutiérrez, Ruiz, & Páez, 2009), college adjustment (Levin, Pistorello, Seeley, & Hayes, 2014), depression (L.L. Hayes et al., 2011), early intervention for depression (Livheim et al., 2012), and chronic pain (Wicksell, Melin, Lekander, & Olsson, 2009). ACT, like other fields of human psychology, has lagged behind in testing models that help young people to grow well.

Livheim, L. Hayes, and colleagues (Livheim et al., 2012) published the outcomes of two school-based studies from Australia and Sweden, which tested the same ACT group protocol in schools. The Australian study showed significant reductions in depression with a medium effect, when compared to the control group who received usual care. The Swedish study, when compared to the control group, reported significantly lower level of stress with a large effect size and increased mindfulness skills, also with a large effect size. L. Hayes et al. (2011), conducted an RCT (N = 30) using ACT for adolescent depression. Compared to treatment as usual, about 60% showed clinically significant change in ACT condition; d = 0.38 at post and 1.45 at follow up. Further, Wicksell et al. (2009) conducted an RCT (n = 32) for chronic pediatric pain, comparing a brief ACT intervention (ten individual sessions) to multidisciplinary treatment plus amitriptyline (MDT), and showed that ACT performed significantly better than MDT on perceived functional ability in relation to pain, pain intensity, and pain-related discomfort (intent-to-treat analyses). At post-treatment, before the dose differences happened, significant differences in favour of the ACT condition were also seen in fear of re/injury or kinesiophobia, pain interference, and in quality of life.

While the beginnings of the work are there, two advances are needed: (1) models for young people, and (2) research investment in trials with young people. We argue our DNA-V model (L.L. Hayes & Ciarrochi, 2015) can address the former issue.

How can we use CBS developmentally for young people?

We began with the question, can ACT, with its broad foundation of CBS, be strengthened to help young people grow? Can it help not just with psychopathology, but with all aspects of their learning and growing? This is the question we grappled with as we tried to adapt ACT, a model that arose from therapy, onto our developmental landscape of adolescents. It felt as if we were working top down, from adults to young people, instead of bottom up, from birth to adulthood. Finally, we came to the belief that we could not answer this question by just using ACT as an adult model. ACT, like CBT and many other therapeutic models, typically seeks to compare 'normal adults' to clinical groups and then suggest interventions that help the clinical group become more 'normal'. Too many models begin this way and are then foisted on young people.

However, ACT is not merely a therapeutic technology, and we were confident that we could build a model of development if we broadened our view beyond ACT and brought in all the CBS layers. That is, we could model what a young person might need to grow up strong and flexible if we used evolutionary science to understand adaption, variation, and selection; functional contextualist philosophy to consider the context in which a young person grows up; operant principles to examine how a child's behaviour is shaped over time; relational frame theory to consider how verbal behaviour is shaped through history; and ACT as a therapeutic technology which brings all these together, helps normalize being human, and addresses the success and struggles of life.

We arrived at a model that we call DNA-V (L. L. Hayes & Ciarrochi, 2015), which brings together the elements of behavioural science to help young people thrive. We start with the child, and seek to describe the conditions that lead a child to develop into a strong and healthy young person.

DNA-V is for promoting valued living and vitality

DNA-V has the primary purpose of helping young people to create values and learn how to engage in valued action as they grow. Value is the verbal construction of ongoing intrinsically reinforcing behaviour. Our model helps with that verbal construction. Once we have value statements they lead us to growth and vitality, and they can act like a compass and direct us through the storms and confusing times, towards the things we care about. Values often come from answering questions of 'what for?'

- *What do I care about in this moment?*
- *What kind of person do I want to be?*
- *What do I want my life to stand for?*
- *What is this learning for?*
- *What is counselling for?*
- *What is anything for?*
- *What for?*

When we live a life inside valuing, we tend to have more vitality. One flows from the other. Vitality can be defined as the capacity to live, grow, and develop; physical or intellectual vigour; energy; power to not just survive but thrive. Research has identified six general patterns of vital activity.

1. Connecting (with others, nature, animals, the universe or god)
2. Giving to others and having a positive influence on the world
3. Being active
4. Enjoying the moment
5. Engaging and challenging ourselves/learning
6. Caring for ourselves

The three DNA skills or 'behaviours'

DNA, as it is used in this model, comprises three expressions or clusters of behaviour that we call *Discoverer, Noticer,* and *Advisor*. We can think of these as metaphorically as 'spaces we can move to – D, N or A' or as different 'expressions' of ourselves, or different skills we can develop. They are groups of behaviour, not things, but expressions of us, and what we do. A key goal of the DNA-V model is to help young people move flexibly between the three processes in a way that helps them develop them all, and ultimately live in vitality and value. Figure 7.1 shows the DNA-V model visually, while Table 7.1 displays the low and high skills that we see in the Discoverer, Noticer, and Advisor behaviours. We use the model to examine a young person's strengths and weaknesses, to plan interventions and classroom lessons, and to reinforce and shape their growing skills (L.L. Hayes & Ciarrochi, 2015).

We use DNA as a metaphor to describe our model because it encompasses behaviours that all young people express in different ways – just as cellular DNA is expressed in certain ways. There are at least two advantages to using the DNA acronym. First, DNA implies that these skills are basic capabilities, a bit like our basic biology. Naturally there is individual variation, but the same core DNA components are present in all typically developing children. Every

112 *Using Acceptance and Commitment Therapy to Help Young People*

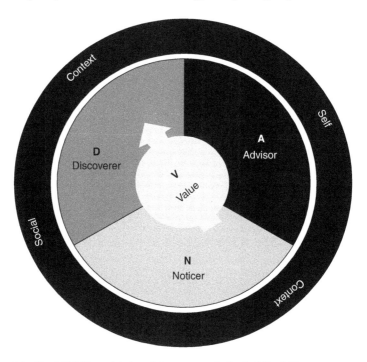

Figure 7.1 The DNA-V model for adolescent psychological flexibility
Source: L.L. Hayes and Ciarrochi (2015).

young person is capable of developing their DNA skills. Second, the DNA-V model does not exist in a vacuum. Like biological DNA, the DNA processes in our model need the right environmental contexts to find optimal expression. Although we are all capable of the core DNA expressions – Discoverer, Noticer, and Advisor – one or all skills might be underdeveloped.

DNA-V has value at its core: this is to remind young people that any of the DNA behaviours are not inherently good or bad. Rather, in a given context, one behaviour is likely to be more or less helpful in supporting valued action and vitality.

DNA-V also rests inside a context. Context refers to all historical and situational events that can exert influence on behaviour. This includes intrapersonal factors such as memories and one's personal history, as well as interpersonal factors such as social relationships. It also includes situational factors such as school and community. DNA behaviour, in turn, exerts an influence on context. There is a bidirectional flow from the skills to the context.

For example, imagine a young person named Jane grows up in an environment that punishes the expression of emotions and teaches her that

Table 7.1 DNA-V high and low skills

DNA process	High skill	Low skill
Advisor	Workable beliefs guide action	Unworkable beliefs guide action
	Ability to unhook from unworkable beliefs	
Noticer	Mindful of self, others, and life	Mindless and unaware
		Highly reactive to emotions
	Able to make space for difficult inner experience to come and go, without reacting to it or seeking to control it	Excessive attempts to control emotions
Discoverer	Expanding, learning, creating, testing, finding new behaviour that promotes vitality and valued living	Impulsive exploration that provides short-term reinforcement but long-term negative consequences
	Spotting and developing values and strengths	Failure to try new behaviour when old behaviour is not working
Self-perspective	Can see oneself from an outside, observer perspective	Can't see oneself from an observer perspective
	Recognizes self is more than self concepts. Can see self as holding self concepts	Believes self-concepts are physical descriptions of self
	Sees that growth and improvement is possible Can view self with compassion	Believes self to be fixed owing to history, and unchangeable
Social perspective	Recognizes the value of social connection, is able to have empathy and compassion, cooperate, and build friendships and love	Fails to recognize the value of social connection, lacks empathy and compassion, fails to build supportive relationships
	Sees that their history with others influences present interactions, and believes they can change	Does not see that their history with others influences present. Reacts without awareness
	Sees personal agency, 'I can choose'	Blames others, 'they made me like this'

Source: L.L. Hayes and Ciarrochi (2015).

emotions are to be suppressed: 'don't cry or I will give you something to cry about'. Given this context, Jane may have little ability to notice her emotions or accept them. When she experiences strong feelings, Jane engages in value-inconsistent behaviour, such as cutting herself, drinking, and risk-taking. Jane's context is not static. Her counsellor now becomes part of Jane's context. This counsellor teaches Jane to notice her feelings and to see that all feelings are normal. Once Jane is able to notice her feelings, she becomes less likely to feel overwhelmed by these physical messages. She learns to soothe herself when distressed, and accept her feelings are messages, not always requiring suppression or lashing out. This acceptance then leads to increased opportunities for relationships and a consequent altering of Jane's social context. Reciprocally, Jane's improved relationships strengthen her DNA skills.

Navigating the world with DNA skills

DNA describes three functional classes of behaviour. We use the metaphorical name of Discoverer, Noticer, and Advisor to describe each class. They are not discrete behaviours or experimental terms; they are useful skill-building terms. 'Function' refers to the purpose of the behaviour, or, metaphorically, why it is used.

Every single person begins life in noticing. Early in life there are no verbal judgements, just experiences, just sensations from the world. Very early on we also engage in the basic skill of the Discoverer, exploring, testing, and broadening our world. It is only in our second year that we develop language, and become capable of entering into a symbolic world, a world of words and judgements rather than just sensory reactions. Our language skill becomes so powerful that the world becomes viewed through it, as if through the eyes of our very own interpreter, or 'Advisor.' The Discoverer's role is to examine the workability of behaviour and to expand behavioural repertoires, the Advisor's role is to use past teaching and experience to navigate the present, and the Noticer's role is to detect psychological and environmental events as they occur. Flexibility is built into DNA-V skills, where we help young people recognize when something is not working and ask them to try stepping into a different DNA space. Let's now take a closer look at the DNA skills.

Discoverer – The Discoverer finds new ways to be in the world. The key behaviours seen in the Discoverer are creating experience by testing, exploring, taking risks, moving out into the world in new ways. When in the Discoverer space, we are behaving in ways that cause us to grow, learn, and expand our behavioural repertoire. One might consider the toddler years as the beginning of the Discoverer skills, as we find out that we can make physical objects move by pushing them, we must take risks in order to learn to walk, finding out that we must get up over and over again, and we learn to avoid things that cause pain. Risk-taking increases in the adolescent years. The Discoverer harnesses this tendency and directs it towards values-based rather than unhelpful impulses.

Example metaphor for young people. Imagine stepping into a new and strange city, one that has no maps to guide you. How do we get around? We must rely on trial-and-error experience. We take different routes and find the cool places to hang out, the places to eat, the parks to rest in, and the dangerous places to avoid. Hopefully, we will not starve to death or be stabbed before we find the useful routes. For the Discoverer to know the city, he or she must explore it to find out for him- or herself.

Noticer – The Noticer senses psychological events as they occur and uses the five senses to receive information from the environment. When in the Noticer space, we are behaving in ways that allow us to receive information from the world through sight, taste, sound, touch, and feel, and through the reactions of our own bodies (e.g., feelings). Developmentally one might say we are all born into the world as Noticers: as babies we experience the world through our physical senses. The world is what we see, hear, touch, taste, and smell.

The Noticer allows inner experience to come and go, rather than trying to change it or cling to it. Noticing creates the space between our difficult inner experience and our outward behaviour, such that when difficult inner experience shows up we don't simply react to it. If angry, we don't automatically strike out. If afraid, we don't automatically flee. If we experience the thought 'I'm not good enough', we don't automatically give up. We cease reacting to this inner experience and are able to better choose our actions in the service of what we care about. Becoming Noticers is the key to breaking free from old patterns of behaviour that are no longer working. Noticing can often be likened to 'neutral gear'. Noticers are not necessarily moving forward (Discoverer) or looking back (Advisor). It is 'taking a look around'.

Example metaphor for young people. The Noticer stands back from the scene of the busy city, witnessing all that is happening but not necessarily seeking to alter events in any way. The Noticer uses all her senses and her bodily reactions to take everything in. Emotions come and go and do not automatically provoke reactions. Anger does not automatically lead to hitting, fear to fleeing, or anxiety to withdrawing from the social world.

Advisor – The Advisor is a metaphor for a key part of our symbolic world. This comprises our verbal history of learning. As we grow into a language-capable being, we gradually build up a verbally interpreted world history of our own memories, words, and images. This world is unique to each of us. Our Advisor is the inner voice, the inner critic and guide. A pre-schooler may not always know the distinction between their Advisor-created world and the physical world, pretending he is Superman, and believing he 'really' is Superman.

Over time our Advisor becomes life director, making conclusions about the present environment based on what others have told us or on our adaptations to past environmental niches. When in Advisor space, we are behaving in ways that allow us to find reward or escape aversive stimuli, with little trial-and-error behaviour or input from the physical world. We rely on past learning, teachings, judgements, verbal rules, and/or reasoning and problem-solving.

We can easily become stuck in this Advisor space, believing that our thoughts about the world are the world. For example, the young person who is physically abused at home may assume that the same risk of abuse is present at school. Consequently he becomes guarded, withdrawn, and fearful both at home, where it is adaptive, and also at school, where it is usually less adaptive. The abused boy follows his 'Advisor' and seems to 'know' that people are not to be trusted. In doing so he avoids relationships and the risk of further abuse, but he also misses opportunities to discover friendship.

Example metaphor for young people. When we are in Advisor space, it is as if we are navigating by a GPS (the inner voice). This GPS often helps us to quickly get to where we want to go. We avoid wasting time going in the wrong direction and avoid fatal mistakes such as driving off a bridge. However, the GPS is sometimes wrong and decidedly unhelpful. For example, we might use the GPS to get to a park, but it leads us incorrectly to an alley. When the GPS fails us, we need to unhook from what it is saying, and shift into noticing and discovery to find a new way forward.

What exactly is DNA?

We have given the three classes of behaviour names, and this can lead to certain misunderstandings. First, by giving these behavioural patterns names, it may seem as if we are talking about cognitive 'things', when what we are actually doing is using terms in a pragmatic way to aid intervention.

Second, it may incorrectly seem as if the behaviours are always discrete; for example, if you engage in Noticer behaviour, you can't be engaged as a Discoverer. In truth, it is possible for behaviour to have multiple functions. Thus, although we will talk about discrete DNA spaces, the reader should keep in mind that these 'spaces' overlap all the time. For example, over-reliance on our verbal understanding (Advisor) may reduce the range of behaviours we try, test, and explore (Discoverer). Over-reliance on our verbal understanding may also reduce our Noticer skills. Thus, at times different expressions of DNA can interfere with each other.

DNA can also work together to produce effective behaviour. For example, when we feel angry, we predict (with Advisor) that hitting our peer will lead to bad things, such as getting expelled from school. Thus we may try a series of new ways of responding, including ignoring the problem, reporting the problem to our teacher, asserting ourselves with the person (Discoverer).

We may also use Noticer skills to gather information, sensing how we are feeling before and after we respond, and detecting how the peer feels and responds towards us. The Noticer is the central skill in the DNA-V model and is most related to the popular term 'mindfulness'. We can use Noticer to create a space between stimulus and response. We don't *have* to react badly to a toxic environment or to our own feelings and thoughts. Noticer gives us choice.

Psychological flexibility is our ultimate goal

By using DNA-V processes, we aim to ultimately build psychological flexibility as young people grow. We stated the adult definition of psychological flexibility above, but for young people we modify this definition somewhat as follows:

> The ability of people to contact the present moment, move between DNA processes in a way that promotes learning and growth, and change or persist in behaviour, in the service of connecting with and building their valued life.

Whilst our definition is similar to the adult one, we are emphasizing that young people are at the stage of **learning** about thoughts and feelings and what it means to be a human being. Second, we are emphasizing that there is a need for adolescents to psychologically **grow**. This requires them to test out new behaviour and explore if the new behaviour meets valued ends. One of the most efficient ways in which humans learn is by trying things out, so adolescents must try many new things, and that might include taking risks, trying on new selves, and testing boundaries set by adults. Finally, we have de-emphasized moving towards 'values' and placed the emphasis on connecting, and building a valued life. We don't assume adolescents 'have' values so much as they are discovering and creating their values as they journey into adulthood.

Psychological inflexibility comes from history and habit, but particularly from excessive verbal control (what we are calling 'Advisor') combined with resultant low situational awareness and attempts to avoid and manipulate inner experience (low Noticing) and sometimes with impulsive sensation-seeking disconnected from workability (low Discoverer). Flexibility is increased by learning to shift to Noticer space, unhook from unhelpful verbal control (Advisor), and then to trial new behaviour, and take calculated risks in order to broaden and build behavioural repertoires (Discovery).

DNA-V is a model that helps give young people choice and control in their life. It does not dictate what young people 'should' do. All actions are evaluated according to their workability measured against the young person's values (what the young person chooses as important). The DNA-V model does not assume that young people are broken in any away or 'missing something'. Every young person can develop the skills needed to shift between Discoverer, Noticer, and Advisor.

DNA-V develops self and social understanding

Perhaps no contextual factor is more important to a young person than their understanding of their self and their social world. Social contexts such as family, school, community, and culture all play a major role in how we grow. Similarly, the creation of 'self' is a key task for the young. We use DNA-V to develop flexible ways of looking at the self and the social world.

Self-perspective

Our self, who we think we are, has such an impact on our lives that we will take a special look at self through our DNA-V model. Of course, self is also a very special task in the adolescent period, so we look carefully at how self develops in this dramatic time. Flexible view of self does not involve additional skills, but a special focus on how DNA skills are used to shape the self. We take the three core DNA expressions of Discoverer, Noticer, and Advisor and look at how we create our self, can come to understand our self, and how we can grow into the kind of self we hope for.

The self is born with language. Relational frame theory helps us understand how it develops (Mchugh, Barnes-Holmes, & Barnes-Holmes, 2004). At birth our primary caregiver, usually our mother, uses language for us, by saying things like, 'you are tired' or 'you are hungry'. She is the primary source of all language information. Over time we begin to use language for ourselves, and we 'grow' a verbal understanding of the self. We come to learn through language that there is a 'me' and there is a 'you'. The self begins with a simple verbal frame:

$$\text{Me} \neq \text{You}$$

You and me are not the same. Through the use of language and thousands of repetitions of 'I' *versus* 'you', we gradually learn a view of the world that is called 'me'. Everything I see in the world, I see through my eyes.

As we develop into our teens, our verbal world, the 'Advisor', becomes increasingly dominant. It can become so powerful that we come to think that what the voice in our heads says about us is true. Thoughts such as 'I am weird', 'I am stupid', 'I can't change', and 'I am not good enough' seem like descriptions of our essence, rather than events that come and go. We can lose the ability to notice our physical self, or to discover new things about our self. We use DNA skills to build a flexible view of the self, and show young people how to unhook from unhelpful self-concepts, see themselves with compassion, broaden their skills and strengths, and recognize that they are always capable of growing and improving.

Social-perspective

Even though our self becomes a dominant force, we are never just a self. We are always connected to other people. Just like a flexible self-perspective, we consider social-perspective as a special approach to harnessing DNA skills. We use the skills of Discoverer, Noticer, and Advisor to see how we develop inside the world of others.

Our brains are wired for social connection (Hrdy, 2009). From the moment of birth, we seek out connection with others and try to gaze into their eyes. It is not long before we start imitating others and mirroring their emotional states. However, despite our biological readiness to connect with others, there are still a number of contextual factors that can undermine our ability to take their perspective. For example, we may not be reinforced for considering others' viewpoints (e.g., narcissism), we may be misled (e.g., 'Nobody likes you'), or we may not be taught to recognize and label emotions in ourselves or others ('alexithymia').

We use social perspective to build social connection in two ways. Firstly, we help young people to take other people's perspective and see the value in relationships. We must learn to use our Advisor wisely in judging others, to become Noticers in order to manage the tsunami of emotions that another person can elicit in us, and to become Discoverers so we build strong relationships that matter. Secondly, we use social-perspective to build our cooperative skills, to help young people participate in and create positive communities. This human ability to cooperate has led us to overcome physical hardship, dangerous foes, and become the most powerful animal species on Earth (S.C. Hayes & Sanford, 2014). DNA-V explicitly seeks to develop this ability (see, L.L. Hayes & Ciarrochi, 2015 for more info).

Conclusion

Perhaps the greatest strength of ACT comes from its CBS foundations, where evolutionary science, functional contextualism, operant principles of behaviour, and relational frame theory all come together to provide a solid foundation on which to build interventions. Its second strength is a comprehensive approach, where researchers and clinicians are working together across science and clinical applications. The ACT model for therapy and training has many useful applications and has begun to be used well with adolescents across a small number of trials. We present a new model of ACT, DNA-V, that was purposefully constructed to account for development and the skills that all young people need as they grow and reach their full potential.

References

Bach, P.A., & Moran, D.J. (2008). *ACT in Practice: Case Conceptualizations in Acceptance and Commitment Therapy*. Oakland, CA: New Harbinger.

Blackledge, J.T. (2003). An introduction to relational frame theory: basics and applications. *The Behavior Analyst Today, 3*(4), 421–433.

Brestan, E.V., & Eyberg, S.M. (1998). Effective psychosocial treatments of conduct-disordered children and adolescents: 29 years, 82 studies, 5,272 kids. *Journal of Clinical Child Psychology, 27*(2), 180–189.

Ciarrochi, J. Hayes, L., & Bailey, A. (2012). *Get Out of Your Mind and Into Your Life for Teens*. Oakland, CA: New Harbinger.

Ciarrochi, J., Heaven, P.C.L., & Supavadeeprasit, S. (2008). The link between emotion identification skills and socio-emotional functioning in early adolescence: a one-year longitudinal study. *Journal of Adolescence, 31*, 564–581.

Ciarrochi, J., Kashdan, T., Leeson, P., Heaven, P.C.L., & Jordon, C. (2011). On being aware and accepting: a one-year longitudinal study into adolescent well-being. *Journal of Adolescence, 34*, 695–703.

Ciarrochi, J., Robb, H., & Godsell, C. (2005). Letting a little non-verbal air into the room: insights from acceptance and commitment therapy Part 1: philosophical and theoretical underpinnings. *Journal of Rational-Emotive and Cognitive Behavior Therapy, 23*(2), 79–106.

Foa, E.B., McNally, R.J., Steketee, G.S., & McCarthy, P.R. (1991). A test of preparedness theory in anxiety-disordered patients using an avoidance paradigm. *Journal of Psychophysiology, 5*(2), 159–163.

Foody, M., Barnes-Holmes, Y., & Barnes-Holmes, D. (2012). The role of self in acceptance and commitment therapy. In: L. McHugh & I. Stewart (eds), *The Self and Perspective Taking: Contributions and Applications From Modern Behavioral Science*. Oakland, CA: New Harbinger.

Hawley, P.H. (2011). The evolution of adolescence and the adolescence of evolution: the coming of age of humans and the theory about the forces that made them. *Journal of Research on Adolescence (Blackwell Publishing Limited), 21*(1), 307–316. doi: 10.1111/j.1532-7795.2010.00732.x.

Hayes, L.L., Boyd, C., & Sewell, J. (2011). Acceptance and commitment therapy for the treatment of adolescent depression: a pilot study in a psychiatric outpatient setting. *Mindfulness, 2*(2), 86–94. doi: 10.1007/s12671-011-0046-5.

Hayes, L.L., & Ciarrochi, J. (2015). *The Thriving Adolescent: Using Acceptance and Commitment Therapy and Positive Psychology to Help Teens Manage Emotions, Achieve Goals, and Build Connection*. Oakland, CA: New Harbinger.

Hayes, S.C. (1993). Analytic goals and the varieties of scientific contextualism. In: S.C. Hayes, L.J. Hayes, H.W. Reese & T.R. Sarbin (eds), *Varieties of Scientific Contextualism*, pp. 11–27. Reno, NV: Context Press.

Hayes, S.C. (ed.). (2004). *Acceptance and Commitment Therapy and the New Behavior Therapies: Mindfulness, Acceptance and Relationship*. New York: Guilford Press.

Hayes, S.C., Barnes-Holmes, D. & Roche, B. (eds). (2001). *Relational Frame Theory: A Post-Skinnerian Account of Human Language and Cognition*. New York: Kluwer Academic.

Hayes, S.C., Barnes-Holmes, D., & Wilson, K.G. (2012). Contextual behavioral science: creating a science more adequate to the challenge of the human condition. *Journal of Contextual Behavioral Science, 1*(1–2), 1–16. doi: 10.1016/j.jcbs.2012.09.004.

Hayes, S.C., Luoma, J.B., Bond, F.W., Masuda, A., & Lillis, J. (2006). Acceptance and commitment therapy: model, processes and outcomes. *Behavior Research and Therapy, 44*(1), 1–25.

Hayes, S.C., & Sanford, B.T. (2014). Cooperation came first: evolution and human cognition. *Journal of the Experimental Analysis of Behavior, 101*(1), 112–129.

Hayes, S.C., Strosahl, K.D., Bunting, K., Twohig, M., & Wilson, K.G. (2004). What is acceptance and commitment therapy? *Practical Guide to Acceptance and Commitment Therapy*, pp. 3–29. New York: Springer.
Hayes, S.C., Strosahl, K.D., & Wilson, K.G. (1999). *Acceptance and Commitment Therapy: An Experiential Approach to Behavior Change*. New York: The Guilford Press.
Hayes, S.C., Strosahl, K.D., & Wilson, K.G. (2012). *Acceptance and Commitment Therapy, Second Edition: The Process and Practice of Mindful Change*. 2nd edition. New York: Guilford Publications.
Hrdy, S.B. (2009). *Mothers and Others: The Evolutionary Origins of Mutual Understanding*. Cambridge, MA: Harvard University Press.
Kabat-Zinn, J. (2005). *Full Catastrophe Living: Using the Wisdom of Your Body and Mind to Face Stress, Pain, and Illness: Fifteenth Anniversary Edition*. New York: Delta Trade Paperback/Bantam Dell.
Levin, M.E., Pistorello, J., Seeley, J.R., & Hayes, S.C. (2014). Feasibility of a prototype web-based acceptance and commitment therapy prevention program for college students. *Journal of American College Health, 62*(1), 20–30.
Livheim, F., Hayes, L.L., Ghaderi, A., Magnusdottir, T., Högfeldt, A., Rowse, J., & Tengström, A. (2012). *Acceptance and Commitment Therapy as an Early Intervention Group Program for Adolescent Depression and Stress: Two Randomised, Controlled Pilot Trials in Two Countries*. Melbourne, Australia.
Luciano, C., Valdivia, S., Gutiérrez, O., Ruiz, F., & Páez, M. (2009). Brief acceptance-based protocols applied to the work with adolescents. *International Journal of Psychology and Psychological Therapy, 9*(2), 237–257.
Mchugh, L., Barnes-Holmes, Y., & Barnes-Holmes, D. (2004). Perspective-taking as relational responding a developmental profile. *The Psychological Record, 54*, 115–144.
Ollendick, T.H., & King, N.J. (2004). Empirically supported treatment for children and adolescents: Advances toward evidence-based practice. In: P. Barrett & T. Ollendick (eds), *Handbook of Interventions That Work With Children and Adolescents*. Chichester, England: John Wiley.
Patterson, G.R. (1982). *Coercive family process*. Eugene, OR: Castalia.
Patterson, G.R. (2002). Etiology and treatment of child and adolescent antisocial behavior. *The Behavior Analyst Today, 3*(2), 133–144.
Ruiz, F. (2010). A review of Acceptance and Commitment Therapy (ACT) empirical evidence: correlational, experimental psychopathology, component and outcome studies. *International Journal of Psychology and Psychological Therapy, 10*, 125–162.
Ruiz, F.J. (2012). Acceptance and commitment therapy versus traditional cognitive behavioral therapy: a systematic review and meta-analysis of current empirical evidence. *International Journal of Psychology and Psychological Therapy, 12*(2), 333–357.
Schlegel, A., & Barry, H. (1991). *Adolescence: An Anthropological Inquiry/Alice Schlegel, Herbert Barry III*: New York: Free Press; Toronto: Collier Macmillan Canada; New York: Maxwell Macmillan International, c1991.
Segal, A.V., Teasdale, J.D., & Williams, J.M.G. (2004). Mindfulness-based cognitive therapy: theoretical rationale and empirical status. In: S. C. Hayes, V.M. Follette & M.M. Linehan (eds), *Mindfulness and Acceptance: Expanding the Cognitive-Behavioral Tradition*, pp. 45–65. New York: The Guilford Press.
Skinner, B.F. (1969). *Contingencies of Reinforcement: A Theoretical Analysis*. Englewood Cliffs, NJ: Prentice-Hall.

Smout, M.F., Hayes, L., Atkins, P.W.B., Klausen, J., & Duguid, J.E. (2012). The empirically supported status of acceptance and commitment therapy: an update. *Clinical Psychologist, 16*(3), 97–109. doi: 10.1111/j.1742-9552.2012.00051.x.

Wicksell, R., Melin, L., Lekander, M., & Olsson, G. (2009). Evaluating the effectiveness of exposure and acceptance strategies to improve functioning and quality of life in longstanding pediatric pain: a randomized controlled trial. *Pain, 141*, 248–257.

Wilson, K.G., & with Du Frene, T. (2009). *Mindfulness for Two: An Acceptance and Commitment Therapy Approach to Mindfulness in Psychotherapy.* Oakland, CA: New Harbinger.

Zinbarg, R.E., Barlow, D.H., Brown, T.A., & Hertz, R.M. (1992). Cognitive-behavioral approaches to the nature and treatment of anxiety disorders. *Annual Review of Psychology, 43*, 235–267.

8
Child Well-Being: Indicators and Measurement

Axel Schölmerich, Alexandru Agache, and Birgit Leyendecker

Introduction

Everybody wants to contribute to child and adolescent well-being. Politicians, parents, educators, health care specialists, lawyers, judges, clinical psychologists, all claim to have this goal in mind, and some even seem to think they are the only one. But what exactly is child well-being? It is easier to say what child well-being is not: risky adolescent behaviour, unhealthy lifestyle, drug addiction, disrupted parent–child relationships, and so forth. Can we then conclude that the absence of negative things constitutes well-being? Certainly not. In this chapter, we will discuss the current use and meaning of well-being in the context of child and adolescent development with a focus on methodological requirements for indicators informing policymakers and community leaders. It is important to acknowledge the difference between results of political decisions (e.g., the establishment of a health care system, providing institutions for day care, or passing laws allowing parental leave), which we label output variables, and the effects such decisions have on child well-being. We argue in favour of using child-oriented data indicating developmental progress as the essential basis for the evaluation of such investments.

Child well-being in a developmental perspective

Human development is in essence a continuous adaptation to challenges. The adaptation occurs with a natural variation: some developmental trajectories are steeper than others; and there can be delayed development as well as precocious maturation. After birth, the establishment of regulatory capacities is essential, not only sleep-wake cycles and temperature regulation, but also regulating emotions and interactions. This regulation happens with contextual support, typically by the parents. Consequently, the establishment of stable relations to other people becomes focal; attachment to caregivers is one central task. Through those same interactions new modalities become available; the pragmatic use of language develops. In parallel, motor development proceeds to refined motor skills, leading to better everyday activities such as eating and dressing. Peer relations become increasingly important, friendships and social hierarchies develop mainly in the preschool age. Knowledge acquisition happens in informal and later formal settings, and attending school provides the essential tools for successful exchange with the cultural environment. During early adolescence, a heightened self-consciousness and feedback of the social environment provide the building blocks of a personal identity, which continues to develop during the rest of our lives. Eventually, developing intimate and sexual relationships forms the end of adolescence and the beginning of psychological adulthood. This very condensed overview of human development shows the magnitude of the task to define well-being of children and adolescents. It is definitely impossible to use similar variables or even identical scales across childhood and adolescence: We have to make decisions about which aspects of that multitude of developmental domains we want to focus on. Generally, age-appropriate achievement of developmental milestones can be considered to be 'good', sometimes earlier than average is better, but not always (e.g., pubertal development).

A second consequence of a developmental view of child well-being is that categories such as 'single parenthood' become quite difficult, since they are obviously state-oriented. The child perspective is a biographical one, and family composition changes over time. Married couples become separated, single parents find new partners or form patchwork families.

Figure 8.1 shows one such example from a data set, with the target child classified as a member of a two-parent family with one sibling (family status 1 in the figure) during her first two years of life, subsequently as a child with a single parent (family status 3). At the end of 2003, her mother remarries a man with one child (family status 6), and in 2006, a new sibling is born, making them a complete patchwork family (family status 7). It seems appropriate to expect the well-being of that girl to in some way reflect these different stages in her biography, but how should we classify her if we were to measure in 2005? Is it the duration of single parenthood, or the age at which it occurs, or a combination of both? At least we should keep in mind that comparisons of family status as an explanatory construct for child well-being may be an oversimplification of a fundamental developmental process.

Existing indicators

The context for the development of indicators of well-being was the attempt to compare communities, regions, countries, and even continents. For the evaluation of programmes targeting a defined problem, such indicators serve an indispensable purpose. UNICEF uses health-related (among them the

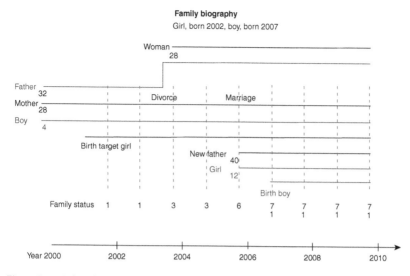

Figure 8.1 A family biography showing transition from two-parent family to single motherhood to patchwork family

child mortality rate) to distribute funds among participating countries. The OECD has made child well-being a focus, and uses six dimensions to monitor progress in the participating countries in the form of reports (OECD, 2009). The indicators for the six dimensions will be briefly introduced.

Material Well-Being. The percentage of children living in households with less than 50% of the adjusted median household income, or in households without any job-related income, or where children report low material resources, low access to educational opportunities and having less than 10 books at home make up material well-being.

Education. The percentage of 15 year olds who participate in any kind of institutionalized education, as well as their success in school (measured in grades), is combined with a negative indicator as the percentage of adolescents who work in unqualified labour.

Health and Safety. Infant mortality, percentage of births with low birthweight, use of vaccinations and death by accident and injury are reported for this factor.

Family and Environment. The percentage of children living in single-head households or with step-parents, percentage of children having a meal with their parents more than once a week, or percentage of children reporting their parents spend time just talking to them is combined with the percentage of 11–13 year olds who report experiencing their peers as friendly and helpful.

Risk Behaviour and Lifestyle. Here a combination of the percentage of children receiving daily breakfast and fruit and are physically active are contrasted with those who are overweight or obese. Risk indicators are percentage of under 15 year olds who smoke tobacco, are sexually active, use cannabis, or have been drunk more than twice. In addition, the rate of condom use and teen pregnancies is reported, as well as the percentage of 11, 13, and 15 year olds who have been involved in physical fights or report bullying.

Subjective Well-Being. The percentage of children and adolescents who describe their own health as sufficient or bad, those who report that they like to go to school, and the percentage of children who score above the mean of the Satisfaction with Life Scale.

The list of indicators used in international comparisons and policy evaluation appears to be *broad*, *selective*, and *specific*. They describe important aspects of child well-being, and they are useful because data can be aggregated on a national level. As such, their main use is the comparison of living conditions across countries. However, they appear to have very limited use for assessing individual well-being. More importantly, the single indicators are selected with specific problem areas in mind, such as teen pregnancy, so they will probably react to specific policy interventions, but they cannot be combined into more comprehensive dimensions. They are sorted by content into the dimensions described above; no weighting or statistical model fit information is available, so even for international comparisons it remains a matter of political judgement to weight advantages in one area against shortfalls in another.

Age-limited indicators

Other established sets of indicators are typically more age-specific. The Early Childhood Longitudinal Study (ECLS, http://nces.ed.gov/ecls/) uses a number of core variables to assess developmental progress of individual children in several domains (motor, cognitive, language, and executive functions), and a set of contextual variables (family, educational institutions) to monitor contextual influence on educational outcomes.

The Atlas of Child Development (Kershaw, Irwin, Trafford, & Hertzman, 2005) uses a standardized set of variables grouped into five categories (physical health and well-being, social competence, emotional maturity, language and cognitive development, and communication skills and general knowledge). The Early Development Index (EDI) used in this study is developmental in focus, and the authors use the outcome measures to relate developmental progress to contextual variations in childcare, public health investments, socio-economic status of families, and other resources. Since data are available for individual children, differences on the community level can be detected.

Variations of the Atlas of Child Development have been commissioned in other settings as well. In Germany, the Bertelsmann Foundation has developed an Instrument (KOMPIK) for the pre-school age, where educators in child care centres provide information on the developmental status of individual children in the domains of motor, social, and emotional competences, motivation, language and early literacy, mathematics, science, music, and artistic skills as well as health status and subjective well-being (Bertelsmann-Stiftung, 2011). Again, a strength is the opportunity to relate individual developmental status to contextual variations in communities and neighbourhoods.

Overall, the development of indicators for child well-being can be traced from the Child and Youth Well-Being Index in the United States (Land, Lamb, & Mustillo, 2001; Land, Lamb, Meadows, & Taylor, 2007) to those used by UNICEF and the OECD: the Index of Child Well-Being in the European Union (Bradshaw, Hoelscher, & Richardson, 2007), a variation for Europe (Bradshaw & Richardson, 2009), and again with variations for specific countries such as Germany (Bertram, Kohl, & Rösler, 2011). The newer versions typically have a stronger focus on microdata, as in analyses based on the US-National Survey of Children's Health (Moore et al., 2008). However, there are no statistical tests of the dimensionality of the scales, and if at all, z-standardization is used to combine variables into dimensions. This results in numerous difficulties when using such indicators in research, and interpretation across gender, age, and culture remains tentative owing to lack of measurement equivalence. No study has an empirically based validation of the dimensions, variables are sometimes grouped in different domains, there is no weighting formula for the combination of variables, and different indices are useful for different age groups. As such, those indices do not represent child well-being on a broader level. Conversely, these indices are very useful when constructing time-series within a defined social setting. Recently, the OECD has published guidelines on measuring subjective well-being in adults, which address some of the critical points above (OECD, 2013).

Five axes of indicators for child well-being

In their extensive review, Amerijckx and Humblet (2013) summarize the existing literature on measures of child well-being. They postulate five structural theoretical axes to combine different aspects of child well-being and argue for a comprehensive model. The first axis is *positive versus negative*. Most papers focus on negative manifestations. However, there is increasing interest in the study of positive development. The second axes contrasts *objective versus subjective* measures. One interesting aspect here is that objective measures are not necessarily reflected in the subjective experience of children. The necessity of including subjective measures has also been noted in the work commissioned by the OECD (Bertram et al., 2011). The third axis distinguishes *state versus process*. Given the interest in lifespan development, the process orientation is clearly of great importance. Child and adolescent development is obviously a process, which may include unpleasant yet beneficial phases, and not a state. The process orientation is sometimes referred to as the eudemonic perspective, while the state perspective is called the hedonic ('here and now') approach. Again, the vast majority of existing measures are state oriented. The fourth axis encompasses *material versus spiritual orientation*. Particularly on the objective and state poles of axes two and three, we have a lot more information about material aspects. However, people consider the spiritual aspects of their lives to be of central importance, and this should be reflected in the measures we use to describe well-being. The fifth and final axis focuses on the *individual versus the community*. Here, cultural models come into play; and the typical Western approach to this issue can be contrasted with cultures that focus more on interdependence than on independence. Still psychologists and economists are trained to focus on individual perspectives. A number of measures include the family as a unit of measurement; typically in state orientation as in contrasting single parents with two-parent families. Only rarely are communities and broader social contexts considered. The authors conclude: 'for each research, a specific combination of positioning on each one of the five axes could and should apply. We thus argue in favour of overriding a one-dimensional, single-level, unipolar approach to child well-being, and for further development of its positive, hedonic, subjective, spiritual and collective dimensions' (Amerijckx & Humblet, 2013, p. 8).

Positive youth development

Another approach towards measurement of well-being has become popular under the title positive youth development. In defining five domains under the label '5C', consisting of Competence (cognitive, social, academic, and vocational), Character (self-control, moral, and spirituality), Confidence (self-confidence, identity), Connection (positive bonds to parents, peers, educational institutions, and the community), and Caring (empathy, prosocial behaviour), Lerner and colleagues (Lerner et al., 2005) have provided a framework for developmental contextualism allowing not only the study of risk factors and their developmental consequences, but also to include the potential benefits of assets for adolescent development. This is a significant shift in theoretical orientation, away from the diathesis-stress model so pertinent in developmental and clinical psychology. While this model in the original formulation is exclusively targeted at youth and not younger children, it is worth exploring in more detail. In essence, the basic assumption is that whenever there is an 'alignment' of individual strengths and ecological assets, positive youth development will take place. Eventually, through a process of thriving, an 'idealized personhood' contributing to self-development and to community and society at large will develop. The contribution is sometimes referred to as the 'sixth C'. The 4-H study included 1,700 fifth-graders who answered surveys; for two-thirds of the sample one parent, mostly mothers, provided information. With extensive surveys for both youth and parent, data were collected to validate the construct of positive youth development consisting of competence, confidence, connection, character, and caring; and to find evidence for a relationship between positive youth development, contribution to the community as well as to risk behaviours. Through a series of regression models, the relationships of demographic variables (gender, race, ethnicity, mother's education and household income) were analyzed. The plethora of measures drawn from extant surveys including external and internal assets from the Profiles of Student Life – Attitudes and Behavior Survey, the Teen Assessment Project Survey Question Bank, the Child's Report of Parenting Behaviors Inventory, the Parental Monitoring Scale, the Target-Based Expectations Scale, the Self-Perception Profile for Children, the Peer Support Scale, the Eisenberg Sympathy Scale, and the Social Responsibility Scale were subjected to a theoretical judgement to organize them according to the 5C model. Risk behaviours were assessed using the Center of Epidemiological Studies Depression Scale and questions developed as indicators of risk behaviour and delinquency. In addition, school and career aspirations and future orientation were measured, as well as puberty development and the Erikson Psychosocial Stage Inventory. After piloting the instruments and restructuring the scales based on a theoretical alignment with the 5C-model, confirmatory factor analysis was used to assess model fit and improve the measurement model by allowing correlations among sets of indicators. This resulted in a set of 19 manifest variables, which were indicators for the 5Cs. Positive Youth Development was a second order latent variable, explaining 60% of variance in the manifest variables. Without going into any detail of the rich findings of this study, we want to emphasize that the measurement model is an excellent example to approach complex and multidimensional issues of child and adolescent well-being.

Cultural aspects

Well-being is both a normative construct and a subjective product. In both ways, it is influenced by the culture in which it is defined. However, the cultural dimension of well-being is almost never discussed. The literature distinguishes two different models of the conception of the self, the independent and the interdependent orientation (Markus & Kitayama, 1991). The independent model focuses on the self as separated from others, with individual preferences and intentions, a high degree of agency as well as stable attributes such as personality traits and internal emotions, while the interdependent model focuses on interconnectedness with a social reference group, leading to more permeable boundaries of the self and an embedded perception of subjective feelings. The independent model describes Western middle-class ideals, and the interdependent model Eastern, particularly Asian personality models. Keller (2013) has reformulated the concepts with respect to adaptation to the cultural context as psychological autonomy and hierarchical relatedness, building on and extending research by Kagitcibasi (2005) and maintaining the general importance of autonomy and relatedness as universal human needs. When Western parents describe aspects of personality, they wish to see in their children as socialization goals, they more frequently refer to self-maximization, happiness, and developing one's own potential, while Latin-American and Asian parents put more emphasis on respect, proper demeanour, and fulfilling expectations (Harwood, Schölmerich, Ventura Cook, Schulze, & Wilson, 1996; Leyendecker & Schölmerich, 2007). Interestingly, the approach to positive youth development described above is meant to be normative for the Western (e.g., US) world; however, the characteristics and indicators to measure well-being appear to focus much more on interdependence with caring and connection as two pivotal aspects. Moreover, the sixth C, contribution as the characteristic of the idealized personhood, is almost the exact opposite of self-maximization. Obviously, there are features compatible with the independent view of the person in the concept of positive youth development as well; for example, competence and confidence allowing fulfilment of the person's potential. It is interesting that in the context of development of children and adolescent well-being, the often-contrasted cultural models appear to be much more in balance than when the focus is on how cultures are different from each other. This observation makes the process orientation of a developmental approach to well-being necessary, acknowledging the adaptation to the different developmental tasks over the lifespan (Leyendecker & Schölmerich, 2007).

A developmentally appropriate empirically derived indicator of child well-being

In our own work, we have recently analysed child well-being among children up to the age of 10 years using data from the German Socio-Economic Panel-study (GSOEP) (Schölmerich, Agache, Leyendecker, Ott, & Werding, 2013), combining the positive development approach with a truly developmental perspective. The GSOEP is a panel study of over 20,000 participants, and since 2003 every child born during the last year into that representative sample has been assessed with age-specific instruments using mother reports gathered by trained interviewers (Wagner, Frick, & Schupp, 2007). In addition, data were gathered with similar instruments in 2007–2009 in the 'Familien in Deutschland (FiD)' study for a somewhat broader age range and oversampling specific populations. There is one questionnaire for newborns, one for children 2–3 years of age, one for 5–6 year olds, one for 7–8

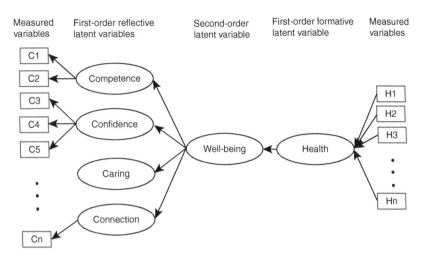

Figure 8.2 Theoretical model of measured variables, reflective and formative latent variables, and second-order latent variable. Not all variables and connections are shown

year olds, and one for 9–10 year olds. As the enrolled children grow older, additional questionnaires are developed. Across all age groups, data from over 5,000 children were available. Obviously, such a study has limitations, most notably the absence of standardized behavioural tests and sole reliance on the mother report. On the other hand, the sample size of this group is very impressive and allows statistical analysis techniques requiring large samples.

The theoretical model in Figure 8.2 consists of four reflective latent variables (competence, confidence, caring, and connection), where the variables in the data set are 'symptoms' of those constructs, and one formative latent variable (health), where the available variables 'cause' the construct. The distinction between formative and reflective variables has consequences in modelling beyond the scope of this chapter. Well-being was then defined as the second-order latent variable combining the five first-order latent variables. This allows using general well-being as an outcome reflecting socio-demographic contexts and other sources of influence in analyses using structural equation models and multiple regression.

The questionnaire for new-borns focuses on temperamental constructs as well as health indicators, and the somatic and psychological well-being of the mother. For 2–3 year olds, those variables are included in some more detail, and parent–child activities, language development, motor development, and social competencies are assessed using an adapted version of the Vineland Social Maturity Scale. For the 5–6 year olds, everyday behaviours and media usage are added, 17 items from the Strength and Difficulties Questionnaire, and childcare arrangements are recorded. For 7–8 year olds, education and academic performance are reported, as well as everyday behaviours and out-of-school activities. For the 9–10 year olds, friendships and social networks of the children are included. The theoretical measurement model depicted in Figure 8.2 was then applied to each age group and the contribution of the available items was estimated using structural equation modelling. Conventional Goodness-of-Fit limits were used including RMSEA, SRMR, and CFI to assess model fit (i.e., by exclusion of items which were only loosely causally connected to our well-being constructs). All final models had good fit to the data and comprised different numbers of observed variables (e.g., 29 items were included in the model for 2–3 year olds). In a series of factor analyses with multiple group comparisons, we established measurement equivalence for the reflective part of the model (i.e., without the Health variable) in comparing boys and girls, single parents with two-parent families, families with and without migratory background, as well as data source (SOEP vs. FiD). Configural equivalence means that the same items load on the same factor and is the most basic requirement to use the measurement model across groups. Metric equivalence indicates that the items on the factors have similar loadings; however, factor scores may still differ between groups. Finally, scalar equivalence was tested, which indicates that means of factors across groups can be compared. With this procedure, we have an empirically derived and meaningful parameter to describe child well-being across different groups and ages. Longitudinal analyses showed that slightly more than half of the available sample remained within the same range of general well-being over time, and about a quarter changed for better or for worse. This is not surprising considering the dynamic plasticity of development, even though correlation coefficients were in the low range. In the analyses of material resources available to the family, we found no overall effect of household income; however, those under 60% of median income had lower general well-being scores. Using childcare arrangements turned out to be a protective factor against lack of economic resources, as did frequent dyadic parent–child activities, but not just spending time with the child while shopping, media use, or going for a walk in the park. In sum, the parameter developed to describe child well-being was sensitive to developmental contexts in a meaningful way (Schölmerich, Agache, Leyendecker, Ott, & Werding, 2014).

Conclusion

While the concept of child well-being remains complex and elusive, we have shown that it is possible to approach the issue in an empirical way. Rather than focusing on aggregated binary data (percentages of children with a certain characteristic, e.g., teenage pregnancy or smoking), we suggest considering developmental progress in various domains to be the hallmark of well-being during childhood. It would certainly be desirable to have more behaviourally anchored information, but there are serious age limitations, as there are for subjective assessments of well-being (e.g., 'to cry a lot' may have a different meaning as indicator at age 0–1 compared to age 5–6). Therefore, parental reports of such measures are the main source of information during childhood, complemented by self-report and objective measures (e.g., school grades and educational biographies). In interpreting well-being indicators for children and adolescents, the multidimensional nature of the construct, its developmental character, and the cultural embeddedness should be considered. Well-being indicators need to be valid for all children in a society, without limitations by gender, race, ethnicity, or cultural orientation. This requires establishment of measurement equivalence for such indicators by statistically sound procedures. The focus on general well-being should, however, not be confused with neglecting those in need of extraordinary support.

References

Amerijckx, G.e., & Humblet, P.C. (2013). Child well-being: What does it mean? *Children and Society*, 1–12. doi: 10.1111/chso.12003.
Bertelsmann-Stiftung. (2011). *KECK-Atlas*. Retrieved 11.3.2014, from http://www.keck-atlas.de/keck.html
Bertram, H., Kohl, S., & Rösler, W. (2011). *Zur Lage der Kinder in Deutschland 2011/2012: Kindliches Wohlbefinden und gesellschaftliche Teilhabe*. Köln: Deutsches Komitee für UNICEF.
Bradshaw, J., Hoelscher, P., & Richardson, D. (2007). An index of child well-being in the European Union. *Social Indicators Research*, 80(1), 133–177.
Bradshaw, J., & Richardson, D. (2009). An index of child well-being in Europe. *Child Indicators Research*, 2, 319–351.
Harwood, R., Schölmerich, A., Ventura Cook, E., Schulze, P., & Wilson, S. (1996). Culture and class influences on Anglo and Puerto Rican mothers' beliefs regarding long-term socialization goals and child behavior. *Child Development*, 67(5), 2446–2461.
Kagitcibasi, C. (2005). Autonomy and relatedness in cultural context: implications for self and family. *Journal of Cross-Cultural Psychology*, 36(4), 403–422.
Keller, H. (2013). Infancy and well-being. In: A. Ben-Arieh, I. Frones, J. Casas & J. Korbin (eds), *Handbook of Child Well-Being*, pp. 1–23. Dordrecht, NL: Springer Science and Business Media.
Kershaw, P., Irwin, L., Trafford, K., & Hertzman, C. (2005). Human early learning partnership. The British Columbia Atlas of Child Development. In: P. Kershaw, L. Irwin, K. Trafford & C. Hertzman (eds), *The British Columbia Atlas of Child Development*, Vol. 40. Vancouver, BC: Human Early Learning Partnership, Western Geographical Press.
Land, K.C., Lamb, V.L., Meadows, S.O., & Taylor, A. (2007). Measuring trends in child well- being: an evidence-based approach. *Social Indicators Research*, 80(1), 105–132.

Land, K.C., Lamb, V.L., & Mustillo, S.K. (2001). Child and youth well-being in the United States, 1875–1998: some findings from a new index. *Social Indicators Research, 56*, 241–320.
Lerner, R., Lerner, J., Almerigi, J., Theokas, C., Phelps, E., Gestsdottir, S., & Von Eye, A. (2005). Positive youth development, participation in community youth development programs, and community contributions of fifth grade adolescence: findings from the first wave of the 4-H study of positive youth development. *Journal of Early Adolescence, 25*(1), 17–71.
Leyendecker, B., & Schölmerich, A. (2007). Interdependente und independente Orientierungen in Kindheit und Jugend. In: G. Trommsdorff & H.J. Kornadt (eds), *Enzyklopädie der Psychologie*, Vol. C/VII/2, pp. 557–597. Göttingen: Hogrefe.
Markus, H., & Kitayama, S. (1991). Culture and the self: implications for cognition, emotion and motivation. *Psychological Review, 98*, 224–253.
Moore, K.A., Theokas, C., Lippman, L., Bloch, M., Vandivere, S., & O'Hare, W. (2008). A microdata child well-being index: conceptualization, creation, and findings. *Child Indicators Research, 1*, 17–50.
OECD. (2009). *Doing Better for Children: Organisation for Economic Co-Operation and Development.* www.oecd.org/els/social/childwellbeing
OECD. (2013). *OECD Guidelines on Measuring Subjective Well-Being.* Retrieved from http://dx.doi.org/10.1787/9789264191655-en
Schölmerich, A., Agache, A., Leyendecker, B., Ott, N., & Werding, M. (2013). *Endbericht des Moduls Wohlergehen von Kindern: Geschäftsstelle Gesamtevaluation der ehe- und familienbezogenen Leistungen in Deutschland* im Auftrag des Bundesministeriums der Finanzen und des Bundesministeriums für Familie, Senioren, Frauen und Jugend. Berlin: BFM & BMFSFJ.
Schölmerich, A., Agache, A., Leyendecker, B., Ott, N., & Werding, M. (2014). Das Wohlergehen von Kindern als Zielgröße politischen Handelns. *Vierteljahreshefte zur Wirtschaftsforschung, 83*, 69–86.
Wagner, G.G., Frick, J.R., & Schupp, J. (2007). The German Socio-Economic Panel Study (SOEP) – scope, evolution and enhancements. *Schmollers Jahrbuch, 127*(1), 139–169.

9
Child Mental Health and Risk Behaviour Over Time

Kathleen Ares, Lisa M. Kuhns, Nisha Dogra, and Niranjan Karnik

Defining risk

In the US, more children aged 1–14 die annually from preventable injury than from all childhood diseases combined (Kennedy & Lipsitt, 1998). However, mortality is only a small percentage of the results accounted for by childhood risk-taking behaviours. For every one child who dies from injury in the US, 42 more are hospitalized and over 1,000 visit the emergency room. Similar trends are documented in the UK, where accidental injury is one of the major causes of death in children over the age of one. Accidents cause more deaths than illnesses such as leukaemia or meningitis (Anderson & Moxgam, 2009). These alarming statistics have led researchers to question how children are exposed to such environments that promote injury and how the predisposition to such risk-taking behaviours develops.

Risk-taking behaviour is defined here as an individual's decision to take chances with the potential for negative consequences (Eaton et al., 2012). Despite the deleterious effects such a decision could result in, one's disposition to such choices does not calculate the seriousness of the actions. Certain risky behaviours such as drug use, criminal activity, unprotected sexual behaviour, and self-harm can be viewed as 'thrill seeking', meaning that individuals see few aversive results from their behaviour owing to their concentration on the perfunctory excitement of the action. While risk-taking behaviour does not always lead to injury, it increases the probability of exposure to aversive environments and hazardous situations. It has been noted that individuals who are inclined to participate in risky behaviours recognize the danger in their actions but deliberately minimize the outcomes and refuse to take the necessary precautions (Arnett, 1992).

In 2011, the Centers for Diseases Control and Prevention conducted a national study of students in grades 9–12 in high schools using the Youth Risk Behavior Survey (YRBS) to gain a better understanding of national trends, gender differences, and racial/ethnic comparisons (CDC, 2011). The study examined six types of health-risk behaviours that contribute to the leading causes of death and illness among youth: alcohol and drug use, tobacco use, risky sexual behaviours, youth violence, unhealthy eating, and inadequate physical activity.

Substance Use. While the percentage of high school students who reported current alcohol use has decreased since 1991, still almost 40% of national high school students report that they had had at least one drink of alcohol on at least one day during the 30 days before the sample. Binge drinking emerged as a concerning statistic among high school students, with 21.9% of students reporting drinking five or more drinks in a row on at least one day prior to the survey. Within this sample, males in the twelfth grade reported the highest prevalence, with occurrence decreasing by school year. Interestingly, the opposite trend was observed in the percentage of 9–12th graders who reported ever using marijuana. Since 1991, the number of teens experimenting with cannabis use has increased almost 10%.

Developmental psychology provides insight on the initial risk factors for substance use disorder (SUDs) that may exist from early childhood. One developmental factor that is postulated to play a role in the pathway is the central concept of disinhibited or externalizing behaviours. Concurrently, emotional regulation associated with internalizing symptomatology may also serve as a potential road to the development of this certain psychopathology (Zeman, Shipman, & Suveg, 2002). In infancy, behavioural disinhibition (i.e., impulsivity) is believed to be the initial precursor for the pathway to risk formation. This temperament usually reflects an inability to inhibit socially undesirable or restricted action, and is typically followed by acting out behaviours, such as aggression and conduct problems. A combination of behavioural dysregulation, high-risk environment, and negative social relationships culminates in the progression of symptoms to include harmful substances (Tarter, 2002). In support of an internalizing pathway to SUDs, children as young as 2 to 5 years of age who presented with internalizing symptoms were identified later in life as having substance use problems in early adolescence (Zucker, Chermack, & Curran, 2000). The internalized developmental risk pathway is expected to develop cumulatively. That is, internalizing symptoms that develop at birth may continue to progress into adolescence, at which time they contribute to poor social functioning, positive expectancies and coping uses of substances, and moderate-to-heavy substance use (Hussong et al., 2011).

Another interesting finding in the pathway of substance use is the *stepping stone* theory. This effect describes how using one harmful drug increases the risk of more varieties and increased frequency. Pedersen's longitudinal study 'Youth, Lifestyle, and Health' (Brunswick & Messeri, 1986) notes that early exposure to cigarette smoking is strongly correlated with the use of illicit drugs in adulthood. Moreover, it is also a predisposition to later development of alcohol problems, use of cannabis, and other illicit drugs.

Sexual Risk Behaviour. Risky sexual behaviour was measured in multiple facets with high school students: those who had sexual intercourse for the first time before the age of 13, those who had had sexual intercourse with four or more persons during their life, those who drank alcohol or used drugs before their last intercourse, and those who did not use any method to prevent pregnancy. The Youth Risk survey reported a decreasing trend in the number of students who had sexual intercourse for their first time before the age of 13, from 10.2% of students in 1991 to 6.2% in 2011. Furthermore, it was found that nationwide high school males reported more sexual partners than females, but were also more likely to use a method of contraception than females. Among the 33.7% of high school students who were currently sexually active, in 2011, 22.1% drank alcohol or used drugs before their last sexual intercourse. This sexual risk-taking behaviour was heightened for males more so than females. These trends shed light on patterns of risk behaviour and how gender, age, and development may influence these behaviours.

While sexuality is considered a normative aspect of adolescent development, sexual risk continues to be an important source of preventable youth morbidity. Sexual risk behaviour places adolescents at an increased risk for HIV infection, sexually transmitted diseases (STDs), and unintended pregnancy. Important indicators of risk include age at first intercourse, frequency of sexual intercourse, frequency of condom use, and number of partners. Individual-level factors such as gender and age are related to risk. For example, sexual activity increases each year during the adolescent period, as parental monitoring decreases and young people begin to assert independent decision-making. With regard to gender, boys are more likely to take sexual risks than girls, including a greater number of partners and more frequent use of alcohol or drugs before intercourse.

Co-morbid conditions are also strongly related to sexual risk. Individuals with a history of childhood sexual abuse, depression, alcohol, and drug abuse, or a lack of connection to trusted adults and family have an increased likelihood of engaging in sexual risk-taking behaviours. In addition, sexual risk behaviour is associated with other academic and social problem behaviours such as delinquency, truancy, and repeating a grade. The association of these problem behaviours with sexual risk supports Problem Behavior Theory, which suggests the clustering together of problem behaviour (Jessor & Jessor, 1977). This clustering may be explained by personality characteristics, such as a predominance of sensation-seeking or impulsivity in some youths.

In addition to individual-level factors, pathways to risky sexual behaviours may also be influenced by environmental domains such as peers and family. Peer relations and perspectives play an influential role in sexual risk behaviour among the youth because peers confer support and both model and reinforce behaviour particularly as they become an important reference group, shifting away from the family. Two specific peer-related pathways include the influence model and selection model. Adolescents may adopt peer values and behaviours to become more similar to them in hopes of acceptance through the influence model. Through the selection model, peers select their friends based on common interests and behaviours. Both pathways have strong influences on peer affiliation and may contribute to risk behaviour via modelling or reinforcement through perceived risky peer norms or affiliation with risk-taking peers.

During adolescence peers represent the leading source of information for other teens on topics such as substance use, social norms, and sexual activity. Adolescents' attitudes toward sexual activity and understanding of sexual norms are largely based on the perception of their peers regarding the subject. When adolescents perceive their peer group to be sexually active, the risk that they engage in sexual activity is six times as great (Potard, Courtois, & Rusch, 2008). A difference in gender was also noted to influence the way teens feel about emotions regarding sex. Boys were determined to think more frequently than girls that their friends do not feel that one must be in love to have sexual relations. Owing to this peer perception, they are twice as likely to have sex when they perceive their peers to favour sexual relations without feelings of intimacy (Potard et al., 2008).

In addition to peers, family influences, particularly parenting behaviour, is an important influence on youthful sexual behaviour. For example, mother-child communication about sex and the availability of condoms at school were related to a decrease in the frequency of intercourse while positive self-attitudes about risk-taking, lack of parental monitoring, conceived peer norms, and male dominance were positively associated with girls' sexual risk-taking behaviour. Parental monitoring and supervision have been found to significantly decrease teen sexual risk-taking by lessoning the opportunity of youths to become involved in sexual activity and other risk behaviours. Families who are available and supportive, as well as connected to their teens and with low levels of relational hostility, are at decreased risk for adolescent sexual risk-taking (Donenberg & Pao, 2005). In addition, culture plays an influential role in mitigating the likelihood of adolescent sexual involvement. In particular, teens who identified as being solely belonging to the Indian culture were found to have lower rates of substance use when compared to their Caucasian peers (Dogra, Svirydzenka, Dugard, Singh, & Vostanis, 2013). This may suggest that cultural identification and community uniformity may influence adolescent risk-taking. Having discussions with adolescents about the importance of contraceptives and positive social relationships are important to the prevention and education about communicable diseases.

Criminality/Violence. Nationwide in 2011, 16.6% of students responded positively to carrying a weapon (gun, knife, or club) in the 30 days prior to the survey. Over 30% of nationwide high school students indicated that they had been in a physical fight one or more times in the previous year. These physical altercations do not include the prevalence of bullying, which is currently a widespread epidemic. In 2011, 20% of high school students reported being bullied on school property, and 16% stated that they had received the bullying electronically within the past 12 months (CDC, 2011). Victims of this type of abuse are at increased risk of academic problems, violence later in life, and substance use.

Both genetic and environmental factors have been attributed as causal factors in the specific pathways formulated to lead to the development of antisocial behaviours and criminality. Gender, low socio-economic status, poor parental interaction, parental alcoholism, and neighbourhood crime are all factors influencing the development of risk behaviour. An interactional style termed 'ill-tempered' was proposed by Caspi et al. (1990) to explain how a combined effect of all these risk factors from childhood persists through adolescence to result in antisocial behaviour. It was theorized that this predisposition is a result of neuropsychological deficits and criminological environments that inadvertently reward aggressive behaviour (Compas et al., 1995). This type of negative thinking, which becomes most salient during periods of transition, results in individuals relying on specific environments that support their faulty belief. In turn, this perpetuates their cycle of antisocial behaviour and irrational beliefs.

In a 1988 survey reporting perception of causes of violent behaviour, 53% of the sample implicated lack of parental discipline to be the leading factor. Smith and Stern (1997) went on to further examine the role of parenting on developing delinquency and concluded:

> We know that children who grow up in homes characterized by lack of warmth and support, whose parents lack behavior management skills, and whose lives are characterized by conflict or maltreatment will more likely be delinquent, whereas a supportive family can protect children even in a very hostile and damaging external environment. Parental monitoring or supervision is the aspect of family management that is most consistently related to delinquency.

Other family constructs have also been found to influence the development of criminality. Having parents and siblings who engage in criminal activity or display antisocial behaviours influences the way in which one views these actions, and beliefs about socially acceptable lifestyles. Other familial aspects, large family size, parental conflict and disrupted families, young parental age, and poor child-rearing methods, all contribute to the emergence of antisocial behaviours in youth (Farrington et al., 1998).

Neuroimaging research, being conducted at the Mind Research Network in Albuquerque, New Mexico, examining recidivism in male offenders, has determined that those with decreased activation in the anterior cingulate cortex, the brain region associated with error processing, were more likely to reoffend. Decreased activity in this area of the brain results in disruptive problems, ranging from impulsivity to distractibility and conflict- or excitement-seeking tendencies (Mind Research Network, 2012). These individuals may display symptoms similar to those with an Attention Deficit Hyperactivity Disorder diagnosis, and are less likely to learn from experience and mistakes. Additionally, structural techniques, such as brain imaging and functional approaches such as Magnetic Resonance Imaging (MRI) and Computed Tomography (CT) scans, have identified correlates between neuronal activity and antisocial behaviours. CT scans have implicated temporal lobe abnormalities in sex offenders, affecting their ability to make socially appropriate decisions and moral judgement. However, MRI studies have provided evidence that men with antisocial personality disorder have approximately 11% less prefrontal grey matter when compared to control participants (Bassarath, 2001). This deficit is the first to provide structural evidence implicating the brain region in the low arousal, poor fear condition, lack of conscience, and decision-making problems characterizing individuals with antisocial personality disorder. Findings from other research into PET scans and SPECT analysis suggest that a biological underpinning to violence and maladaptive behaviour exists. One such study (Raine et al., 1994) found that violent offenders showed significantly reduced glucose metabolism in their prefrontal cortex, resulting in a greater predisposition to violence. SPECT studies suggest that these behaviours may be due to hypoperfusion, or the brain's inability to manage increased blood flow, in the frontal lobes of individuals with antisocial personality disorder, in addition to subjects who have committed violent offences (Kuruofülu et al., 1996).

Normative development/exploration of world

Throughout child development, infants are disposed and expected to explore their environment and test the limits of their skills, albeit with boundaries placed by parents to manage the risk involved in the exploration. Adolescents act in much the same fashion, by pushing their boundaries and acting out of impulse. Recent neuroimaging studies suggest possible biological answers to explain why adolescents are so likely to partake in risk-taking behaviours. One explanation for teens' susceptibility to peer pressure and risky behaviours during puberty may be due to the increased volume of testosterone and decreased medial oribitofrontal cortex (OFC) volume found during the decision-making process (Peper, Koolschijn, & Crone, 2013). Increased levels of testosterone are associated with increased impulsivity and riskier decision-making, while decreased OFC volume has been implicated in the inability to effectively regulate aggression and impulsivity. The OFC is the region of the brain responsible for weighing options and assessing decisions. Research has found that this region of the brain does not fully develop until the age of 25, thus presenting one possible explanation for deficits in adolescent problem-solving. The positive trend in risk-taking between childhood and adolescence has also been connected to increases in sensation-seeking behaviours that are linked to changes in activity patterns of the neurotransmitter, dopamine, around the time of puberty (Laucht et al., 2007). Dopamine, a chemical in the brain, is associated with the desire for risk-taking behaviour as a result of the neural pathways related to intrinsic reward and pleasure centers. This vulnerability to risk-taking and reward-seeking behaviour may be further enhanced by interactions with peers. Steinberg (2007) found that the number of risks teens took in a video driving game more than doubled in the presence of their peers, compared to when they engaged in the same game alone. This is also true for driving, where adolescent drivers with passengers of similar ages are at increased risk of accidents. The presence of peers increased risk-taking by 50% in college undergraduates who also participated in the study, but it did not influence the number of risks older adults took. A possible biological explanation for the decrease in risk-taking through maturity suggests that higher level cognition develops, including abstract reasoning and deliberative action, in the late 20s. The maturation of this cognitive control system is consistent with evidence that structural and functional changes occur in the prefrontal cortex, which plays a substantial role in self-regulation. Maturation of neural connections between the prefrontal cortex and the limbic system permits the better coordination of emotion and cognition. These changes allow an individual to suppress impulsive sensation-seeking behaviour and resist peer influence on decision-making. Other research endeavours implicate risky behaviour in adolescence to have an association with different neuronal trajectories of reward systems between late childhood through adolescence (Bjork et al., 2007; Burnett et al., 2010; Van Leijenhorst et al., 2010). Limited but salient research has found that changes in the dopaminergic system, or in reward processing, take place in late adolescence that alter reward sensitivity, and, in turn, diminish reward-seeking.

In addition to understanding the biological substrates and evidentiary support as to why adolescents are disposed to make such risky decisions, it is also important to consider how these behaviours can be advantageous. A recent study by Burnett and Blakemore (2010) found that teens took risks because they liked the *thrill* of risk-taking as opposed to not being able to understand the consequences of their behaviour. Positive risk-taking has been found to promote healthy neurological development as well as independence and identity formation. In males, risk-taking may also serve as a dominance display through 'sexual selection'. From a developmental perspective, females are more inclined to be attracted to males who have higher chances of surviving and reproducing. Likewise, males are more prone to risky behaviours to attract females. With respect to dominance theory, adolescent males are suggested to engage in risk behaviours in order to state their supremacy and maintain social dominance (Pellegrini, 2003).

Development of adolescent cognition and emotions related to risk. Adolescence is a transition time marked by impulsive decision-making and emotional lability. Some may question why adolescents are so prone to making faulty decisions that often lead to physical injury, criminal involvement, or relational turmoil. The answer is rooted in the development of cognitive and psychological control. Adolescents have yet to develop a sense of maturity that allows them to observe their actions in perspective. This includes thinking about how another person would think or feel, imagining performing an action, and visualizing alternative probabilities. The brain regions responsible for perspective have been found also to be those that undergo the most significant development during adolescence. Viewing potential actions in perspective plays an integral role in adolescent decision-making, which includes goal-setting, evaluation of options, and implementation of weighed risks. Adolescents develop the ability to make competent decisions over time as their metacognition develops. They are then more able to use insight into the factors that affect the quality of decision-making to make sound choices. Without this awareness of their own cognitive immaturity, adolescents resort to reward-seeking behaviours that satisfy immediate gratification but may have serious implication in the long term. As their egocentrism develops, teens believe they are invulnerable to the consequences of dangerous or risky behaviour, rendering them 'invincible' (Wickman, Anderson, & Greenberg, 2008). They do not foresee the dangers of these decisions as possible side effects and will minimize the risks involved.

Just as youngsters must learn how to control their cognitions, they must also develop ways of regulating the intense emotions that they experience during this time. Emotional self-efficacy refers to the ability to manage emotions internally rather than by acting out, such as tantrums in childhood. During adolescence, self-efficacy is defined by the ability to identify, understand, and cope with emotions in a healthy manner. Some researches have argued that owing to parallel cognitive development, adolescents develop executive control that assists in the management of emotions and regulation of negative states. Teens also learn how to navigate their emotions among alternating environments that place different demands on youth. While emotional regulation has been tied to early attachment figures, adolescents spent more time at school and with peers than with their caretakers. They are exposed to 'peer contagion' influences such as social rejection, peer pressure, and a myriad of experiences that require emotional maturity to withstand. Without the ability to develop these self-efficacy skills, adolescents often fall victim to these teenage plights and increase their risk of drug use, delinquency, and violence in late adolescence (Dishion & Tipsord, 2011).

Etiological factors that increase risky behaviours

Familial Environment. Youths' risk-taking behaviour manifests as a culmination of biological, cultural, and environmental conflicts. In addition to a child's individual disposition, parental behaviour and home environment should also be examined in order to gain a comprehensive understanding of risky behaviours. In order to assess family dynamics' influence on adolescent risk-taking behaviour, Blum et al. (2000) conducted a longitudinal study on a national representation of 7th to 12th graders. Results showed that in terms of factors related to cigarette smoking, alcohol consumption, weapon-related violence, and sexual behaviour, students from single parent families were significantly more at risk than peers from dual parent households. Moreover, family income had a positive effect on alcohol use in high school students and an inverse relationship with weapon-related violence. Measures of familial hindrance, single parent households, and low familial socio-economic status were implicated with youth cannabis use in two youth studies in Australia. However, in Blum's US study, familial characteristics were important determinants of marijuana use only among young men (Blum et al., 2000).

Some studies have also linked parental alcohol and substance use to adolescent initiation of use. Dishion et al. (1998) demonstrated that parental drug use had an influencing relationship on adolescent drug experimentation, known as the social interactional theory. According to this theory, it is believed that teens' risky decision-making is due to poor parental monitoring as a result of parental drug use. In turn, children aligned themselves with peer drug use and delinquency, leading to poor decision-making skills and peer pressure. Teens with alcoholic parents are also subject to negative models of drinking and access to illegal substance use. This socialization mechanism was found to significantly increase substance use in adolescents owing to a reduction in parental monitoring, and increases in environmental stress and negative affect (Chassin et al., 1993). Parental monitoring has also been linked to adolescent sexual risk-taking as well. Donnenberg et al. (2002) evaluated the link between parental permissiveness and sexual activity, and found that when parental permissiveness was high, girls demonstrated increased sexual risk-taking, decreased use of contraceptives, and increased use of drugs and alcohol before having sex.

Community Influences. Bronfenbrenner (1992) proposed a longstanding theoretical framework for better understanding how an individual's community and environmental context influence their adjustment. Community characteristics, such as a child's school, peer influence, and geographical location, add unique contributing factors to their decision-making process and reward appraisal. In 1990, Jencks and Mayer provided insight into the mediating processes responsible for these links, in this case between neighbourhood poverty and children's health. Community-based research demonstrated that the more resources (e.g., activities for youth, adults as role models) the community is perceived to have, the lower the levels of risky behaviour in the community. In one larger-scale (Mayer & Jencks, 1989) study examining how neighbourhoods affect behaviour, four main theories were developed to demonstrate the causal relationship of community on behaviour. The first theory, or 'contagion model', suggests that disadvantaged neighbours act as a hindrance to their community. If neighbourhood children are exposed to their neighbours, peers, and even siblings committing delinquent activity or impulsivity in their community, they will be influenced towards accepting these behaviours as well. In contrast, individuals who are typically in higher socio-economic status (SES) neighbourhoods follow the 'social control' model, in which rule-following adults are seen as enforcers who maintain peace and promote sound decisions. In the second theory, advantaged neighbours are a disadvantage, which illustrates the 'relative deprivation' model, in that lower SES neighbours resent the affluence displayed in the neighbourhood and feel the need to create a deviant subculture. For example, students from higher SES neighbourhoods may find schoolwork easier than their peers from less affluent areas owing to the availability of more resources and additional help at home. As a result, those students who do not have these privileges are more likely to rank lower in class, devote less dedication to their schoolwork, and are more likely to act up. The third model suggests that certain individuals disregard their neighbourhood entirely and can either align themselves with perceptions similar to their own or seek out negative influence. Finally, the last theory directly implicates neighbourhoods in the development of an individual's decision-making skills. Bronfenbrenner refers to the environment that one lives in as one's microsystem. The final theory assumes that individuals have preconceived notions about their microsystem, which directly influence possible delinquency despite the characteristics of those living in the area. The belief that low SES schools have less dedicated teachers and worse learning environments directly affects a student's willingness to learn and enrolment in class. The interaction between a child's microsystems, also referred to as their *Mesosystem* by Bronfenbrenner, influences the way a child views their role in their community and their behaviours in each of their environments.

Individual child characteristic. Gender studies have compared aspects of gender and sex characteristics to gain a better understanding of how these factors may attribute to differences in risk-taking behaviour. It was uniformly recorded that young boys experience two to four times as many injuries as girls of the same age (Morrongiello & Rennie, 1998). By the age of three, boys are at higher risk of injury, and this continues on a similar trajectory throughout childhood. This pattern was attributed to males' assumption that they are impermeable to injury, their lower severity ratings of potential injury, and attribution of injury to bad luck (Morrongiello & Dawber, 1998). In addition, observational studies found that as toddlers, boys were granted more independence from their parents and were provided less direct supervision. They were allowed to roam further than girls of the same age, and were granted more opportunities to play alone (Fagot, 1978). These factors influence and potentially yield more chances to engage in risk-taking behaviours without the feedback from parents and fear of parental chastisement.

A child's individual temperament also plays a determining role in his or her disposition to take chances. Research into children who are more prone to injury and risky behaviours has determined that those with an impulsive temperament and externalizing behavioural problems are more likely to engage in these decision-making situations with injurious consequences. Owing to a child's inability to delay gratification, they make impulsive decisions that satisfy their fleeting need (Kennedy & Lipsitt, 1998). In an attempt to examine this in a controlled setting, Conner (2012) compared impulsive children with those who exemplified reflective cognitive styles on the Matching Familiar Figures task. Reflective children were found to be more thoughtful in their responses and scanned alternative stimuli more frequently than impulsive children, which was also evident in their risk-taking.

Individual personality characteristics in youth may also account for their disposition towards riskier behaviours, such as gambling. In a study of over 1,200 adolescent high school students, personality traits related to excitability, conformity, self-discipline, and cheerfulness significantly differed in students with high-risk gambling addictions. These personality characteristics were reflected in behaviours of impulsivity, distractibility, over-activity, self-indulgence, and difficulty conforming to group norms. These individuals also reported higher overall risk-taking tendencies, being socially disinhibited (i.e., drinking and substance use), adventure seekers, and easily bored with routine. These results indicate that individual personality characteristics are important to consider when examining the profile of a risky adolescent.

Developmentally, adolescents have been deemed the optimal manifestation of Zuckerman's (1979) 'sensation seeking' personality dimension. In adolescents, teens are thought to have consolidated Piaget's formal operation stage by the age of 16. It is during this cognitive development stage that adolescents develop skills such as logical thought, reasoning, and problem-solving. However, an abundance of research has indicated that deficiencies in the adolescent cognitive development lead to the conception of adolescent egocentrism. Piaget theory describes egocentrism as 'a failure to differentiate between subject and object, a failure to understand clearly where the self ends and other begins' (Greening, Stoppelbein, Chandler, & Elkin, 2005). According to this view, egocentrism contributes to adolescents' belief that others are preoccupied with their behaviour and appearance. This flawed cognition results in the conviction that they are unique, and thus invulnerable to the consequences of reckless behaviour.

Exposure to Trauma. Adolescents exposed to trauma report a myriad of psychological and physical reactions. Through direct or indirect exposure to violence, such as being a victim of physical or sexual abuse or learning about the untimely death of a loved one, adolescents may react to trauma by use of anger or self-preservation. Statistically, it has been determined that males are more likely to experience events such as natural disasters, accidents, or wartime action, whereas females are inclined to be victims of assault and sexual abuse (Ben-Zur & Zeidner, 2012). Witnessing or being a victim of trauma affects one's ability to self-regulate and commonly results in both internalizing (i.e., self-mutilation and suicidality) and externalizing (i.e., delinquency and risk-taking) conduct behaviours.

Sexual trauma, predominantly women victims, has been well documented to be a stimulus in the development of negative consequences such as risky sexual behaviour. Hypersexuality in victims of sexual abuse has resulted in an increased number of unwanted pregnancies and sexual partners, and greater transmission of STDs (Mullen, Martin, Anderson, Romans, & Herbison, 1996). Sexual trauma victims are also more likely to make risky decisions without use of contraceptives and consume alcohol before sexual activity. In addition, sexual trauma has been acknowledged to yield a larger number of women who enter into prostitution as compared to women who are not victims. One possible explanation for increased risk behaviour in sexual trauma survivors is the development of mental illness and use of substances as a coping mechanism (Senn, Carey, & Vanable, 2008). Owing to their poor self-esteem and decreased feeling of self-worth, these individuals use substances to temporarily alleviate their emotional distress and give themselves temporary respite from the adverse psychological effects.

Communal trauma, although possibly not directly affecting one's well-being, also serves as a catalyst to risk-taking behaviours and choices. Communal trauma may include disasters from natural causes (i.e., floods and tornadoes), human-caused (i.e., war violence and terrorism) or severe damage to communal property. Such disasters lead to grave loss, psychological upheaval, and risk-taking behaviours posing a threat to one's life. In an extensive review conducted by Norris et al. (2002), risky behaviours such as alcohol use, cigarette smoking, and substance abuse significantly increased following the exposure to communal trauma. The amount of time following a traumatic event is also an important quantitative factor to consider when assessing risk behaviour. After 9/11, Manhattan residents reported significant increases in substance use five to eight weeks after the terrorist attacks (Vlahov et al., 2006). Two years after the attacks, New York City residents continued to report significant increases in alcohol consumption as compared with that before the event. In addition, sexual risk-taking was also assessed in comparison to before the 9/11 attacks, and results showed that unprotected sexual acts increased after the communal trauma (Chiasson et al., 2005).

War and other community-wide disasters can have devastating effects on children because of effects on parents, unmet survival needs, and interference with developmental tasks. Many of the symptoms displayed by youth post-war are believed to be due to a co-occurrence of post-traumatic stress disorder (PTSD). Regardless, adolescents who experience war-related trauma are at risk for a range of negative outcomes, including internalizing (PTSD, other anxiety disorders, depression) and externalizing (e.g. risk-taking) problems. In examining the post-war effects on risky sexual behaviour in Uganda (Strom, 2012), transactional sex, sexual predation, multiple partners, early marriages, and forced marriage resulted from economic destruction and the vulnerability of effected populations. Dishonour through transactional sex and incest were found to directly result from exposure to conflict. High sexual behaviour was associated with the volume of people in camps, where unemployment and indolence were the norm.

Resiliency

Despite adolescents' exposure and involvement in risk behaviours that directly impact their social, emotional, and physical well-being, certain resiliency factors exist that may provide a positive influence. Resilient factors are people, circumstances, or environments that promote recovery from adversary (Fergus & Zimmerman, 2005). In children, resiliency has been referred to as the capacity of those who are exposed to identifiable risk factors to overcome those risks and avoid negative outcomes such as delinquency and behavioural problems, psychological maladjustment, academic difficulties, and physical complications (Rak & Patterson, 1996). While many youths are exposed to negative and debilitating situations, the majority of them have the capability to prevail. Investigating the resiliency phenomenon, Werner and colleagues examined 200 high-risk children in a longitudinal study over the course of 32 years. Despite poverty, parental stress, family discord, divorce, parental alcoholism, and mental illness, one out of every three children overcame the adverse conditions and developed into well-adjusted adults (Werner, 1992).

Individuals at risk, who have surrounded themselves with supportive family members and positive peers, have been found to experience better longitudinal outcomes then those with no resiliency factors. Of most importance, those with prosocial relationships within their family or peer network have described feelings of being cared for, acknowledged, trusted, and empowered, resulting in more positive outcomes. In addition, families that have clearly stated expectations for their children and exert pressure to achieve these goals were found to develop fewer risk-taking behaviours than those families with no expectations (Guerra & Bradshaw, 2008). Studies have also proposed that familial protective factors such as frequently shared activities with parents, ability to discuss problems, and the consistent presence of a parent during arrival from school, and at mealtimes and bedtimes, are associated with lower levels of youth violence and risk behaviours (Resnick et al., 2004). However, how does familial resiliency impact the pressure an adolescent feels from their peers? According to the National Longitudinal Study of Adolescent Health (2010), family-resilience, in the absence of peer/community resilience, was inadequate to prevent participation in risky behaviours, such as smoking, drinking, and using drugs. Lack of academic success can lead to poor self-esteem, behavioural problems, and marginalization, which can lead to risky behaviours. As Mortimore (1995) identified, where young people are 'committed' to the school through their peers and staff, they do better academically. Where schools are unsupportive with poor relationships, there are problems with absenteeism and depression for staff and students. Having a supportive adult outside a dysfunctional family, such as a teacher, can also be a significant factor in helping children avoid risk-taking trajectories.

Outside the family influence, involvement in some form of extracurricular activity has been found to increase self-esteem in youth, thus having an inverse relationship to the likelihood of becoming involved in risky activities. Research indicates that physical activity yields a psychological benefit, including improvement in depressed mood, decrease in anxiety and stress, and possibly protection against suicidality (Taliaferro et al., 2008). Although there are mixed findings on the subject, it has been noted that sports participation protected against suicidal behaviour in both men and women compared to non-participants, who were between 1.5 and 2.5 times more likely to report suicidal behaviour depending on their gender. In addition, females who participate in sports are less likely to be involved in risky sexual behaviour and half as likely to become pregnant in comparison to girls who do not participate in sports (Brown & Blanton, 2002). Youth may also receive psychosocial advantages from sports involvement, as the cohesive nature of sports promotes team building and trust.

Early Intervention Programmes. Early interventions are programmes established for individuals to enrol in at an early age in an attempt to prevent risk behaviours that may emerge in later years. In the primary years of life, such skills develop that are essential to cognitive, emotional, and social growth. In the US, there is an increasing number of children being born into disadvantaged families who lack the resources and support to allow their children to thrive (Hart & Risley, 2003). Without this kind of help, children are susceptible to poorer academic performance, increased risk-taking, and predisposition to criminality. The quality of parenting is an essential factor to examine when assessing individuals for early intervention programmes. Available research suggests that the influence on disadvantaged youth is not primarily due to family income or parental education, but rather based on the quality of support and parenting that they receive.

Early intervention programmes, designed to promote educational readiness for unprivileged youth, have been found to increase students' non-cognitive skills, which are related to success later in life. Heckman (2008) speculates that early intervention programmes enrich the environments of disadvantaged children, resulting in higher IQ scores. Early intervention programmes have been found to improve both cognitive and personality factors (i.e., motivation) in low-income families. These programmes have found that non-cognitive skills such as personality, drive, and willingness to learn are the essential pathway to improvement (Heckman et al., 2008). Two specific programmes, the Perry Preschool Program and the Abecedarian Program, yielded significant positive effects on school achievement, job performance, social behaviours, and cognitive performance (Campbell, Ramey, Pungello, Sparling, & Miller-Johnson, 2002). Such programmes as these are built on the foundation that learning occurs early in life, and interventions at a young age will lead to early mastery of a range of cognitive, social, and emotional attributes. This in turn will allow for easier and more efficient learning at later ages with an inherent self-reinforcing motivation to learn more.

Summary and lessons for clinical practice

Owing to the trends in adolescent risk-taking behaviour over the past ten years, it is important to be informed about the causes and pathways that result in these types of behaviours. While some believe that there is a biological underpinning to sensation-seeking behaviour, and that it is caused by neuronal volume and reward systems, others attribute the predisposition to cognitive and emotional development during adolescence. The community and familial influences that a child is exposed to also play a vital role in their development of self-esteem as well as moral judgement. Well connected families marked by high levels of parental monitoring and involvement serve as protective factors for sexual and physical risk behaviours. In addition, involvement in extracurricular activities and early age intervention programmes are key to mitigating the deleterious effects of risk.

Clinicians need to be mindful of these shifts and changes in children's and adolescents' behavioural patterns as they plan interventions. There are some basic lessons that can be distilled from what we have reviewed in this chapter. First, early assessment and intervention is always a good idea. Many practitioners are used to taking a 'wait and see' approach to problems which they ascertain as lower acuity. Behaviours including drugs, alcohol, and sexual risk are sometimes seen as experimental phases through which children and adolescents will pass. Nevertheless, a 'wait and see' approach risks much, and it may be better to refer individuals for an assessment with a specialist. The referral serves two purposes. It will enable a more in-depth evaluation and assessment than the front-line practitioner can reasonably make and may uncover other elements or deeper issues meriting treatment. Next, in the event that the specialist determines that there is no major concern, the child and family now have a connection in the event that the behaviours or the situation worsen. Either pathway is a best practices scenario that front-line clinicians need to promote and support by making early referrals. Second, in any of the scenarios we have outlined, early interventions with the child and family hold much more promise for better outcomes than later interventions. Finally, the overwhelming evidence is that the involvement and support of families is essential for the mitigation of risk behaviour and promotion of resilience in children and adolescents. Clinicians need to gradually learn the basic technique of good parenting practices so that we can help families function better and increase the likelihood of good outcomes for all children.

References

Anderson, R., & Moxham, T. (2009). *Preventing Unintentional Injuries in Children: Review – Final Report. Systematic Review to Provide an Overview of Published Economic Evaluation of Relevant Legislation, Regulations, Standards, and/or Their Enforcement and Promotion by Mass Media*. Exeter: Peninsula Technology Assessment Group, Peninsula Medical School, Universities of Exeter and Plymouth. Report commissioned by NICE Centre for Public Health Excellence.

Arnett, J. (1992). Reckless behavior in adolescence: a developmental perspective. *Developmental Review, 12*(4), 339–373.

Bassarath, L. (2001). Neuroimaging studies of antisocial behaviour. *Canadian Journal of Psychiatry, 46*(8), 728.

Ben-Zur, H., & Zeidner, M. (2012). Gender differences in loss of psychological resources following experimentally-induced vicarious stress. *Anxiety, Stress & Coping, 25*(4), 457–475.

Bjork, J.M., Smith, A.R., Danube, C.L., & Hommer, D.W. (2007). Developmental differences in posterior mesofrontal cortex recruitment by risky rewards. *The Journal of Neuroscience, 27*(18), 4839–4849.

Blum, R.W., Beuhring, T., Shew, M.L., Bearinger, L.H., Sieving, R.E., & Resnick, M.D. (2000). The effects of race/ethnicity, income, and family structure on adolescent risk behaviors. *American Journal of Public Health, 90*(12), 1879.

Bronfenbrenner, U. (1992). *Ecological Systems Theory*. London: Jessica Kingsley Publishers.

Brown, D., & Blanton, C. (2002). Physical activity, sports participation, and suicidal behavior among college students. *Medicine & Science in Sports & Exercise, 34*(7), 1087–1096.

Brunswick, A.F., & Messeri, P. (1986). Drugs, lifestyle, and health: a longitudinal study of urban black youth. *American Journal of Public Health, 76*(1), 52–57.

Burnett, S., Bault, N., Coricelli, G., & Blakemore, S.J. (2010). Adolescents' heightened risk-seeking in a probabilistic gambling task. *Cognitive Development, 25*(2), 183–196.

Burnett, S., & Blakemore, S. (2010, March 25). Teenagers programmed to take risks. *Science Daily*. Retrieved 4 October 2013, from http://www.sciencedaily.com.

Campbell, F.A., Ramey, C.T., Pungello, E., Sparling, J., & Miller-Johnson, S. (2002). Early childhood education: young adult outcomes from the Abecedarian Project. *Applied Developmental Science, 6*(1), 42–57.

Caspi, A., Elder, G., & Herbener, E. (1990). Childhood personality and the prediction of life-course patterns. In: L. Robins & M. Rutter (eds), *Straight and Devious Pathways from Childhood to Adult life*, New York: Cambridge University Press.

Centers for Disease Control and Prevention (CDC) (2011). *Youth Risk Behavior Surveillance – United States, 2011*. Atlanta: CDC. http://www.cdc.gov/mmwr/preview/mmwrhtml/ss6104a1.htm?s_cid=ss6104a1_whttp://www.cdc.gov/mmwr/preview/mmwrhtml/ss6104a1.htm?s_cid=ss6104a1_w (13 March 2011).

Chassin, L., Pillow, D.R., Curran, P.J., Molina, B.G., & Barrera, M.R. (1993). Relation of parental alcoholism to early adolescent substance use: a test of three mediating mechanisms. *Journal of Abnormal Psychology, 102*(1), 3–19.

Chiasson, M.A., Hirshfield, S., Koblin, B.A., & Remien, R.H. (2005). Increased high risk sexual behavior after September 11 in men who have sex with men: an internet survey. *Archives of Sexual Behavior, 34*(5), 527–535.

Chen, X., Unger, J.B., & Johnson, C.A. (1999). Is acculturation a risk factor for early smoking initiation among Chinese American minors? A comparative perspective. *Tobacco Control, 8*(4), 402–410.

Compas, B.E., Hinden, B.R., & Gerhardt, C.A. (1995). Adolescent development: pathways and processes of risk and resilience. *Annual Review of Psychology, 46*(1), 265–293.

Conner, E. (2012). *The Relative Effectiveness of Two Cognitive Intervention Approaches With Attention Deficit Disordered Children* (Doctoral Dissertation). Retrieved from ProQuest Dissertations and Theses. (Accession Order No. AAT 9929173)

Dishion, T.J., & McMahon, R.J. (1998). Parental monitoring and the prevention of child and adolescent problem behavior: a conceptual and empirical formulation. *Clinical Child and Family Psychology Review, 1*(1), 61–75.

Dishion, T.J., & Tipsord, J.M. (2011). Peer contagion in child and adolescent social and emotional development. *Annual Review of Psychology, 62*, 189.

Dogra, N.N., Svirydzenka, N.N., Dugard, P.P., Singh, S.P., & Vostanis, P. P. (2013). Characteristics and rates of mental health problems among Indian and White adolescents in two English cities. *British Journal of Psychiatry, 203*(1), 44–50.

Donenberg, G.R., & Pao, M. (2005). Youths and HIV/AIDS: psychiatry's role in a changing epidemic. *Journal of the American Academy of Child and Adolescent Psychiatry, 44*(8), 728–747.

Donenberg, G.R., Wilson, H.W., Emerson, E., & Bryant, F.B. (2002). Holding the line with a watchful eye: the impact of perceived parental permissiveness and parental monitoring on risky sexual behavior among adolescents in psychiatric care. *AIDS Education and Prevention: Official Publication of the International Society for AIDS Education, 14*(2), 138.

Eaton, D.K., Kann, L., Kinchen, S., Shanklin, S., Flint, K.H., Hawkins, J.,...& Wechsler, H. (2012). Youth risk behavior surveillance-United States, 2011. *Morbidity and Mortality Weekly Report: Surveillance Summaries, 61*(4), 1–162.

Fagot, B. (1978) The influence of sex of child on parental reaction to toddler children. *Child Development*, 53, 459–465.

Farrington, D.P., Tonry, M., Mark M., H (1998). Predictors, causes, and correlates of male youth violence. *Youth Violence, 24*, 421–475.

Fergus, S., & Zimmerman, M.A. (2005). Adolescent resilience: a framework for understanding healthy development in the face of risk. *Annual Review of Public Health, 26*, 399–419.

Greening, L., Stoppelbein, L., Chandler, C.C., & Elkin, T.D. (2005). Predictors of children's and adolescents' risk perception. *Journal of Pediatric Psychology, 30*(5), 425–435.

Guerra, N.G., & Bradshaw, C.P. (2008). Linking the prevention of problem behaviors and positive youth development: core competencies for positive youth development and risk prevention. *New Directions for Child and Adolescent Development, 122*, 1–17.
Hart, B., & Risley, T.R. (2003). The early catastrophe: the 30 million word gap by age 3. *American Educator, 27*(1), 4–9.
Heckman, J.J. (2008). Schools, skills, and synapses. *Economic Inquiry, 46*(3), 289–324.
Hussong, A.M., Jones, D.J., Stein, G.L., Baucom, D.H., & Boeding, S. (2011). An internalizing pathway to alcohol use and disorder. *Psychology of Addictive Behaviors, 25*(3), 390.
Jencks, C., & Mayer, S.E. (1990). The social consequences of growing up in a poor neighborhood. *Inner-city poverty in the United States, 111*, 111–186.
Jessor, R., & Jessor, S.L. (1977). *Problem Behavior and Psychosocial Development: A Longitudinal Study of Youth*. New York: Academic Press.
Kuruofülu, A.C., Arikan, Z., Vural, G., Karata, M., & Ara, M. (1996). Single photon emission computerised tomography in chronic alcoholism. Antisocial personality disorder may be associated with decreased frontal perfusion. *The British Journal of Psychiatry, 169*(3), 348–354.
Kennedy, C.M., & Lipsitt, L.P. (1998). Risk-taking in preschool children. *Journal of Pediatric Nursing, 13*(2), 77–84.
Mayer, S.E., & Jencks, C. (1989). Growing up in poor neighborhoods: how much does it matter. *Science, 243*(4897), 1441–1445.
Laucht, M., Becker, K., Blomeyer, D., & Schmidt, M.H. (2007). Novelty seeking involved in mediating the association between the dopamine D4 receptor gene exon III polymorphism and heavy drinking in male adolescents: results from a high-risk community sample. *Biological Psychiatry, 61*(1), 87–92.
Mortimore P (1995) The positive effects of schooling. In: Rutter, M. (ed.), *Psychosocial Disturbances in Young People: Challenges for Prevention*, pp. 333–365. Cambridge: Cambridge University Press.
Morrongiello, B.A., & Dawber, T. (1998). Toddlers' and mothers' behaviors in an injury-risk situation: implications for sex differences in childhood injuries. *Journal of Applied Developmental Psychology, 19*(4), 625–639.
Morrongiello, B.A., & Rennie, H. (1998). Why do boys engage in more risk taking than girls? The role of attributions, beliefs, and risk appraisals. *Journal of Pediatric Psychology, 23*(1), 33–43.
Mullen, P.E., Martin, J.L., Anderson, J.C., Romans, S.E., & Herbison, G.P. (1996). The long-term impact of the physical, emotional, and sexual abuse of children: a community study. *Child Abuse & Neglect, 20*(1), 7–21.
Norris, F.H., Friedman, M.J., Watson, P.J., Byrne, C.M., Diaz, E., & Kaniasty, K. (2002). 60,000 disaster victims speak: Part I.An empirical review of the empirical literature, 1981–2001. *Psychiatry: Interpersonal and Biological Processes, 65*(3), 207–239.
Pellegrini, A.D. (2003). Perceptions and functions of play and real fighting in early adolescence. *Child Development, 74*(5), 1522–1533.
Pellegrini, A.D. (2009). Research and policy on children's play. *Child Development Perspectives, 3*(2), 131–136.
Peper, J.S., Koolschijn, P.C.M., & Crone, E.A. (2013). Development of risk taking: contributions from adolescent testosterone and the orbito-frontal cortex. *Journal of Cognitive Neuroscience, 25*(12), 2141–2150.

Potard, C., Courtois, R., & Rusch, E. (2008). The influence of peers on risky sexual behaviour during adolescence. *European Journal of Contraception and Reproductive Healthcare, 13*(3), 264–270.

Rak, C.F., & Patterson, L.E. (1996). Promoting resilience in at-risk children. *Journal of Counseling & Development, 74*(4), 368–373.

Raine, A., Buchsbaum, M.S., Stanley, J., Lottenberg, S., Abel, L., & Stoddard, J. (1994). Selective reductions in prefrontal glucose metabolism in murderers. *Biological Psychiatry, 36*(6), 365–373.

Resnick, M.D., Ireland, M., & Borowsky, I. (2004). Youth violence perpetration: what protects? What predicts? Findings from the National Longitudinal Study of Adolescent Health. *Journal of Adolescent Health, 35(5),* 424–e1.

Senn, T.E., Carey, M.P., & Vanable, P.A. (2008). Childhood and adolescent sexual abuse and subsequent sexual risk behavior: evidence from controlled studies, methodological critique, and suggestions for research. *Clinical Psychology Review, 28*(5), 711–735.

Smith, C.A. & Stern, S.B. (1997). Delinquency and antisocial behavior: a review of family processes and intervention research. *Social Service Review, 71,* 382–420.

Steinberg, L. (2007) Risk-taking in adolescence: new perspectives from brain and behavioral science. *Current Directions in Psychological Science, 16,* 55–59.

Steinberg, L. (April 2007). *Current Directions in Psychological Science.* Laurence Steinberg, PhD, professor of psychology, Temple University, Philadelphia. Gardner and Steinberg (2005). *Developmental Psychology, 41,* 625–635.

Strom, T.Q., Leskela, J., James, L.M., Thuras, P.D., Voller, E., Weigel, R., & Holz, K. (2012). An exploratory examination of risk-taking behavior and PTSD symptom severity in a veteran sample. *Military Medicine, 177*(4), 390–396.

Taliaferro, L.A., Rienzo, B.A., Miller, M.D., Pigg, R.M., & Dodd, V.J. (2008). High school youth and suicide risk: exploring protection afforded through physical activity and sport participation. *Journal of School Health, 78*(10), 545–553.

Tarter, R.E. (2002). Etiology of adolescent substance abuse: a developmental perspective. *The American Journal on Addictions, 11*(3), 171–191.

Van Leijenhorst, L., Moor, B.G., Op de Macks, Z.A., Rombouts, S.A., Westenberg, P.M., & Crone, E.A. (2010). Adolescent risky decision-making: neurocognitive development of reward and control regions. *Neuroimage, 51*(1), 345–355.

Vlahov, D., Galea, S., Resnick, H., Ahern, J., Boscarino, J.A., Bucuvalas, M., Gold, J., & Kilpatrick, D. (2002). Increased use of cigarettes, alcohol, and marijuana among Manhattan, New York, residents after the September 11th terrorist attacks. *American Journal of Epidemiology, 155*(11), 988–996.

Werner, E.E. (1992). The children of Kauai: resiliency and recovery in adolescence and adulthood. *Journal of Adolescent Health, 13*(4), 262–268.

Wickman, M.E., Anderson, N.L.R., & Smith Greenberg, C. (2008). The adolescent perception of invincibility and its influence on teen acceptance of health promotion strategies. *Journal of Pediatric Nursing, 23*(6), 460–468.

Zeman, J., Shipman, K., & Suveg, C. (2002). Anger and sadness regulation: predictions to internalizing and externalizing symptoms in children. *Journal of Clinical Child and Adolescent Psychology, 31*(3), 393–398.

Zucker, R.A., Chermack, S.T., & Curran, G.M. (2000). Alcoholism. In: Sameroff, A.J., Lewis M. & Miller, S.M. (eds), *Handbook of Developmental Psychopathology,* pp. 569–587. US: Springer.

Zuckerman, M. (1979). *Sensation Seeking: Beyond the Optimal Level of Arousal.* Hillsdale, NJ: New York : L. Erlbaum Associates.

10
Psychosocial Factors and Suicidal Behaviour in Adolescents

Alexander-Stamatios Antoniou, Eftychia Mitsopoulou, and George P. Chrousos

Introduction

Suicides as well as suicidal behaviours are considered to be one of the main health problems in the world, rated as the second most common cause of death among young people globally and the 15th leading cause of death worldwide among all populations (World Health Organization, 2012). According to statistical data and epidemiological reports, in Europe suicide is the second leading cause of death among people 15 to 29 years old (Blum & Nelson-Mmari, 2004), while in a study by Kokkevi, Rotsika, Arapaki, and Richardson (2011) among Greek adolescents throughout a period of 23 years (1984–2007), self-reported suicide attempts doubled in prevalence from 7.0% to 13.4%.

According to the world report on violence and health (2002) by the World Health Organization (WHO) there are three types of violence, the self-directed, the interpersonal, and the collective, with the former including suicidal behaviour and self-abuse, such as self-mutilation. According to the report: 'Suicidal behaviour ranges in degree from merely thinking about ending one's life, to planning it, finding the means to do so, attempting to kill oneself, and completing the act. However, these should not be seen as different points on a single continuum. Many people who entertain suicidal thoughts never act on them, and even those who attempt suicide may have no intention of dying' (p. 5).

Suicidal behaviour: The construct

But is suicidal behaviour a concrete construct or does it involve different patterns? According to Osman et al. (2005), who were based on Lewinsohn,

Rohde, and Seeley's (1996) conceptualization, suicidal behaviour encapsulates the following: suicide ideation, suicide attempt, and suicide completion. Suicide ideation is defined as self-reported thoughts or wishes to be dead or to take one's own life, while suicide attempt has to do with self-inflicted or harmful behaviour with the intent to take one's own life. Lastly, suicide completion is defined as self-inflicted death.

Investigating the relevant studies and the bibliography about suicidal behaviour in adolescents, we came to the conclusion that sometimes self-harm and suicidal behaviour are used interchangeably; that is why, at this point, it is convenient to differentiate these two terms. According to the International Society for the Study of Self-Injury (2007), self-injury is the deliberate, self-inflicted destruction of body tissue without suicidal intent and for purposes not socially sanctioned, and is distinguished from suicidal behaviours such as an intention to die or drug overdoses. On the other hand, self-harm includes both intentional self-injury and intentional self-poisoning irrespective of whether there is suicidal intent, while in adolescents it is likely to be associated with a spectrum of suicidal intent (Ougrin, 2012). While there is a clear distinction between non-suicidal self-injury (NSSI) and suicide attempt, as in the former there is no suicide intent involved, there is evidence showing that NSSI co-occurs with suicidal ideation and attempted suicide (Cheung et al., 2013).

The rates of suicidal ideation and suicide attempts increase dramatically during adolescence, making it a critical period during which potential environmental psychiatric, psychological, social, and cultural a etiological factors intervene. In the last decades there has been an increase in research studies dealing with suicide in adolescents, as this part of the population is considered vulnerable. Because the transition from middle childhood to adolescence and then to adulthood is marked by critical changes in emotional, cognitive, social, and physical/biological development, the adolescent struggles to find his/her own identity and place himself/herself in the wider picture. While most adolescents do not face severe difficulties as they develop, and negotiate this transition quite successfully, there is still a percentage of them who are susceptible to various disorders. These adolescents may end up using maladaptive coping methods, such as thinking of suicide or attempting to take their own lives.

Psychosocial determinants of suicidal behaviour

Apart from the psychiatric factors that are responsible for adolescent suicidal behaviour, we cannot ignore the psychosocial factors that are directly correlated with suicidal behaviour. One important psychosocial factor is family dynamics. Family dysfunction is associated with thinking, planning, and attempting suicide as well as deliberate self-harm among adolescent' (Martin, Gozanes, Pearce, & Allison, 1995), while family conflict (Kuł et al., 2011) may also be a risk factor. At a greater risk for subsequent suicidal behaviour are young people who are exposed to dysfunctional and abusive childhood environments (Kim & Kim, 2008). When a parent is absent, adolescents are at a higher risk of committing suicide, especially when there is lack of stability in the parental marital status (Nrugham, Herrestad, & Mehlum, 2010), and even those adolescents who have lost one parent and live in a single parent family may feel the stigma or be pressured by the other parent (Tang et al., 2010; Yang, 2012). Thus, a nonintact parental unit is a significant risk factor for adolescents (Kokkevi et al., 2011).

The probability of having a parent who has attempted or committed suicide is also a factor that may influence an adolescent in practising the same (Larsson & Ivarsson, 1998). As Hung and Rabin (2009) state, 'much is still unknown about the sequelae, determining factors, and experiences of those surviving suicide bereavement' (p. 782). According to Silverman, Baker, Cait, and Boerner (2002–2003), there exist five types of negative legacies that concern the deceased parent, one of which has to do with the fact that the suicide-bereaved child is likely to form a dangerous identification with the parent who has committed suicide around the act itself. Quin, Agerbo, and Mortensen (2005) found that family history has a large impact on the child's decision to commit suicide, while in another study young people under 21 had a risk of suicide 4.8 times more likely among the offspring of mothers who had completed suicide and 2.3 times as common among the offspring of fathers who had committed suicide (Agerbo, Nordentoft, & Mortensen, 2002). Taking into account the fact that stigma occurs when a family has lost a member by suicide (Murray, Toth, & Clinkinbeard, 2005), we can imagine how painful it is for an adolescent to try to cope with this loss, especially when there is no supportive system. Children are also at risk when one parent or family member committed suicide and the child was not told the truth or was misinformed (Hung & Rabin, 2009).

Studies have also shown that adolescents who do not live with their families, but, rather, in out-of-home placements or state care, may face more emotional, social, and behavioural problems and be at risk of committing suicide or engaging in deliberate self-harm (Cousins, Taggart, & Milner, 2010). In general, the displacement in the relationship between the adolescent and the parent, for example foster homes, primary caretakers, and parental death, is consistently associated with adolescent suicidal ideation and behaviours (Timmons, Selby, Lewinsohn, & Joiner, 2011). For inpatient adolescents, depression, thwarted belongingness, and suicide-related thoughts are also significantly correlated with maternal attachment insecurity (Venta, Mellick, Schatte, & Sharp, 2014).

Vulnerable populations, such as dislocated adolescents (e.g., homeless and street youths), are more vulnerable to impaired psychological health, with a high percentage of them, mainly those who are characterized by family dysfunction, and use of alcohol and other drugs, attempting suicide (Adlaf, 1999). In an Australian study of homeless youth, 40% to 80% had suicidal ideation, while 23% to 67% had attempted to commit suicide (Kamieniecki, 2001). In a United States study of youth under the age of 23, 39% had a history of suicide attempt (Unger, Kipke, Simon, Montgomery, & Johnson, 1997). It was also found elsewhere that adolescents who were highly displaced and at the same time felt that they did not belong anywhere, had increased probabilities of a suicide attempt (Timmons et al., 2011).

Peer relationships serve also as another significant factor connected to suicidal behaviour among adolescents, as having friends serves as a protective factor against suicide for both genders (Fotti, Katz, Afifi, & Cox, 2006), and peer relationships have a dominant role in how the adolescent constructs his/her self-image. Perceiving other adolescents in school as unkind and unhelpful, as well as not having close friends, makes it more likely for a person to have suicidal ideation or attempt to commit suicide (Cui, Cheng, Xu, Chen, & Wang, 2010). Socially isolated adolescents have increased odds of suicide attempts, lower levels of self-esteem, and higher levels of depression (Hall-Lande, Eisenberg, Christenson, & Neumark-Sztainer, 2007). Their depression is associated with reduced psychosocial functioning (Eskin, Ertekin, & Demir, 2008). It is also noteworthy that adolescents are influenced by peers who have attempted suicide (Larsson & Ivarsson, 1998), while socially maladjusted adolescents are also at risk of suicidal behaviour (Kuba et al., 2011).

Psychiatric disorders

Borderline personality disorder and, mainly, unstable interpersonal relations and confusion about oneself are correlated with non-suicidal self-injury as well as suicide attempts (Muehlenkamp, Ertelt, Miller, & Claes, 2011). According to Eskin (2012): 'most people find what makes life beautiful is the time they share with loved ones. Yet, another thing that we learn in life is that those people who make our lives beautiful, liveable, and meaningful can be the major source of our problems. Interpersonal relations can be the source of both happiness and unhappiness' (p. 3). If an adolescent feels not welcomed by peers, he or she may take this rejection as a personal failure and may wish to harm himself/herself, as a way of self-punishment.

Poor peer relations are also associated with bullying and subsequently with suicidal behaviour. According to Tikkannen, Alaräisänen, Hakko, Räsänen, and Riala (2009), those students who have prodromal symptoms of psychotic disorders and, thus, are more at risk of committing suicide and perform well in school could be more susceptible to bullying than their peers who do not perform accordingly. Based on other studies, Kretschmar, Butcher, and Flannery (2014) reached the conclusion that there is a ubiquitous relation between bullying behaviour and suicide ideation and attempts, with both bullies and victims having a higher risk of suicidal behaviour. This is in accordance with other studies (Kim, Koh, & Leventhal, 2005; Hidaka et al., 2008; Cui et al., 2010).

Depression is considered one of the main clinical characteristics of adolescents who have attempted suicide (Larsson & Ivarsson, 1998). As depression applies as a pre-stage of suicidal ideation, the victims of bullies may attempt suicide or think about it when they do not receive social support (Yen, 2010). Even when the depression is mild rather than moderate or severe, there is a high risk for an adolescent to attempt suicide, probably because this type of depression contains higher degrees of agitated depression, as well as more existential cognition about hopelessness (Christiansen & Larsen, 2012). Adolescents who are not optimistic in their life and have lower levels of life satisfaction are at greater risk of committing suicide, as they feel they fail to cope with unpleasant situations in their life (Kim & Kim, 2008).

Sexual orientation may also play a significant role in suicidal ideation and suicide attempts among adolescents. According to a study by Renaud, Berlim, Begolli, McGirr, and Turecki (2010), although there were no significant differences between suicide victims and control subjects regarding same-sex orientation, the suicide victims with same-gender sexual orientation were more prone to anxiety disorders that the suicide victims who did not have a same-gender sexual orientation. This is in accordance with Russell and Joyner (2001) who found that adolescent boys and girls with same-gender sexual orientation reported significantly more alcohol abuse and depression, signs that predict the probability of a suicide attempt, while boys being homosexual or bisexual had a greater chance of reporting an attempted suicide (Hidaka et al., 2008).

According to Brown (2002), 'the dynamics of family relationships often make it difficult for young people to feel safe about "coming out", instead preferring to keep their feelings hidden, which can also result in suicide ideation and attempted suicide' (p. 3). This is probably why gay, lesbian, or bisexual youths, afraid of discrimination, belong to a high-risk group that considers suicide as a means of overcoming oppression (Proctor & Groze, 1994). Another reason for the above is that being gay, lesbian, or bisexual and having low family acceptance during adolescence makes it more likely for the individual to report both suicidal ideation and suicide attempt than those who have high levels of family acceptance (Ryan, Russell, Huebner, Diaz, & Sanchez, 2010), as a family that embraces diversity facilitates the adolescent's embracing of his/her own sexual identity, rather than denying it.

Sexual traumatic events, such as sexual abuse, seem to be a very significant risk factor correlated with suicide attempts, rather than suicide ideation (Plener, Singer, & Goldbeck, 2011). Childhood sexual abuse, physical abuse, emotional abuse, and neglect are strongly associated with suicidal ideation and attempts (Miller, Esposito-Smythers, Weismoore, & Renshaw, 2013). Even personal matters, such as relationships with another person, may serve as risk factors. Dating violence, as a type of intimate partner violence that has a physical, emotional, or sexual character, may lead to depression or suicide thoughts (Lutwak, Dill, & Saliba, 2013).

The influence of media and Internet

Mass media are also associated with adolescent suicidal behaviour. Many suicide attempters may face cyber-bullying, peer victimization through social media and the new term in Internet slang: trolling. Klomek, Marrocco, Kleinman, Schonfeld, and Gould (2007) found that girls who were cyber-bullied reported higher levels of depression and suicide ideation, while boys were more likely to report that they had suicide ideation. Internet sites that promote suicide or facilitate suicide among strangers, such as Internet suicide pacts, which are agreements among strangers who meet online and are planning to commit suicide, serve as risk factors.

Is the Internet to blame for the increase in suicides among adolescents during the last years? Baker and Fortune (2008) claimed that people who visit suicide and self-injury forums usually seek help to solve their psychological and social problems, while they perceive these sites as sources of empathy. Adolescents also use social networking sites, for example MySpace, to discuss suicidal thoughts and intentions, probably as a way to ask for help and support (Cash, Thelwall, Peck, Ferrell, & Bridge, 2013). Still, being a member of a chat room and discussion forum, the so-called social media platforms, may reduce fears and doubts for those who were thinking of suicide but were ambivalent about it (Luxton, June, & Fairall, 2012) and, consequently, make the decision to commit suicide.

As far as pro-suicide websites are concerned, the messages that these sites communicate, such as that each person has a natural right to take his/her life and that society and institutions are threats to this right, influence those who have psychosocial problems and seek help online (Durkee, Hadlaczky, Westerlund, & Carli, 2011). According to Durkee et al. (2011), 'as global Internet user rates are rising, the reliance on the Internet and ensuing online risks are increasing as well' (p. 3940). In many cases, the Werther effect may be encountered as far as adolescent suicide attempters are concerned.

According to the Werther effect, or copycat suicide, someone emulates the suicide of another person, and usually this suicide is strongly influenced by media reports (Hepp, Stulz, Köppel-Unger, & Gross-Ajdacic, 2012). There are numerous examples of the Werther effect. The suicide of a famous singer in Taiwan was followed by other suicides among young groups and with the same method (burning by charcoal) among females (Chen et al., 2012), while researchers have found that newspaper reporting of suicides and the methods used has a great impact on individuals, as it provokes imitative attempts (Hagihara, Abe, Omagari, Motoi, & Nabeshima, 2014).

Impact of traumatic and/or catastrophic events

As far as natural disasters are concerned, evidence shows that experiencing a natural disaster and surviving it may serve as a prerequisite for suicidal ideation. In research by Warheit, Zimmerman, Khoury, Vega, and Gil (1996) relating to 4,978 adolescents who survived Hurricane Andrew, it was found that factors such as gender (being female), having prior suicidal ideation, low family support, and hurricane-generated stress, served as direct and indirect paths to suicidal ideation after the hurricane. Even when the adolescent has experienced a natural disaster, for example flood, and is suffering from a post-traumatic stress disorder (PTSD), the role of the family is highly significant, as an overprotective family may harm the recovery process of the adolescent (Bokszczanin, 2008).

Tang et al. (2010) found that adolescents who had experienced Typhoon Morakot and the associated mudslides had a higher suicide risk, and this risk was mediated by PTSD as well as, in some cases, major depressive disorder. Natural disasters and adolescent suicidal ideation and suicide attempts may not be directly connected, as it is depression and post-traumatic stress that occur and are considered pre-stages of suicidal behaviour. For example, Madianos and Koukia (2010), who used epidemiological data to assess findings about the psychological and traumatic consequences of earthquakes in Greece over the last 40 years, reached the conclusion that the large majority of survivors, among them adolescents, had developed anxiety, depression, PTSD, and protracted acute stress syndrome.

Self-esteem and self-acceptance are important intermediate factors associated with suicide risk (Walker, Ashby, Hoskins, & Greene, 2009). According to Kuhlberg, Pena, and Zayas (2010), individual factors such as depression, anxiety, and low self-esteem are predictors of suicidal behaviour. Nrugham et al. (2010) reviewed previous research on risk factors and interventions regarding the suicidality among Norwegian youth, and found that lower self-esteem was consistently related to suicidal phenomena. And this is also the case in other countries, as it was found that psychological vulnerability, such as low self-esteem, was a determinant for suicide attempts among Japanese adolescents (Hidaka et al., 2008).

Other factors involved in susceptibility to suicidal behaviour

Problem-solving skills are important life skills for young people who assist with coping with the difficulties and challenges they face during such a vulnerable period of their lives (Eskin et al., 2008). Deficits in problem-solving and decision-making (Oldershaw et al., 2009) may make adolescents harm themselves as they have a trend towards high-risk choices. Ineffective problem-solving serves as a significant vulnerability factor for suicidal behaviour in adolescents (Speckens & Hawton, 2005) as it is closely associated with chronic stress (Grover et al., 2009), while problem-solving skill deficits may be a risk factor for the onset, as well as the maintenance, of different types of emotional or behavioural problems (Eskin, 2012).

Even a lack of sufficient sleep may influence an adolescent towards having suicidal ideation, as data show that the less adolescents sleep the more they tend to think about taking their lives, while sleeping less than four hours per night is a risk factor associated with suicidal ideation (Park, Yoo, & Kim, 2013). Socio-economic status also plays an important role, although it is more related to thoughts of self-harm than suicide attempts (Kokkevi, Rotsika, Arapaki, & Richardson, 2012a). As far as academic performance is concerned, the adolescents who struggle to perform academically show high vulnerability to suicidality (Yang, 2012). While most of the public and researchers believe that suicidal ideation may be a feature of adolescents who do not perform well at school, there is evidence that boys, mainly, those with a psychotic disorder and have good school performance, are at high risk of committing suicide (Tikkanen et al., 2009).

Afifi, Cox, and Katz (2007) found that the health risk behaviours that were associated with suicidal ideation and attempts for both male and female adolescents included being in a physical fight, carrying a knife, having sexual intercourse, smoking cigarettes, and using marijuana. According to the authors, engaging in a health risk behaviour is a way of acting against both self and others, which has broader implications as 'suicide may be similar, because it is also an unsafe and often violent act and could be considered violence against oneself' (p. 672). The adolescent perceives others as a threat, and instead of using violence against them or being hostile and aggressive, turns against himself/herself.

Another point that has to be acknowledged is that there are cultural differences in suicide. For example, Goodkind, LaNoue, and Milford (2010) reported that in the US, American Indian adolescents, as well as Alaska Natives, experience higher rates of psychological symptoms than the overall United States adolescent population, thus resulting in higher rates of suicide attempts, which may be due to trauma exposure, such as victimization.

Chemical and drug abuse

Illegal use of drugs, as well as use of legal substances, including tobacco and sedatives, is highly associated with self-reported suicide attempts (Kokkevi et al., 2012b), and alcohol use disorders are associated with suicide risk as well (Pompili et al., 2012b). Lastly, Pena, Matthieu, Zayas, Masyn, and Caine (2012) found a correlation between substance use, such as binge drinking and drug use, violent behaviour, such as physical fights and carrying a weapon, and suicide attempts. Many of the factors analysed previously may coexist. In a sample of 1908 Korean adolescent delinquent students,

221 reported having attempted suicide. The factors that were responsible for these attempts were intrafamiliar sexual abuse, depression, psychotic disorders, as well as other adverse conditions, such as alcoholism or epilepsy of a family member (Kim & Kim, 2008).

There are also sex differences in suicidal behaviour (Afifi et al., 2007). One has to do with the method adolescents use to commit suicide. Usually, males prefer to use firearms, hanging, railway suicides, and jumping from heights, while females have a tendency towards railway suicides, jumping from heights, hanging, and intoxication (Hepp et al., 2012). There are research data suggesting that the use by girls of more lethal suicide methods in recent years may be a product of changes in cultural patterns that allow girls to engage in similar roles to males (Pompili, Vichi, de Leo, Pfeffer, & Girardi, 2012a). Tang et al. (2010) found that there are sex differences in suicide risk when adolescents have experienced a natural disaster, with girls having higher levels of PTSD, while, according to Miller et al. (2013), there is a stronger association between childhood physical abuse and suicide attempts among adolescent males than females. Still, evidence shows that girls report higher rates of suicide attempts (Hall-Lande et al., 2007).

Fedyszyn, Harris, Robinson, Edwards, and Paxton (2011) point out that the majority of suicide attempts are impulsive and, therefore, difficult to anticipate. According to Hepp et al. (2012), many young suicide attempters report that they spent only minutes between the decision to commit suicide and the actual attempts, thus indicating a high degree of impulsiveness. In general, impulsivity, along with depression, low self-esteem, and anxiety, is predictor of deliberate self-harm (Madge et al., 2011). As impulsivity is a dominant characteristic in the adolescent's personality, we can conclude that not planning the suicide carefully may mean that the adolescent is not completely sure of what he/she is about to do, does not understand fully the consequences, and does not consider the implications, permanence, and non-reversibility of the act.

Still, keeping in mind that the adolescent who harms himself/herself or commits suicide had probably attempted to do the same in the past, it is very important to note the following: 'suicide attempts therefore represent an invaluable signal for preventing fatal incidents of suicidal behaviour among young people, and the timely identification of factors associated with suicidal behaviour could contribute to the effective guidance of policies and interventions' (Kokkevi et al., 2012a, p. 381). After all, self-harm, if considered a step before suicide attempt, is usually repetitive and does not only occur once prior to the suicide attempt (Hawton et al., 2012).

But why do adolescents think of or attempt to commit suicide? What are the factors underlying this type of thought and act, and what are the thoughts of the ideator or attempter? Apart from the factors analysed previously, there must be something more to our knowledge on suicidal behaviour. According to Macedo and Werlang (2011), for a person who had lost her father, had a difficult relationship with her mother, and had problems with her sexual identity, thus engaging in marijuana and alcohol use, while at the end attempting to take her life, 'the attempt at suicide turns the pain into an act, and sets a requirement on the Other: something in this pain act needs to be listened to so that the subject herself need not devour herself in the solitude and in the irreversibility of a fatal act' (p. 24).

Do these adolescents really need to be listened to? Do they struggle to raise their voice and make a statement or do they simply want to be left alone to make decisions by themselves? Is suicide for adolescents an act of rebelliousness, an opposition to authority, which may be the family, teachers, society? We cannot conclude with certainty why an adolescent will think of taking his/her life, as suicide itself is not merely one thing. Practitioners should keep in mind that suicide is not just a thought and an act that sometimes is interrupted by a plan. It is not a two-step path to death; it is more than that.

Maybe it is true that 'suicide attempts may occur to resolve or avoid personal difficulties and stress associated with exposure to adverse life events' (Kim & Kim, 2008, p. 232). If the struggle of an adolescent to resolve inauspicious life events is the answer to understanding suicidal behaviour, then this is the first thing that practitioners should realize. Knowing the factors that undermine an adolescent's desire to live is just not enough. The approach to this type of behaviour should be manifold and pluralistic. Youth suicide should be addressed using evidence-based clinical, preventive, and health promotion strategies, as it is an important health issue (Szumilas & Kutcher, 2009). Although most people believe that suicidal behaviour in adolescents is an individual character and a personal health problem, we claim that it is primarily a public health concern. If we estimate the economic and human cost that suicidal behaviour has for both families and society, we can see the tragic implications it has for the present and the future.

Most health practitioners would claim that referring an adolescent to a mental health service unit is the most appropriate solution, and that contacting such a person or centre would serve as a protective factor. It is true that, as a health issue, suicidal behaviour needs to be addressed appropriately, with trained staff and adequate resources. Still, evidence does not support that this is always the most successful solution. Contacting health services, for example an outpatient physician or an emergency department, is not a panacea, as there is evidence stating that although there is contact with this type of service prior to the action, an adolescent may *still* commit suicide (Rhodes et al., 2013).

Consequently, the role of health services is highly significant, as there are data supporting that adolescents are at a higher risk of committing suicide *after* their discharge from a psychiatric service (Christiansen & Larsen, 2012). If an adolescent who entered an inpatient unit and was discharged after treatment tried again to hurt himself/herself, then this implies that the health system failed to provide the adolescent with all the necessary skills to fight his/her suicidal tendency. Thus, what needs to be changed is more than the standard treatment of suicidal adolescents.

According to Windfuhr et al. and the National Confidential Inquiry into Suicide and Homicide by People with Mental Illness (2008), health professionals who are dealing with incidents of suicide in adolescents tend to evaluate the incident after the suicide was committed rather than before, thus engaging in a 'culture of blame' as to why the action was not prevented. Still, there is a shift to a 'culture of learning', where clinicians learn from these kind of adverse incidents. Culture and all the relevant elements that constitute it play an important role in suicidal ideation and attempts. As Yang (2012) mentions: 'It is through culture that researchers and therapists begin to understand the personal meaning people give to situations that may lead to suicide' (p. 254). It is this new culture in the study and treatment of suicidal behaviour that asks for more than just 'talking', but rather 'listening', as a way for adolescents to communicate hopes and fears.

Lessons for the practitioner

What should clinicians know? First, they should know that each adolescent is a single and unique case that has his/her own personality, background, aspirations, fears, and experiences. Thus, when clinicians treat an adolescent they should bear in mind that there may be more to what they have learned during their studies and practice. Using a single approach to assess and possibly intervene in all at-risk adolescents is not listening to what the individual has to say and not accepting his or her individuality. Keeping in mind that adolescents display suicidal behaviour as a means through which to be listened, we can imagine the dreadful consequences this will have for the adolescent.

For example, Quin et al. (2005) suggested that gender differences should be taken into account by the strategies practitioners implement, and that the effects of interventions may differ by gender, as the roles men and women have in society may affect the way they react when they encounter difficulties and are exposed to risk factors, such as those mentioned earlier in the chapter. Moreover, greater attention should be paid to race and ethnicity so that targeted efforts can reach different types of population (Pena et al., 2012).

Furthermore, practitioners should keep in mind the importance of discovering and assessing the protective factors that may prevent an adolescent from displaying suicidal behaviour, when implementing methods that are targeted to vulnerable populations, such as adolescents. Usually, in the past, emphasis was placed on the risk factors and ways to battle against them, such as psychoanalysis, cognitive behavioural therapy, medication, and so on. If most adolescents are enjoying life as it is and cope effectively with their everyday difficulties and life events, then there is something to which greater attention needs to be paid in their management – protective factors. Thus, it is preferable for practitioners to identify, assess, and use these protective factors to benefit at-risk adolescents, than target only the risk factors. Whether these protective factors are personal/internal or external, it is something that needs to be thoroughly investigated to be correctly implemented in the everyday life of adolescents. As these protective factors nourish resilience in most adolescents, then it is worth promoting them in the lives of at-risk adolescents.

The last and most important aspect in tackling suicidal behaviour among adolescents, as well as other populations, is prevention. Prevention means approaching the adolescent before even he/she displays suicidal behaviour, by intervening before the behaviour occurs. The most useful way is through schools, as 'given their access to children and adolescents, schools are commonly viewed as a promising venue for enhanced youth suicide prevention efforts' (Stein et al., 2010, p. 339), while the intervention programmes schools implement are considered a cost-effective and convenient way in which to reach adolescents (Wyman et al., 2010).

Stein et al. (2010) reported three main approaches used by schools to prevent suicide. The first is the curricular suicide prevention programmes that aim to inform students about suicide and suicide risks. The second is the screening-based prevention programmes, which plan to identify youths who are at risk of committing suicide, while gatekeeper methods, the third approach, aim to train students, teachers, and school staff to be able to identify those students who may be at risk of suicide and help them to take part in social support networks, as well as other counselling and treatment facilities.

Self-report measures contribute clinically useful information in the assessment of internalizing symptoms (Osman et al., 2005). However, because self-report questionnaires are usually used, there is the probability of not receiving true answers, as people tend to reply according to social desirability rules, thus providing researchers with response bias, especially in the case of adolescents (King, Hill, Wynne, & Cunningham, 2012). As far as gatekeeper programmes are concerned, the so-called peer gatekeepers programmes, a type of peer helper programme whereby trained adolescents help peers with difficulties to overcome them, are considered beneficial social ties, as trust and interdependence occur more readily among similar groups rather than dissimilar ones (Walker et al., 2009).

Concluding comments

According to the WHO (2002), there is no single factor to explain why someone behaves in a violent manner, including those who act against themselves, by thinking of or attempting suicide. The ecological theory

(Bronfenbrenner, 1979) proposes that children's development is influenced by multiple contexts, as the person develops through the interaction with others. That is why WHO is proposing an ecological model that helps understand the multi-faceted nature of violence, which divides the factors into four levels: the first identifies personal and history factors, the second examines relationships between persons, the third explores community and the relationships therein, while the fourth examines societal factors that engage in violence.

Drawing from the above paradigm, we can use the notion of ecological contexts in referring to suicidal behaviour. The first significant context is family. When there is family connectedness, this serves as a protective factor against suicide attempts, even if the child is socially isolated or has low self-esteem (Hall-Lande et al., 2007). Providing a healthy and stable support system for adolescents at risk of suicidal behaviour serves as a way of overcoming difficulties. For example, when gay, lesbian, or bisexual youths rely on a highly functioning support system, they draw from their support system rather than consider suicide (Proctor & Groze, 1994). Another context is social engagement with peers.

Wyman et al. (2010), by evaluating the prevention programmes implemented in schools to forestall suicide attempts, proposed modifying socio-ecological factors at the population level, by focusing on the social ties and norms that adolescents have, such as communication with peer groups. Lastly, the cultural context provides children with a framework of references, such as values and beliefs. As Goldston et al. (2008) claim, suicidal behaviour and help-seeking occur in a cultural context and may be associated with different precipitating factors, different vulnerability and protective factors, differing reactions to and interpretations of the behaviour, as well as different resources and options for help-seeking.

Reaching the end of this analysis, it would be reasonable to wonder whether sometimes suicidal behaviour gives someone a reason to live. Yang (2012) case-studied an adolescent girl from South Korea who tried to take her own life. The subject released her stress through a suicide attempt, showed her resolution not to put up with things that served as burdens any more, and in the end, the act inspired her to live. On the other hand, infrequent help-seeking before a suicide attempt may suggest that the individual has a genuine desire to die at the moment of the attempt, and this explains the fact that in many cases, suicidal intent or regret that the attempt was not successful persisted for some hours after the act (Fedyszyn et al., 2011). Although these two examples are contradictory, we can only be confident that when there is a real interest in what the adolescent wants to express, then we are providing him/her with a helping hand, which for many may be inconsequential, but for an adolescent may be a lifeline.

References

Adlaf, M.E. (1999). A cluster-analytic study of substance problems and mental health among street youths. *American Journal of Drug and Alcohol Abuse, 25*, 639–660.

Afifi, T.O., Cox, J.B., & Katz, Y.L. (2007). The associations between health risk behaviours and suicidal ideation and attempts in a nationally representative sample of young adolescents. *Canadian Journal of Psychiatry, 52*, 666–674.

Agerbo, E., Nordentoft, M., & Mortensen, P.B. (2002). Familial, psychiatric, and socioeconomic risk factors for suicide in young people: nested case-control study. *British Medical Journal, 325*, 74–79.

Baker, D., & Fortune, S. (2008). Understanding self-harm and suicide websites: a qualitative interview study of young adult website users. *Crisis, 29*, 118–122.

Blum, R.W., & Nelson-Mmari, K. (2004). The health of young people in a global context. *Journal of Adolescent Health, 35*, 402–418.

Bokszczanin, A. (2008). Parental support, family conflict, and overprotectiveness: predicting PTSD symptom levels of adolescents 28 months after a natural disaster. *Anxiety, Stress & Coping: An International Journal, 21*, 325–335.

Bronfenbrenner, U. (1979). *The Ecology of Human Development: Experiments by Nature and Design.* Cambridge, MA: Harvard University Press.

Brown, R. (2002). Self harm and suicide risk for same-sex attracted young people: a family perspective. *Australian e-Journal for the Advancement of Mental Health, 1*, 3–11.

Cash, J.S., Thelwall, M., Peck, N.S., Ferrell, Z.J., & Bridge, A.J. (2013). Adolescent suicide statements on MySpace. *Cyberpsychology, Behaviour, and Social Networking, 16*, 166–174.

Chen, Y.-Y., Liao, S.-F., Teng, P.-R., Tsai, C.-W., Fan, H.-F., Lee, W.-C., & Cheng, T.-A. (2012). The impact of media reporting of the suicide of a singer on suicide rated in Taiwan. *Social Psychiatry & Psychiatric Epidemiology, 47*, 215–21.

Cheung, D.T. Y., Wong, C.W.P., Lee, M.A., Lam, H.T., Fan, S.S.Y., & Yip, F.S.P. (2013). Non-suicidal self-injury and suicidal behaviour: prevalence, co-occurrence, and correlates of suicide among adolescents in Hong Kong. *Social Psychiatry & Psychiatric Epidemiology, 48*, 1133–1144.

Christiansen, E., & Larsen, J.K. (2012). Young people's risk of suicide attempts after contact with a psychiatric department – a nested case-control design using Danish register data. *The Journal of Child Psychology and Psychiatry, 53*, 16–25.

Cousins, W., Taggart, L., & Milner, S. (2010). Looked after or overlooked? An exploratory investigation of the mental health issues of adolescents living in state care in Northern Ireland. *Psychology, Health & Medicine, 15*, 497–506.

Cui, S., Cheng, Y., Xu, Z., Chen, D., & Wang, Y. (2010). Peer relationships and suicide ideation and attempts among Chinese adolescents. *Child: Care, Health and Development, 37*, 692–702.

Durkee, T., Hadlaczky, G., Westerlund, M., & Carli, V. (2011). Internet pathways in suicidality: a review of the evidence. *International Journal of Environmental Research and Public Health, 8*, 3938–3952.

Eskin, M., Ertekin, K., & Demir, H. (2008). Efficacy of a problem-solving therapy for depression and suicide potential in adolescents and young adults. *Cognitive Therapy & Research, 32*, 227–245.

Eskin, M. (2012). *Problem Solving Therapy in the Clinical Practice.* Elsevier Insights. New York, Berlin: Springer.

Fotti, S.A., Katz, L.Y., Afifi, T.O., & Cox, B.J. (2006). The associations between peer and parental relationships and suicidal behaviours in early adolescents. *Canadian Journal of Psychiatry, 51*, 698–703.

Fedyszyn, E.I., Harris, G.M., Robinson, J., Edwards, J., & Paxton, J.S. (2011). Characteristics of suicide attempts in young people undergoing treatment for first episode psychosis. *Australian and New Zealand Journal of Psychiatry, 45*, 838–845.

Goldston, D.B., Molock, D.S., Whitbeck, B.L., Murakami, L.J., Zayas, H.L., & Nagayama Hall, G.C. (2008). Cultural considerations in adolescent suicide prevention and psychosocial treatment. *American Psychologist, 63*, 14–31.

Goodkind, R.J., LaNoue, D.M., & Milford, J. (2010). Adaptation and implementation of cognitive behavioural intervention for trauma in schools with American Indian youth. *Journal of Clinical Child & Adolescent Psychology, 39*, 858–872.

Grover, E.K., Green, L.K., Pettit, W.J., Moneteith, L.L., Garza, J.M., & Venta, A. (2009). Problem solving moderates the effects of life events stress and chronic stress on suicidal behaviours in adolescence. *Journal of Clinical Psychology, 65*, 1281–1290.

Hagihara, A., Abe, T., Omagari, M., Motoi, M., & Nabeshima, Y. (2014). The impact of newspaper reporting of hydrogen sulfide suicide on imitative suicide attempts in Japan. *Social Psychiatry & Psychiatric Epidemiology, 49*, 221–229.

Hall-Lande, A. J., Eisenberg, E.M., Christenson, L.S., & Neumark-Sztainer, D. (1997). Social isolation, psychological health, and protective factors in adolescence. *Adolescence, 42*, 265–286.

Hawton, K., Bergen, H., Kapur, N., Cooper, J., Steeg, S., Ness, J., & Waters, K. (2012). Repetition of self-harm and suicide following self-harm in children and adolescents: findings from the Multicentre Study of Self-harm in England. *Journal of Child Psychology and Psychiatry, 53*, 121–1219.

Hepp, U., Stulz, N., Köppel-Unger, J., & Gross-Ajdacic, V. (2012). Methods of suicide used by children and adolescents. *European Journal of Adolescent Psychiatry, 21*, 67–73.

Hidaka, Y., Operario, D., Takenaka, M., Omori, S., Ichikawa, S., & Shirasaka, T. (2008). Attempted suicide and associated risk factors among youth in urban Japan. *Social Psychiatry & Psychiatric Epidemiology, 43*, 752–757.

Hung, N.C., & Rabin, A.L. (2009). Comprehending childhood bereavement by parental suicide: a critical review of research on outcomes, grief processes and interventions. *Death Studies, 33*, 781–814.

International Society for the Study of Self-injury (2007). *Definitional Issues Surrounding our Understanding of Self-injury.* Conference proceedings from the annual meeting.

Kamieniecki, G.W. (2001) Prevalence of psychological distress and psychiatric disorders among homeless youth in Australia: a comparative review. *Australian & New Zealand Journal of Psychiatry, 35*, 352–358.

Kim, Y.-S., Koh, Y.-J., & Leventhal, B. (2005). School bullying and suicidal risk in Korean middle school students. *Pediatrics, 115*, 357–363.

Kim, S.H., & Kim. S., H. (2008). Risk factors for suicide attempts among Korean adolescents. *Child Psychiatry & Human Development, 39*, 221–235.

King, A.C., Hill, M.R., Wynne, A.H., & Cunningham, M.R. (2012). Adolescent suicide risk screening: the effect of communication about type of follow-up on adolescents' screening responses. *Journal of Clinical Child & Adolescent Psychology, 41*, 508–515.

Klomek, A.B., Marrocco, F., Kleinman, M., Schonfeld, I.S., & Gould, M.S. (2007). Bullying, depression, and suicidality in adolescents. *Journal of the American Academy of Child and Adolescent Psychiatry, 46*, 40–49.

Kokkevi, A., Rotsika, V., Arapaki, A., & Richardson, C. (2011). Increasing self-reported suicide attempts by adolescents in Greece between 1984 and 2007. *Social Psychiatry and Psychiatric Epidemiology, 46*, 231–237.

Kokkevi, A., Rotsika, V., Arapaki, A., & Richardson, C. (2012a). Adolescents' self-reported suicide attempts, self-harm thoughts and their correlates across 17 European countries. *The Journal of Child Psychology and Psychiatry, 53*, 381–389.

Kokkevi, A., Richardson, C., Olszewski, D., Matias, J., Monshouwer, K., & Bjarnason, T. (2012b). Multiple substance use and self-reported suicide attempts by adolescents in 16 European countries. *European Child & Adolescent Psychiatry, 21*, 443–450.

Kretschmar, J., Butcher, F., & Flannery, D. (2014). Aspects of bullying and its relationship to suicide. In: M. Van Dulmen, R. Bossarte & M. Swahn (eds), *Developmental and Public Health Perspectives on Suicide Prevention: An Integrated Approach*, pp.58–83. Kent, OH: Kent State University Press.

Kuba, T., Yakushi, T., Fukuhara, H., Nakamoto, Y., Singeo, S.T.S., Tanaka, O., & Kondo, T. (2011). Suicide-related events among child and adolescent patients during short-term antidepressant therapy. *Psychiatry and Clinical Neurosciences, 65*, 239–245.

Kuhlberg, A.J., Pena, B.J., & Zayas, H.L. (2010). Familism, parent-adolescent conflict, self-esteem, internalizing behaviours and suicide attempts among adolescent Latinas. *Child Psychiatry & Human Development, 41*, 425–440.

Larsson, B., & Ivarsson, T. (1998). Clinical characteristics of adolescent psychiatric inpatients who have attempted suicide. *European Child & Adolescent Psychiatry, 7*, 201–208.

Lewinsohn, P.M., Rohde, P., & Seeley, J.R. (1996). Adolescent suicidal ideation and attempts: prevalence, risk factors, and clinical implications. *Clinical Psychology: Science and Practice, 3*, 25–46.

Lutwak, N., Dill, C., & Saliba, A. (2013). Dating violence must be addressed in the public health forum. *Journal of Women's Health, 22*, 393–394.

Luxton, D.D., June, D.J., & Fairall, M.J. (2012). Social media and suicide: a public health perspective. *American Journal of Public Health, 102*, 195–200.

Macedo, K.M. M., & Werlang, G.S.B. (2011). A case of trauma and attempted suicide in an adolescent patient. *International Forum of Psychoanalysis, 20*, 18–25.

Madge, N., Hawton, K., McMahon, E.M., Corcoran, P., De Leo, D., de Wilde, E.J., Fekete, S., van Heeringen, K., Ystgaard, M., & Arensman, E. (2011). Psychological characteristics, stressful events and deliberate self-harm: findings from the Child & Adolescent Self-harm in Europe (CASE) Study. *European Journal of Adolescent Psychiatry, 20*, 499–508.

Madianos, G.M., & Koukia, E. (2010). Trauma and natural disaster: the case of earthquakes in Greece. *Journal of Loss and Trauma, 15*, 138–150.

Martin, G., Gozanes, P., Pearce, C., & Allison, S. (1995). Adolescent suicide, depression and family dysfunction. *Acta Psychiatrica Scandinavica, 92*, 336–344.

Miller, B.A., Esposito-Smythers, C., Weismoore, T.J., & Renshaw, D.K. (2013). The relation between child maltreatment and adolescent suicidal behaviour: a systematic review and critical examination of the literature. *Clinical Child and Family Psychology Review, 16*, 146–172.

Muehlenkamp, J.J., Ertelt, W.T., Miller, L.A., & Claes, L. (2011). Borderline personality symptoms differentiate non-suicidal and suicidal self-injury in ethnically diverse adolescent outpatients. *The Journal of Child Psychology and Psychiatry, 52*, 148–155.

Murray, C.I., Toth, K., & Clinkinbeard, S. (2005). Death, dying and grief. In: P.C. McKenry & S. Price (eds), *Families and change: Coping With Stressful Events*, 3rd edition, pp. 75–102. Thousand Oaks, CA: Sage.

Nrugham, L., Herrestad, H., & Mehlum, L. (2010). Suicidality among Norwegian youth: review of research on risk factors and interventions. *Nordic Journal of Psychiatry, 64*, 317–326.

Oldershaw, A., Grima, E., Jollant, B., Richards, C., Simic, M., Taylor, L., & Schimdt, U. (2009). Decision making and problem solving in adolescents who deliberately self-harm. *Psychological Medicine, 39*, 95–104.

Osman, A., Gutierrez, M.P., Brrios, X.F., Bagge, L.C., Kopper, A.B., & Linden, S. (2005). The inventory of suicide orientation-30: further validation with adolescent psychiatric inpatients. *Journal of Clinical Psychology, 61*, 481–497.

Ougrin, D. (2012). Commentary: self-harm in adolescents: the best predictor of death by suicide? – reflections on Hawton et al. (2012). *Journal of Child Psychology and Psychiatry, 53*, 1220–1221.

Park, H.J., Yoo, J.-H., & Kim, H.S. (2013). Associations between non-restorative sleep, short sleep duration and suicidality: findings from a representative sample of Korean adolescents. *Psychiatry and Clinical Neurosciences, 67*, 28–34.

Pena, B.J., Matthieu, M.M., Zayas, H.L., Masyn, E.K., & Caine, D.E. (2012). Co-occurring risk behaviours among White, Black, and Hispanic US high school adolescents with suicide attempts requiring medical attention, 1999–2007: implications for future prevention initiatives. *Social Psychiatry and Psychiatric Epidemiology, 47*, 29–42.

Plener, L.P., Singer, H., & Goldbeck, L. (2011). Traumatic events and suicidality in a German adolescent community sample. *Journal of Traumatic Stress, 24*, 121–124.

Pompili, M., Vichi, M., de Leo, D., Pfeffer, C., & Girardi, P. (2012a). A longitudinal epidemiological comparison of suicide and other causes of death in Italian children and adolescents. *European Child & Adolescent Psychiatry, 21*, 111–121.

Pompili, M., Serafini, G., Innamorati, M., Biondi, S., Siracusano, A., di Giannantonio, M., Giupponi, M., Amore, M., Lester, D., Girardi, P., & Leimkühler-Möller, A.M. (2012b). Substance abuse and suicide risk among adolescents. *European Archives of Psychiatry and Clinical Neuroscience, 262*, 469–485.

Proctor, D.C., & Groze, K.V. (1994). Risk factors for suicide among gay, lesbian, and bisexual youths. *Social Work, 39*, 504–513.

Quin, P., Agerbo, E., & Mortensen, B.P. (2005). Factors contributing to suicide: The epidemiological evidence form large-scale registers. In: K. Hawton (eds), *Prevention and Treatment of Suicidal Behaviour: From Science to Practice*, pp.11–28. Oxford, UK: Oxford University Press.

Renaud, J., Berlim., T.M., Begolli, M., McGirr, A., & Turecki, G. (2010). Sexual orientation and gender identity in youth suicide victims: an exploratory study. *The Canadian journal of Psychiatry, 55*, 29–34.

Rhodes, E.A., Khan, S., Boyle, H.M., Tommyr, L., Wekerle, C., Goodman, D., Bethell, J., Leslie, B., Lu, H., & Manion, I. (2013). Sex differences in suicides among children and youth: the potential impact of help-seeking behaviour. *Canadian Journal of Psychiatry, 58*, 274–282.

Russell, T.S., & Joyner, K. (2001). Adolescent sexual orientation and suicide risk: evidence from a national study. *American Journal of Public Health, 91*, 1276–1281.

Ryan, C., Russell, T.S., Huebner, D., Diaz, R., & Sanchez, J. (2010). Family acceptance in adolescence and the health of LGBT young adults. *Journal of Child and Adolescent Psychiatric Nursing, 23*, 205–213.

Silverman, P.R., Baker, J., Cait, C.-A., & Boerner, K. (2002–2003). The effects of negative legacies on the adjustment of parentally bereaved children and adolescents. *Omega: The Journal of Death and Dying, 46*, 335–352.

Speckens, A.E. M., & Hawton, K. (2005). Social problem solving in adolescents with suicidal behaviour: a systematic review. *Suicide and Life-Threatening Behaviour, 35,* 365–387.
Stein, D.B., Kataoka, H.S., Hamilton, B.A., Schultz, D., Ryan, G., Vona, P., & Wong, M. (2010). School personnel perspectives on their school's implementation of a school-based suicide prevention program. *Journal of Behavioural Health Services & Research, 37,* 338–349.
Szumilas, M., & Kutcher, S. (2009). Teen suicide information on the internet: a systematic quality analysis. *Canadian Journal of Psychiatry, 54,* 596–604.
Tang, T.C., Yen, C.F., Cheng, C.P., Yang, P., Chen, C.S., Yang, R.C., Huang, M.S., Jong, J.Y., & Yu, S.H. (2010). Suicide risk and its correlate in adolescents who experienced typhoon-induced mudslides: a structural equation model. *Depression and Anxiety, 27,* 1143–1148.
Tikkanen, V., Alaräisänen, A., Hakko, H., Räsänen, P., Riala, K., & the Study-70 Workgroup. (2009). Psychotic boys performing well in school are at increased risk of suicidal ideation. *Psychiatry and Clinical Neurosciences, 63,* 30–36.
Timmons, A.K., Selby, A.E., Lewinsohn, P.P., & Joiner, E.T. (2011). Parental displacement and adolescent suicidality: exploring the role of failed belonging. *Journal of Clinical Child & Adolescent Psychology, 40,* 807–817.
Unger, J.B., Kipke, M.D., Simon, T.R., Montgomery, S.B., & Johnson, C.J. (1997). Homeless youths and young adults in Los Angeles: prevalence of mental health problems and the relationship between mental health and substance abuse disorders. *American Journal of Community Psychology, 25,* 371–394.
Venta, A., Mellick, W., Schatte, D., & Sharp, C. (2014). Preliminary evidence that thoughts of thwarted belongingness mediate the relations between level of attachment insecurity and depression and suicide-related thoughts in inpatient adolescents. *Journal of Social and Clinical Psychology, 33,* 428–447.
Walker, L. R, Ashby, J., Hoskins, D.O., & Greene, N.F. (2009). Peer-support suicide prevention in a non-metropolitan U.S. community. *Adolescence, 44,* 335–346.
Warheit, J.G, Zimmerman, S.R., Khoury, L.E., Vega, A.W., & Gil, G.A. (1996). Disaster related stresses, depressive signs and symptoms, and suicidal ideation among a multi-racial/ethnic sample of adolescents: a longitudinal analysis. *The Journal of Child Psychology and Psychiatry, 37,* 435–444.
Windfuhr, K., While, D., Hunt, I., Turnbull, P., Lowe, R., Burns, J., Swinson, N., Shaw, J., Appleby, L., Kapur, N., & the National Confidential Inquiry into Suicide and Homicide by People with Mental Illness. (2008). Suicide in juveniles and adolescents in the United Kingdom. *Journal of Child Psychology and Psychiatry, 49,* 1155–1165.
World Health Organization. (2002). *World Report on Violence and Health.* Geneva, Switzerland: Author. World Health Organisation. (2012). Mental health: Suicide data. http://www.who.int/mental_health/prevention/suicide/suicideprevent/en/ (downloaded March 2015).
Wyman, P.A., Hendricks Brown, C., Lo, M.M., Schmeelk-Cone, K., Petrova, M., Yu, Q., Walsch, E., Tu, X., & Wang, W. (2010). An outcome evaluation of sources of strength suicide prevention program delivered by adolescent peer leaders in high schools. *American Journal of Public Health, 100,* 1653–1661.
Yang, S. (2012). A life history of a Korean adolescent girl who attempted suicide. *Death Studies, 36,* 253–269.
Yen, F.-C. (2010). School bullying and mental health in children and adolescents. *Taiwanese Journal of Psychiatry (Taipei), 24,* 3–13.

11
It Takes a Global Village: Internet-Delivered Interventions Supporting Children and Their Families

Nicole Pugh, Kathy Chan, and Christine Korol

Introduction

Increasingly people are searching the Internet to address parenting dilemmas, locate community resources, and self-diagnose and treat mental health concerns. According to the Pew Research Centre, approximately 72% of Americans use Internet searches for health-related information (2014). Although it is important to be an informed consumer, it is often challenging to critically evaluate the health and parenting information available over the Internet. This may lead to increased anxiety or distress from self-misdiagnosis, unhelpful online support groups, or the use of ineffective or even harmful parenting interventions. Timely access to accessible and effective support for children and their families is critical to treatment and often prevention of more serious conditions. Psychological interventions are particularly well suited to be offered over the Internet. In particular, therapist-assisted Internet-delivered cognitive behavioural therapy (TAI-CBT) is a growing model of service delivery. In this model, consumers of mental health services complete courses delivered over the Internet that explore common mental health and family issues, such as postpartum depression (PPD), anxiety, child behavioural problems, and sleep. Such programmes can be self-directed or facilitated by a therapist who provides support and encouragement either via email or telephone.

Currently there are numerous Internet-delivered resources that provide parents with information on diverse topics such as parenting strategies, child development, and self-care while parenting. This chapter will review select promising Internet-delivered interventions in the area of parenting as well as Internet-delivered programmes designed to support the well-being of parents. The accessibility and convenience of these programmes make them ideally suited for busy parents who find it challenging to participate in traditional face-to-face group or individual therapy. This chapter concludes with examining advantages and disadvantages of Internet-delivered approaches as well as clinical implications and future research directions.

Internet-delivered parenting interventions

Children's socio-emotional and behavioural problems constitute a major public health concern on personal, familial, and societal levels (Romeo, Knapp, & Scott, 2006). Improving parenting is widely recognized as imperative for promoting optimal child development and the prevention of behavioural and emotional concerns throughout the lifespan (Dretzke et al., 2009; Gutman & Feinstein, 2010; Stack, Serbin, Enns, Ruttle, & Barrieau, 2010; Kirp, 2011). Indeed, evidence-based (EB) practice guidelines recommend behavioural parenting interventions as the gold standard in the prevention and treatment of problem behaviours in children (Chorpita et al., 2011; Kazdin & Blasé, 2011; NICE, 2013). Despite their availability, EB parenting interventions are not widely used across communities (Walker, 2006). To facilitate the incorporation of EB interventions into community practice, researchers and clinicians have increasingly turned to the Internet as a novel avenue for convenient and efficacious service delivery.

Over the past decade, substantial research has evaluated Internet-delivered interventions for the treatment of adult behavioural and mental health concerns (Spek et al., 2007; Barak, Hen, Boniel-Nissim, & Shapira, 2008; Griffiths, Farrer, & Christensen, 2010). The development of Internet-delivered interventions to assist parents who are raising children with difficulties or to provide the parents with personal support is a relatively new phenomenon. Two systematic reviews concluded that many Internet-delivered parenting resources are at the initial development stage, with a few that have progressed to feasibility and efficacy testing (Nieuwboer, Fukkink, & Hermanns, 2013; Breitenstein, Gross, & Christophersen, 2014). Given the importance of EB interventions, rather than examine newly established Internet-delivered interventions (see the above reviews for further details), this chapter will begin by examining Internet-delivered programmes that were derived from EB face-to-face parenting interventions.

Triple P Online (TPOL). The five-level Triple P-Positive Parenting Program (Sanders, 1999) has over 30 years of research support (Sanders, Kirby, Tellegen, & Day, 2014). Derived from Triple P, Triple P Online (TPOL; Turner & Sanders, 2011) is a Level 4 intervention which provides parents with moderate-to-intense training in positive parenting skills (i.e., encouraging positive behaviour, managing misbehaviour, promoting a positive parent–child relationship). TPOL consists of eight Internet-delivered linear modules that are delivered sequentially, with the completion of one module unlocking the next. In keeping with the programme's emphasis on supporting parental self-regulation, TPOL is designed to be entirely self-directed, although therapists working with families may provide the option for individual face-to-face, email, or telephone contact. TPOL is a dynamic and interactive programme and includes: (1) Videos to present didactic content, demonstrate parenting skills, and provide descriptions of actual parents' experiences; (2) Exercises which encourage decision-making and problem-solving skills; (3) Individualized goal-setting, self-evaluation, and feedback; (4) A reminder system (via text and email messaging) to encourage continued participation; and (5) Supplementary downloadable materials (e.g., worksheets, podcast, printable workbook).

Two randomized controlled trials (RCTs) have examined the efficacy of TPOL. Sanders, Baker, and Turner (2012) compared TPOL ($n = 60$) with an Internet-use-as-usual control condition ($n = 56$) for parents of children aged 2–9 years. Parents participating in the TPOL condition reported significantly fewer child behaviour problems and a reduction in their use of ineffective parenting strategies. The results ranged from medium to large effect and the majority of changes were maintained or enhanced at follow-up.

A separate study evaluated the efficacy of TPOL compared to the Triple P self-help workbook for mothers and fathers of children aged 3–8 years (Sanders, Dittman, Farruggia, & Keown, 2014). Results indicated that the intervention effects for TPOL were not significantly different to those found for the self-help workbook. Further, mothers and fathers in both conditions reported clinically significant reductions in disruptive child behaviours and dysfunctional parenting styles. At six-months post-treatment, these effects were maintained for fathers, but mothers reported increases in child behaviour problems and ineffective parenting behaviours, regardless of their treatment condition.

Mixed findings have been reported with regard to parental satisfaction with TPOL. Sanders et al. (2012) indicated that ratings for TPOL were slightly lower than those found for the face-to-face Triple P programme, but were higher than ratings for other self-directed forms of Triple P (Sanders et al., 2000). However, when compared directly, no differences in parental satisfaction ratings were reported between TPOL and the self-help Triple P workbook. Despite these contradictions, overall satisfaction ratings suggest that parents using TPOL find it acceptable, engaging, and easy to use (Sanders et al., 2012).

Internet Parent Management Training (i-PMT). The Internet Parent Management Training programme (i-PMT; Enebrink, Högström, Forster, & Ghaderi, 2012) was developed from the COmmunication METhod (Comet) programme (Hassler & Havbring, 2003; Kling, Sundell, Melin, & Forster, 2006; Kling, Forster, Sundell, & Melin, 2010), a Swedish parenting intervention aimed to reduce negative parent–child interactions. Delivered on a secured website, i-PMT consists of seven sessions which are completed over a period of ten weeks. The i-PMT programme primarily focuses on positive parenting, communication, and positive reinforcement, with limited focus on management of child misbehaviour via response-cost and punishment strategies. Similar to TPOL, videos are used to provide parenting examples and to demonstrate different parent–child interactions. Downloadable content, review of content covered in the previous session, and testing questions (as well as corrective feedback, when necessary) are all used to consolidate parents' learning. Therapist assistance was provided to parents throughout the programme. Each week, therapists provide parents with their new session, monitor a progress diary completed by parents, and offer supportive feedback (i.e., reinforcing progress, problem-solving around specific skills, answering questions). Parents also receive additional support through a monitored discussion board on which they can communicate with other users of the programme.

An RCT examined the efficacy of i-PMT (Enebrink et al., 2012), comparing parent users of i-PMT ($n = 58$) and parents in a waitlist control condition ($n = 46$) in their reports of child behaviour problems. Parents who received the i-PMT programme reported greater reductions in the number and intensity of problem behaviours in children of 3–12 years of age. These effects were in the medium to large range and were maintained in a six-month follow-up. Kling et al. (2010) reported treatment effects in the same range among parent users of Comet when compared to those in a waitlist control group. Parents' satisfaction with and perceived ease of use of i-PMT was not assessed.

Infant-Net. The Play and Learning Strategies programme (PALS; Landry & Smith, 1996) is an 11-session programme which has been shown to be effective in promoting sensitive and responsive parenting behaviours towards infants in order to improve children's socio-emotional behaviours and developmental outcomes (Smith, Landry, & Swank, 2005; Landry, Smith, & Swank, 2006; Akai et al., 2008; Landry, Smith, Swank, & Guttentag, 2008). Infant-Net (Feil et al., 2008) was created as the web-based version of PALS, which teaches skills to be incorporated into parents' day-to-day activities (e.g., feeding, playing, changing, clothing). Parents learn how to better understand infant cues, be more sensitive and responsive in their parenting behaviours, sustain infant focus, find occasions to familiarize infants with objects or social games, and to express themselves both verbally and physically when interacting with their infants. In addition to the elements common to TPOL (i.e., video modelling) and i-PMT (i.e., knowledge testing, summary of important concepts, skills-based homework, online parent discussion board), Infant-Net incorporates professional coaching through the use of video technology, simulating clinicians' direct observations in face-to-face interventions. Each week, parents record five-minute videos of their interactions at home with their infants while practising the assigned skills. Coaches provide personalized support as they review these videos together with parents over the telephone.

Baggett et al. (2010) examined the efficacy of Infant-Net in an RCT, comparing the Internet-delivered programme ($n = 20$) to a control condition ($n = 20$) in which parents received six-month access to a computer, an Internet connection, and Internet-delivered resources for parenting and infant development. When interacting with their mothers, significantly higher levels of infant social and environmental engagement were observed by parents using the Infant-Net programme than those in the control condition, reflecting a medium to large effect size. Further, the mothers using Infant-Net demonstrated higher levels of positive parenting behaviours (i.e., responsiveness, warmth, positive affect) when compared to those in the control condition, and these differences showed a trend towards statistical significance. It is uncertain how these effects were maintained as a follow-up assessment was not completed. While the differences were not statistically significantly, a medium effect size was revealed, suggesting the need for further examination with a higher-powered study. The face-to-face PALS programme has demonstrated a range of small to large effects on both infant and maternal positive behaviour (Landry et al., 2006, 2008). In comparison, it appears that the Internet-delivered Infant-Net produces similar, if not even better, results. The Internet-delivered programme was reported by parents as easy to use and navigate (95%). The use of video-modelling and coaching was regarded by 95–100% of parents as being helpful for learning programme skills. Moreover, parents generally felt connected to the programme, with 85–90% indicating that the coach appeared interested in them and had understood them and their baby. Most (85%) would also recommend the programme to a friend.

Internet-delivered interventions to support parental well-being

Although one of the primary purposes of parenting programmes is to promote healthy child development and to assist parents in parenting skills, they have also been found to be helpful for improving parents' well-being. A meta-analysis consisting of 23 studies found that face-to-face parenting programmes are efficacious in reducing parental depression and anxiety/stress and improving self-esteem and one's relationship with one's partner (for a review, see Barlow, Coren, & Stuart-Brown, 2002). While it is not surprising that improvements in parenting skills and child behavioural problems lead to improvements in the general well-being of parenting, a growing body of research has investigated Internet-delivered programmes designed to support the well-being and mental health of parents.

With the advent of the computer and Internet, traditional neighbourhood, family, and community parental support and face-to-face programmes have been transformed. Indeed, Internet-delivered broadband technologies have allowed for the development of multifunctional social network options that can include asynchronous text-based communication (e.g., email-based mailing lists, Internet discussion forums), synchronous instant messaging (e.g., 'live' support groups), static informational websites, and/or supportive videos (Horrigan, 2009). Similar to traditional face-to-face parenting programmes, Internet-delivered support programmes are often founded by individuals motivated by personal interest, perceptions of marginalization, and frustration regarding the inadequacy of local support services (Kahn, 1991).

Parents may be particularly well suited to utilize parental support over the Internet. For instance, in a national survey of parents residing in the US, married-parent and single-parent homes with children aged under 18 years were found to have higher adoption of high speed Internet, 84% and 66% respectively, compared with 55% reported in homes without children (National Telecommunications and Information Administration, 2011). Parents also indicate interest in learning experience-based information from other parents, rather than receiving information strictly from experts (Doty & Dworkin, 2014). Social isolation in a modern, fast-paced society is an additional reason that parents use Internet-delivered resources to receive support (Plantin & Daneback, 2009). Indeed, through the use of Internet-delivered parental support sites, parents can conveniently congregate with other parents who are faced with similar difficulties, and share coping strategies, as well as offering encouragement and support. This is particularly useful for parents residing in remote and rural communities, where access to specialized support groups may be more limited than in the larger urban centres.

Over the past decade, multiple Internet-delivered parent support groups have emerged. While these are still in their infancy, researchers have started to investigate both the efficacy and perceptions of Internet-support groups for a range of parenting difficulties. For instance, Clifford and Minnes (2013) conducted an RCT on a four-month Internet support group for parents of children with autism spectrum disorders ($n = 20$) compared to a control group ($n = 25$). The intervention included eight Internet-delivered support groups as well as open access to a discussion board. Facilitated by a Master's level clinician, the support groups included synchronous discussion of specific topics as well as the provision of support. Results indicated that the Internet support group was well utilized, with 64% of parents attending three or more groups. No significant differences were revealed between the Internet-delivered support group and the control group for reported mood, anxiety, parental stress, or positive perceptions. However, parents reported satisfaction with the support group and perceived the discussion topics as helpful. In similar fashion, Carter (2009) conducted a qualitative study on the Internet-delivered self-help group experiences of 22 parental advocates who have children diagnosed with Autism Spectrum Disorder. Reported advantages included receiving access to information and services, connecting with other parents of similar background, and increasing advocacy. Reported drawbacks included receiving inaccurate, confusing, or overly negative information, and the lack of success they experienced at times from their advocacy efforts.

Preliminary research suggests Internet-delivered support is efficacious for women afflicted with postpartum depression (PPD). O'Mahen et al. (2013) tested the efficacy of an Internet behavioural activation (iBA) programme compared with treatment as usual (TAU) for the treatment of PPD. The 11-session programme consisted of psychoeducation and behavioural exercises as well as access to an Internet chat room that was moderated by parent supporters and supervised by specialist health visitors. Findings from 910 women with PPD indicated that participants in the iBA group reported greater reductions in depressive symptoms compared to the TAU group; attrition rates were high, however, with less than one-third of the participants completing the programme. Further, the chat room was utilized by only 7% of the participants. Evans and colleagues (2012) conducted a qualitative content analysis to examine the nature of communication that was posted on PPD Internet-delivered support groups over a six-month period. Using directed content analysis, 512 postings were reviewed. Results indicated that the majority of participants' postings included providing emotional support (41.6%) followed by information seeking (37.5%) and instrumental support (20.9%).

Research has also been conducted in the area of Internet support groups for parents of children diagnosed with diabetes. One study interviewed parents of adolescents with diabetes and found that parents were interested in learning ways to support their children as well as receiving personal support for their own well-being. For instance, parents were interested in assisting with fostering self-efficacy regarding their children's management of diabetes. They were also interested in learning from the advice and experience of other parents in addition to the expertise offered by healthcare practitioners. Further, the participants reported that Internet support would be helpful for parents living in rural or remote communities and for parents requiring culturally sensitive support.

A separate study explored the needs and preferences of support groups tailored to parents of adolescents with Type 1 diabetes (Nicholas, Gutwin, & Paterson, 2013). Group interviews were conducted at multiple Canadian sites. Results showed that parents reported an interest in receiving emotional support over the Internet. Notably, parents were interested in discussing the impact of the disease on the whole family, as well as methods to effectively educate other family members and to implement appropriate parenting strategies. Parents were also drawn to the accessibility of Internet social support sites.

More widely established Internet support programmes have also been examined. For instance, Jones and Meier (2012) explored the development and leadership of the Parents of Suicides (POS) Internet community. POS has been active for over a decade and was developed by a parent-survivor after discovering that her community lacked adequate, appropriate support. Information regarding the POS community was gathered through email correspondence with the founder, telephone interviews with the founder and leaders, and an analysis of website variables. Results from qualitative analyses revealed that POS began with a free mailing list service and the Internet support group was characterized by a 'strong sense of intimacy and quick, intense bonding' (Jones & Meier, 2012, p. 107). Progressing from strictly email correspondences, POS has adapted with the changes in technology and now offers chat rooms, memorials, social network pages, and sister groups in response to interest from non-parent survivors (i.e., family and friends). Similar to face-to-face support groups, volunteer moderators facilitate chat sessions held throughout the week. Website analyses indicated that POS has over 400 members and that the site has an active membership with individual members posting approximately 7,100 messages per month. Given the member diversity, guidelines for group interaction and formalized member screening have been implemented. To address the loss of face-to-face contact, yearly in-person retreats are organized for interested members. Outcome statistics on the effectiveness of this website on improving parental well-being were not reported.

Doty and Dworkin (2014) critically reviewed 19 international articles addressing Internet social supports for parents. Results showed that parents typically report using Internet-delivered parenting sites to gather information and for support. Most studies reported that parents found support through informal learning and that they valued other parents' advice more than expert advice. Informal databases of parenting knowledge and experiences created in discussion threads were considered by parents to be useful tools because they could search the site for information when questions emerged. The review further provided evidence that Internet-based support can be helpful for addressing isolation, particularly for new parents. For instance, one study found that 86% of mothers engaged in blogging to stay in touch with family and friends and perceived blogging as a form of social support (Bartholomew et al., 2012 as cited in Doty & Dworkin, 2014). Parental use of the popular social networking website Facebook was positively associated with parental adjustment, and this was found in samples unique to fathers. Single parents and parents with higher self-esteem were also more likely to use Internet parenting websites. The review further noted that Internet-delivered parental support decreased stress and facilitated coping strategies.

Advantages and disadvantages of Internet-delivered interventions for parents

There are multiple benefits associated with Internet delivery to help with parenting and to support the well-being of parents. One of the major benefits of using online interventions is the ability to extend the reach of services. This includes the provision of services to families living in remote or rural locations that otherwise may not have access. Even families unlimited by geographical proximity experience barriers to interventions. One of the main obstacles cited by parents for taking part in parenting interventions is the logistical barrier they encounter, such as problems with scheduling sessions, arranging transportation, and finding childcare (Heinrichs, Bertram, Kuschel, & Hahlweg, 2005; Ingoldsby, 2010). Online interventions can overcome such roadblocks for parents by allowing them the convenience of accessing services anywhere, at a time that suits them and their family. Research has highlighted the importance of social support when it is challenging to leave home (Han & Belcher, 2001) or outside traditional office hours when face-to-face supports are typically not available (Huws, Jones, & Ingledew, 2001). Receiving Internet-delivered treatment from a parent's home is beneficial when raising an infant, a child with developmental or psychological difficulties, or when parenting multiple children, as parents often have limited time to seek face-to-face services.

Receiving online services may be particularly appealing to parents. Parent consumers may appreciate the addition of the online modality in their menu of choices for interventions, which may be especially true for parents who are more inclined towards newer technologies. Additionally, Internet support programmes may be well suited for new parents as it provides an anonymous space to test out a new identity (Madge & O'Connor, 2006). Indeed, the invisibility and anonymity offered through Internet-delivered approaches reduces social pressure (Walther, 1996) and encourages participant openness and self-disclosure (Weinberg et al., 1995).

Lastly, online interventions have the potential of increasing the efficiency of the healthcare system. Internet-delivered programmes have demonstrated to be more cost-effective (Gerhards et al., 2010) and less time- and resource-intensive for service providers (Marks & Cavanagh, 2009). By using a stepped-care approach to service delivery, increased uptake of lower intensity interventions (i.e., Internet-delivered services) by families requiring less intensive care can increase the availability of higher intensity interventions (i.e., face-to-face treatment) for families that need such services. Moreover, delivering services over the Internet helps to increase implementation fidelity. This helps to maximize the effectiveness of evidence-based interventions, further improving the efficiency of services.

Despite the many advantages of Internet-delivered programmes, the drawbacks of this modality should be considered. While computer ownership and Internet access have widely expanded, they are still not universally available. For instance, a 2005 survey of 55% of British Columbia First Nations communities found that less than half of the homes were connected to the Internet (First Nations Technology Council, 2005). Thus, it is possible that not all parents have access to a computer or to the Internet and are less able to participate in Internet-delivered programmes. An additional disadvantage of Internet-delivered programmes is the lack of visual and facial expression information. Aside from reported non-verbal behaviour, such as conveying emotions through emoticons (e.g., :) to convey happiness, :(to convey sadness), written communication presented on chat forums or through synchronous communication does not translate non-verbal behaviours that are undeniably important aspects in the supportive process. In addition, with an absence of spontaneous clarification offered by face-to-face facilitators, Internet-delivered services create the potential for misunderstanding of group moderators or group participants.

Finally, handling crisis situations effectively presents an additional challenge to the safe use of Internet-delivered interventions. Some critics argue that significant problems can arise if individuals using Internet-delivered support services become suicidal or if the support room moderator is concerned about the safety of a participant (Mitchell & Murphy, 1998). To address this concern, it is imperative that Internet programmes collect identifying client information, as well as the client's location and contact information, so that if participants are at risk, then an emergency management team can be contacted and directed to the client if necessary (Rummell & Joyce, 2010).

Future directions

Technology is continuing to evolve and it will be interesting to see the many different ways that parents will reach out for help from the global community in the future. New resources will be created and old ones will be refined through a process of using traditional outcome data (e.g., improvements in symptom ratings) combined with metrics typically associated with marketing research, such as patterns of usage (e.g., bounce rates, return visits, and time spent on page). Both the content and nature of delivery will be important determinants in the success and popularity of future Internet-delivered services.

Research in this area lends itself to the evaluation of various methods of delivering therapeutic or supportive interventions over the Internet. For example, the type of feedback from a therapist could be directly compared to determine whether synchronous or asynchronous supports are equally effective for a particular concern or patient population. Online or face-to-face groups could be readily compared with individual interventions. There is even the possibility of examining the benefits of creating an online community for a particular concern that included experts and consumers of mental health services using self-study materials and live events such as webinars.

It is also difficult to predict what technologies will be available in the near future and how they might impact options for Internet-delivered care. It has been less than ten years since smart phones have become commonplace and we are continuing to integrate their use into daily living in surprising and novel ways. Emerging technologies that may prove promising for providing immediate in-vivo feedback are wearable biometric trackers and smart clothes. Using these tech-savvy trackers, parents could monitor their children's physiological data in real time as they practise the strategies they learn in Internet-delivered interventions. These data could provide feedback on how a child is reacting to an intervention, and how a parent could most effectively respond. For example, a parent may wish to proceed with an intervention if the child's feedback is calm, but may decide to take a break if the child's heart rate and respiration are elevated, to help the child relax before returning to the situation. Physiological data could also be collected to decide if interventions could be tailored to individuals based on their reactivity, or if they are more effective for certain subgroups of children and parents.

Technology is developing at a rapid pace, and it is likely that just as we demonstrate the efficacy of one particular intervention it will need to be modified for delivery on a new platform that did not exist previously. Although it may appear onerous to invest in interventions with short shelf lives owing to quickly changing platforms, the benefits in persisting in this area include being able to reach out in new and innovative ways to improve the lives of families around the globe.

Clinical recommendations

In the light of the emerging research support, clinicians may be interested in how to use Internet-delivered interventions when assisting parents and families in their clinical practice. We offer the following recommendations. To begin, if clinicians recommend parenting sites or support programmes to parents, it is imperative that the clinician continually monitor the site. Given the changing technology and minimal quality control for Internet-delivered interventions, unlike traditional books or face-to-face services, there are a range of Internet-delivered interventions which are constantly in flux. Further, with respect to suggesting Internet-delivered parenting programmes to parents, it is important to understand not only the degree of therapist support required to implement the intervention (i.e., no support required for self-guided programmes versus higher degree of support required for coaching-based programmes), but also the expectations that parents may have about their clinician's involvement. Will the client be working with their face-to-face clinician over the Internet, or will a different therapist or coach offer the Internet-delivered support? Introducing a new service modality presents the responsibility of helping clients familiarize themselves with it and to clarify such questions. Further, when recommending Internet-delivered social support sites, clinicians are encouraged to direct parents to moderated sites where a clinician or volunteer moderates the content of the site to ensure the safety of the group members. Social support sites that are unmoderated could be potentially harmful if group members are unsupportive or offer unhelpful advice.

Summary

Preliminary findings provide support for the efficacy of Internet-delivered parenting programmes for improving behavioural outcomes for children and parents, and of programmes for improving the well-being of parents. While more research is required, early outcomes suggest that Internet-delivered support and interventions are efficacious and desirable for parents struggling with a range of difficulties. Although not expected to replace face-to-face contact, Internet-delivered interventions are a promising use of technology that provide parents with an expanding menu of options, have the potential to increase services and support, and also may improve the cost-efficiency of the healthcare system.

References

Akai, C.E., Guttentag, C.L., Baggett, K.M., Willard-Noria, C., & Centers for the Prevention of Child Neglect. (2008). Enhancing parenting practices of at-risk mothers. *The Journal of Primary Prevention, 29*, 223–243. doi: 10.1007/s10935-008-0134-z.

Baggett, K.M., Davis, B., Feil, E.G., Sheeber, L.L., Landry, S.H., Carta, J.J., & Leve, C. (2010). Technologies for expanding the reach of evidence-based interventions: preliminary results for promoting social-emotional development in early childhood. *Topics in Early Childhood Special Education, 29*, 226–238. doi: 10.1177/0271121409354782.

Barak, A., Hen, L., Boniel-Nissim, M., & Shapira, N. (2008). A comprehensive review and a meta-analysis of the effectiveness of Internet-based psychotherapeutic interventions. *Journal of Technology in Human Services, 26*, 109–160. doi: 10.1080/15228830802094429.

Barlow, J., Coren, E., & Stewart-Brown, S. (2002). Meta-analysis of the effectiveness of parenting programmes in improving maternal psychosocial health. *British Journal of General Practice, 52*, 223–233.

Bartholomew, M.K., Sullivan Schoppe, S.J., Glassman, M., Dush Kamp, C.M., & Sullivan, J.M. (2012). New parents' Facebook use at the transition to parenthood. *Family Relations, 61*, 455–469.

Breitenstein, S.M., Gross, D., & Christophersen, R. (2014). Digital delivery methods of parenting training interventions: a systematic review. *Worldviews on Evidence-Based Nursing, 11*, 168–176. doi: 10.1111/wvn.12040.

Carter, I. (2009). Positive and negative experiences of parents involved in online self-help groups for autism. *Journal on Developmental Disabilities, 15*, 44–52.

Chorpita, B.F., Daleiden, E.L., Ebesutani, C., Young, J., Becker, K.D., Nakamura, B.J., ... Starace, N. (2011). Evidence-based treatments for children and adolescents: an updated review of indicators of efficacy and effectiveness. *Clinical Psychology: Science and Practice, 18*, 154–172. doi: 10.1111/j.1468-2850.2011.01247.x.

Clifford, T., & Minnes, P. (2013). Logging on: evaluating an online support group for parents with children with autism spectrum disorders. *Journal of*

Autism and Developmental Disorders, 43, 1662–1675. doi: 10.1007/s10803-012-1714-6.
Doty, J.L., & Dworkin, J. (2014). Online social support for parents: a critical review. *Marriage and Family Review, 50,* 174–198.doi: 10.1080/01494929.2013.834027.
Dretzke, J., Davenport, C., Frew, E., Barlow, J., Stewart-Brown, S., Bayliss, S., Taylor, R.S., Sandercock, J., & Hyde, C. (2009). The clinical effectiveness of different parenting programmes for children with conduct problems: a systematic review of randomized controlled trials. *Child and Adolescent Psychiatry and Mental Health, 3,* 1–10. doi: 10.1186/1753-2000-3-7.
Enebrink, P., Högström, J., Forster, M., & Ghaderi, A. (2012). Internet-based parent management training: a randomized controlled study. *Behaviour Research and Therapy, 50,* 240–249. doi: 10.1016/j.brat.2012.01.006.
Evans, M., Donelle, L., & Hume-Loveland, L. (2012). Social support and online postpartum depression discussion groups: a content analysis. *Patient Education and Counseling, 87,* 405–410.
First Nations Technology Council. (2005). *Report on an Environmental Scan Conducted by the First Nations Technology Council.* Retrieved from the First Nations Technology Council website: http://www.fntc.info/files/documents/Environmental_Scan___Final_Report.pdf.
Feil, E.G., Baggett, K.M., Davis, B., Sheeber, L., Landry, S., Carta, J.J., & Buzhardt, J. (2008). Expanding the reach of preventive interventions: development of an internet-based training for parents of infants. *Child Maltreatment, 13,* 334–346. doi: 10.1177/1077559508322446.
Gerhards, S.A. H., de Graaf, L.E., Jacobs, L.E., Severens, J.L., Huibers, M.J.H., Arntz, A., Gerhards, S.A.H., de Graaf, L.E., Jacobs, L.E., Severens, J.L., Huibers, M.J.H., Arntz, A., Riper, H., Widdershoven, G., Metsemakers, J.F.M., & Evers, S.M.A.A. (2010). Economic evaluation of online computerized cognitive behavioural therapy without support for depression in primary care: Randomized trial. *British Journal of Psychiatry, 196,* 310–318. doi: 10.1192/bjp.bp.109/065748.
Griffiths, K.M., Farrer, L., & Christensen, H. (2010). The efficacy of Internet interventions for depression and anxiety disorders: a review of randomised controlled trials. *Medical Journal of Australia, 192,* 4–11.
Gutman, L.M., & Feinstein L. 2010. Parenting behaviours and children's development from infancy to early childhood: changes, continuities and contributions. *Early Child Development and Care, 180,* 535–556. doi: 10.1080/03004430802113042.
Han, H.R., & Belcher, A.E. (2001). Computer-mediated support group use among parents of children with cancer – an exploratory study. *Computer, 19,* 27–33.
Hassler, M., & Havbring, L (2003). Föräldracirklar – en metod för att utveckla sitt föräldraskap (FoU-rapport 2003:8) [Parent circles – a method for strengthening parent skills]. Stockholms socialtjänstförvaltning: FoU-enheten.
Horrigan, J. (2009). *Home Broadband Adoption 2009: Broadband Adoption Increases, but Monthly Prices Do Too.* Retrieved from http://pewinternet.org/Reports/2009/10-Home-Broadband-Adoption-2009.aspx.
Huws, J.C., Jones, R.S.P., & Ingledew, D.K. (2001). Parents of children with autism using an email group: a grounded theory study. *Journal of Health Psychology, 6,* 569–584.
Jones, A., & Meier, A. (2012). Growing www.parentsofsuicide: a case study of an online support community. *Social Work with Groups, 34,* 101–120. doi: 10.1080/01609513.2010.543049.
Kahn, S. (1991). *Organizing: A Guide for Grassroots Leaders.* Washington, DC: NASW Press.

Kazdin, A.E., & Blase, S.L. (2011). Rebooting psychotherapy research and practice to reduce the burden of mental illness. *Perspectives on Psychological Science, 6,* 21–37. doi: 10.1177/1745691610393527.

Kirp, D.L. (ed.). (2011). *Kids First: Five Big Ideas for Transforming Children's Lives and America's Future.* New York: Public Affairs.

Kling, Å., Forster, M., Sundell, K., & Melin, L. (2010). A randomized controlled effectiveness trial of parent management training with various degrees of therapist support. *Behaviour Therapy, 41,* 530–542. doi: 10.1016/j.beth.2010.02.004.

Kling, Å., Sundell, K., Melin, L., & Forster, M. (2006). Komet för föräldrar. En randomiserad effektutvärdering av ett föräldraprogram för barns beteendeproblem. (FoU-rapport 2006:14) Stockholms Socialtjänstförvaltning: FoU-enheten.

Landry, S.H. & Smith, K.E. (1996). *Playing and Learning Strategies – I.* Houston, TX: University of Texas – Houston Health Science Center.

Landry, S.H., Smith, K.E., & Swank, P.R. (2006). Responsive parenting: establishing early foundations for social, communication, and independent problem-solving skills. *Developmental Psychology, 42,* 627–642. doi:10.1037/0012-1649.42.4.627.

Landry, S.H., Smith, K.E., Swank, P., & Guttentag, C. (2008). A responsive parenting intervention: the optimal timing across early childhood for impacting maternal behaviors and child outcomes. *Developmental Psychology, 44,* 1335–1353. doi: 10.1037/a0013030.

Madge, C., & O'Connor, H. (2006). Parenting gone wired: empowerment of new mothers on the internet? *Social and Cultural Geography, 7,* 199–220.

Marks, I., & Cavanagh, K. (2009). Computer aided psychological treatments: evolving issues. *The Annual Review of Clinical Psychology, 5,* 121–141.

Mitchell, D.L., & Murphy, L.M. (1998). *Confronting the Challenges of Therapy Online: A Pilot Project.* Retrieved from http://www.therapyonline.ca/files/Confronting_the_challenges.pdf.

National Institute For Health And Care Excellence (NICE) (2013). *Antisocial Behaviour and Conduct Disorders in Children and Young People: Recognition, Intervention and Management.* Retrieved from http://www.nice.org.uk/cg158.

Nicholas, D.B., Gutwin, C., & Paterson, B. (2013). Examining preferences for website support to parents of adolescents with diabetes. *Social Work in Health Care, 52,* 862–879. doi: 10.1080/00981389.2013.827144.

National Telecommunications and Information Administration. (2011). *Digital Nation: Expanding Internet Usage.* Washington, DC: Author.

Nieuwboer, C.C., Fukkink, R.G., & Hermanns, J.M.A. (2013). Online programs as tools to improve parenting. A meta-analytic review. *Children and Youth Services Review, 35,* 1823–1829. doi: 10.1016/j.childyouth.2013.08.008.

O'Mahen, H.A., Woodford, J., McGinley, J., Warren, F.C., Richards, D.A., O'Mahen, H.A., Woodford, J., McGinley, J., Warren, F.C., Richards, D.A., Lynch, T.R., & Taylor, R.S. (2013). Internet-based behavioral activation – Treatment for postnatal depression (Netmums): A randomized controlled trial. *Journal of Affective Disorders, 150,* 814–822.doi: 10.1016/j.jad.2013.03.005.

Pew Research Center (2014) http://www.pewinternet.org/fact-sheets/health-fact-sheet/

Plantin, L., & Daneback, K. (2009). Parenthood, information, and support on the Internet: a literature review of research on parents and professionals online. *MBC Family Practice, 10,* 34. doi: 10.1186/1471-2296-10-34.

Rummell, C.M., & Joyce, N.R. (2010). 'So wat do u want to wrk on 2day?': the ethical implications of online counselling. *Ethics & Behaviour, 20,* 482–496.

Romeo, R., Knapp, M., & Scott, S. (2006). Economic cost of severe antisocial behaviour in children – and who pays it. *British Journal of Psychiatry, 188,* 547–553. doi: 10.1192/bjp.bp.104.007625.
Sanders, M.R. (1999). The Triple P-Positive Parenting Program: towards an empirically validated multilevel parenting and family support strategy for the prevention of behavior and emotional problems in children. *Clinical Child and Family Psychology Review, 2,* 71–90. doi: 10.1023/A:1021843613840.
Sanders, M.R., Baker, S., & Turner, K.M.T. (2012). A randomized controlled trial evaluating the efficacy of Triple P online with parents of children with early-onset conduct problems. *Behaviour Research and Therapy, 50,* 675–684. doi: 10.1016/j.brat.2012.07.004.
Sanders, M.R., Dittman, C.K., Farruggia, S.P., & Keown, L. (2014). A comparison of online versus workbook delivery of a self-help positive parenting program. *Journal of Primary Prevention, 35,* 125–133. doi: 10.1007/s10935-014-0339-2.
Sanders, M.R., Kirby, J.N., Tellegen, C.L., & Day, J.J. (2014). The Triple P-positive parenting program: a systematic review and meta-analysis of a multi-level system of parenting support. *Clinical Psychology Review, 34,* 337–357. doi: 10.1016/j.cpr.2014.04.003.
Sanders, M.R., Markie-Dadds, C., Tully, L.A., & Bor, W. (2000). The Triple P-positive parenting program. A comparison of enhanced, standard, and self-directed behavioral family intervention for parents of children with early onset conduct problems. *Journal of Consulting and Clinical Psychology, 68,* 624–640. doi: 10.1037/0022-006X.68.4.624.
Smith, K.E., Landry, S.H., & Swank, P.R. (2005).The influence of decreased parental resources on the efficacy of a responsive parenting intervention. *Journal of Consulting and Clinical Psychology, 73,* 711–720. doi: 10.1037/0022-006X.73.4.711.
Spek, V., Cuijpers, P., Nyklícek, I., Riper, H., Keyzer, J., & Pop, V. (2007). Internet based cognitive behaviour therapy for symptoms of depression and anxiety: a meta-analysis. *Psychological Medicine, 37,* 319–328. doi: 10.1017/S003329170600894.
Stack, D.M., Serbin, L.A., Enns, L.N., Ruttle, P.L., & Barrieau, L. (2010). Parental effects on children's emotional development over time and across generations. *Infants and Young Children, 23,* 52–69. doi: 10.1097/IYC.0b013e3181c97606.
Turner, K.M. T., & Sanders, M.R. (2011). *Triple P Online (Interactive Internet Program).* Brisbane, QLD: Triple P International.
Walker, H. (2006). *Addressing Social Behavior Needs of Students With Disabilities and Those At-Risk Though Classroom, Program, and School-Wide Systems of Support.* OSEP Project Director Meeting report, Institute on Violence and Destructive Behavior, University of Oregon, Eugene.
Walther, J.B. (1996). Computer-mediated communication: impersonal, interpersonal and hyper-personal interaction. *Communication Research, 23,* 23–43.
Weinberg, N., Schmale, J.D., Uken, J., & Wessel, K. (1995). Computer-mediated support groups. *Social Work with Groups, 17,* 43–54.

12
Becoming Invisible: The Effect of Triangulation on Children's Well-Being

Rudi Dallos

Introduction

The concept of triangulation has been one of the conceptual cornerstones of systemic therapy (Minuchin, 1974; Palazzoli et al., 1978; Dallos & Draper, 2009). It represents the basis of a fundamental shift from linear to systemic thinking and offers the suggestion that triads rather than individuals or dyads are the fundamental building blocks of family life. More specifically in relation to work with children it emphasizes that children can experience severe distress when 'caught in the middle' of their parents' conflicts and tensions (Dubois-Comtois et al., 2008). The long-term effects of such exposure and entanglement can have significant negative impacts on children's mental health. Despite the centrality of this concept to clinical practice, there has been surprisingly little research conducted to explore the nature and experience of triangulation. Arguably most of what we know comes from clinical observation in work with families.

Bowen (1978) has defined triangulation as potentially occurring in any pattern of family relationships and also in terms of a network of interlocking triadic processes. In this paper we are focusing on children's experience of conflictual triadic process in relation to their parents or carers. Further we will consider this from a systemic and attachment perspective.

The patterns of triangulation can be seen to follow a developmental pathway. This can be seen in terms of how the representation of attachment experiences by a child follows the neuro-psychological profiles of developments.

Young infants represent experience prior to the onset of language in terms of sensory and somatic/procedural memories. An infant or young child may experience the tensions, conflicts, and distresses between his parents in terms of an embodied response including arousal, tension, and anxiety. This may be expressed in terms of a variety of somatic states, for example agitation, crying, sleeplessness, vomiting, and so on. These symptoms may have the effect of distracting the parents from their conflicts and temporarily reduce the emotional tension. However, they may be a habituation effect such that the child may need to increase the severity of the symptoms in order to maintain this distracting influence.

With the development of language the possibility arises that in addition to this process the child is recruited to take sides in the conflict between the parents:

> They used to really hurt me because they used to play each other off... And they would be like 'Go on tell me all the bad stuff about the other one'. And I used to sit there and think to myself I am made up of half of each of these people and they hate each other and do they hate me? That used to play on my mind for ages when I was really young and that was the limit of my thought, I didn't analyse it further.
> (Dallos, 2007)

As the child matures, the possibilities for conscious, explicit, and strategic thinking increase and the child may make a choice organized around avoidance or involvement in the process (Shelton and Harold, 2008). In the former the child may decide to try and withdraw from the parents' conflicts, though this may be difficult, as Kathy describes above, in that pressure to take sides may be increased and one solution is to take sides with one parent and avoid a relationship with the other. Involvement consists of the child attempting to manage the parents' conflicts: this can consist of the child attempting to be a peacemaker, trying to calm the parents, or being especially helpful. Alternatively the child may adopt a more angry coercive strategy towards the parents or distract them by engaging in dangerous or disruptive behaviours. Although these forms of mediating may be effective in ending the conflict, over-involvement may only further triangulate the child and increase distress. We use the words 'decide' and 'strategy' here with caution since in our clinical experience these are not conscious choices, and to the contrary children typically appear largely unaware of the distressing and disorienting effect that triangulation has on them.

Both these strategies have costs. Avoidance as a conflict management strategy has also been associated with increased adjustment problems, particularly anxiety and depression. Involvement in marital conflict can cause psychological maladjustment, while avoidance of marital arguments may be differently adaptive for children, depending on the cognitive processes, such as use of self-calming or distracting activity. Shelton and Harold (2008) found children's attributions of threat and self-blame and their avoidant and over-involved coping responses caused by parents' marital arguments could explain the variation in children's long-term internalizing symptoms and externalizing problems.

Attachment and triangulation

Attachment theory has essentially offered a dyadic picture of the development of security in children. Bowlby (1969, 1988) referred to the creation of a 'secure base', which includes fostering an 'internal working model' for the child that she can consistently expect emotional and practical protection from external danger and assistance with managing her own feelings. However, there has been little exploration of how the mother is herself influenced by the anxieties and tensions in her other relationships, in particular with the child's father (Dubois-Comtois et al., 2008). Further, not only the mother's ability to respond empathetically but the wider context of the security of the child's family life is threatened by conflict between the parents. This arguably may produce an even higher level of anxiety since the child runs the risk of losing not only the attachment figure but their home, family, and physical safety. We might suggest that a child has an attachment not just with each parent but with the relationship between them:

- Relationship with each parent
- Pulled to take sides

For some children the parents' relationship represents a context of safety and security. The child may have the experience of seeing her parents being warm with each other, drawing the child into pleasant activities as a threesome, and being cared for, soothed, and guided by both of them jointly. On the other hand, for many children the opposite is true. The parents being together may signal anxiety, distress, or even danger. The child might expect the parents to start to argue, threaten each other, and even threaten the child in their conflicts. Where this is a frequent pattern the child might come to be highly anxious about the parents being with each

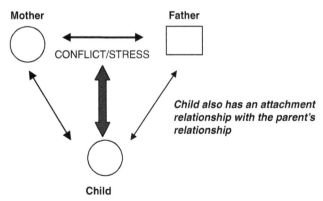

Figure 12.1 Triadic attachment relationships

other and find ways to try and keep them apart or to attempt to mediate and calm their conflicts. Additionally a child might also be able to distract the parents from each other by themselves becoming problematic, angry, shouting at both of them, engaging in risky behaviours, and so on. These have the temporary effect of distracting the parents but may also add to the overall family distress and tension. In turn it may also serve to make the parents feel bad about themselves as parents and their relationship, and to blame each other for producing such a 'problematic' or 'distressed' child.

Such considerations have been central to family therapy, and a key example is the work of Byng-Hall (1995) who offered the conceptualization that children can function as 'marital-distance regulators'. He argued that the child's behaviours could function to draw the parents closer if they were drifting apart but more counter-intuitively could also serve to distance them if they were becoming too emotionally aroused:

> The only thing I ever hear them talking about is me and if I didn't have this [anorexia] it's kind of like, would everything fall apart, at least it's keeping them talking. And they won't argue while I've got this because it might make me worse. So um... that's kind of bought, sort of like, I'm not in control as such, but I've got more control over the situation that way.
> (Kathy (17), in Dallos, 2007)

In the quote above Kathy poignantly exemplifies how her symptoms appear to function in such a distance-regulating manner. She considers that her anorexia both keeps her parents connected – 'keeping them talking' – but at the same time that they will not argue because it 'might make me worse'.

Dallos and Vetere (2010) proposed that unhappy marriages have escalating patterns of anger and fear as distressed parents can trigger each other's negative emotional responses. In turn these patterns may consist of combinations of insecure attachment strategies held between the parents. The patterns between the parents may be matched or mis-matched: Where both parents have secure attachment strategies this is relatively unproblematic for the child, but if both hold avoidant patterns the child may struggle to gain attachment responses, or where both are anxious the child may struggle to gain some emotional space. However, adjusting to combinations of mis-matched patterns might be even more complex in that the child is required to develop 'multiple models' to adapt to the differences. The conflicts between the parents and the emotional pull on the child may be related to these patterns. For example, an anxious parent may draw the child in to offer them emotional support against the other parent whereas the avoidant parent backs off, perhaps leaving the child feeling abandoned by them or feeling guilty that they have rejected them.

Schindler et al. (2007) looked at triads in relation to Drug Dependent Adolescents (DDAs). Evidence of a 'Triangulated pattern' was found in two-thirds of the sample consisting of fearful attachment representations in DDAs, preoccupied in mothers and dismissing in fathers. 'Insecure' patterns were also found in 19% of the sample, with fearful attachments in DDAs, mothers, and fathers. Ringer and Crittenden (2007) also found results relating to triangulation; parents would abdicate their parental function because they were preoccupied with marital problems, leaving the child to feel 'invisible' and perhaps act compulsively compliant. Amato and Afifi (2006) found that loyalty conflict declined in late adolescence, mainly because of alignment with one parent. In contrast, Buchanan et al. (1991) found that older adolescents were more likely to feel caught in between parents. Amato and Afifi (2006) indicate that being dependent on parents contributes to this in terms of needing their financial and emotional continuing support to assist their passage into adulthood. For some children the parent's relationship represents a context of safety and security. The child may have the experience of seeing her parents being warm with each other, drawing the child into pleasant activities as a threesome and of being cared for, soothed and guided by both of them jointly. On the other hand for many children, the opposite is true (Marvin, 2009).

Feeling caught between parents was related to high parental conflict and hostility and low parental cooperation. However, unexpectedly, they found that being close to both parents was associated with low rather than high feelings of being caught, as parents may be more sensitive to their children's feelings and therefore be less likely to behave in ways that put their children in the middle. Amato and Afifi (2006) supported this, though finding that high-conflict marriages make children feel more caught in the middle, and these feelings are associated with lower-subjective well-being and weaker parent–child relationships irrespective of age. Such feelings appeared to affect mother–daughter more than mother–son relationships, and faded following parental divorce.

A wealth of research indicates that children who are exposed to frequent, intense, and poorly resolved conflicts between parents are at greater risk for internalizing symptoms, externalizing problems, poor academic achievement, and weak parent–child relationships (Amato & Afifi, 2006; Shelton & Harold, 2008). Buehler and Welsh (2009) also support this and argue that adolescents need to be left out of marital problems owing to the harmful effects of triangulation: emotional arousal, triggering emotional and physiological responses, and upsetting and agitating adolescents. Shelton and Harold (2008) also state that the two factors most adversely affecting children exposed to parental hostility are the disruption of the parent–child relationship and negative emotions, cognitions, and representations. Davies and Cummings (1998) and Nicolotti, El-Sheikh, and Whitson (2003) add that exposure to conflict is associated with negative psychological symptoms in both children and adolescents (Harold & Conger, 1997; Harold, Shelton, Geoke-Money & Cummings, 2004). Gerard et al. (2006) argue that marital conflict can influence children's adjustment directly by equipping them with faulty working models of behavioural and emotional expression for dealing with social problems. They describe the 'spillover' effect where anger and tension from marital conflict interferes into the parent–child dyad. This can lead to parental punitive discipline or disengagement and negative interaction between parents and children, compromising children's psychosocial development. Marital conflict, parent–child relationship quality, and youth maladjustment influence negative family processes and maintain them over time, leading to increased tension in the family system. Children's noxious behaviours contribute to maintaining the destructive family patterns by increasing friction.

Buchanan, Maccoby, and Dornbusch (1991) propose that feelings of being caught in between parents' conflicts are related to higher levels of depression/anxiety and more deviant behaviour. Effects of the co-parenting relationship on adolescent adjustment were accounted for by its relation to feeling caught between parents. Further to this, Davies and Cummings (1994) proposed the Emotional Security Hypothesis, derived from attachment theory, suggesting that three areas of emotional functioning are disrupted by badly managed conflict between parents: emotional reactivity, representations of family relationships, and children feeling compelled to regulate marital conflict through intervening/withdrawing.

Coping with conflict

Grych (1998) discussed how feeling responsible for marital conflict provides children with a sense of coping efficacy and perceived control over conflict, which increases the likelihood of involvement. Shelton and Harold (2008) argue that adolescents who feel responsible for parents' arguments, yet cannot intervene, may express their distress through anger and acting up. Over-involvement in conflict may also weaken boundaries between marital and parent-child sub-systems, enmeshing children in marital interactions (Minuchin, 1974). The behaviour of 'masking' is also discussed as a coping response to marital conflict (Shelton & Harold, 2008), and as an attempt to inhibit expressions of distress and reduce their presence in the conflict (Davies & Forman, 2002). An increase in masking behaviour was found when adolescents felt they were to blame for their parents' arguments, with girls concealing it more than boys, possibly leading to adjustment problems. Dallos and Denford (2008) found that doubt and anxiety encouraged deceptive and masked communication. Dozier and Kobak (1992) found that adolescents who displayed dismissive strategies reacted with the greatest increase in physiological measures of stress (skin-conductance: sweating) during Adult Attachment Interview (AAI), suggesting that attempting to avoid emotional topics and encounters comes at a high emotional cost. It is possible that older age groups use avoidance more effectively, perhaps because of the autonomy they have to leave the house or call their friends. In terms of age, Johnston et al. (1987) argued that loyalty conflicts are most common at ages 6–8, less so at 9–11 when children become more likely to form alliances with one parent or the other. Buchanan et al. (1991) explain that with age children become increasingly able to distance themselves from parental disputes. However, as they get older they may be able to see multiple points of view, and parents may confide in them or have them relay messages to one another, possibly increasing feelings of being caught. They found that older adolescents were more likely to feel caught, showing that increases in social and cognitive maturity may influence this.

Aside from clinical observation, there has been surprisingly little research which explores in detail the experience of the conflicts and dilemmas experienced by children who are triangulated. These studies have typically employed standardized measures, which, although relevant, fall short of exploring the nature of children's experience in depth.

Experiences of triangulation: Attachment insecurity

The available research and clinical case studies indicate that triangulation, 'being caught in the middle', has a variety of negative consequences on children's lives. One specific question that arises is to what extent being in these situations relates to children's general sense of attachment in security. This is also a broader theoretical question in terms of whether the focus on dyadic relationships in attachment theory ignores the impact of triadic processes. Bowlby (1969) was always interested in these wider family dynamics but felt that they were more difficult to investigate. The subsequent focus by Ainsworth et al. (1978) on dyadic process, for example in the Strange Situation protocol, appears to have cemented such a dyadic focus. Though it has produced a richness of evidence regarding dyadic processes, this has not been integrated with a wider systemic perspective.

We have conducted a number of studies that have explored triadic attachment processes. Our primary interest was to explore how children experienced and understood situations of triadic conflict in contrast to dyadic scenarios. In order to pursue this, we considered a variety of attachment measures that are available for children (Dallos, 2014). The most frequently used of these is the Separation Anxiety Test (SAT), which consists of depictions of a variety of situations involving separation from a parent ranging from what might be considering to be mildly anxiety-provoking separation situations, such as the child going away on a school trip to the mother going into hospital for an operation. These were originally developed as cartoon depictions but have also been produced as photographs (Wright et al., 1995). Since we wanted to include a comparison of the children's responses to triadic scenarios, we chose what were considered to be more extreme separation scenarios. Examples of the photos we employed in our studies are shown below (Table 12.1):

Table 12.1 Dyadic scenario picture prompts

Triadic scenarios

In contrast we have developed a set of scenarios which depict triadic situations that also potentially involve a threat to the child in terms of potential separations and losses. In effect these scenarios represent attachment dilemmas for a child which are wider than those in dyadic situations. For example, the scenarios include a parent leaving the home after an argument between the adults. This represents a loss and separation from the leaving parent but also a loss of the family context and of the relationship the child has with her parents' relationship. We also considered that in ordinary family life a child's separation is not always clearly in terms of a separation from one of the parents. Interestingly, in the SAT pictures the depiction of the child going away on a school trip depicts a triadic scenario, in that both parents are present but the triadic features, such as whether the child might feel more or less anxious if it was just one of the parents present, whether he feels that one parent might miss him more than the other, or that he is likely to show a different separation response. Hence we decided to include this picture as an example of a triadic situation.

We developed a series of triadic scenarios that we felt would trigger the children's attachment responses in terms of anxieties about separation and changes in their relationship with each parent but also in terms of their relationship with the parents' relationship. The pictures devised are shown below (Table 12.2) and included child saying goodbye to both parents as he/she goes away on holiday, parents arguing over an inappropriate present

Table 12.2 Triadic scenario picture prompts

for the child, parents waiting up as the child comes home late, mother/father listening in to child's conversation with the separated parent, parents discussing the child's school report, and father leaving after an argument. These pictures were designed to elicit understandings and emotional responses regarding typical triadic interactions and conflicts. Two sets of pictures were developed, with male or female children in the pictures to facilitate identification with the young people depicted.

Children's experience of triangulation – Early intervention family therapy service

This service, which operated outside the NHS with charitable and some NHS funding, offered a systemic family therapy service for families who were usually referred by their GP or social services, and/or were self-referred. They had relatively little contact with clinical or social services and hence the processes of labelling had not usually been established or internalized by the families to become their dominant understanding of their problems. We initially intended to identify families where there appeared to be clear indication of triangulation processes. This in itself was interesting, because as we attempted to do this it became apparent that a lack of clear evidence of triangulation was the exception not the rule in this context.

The children were shown both sets of pictures on a laptop and invited to respond utilizing the procedure developed by Klagsbrun and Bowlby (1976) and Resnick (1993). This involved asking the children to respond to the pictures in terms of how the child depicted in the picture would respond and secondly how, if they were themselves the child in the picture, they would respond. The rationale between asking for these two types of response is that they allow an exploration of the child's generalized working model (another child) and their own specific responses. It also incorporates the idea that the attachment response may differ (see Table 12.3); for example, children who are more avoidant may show more defensive responses when they are asked to talk about their own responses. However, responding from the other child's perspective they may indicate that they are aware of the dilemmas and show a greater range of emotional responses as 'projected' onto the other child. Conversely children with anxious ambivalent patterns may show a greater emotional responsiveness when asked to respond as themselves and a less emotional response when there is more distance between the scenarios and themselves.

The procedure also involves inviting the children to describe the feelings and thoughts of the child and the adults in the scenarios in order to reveal their working model regarding self and other. This was also designed to assess the children's mentalization – how they thought the adults were thinking and feeling. Related to this, the child is also asked how they think the adults in the picture would respond and how the child would respond. This is intended to elicit their views of the attachment responses that are likely to occur.

We also developed an important reflective component in that we asked the children how they thought the adults in the scenarios understood their thoughts and feelings. We called this 'parental accurate empathy', and it was a measure of how much what they said the parents understood of their thoughts and feelings coincided with the children's statements earlier about how they thought and felt (see Table 12.1)

The children

Dean (11), Rick (11), and Jenny (11) (triplets) were living with their mother and stepfather; the mother and father had separated following the father being found in possession of pornographic pictures of young girls. Dean was seen by his school as defiant, angry, and displaying conduct problems. Jenny was seen as less symptomatic but there was suspicion of sexualized contact/behaviour. Rick, on the other hand, was seen as quiet, withdrawn, and depressed, but again, not as symptomatic as Dean. *John (12) and Peter (16)* (siblings) were adopted and living with their adoptive parents, and had no contact with their birth parents who were reported to have been very neglectful/abusive. Peter was said by his adoptive parents to have problems with drug use, and criminal and defiant behaviour. John was seen as the

Table 12.3 Scoring of dyadic and triadic pictures

Ratings 1 →9	SAT					Triadic			
Picture Number **Line Number** **Picture Title**	1 Holiday	6 Mum hospital	8 Dad arrested	2 Inappropriate present	3 Late home	4 Ring dad	5 School report	7 Argument-dad leaves	9 Mum affair
Avoidant									
Dismissing – minimizing importance of attachments									
Self-blame									
Resistance – avoiding attachment dilemma									
Idealization									
Anxious-Ambivalent									
Pre-occupying affect – anxiety									
Pre-occupying anger									
Derogation of others									
Solutions									
Unrealistically positive									
Catastrophic/destructive									
Avoiding the conflict									
Involvement in conflict									
Reflective Functioning									
Child re. parent/s									
PAE (Parent Accurate Empathy)									
Triadic Processes									
Aware of triadic process									
Aware of emotional impacts of triadic processes									
Traumatic States									
Indications of previous traumas									

'good boy', but he also started exhibiting some behaviour problems after an incident in his family occurred.

Jack (14) was living with his mother but stayed regularly with his birth father, and there was anxiety in the family system caused by the mother's boyfriend. Jack was also exhibiting behaviour problems, such as disrespect, anger, and defiance; however he was calmer when father was around. *Megan (11)* was seen by her single parent mother to be very 'clingy' and suffering with her anxiety caused by witnessing a traumatic incident. *Kate's (11)* parents had divorced but considerable conflict continued, to the extent that Katie decided to stop seeing her father. The mother said that she was stressed and lacked time for her daughter.

Findings (see Figure 12.2)

SAT and triadic pictures

Generally the SAT pictures produced generally lower attachment anxiety scores than those Triadic pictures. The figure below shows visually how the children rated the nine different scenarios:

The findings also indicated that in triadic separation and conflict situations, particularly when the children appear to be the cause of familial conflict and potential separations, the children are much more affected. In contrast to the triadic scenarios in some cases in the dyadic (SAT) pictures, the child produces responses which would indicate secure attachment responses giving a range of affect, showing good reflective functioning and a good relationship with carer. In contrast, in the triadic pictures, particularly, especially the 'school report' scenario insecure responses were evident and these were characterized by with self-blame and very low parent accurate empathy

Self-blame was also a recurrent theme for the children in relation to the triadic scenarios, for example Megan said in relation to the scenario of the parents arguing over a present:

> *They're arguing over my grades and it's my fault. It's not their fault. Mum can't blame it on dad and mum can't blame it on herself.... It's not fair.*
> (Megan: 284–287)

This also indicates the sense of helplessness, as the phrase 'it's not fair' is also repeated in the responses. A common theme also found in the conflict situations was that the children would either avoid or involve themselves in the conflict situation. These mechanisms are a form of coping, and the findings showed that the higher the score on avoiding conflict, the lower the score for catastrophic solutions, and the higher the score for involvement in conflict, the higher the score for catastrophic solutions. In relation

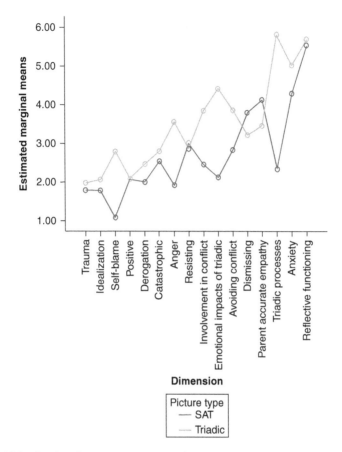

Figure 12.2 Graph of average responses for SAT or triadic pictures across all dimensions (n = 8)

to attachment strategies, involvement in conflict and catastrophic solutions predicts a preoccupied pattern as compared to avoidance of conflict and less catastrophic solutions as indicative of avoidant strategies.

Taking sides, mediating, and role reversal

It was found that children would involve themselves in conflict to mediate or resolve it, for example through trying to reason with the adults:

> I don't know. I might like five minutes later – just let them cool down. Then I might come in and say, 'Oh, just have it. Because I don't want it to make you two fall out just over this little thing.' [...] Mum would probably ground

> me. But if dad argues with it, they have a big argument, so I'm just like, 'Just ground me.'
>
> (Megan: 150–152/201–202)

Megan indicates considerable awareness of mediating her parents' conflict as she describes her tactics of letting them cool down and then going back to reason with them further. She even accepts if it seems to help to reduce the conflict. It was apparent that the children consistently felt drawn in to take sides with one parent against the other:

> *You do not have to go. Because I'm more closer to you than dad.*
>
> (Megan: 554)

In this instance, the scenario is that of 'Mum had an affair and is leaving', and Megan talks about wanting to stop her mother from leaving, and it seems she has to choose sides, preparing to lose one parent over the other. Rick feels he has to take the father's side:

> *She was probably shouting at her son because of the results. She was probably saying, 'It is something to do with your dad isn't it?' Then he is probably to tell her that it wasn't. But then she just doesn't listen to him and phones him to go round and starts shouting.*
>
> (Rick: 212–215)

Rick introduced this scenario, which suggested his feelings of triangulation and obligation to take his father's side in conflict situations.

It was found that children felt very much caught in the middle of family conflicts. Rick clearly demonstrates his dilemma in the 'ring dad' scenario:

> *He can't just speak to his father without someone listening too. So like maybe he will say something different because someone is listening to his conversation. [...] He clearly wants to say something, that he wants to express with his dad. So he could be saying some things like that his mum is being annoying.*
>
> (Rick: 136–142)

Here he indicates he is torn between loyalties; conscripted into a coalition with his father against his mother, but not knowing what he can say with his mother present. This suggests that children can feel caught in terms of divided loyalties.

The children indicated some fluidity in their coping strategies, such that if a certain behaviour during a conflict situation did not work, they would try a different behaviour:

I would either say to them, 'Right, if you want me to give it back, I will.' Or I would either just go in my room and just – yes, just get out of the situation. [...] Well, we just try and walk off and try to just let them calm down and then go back and just say, 'Please stop it. We don't like it. We don't want you to fall out.'

(Megan: 144–6/622–624)

No. I was trying to stop them from arguing and then just kept on arguing. So I got really upset and cried and just like, sort of walked off to my bedroom.

(Jack: 338–340)

It was possible that as children grow up into adolescents, their coping strategies become less fluid and they may settle on one coping strategy that appears to work in high stress situations.

Parent accurate empathy and invisible children

Parent Accurate Empathy (PAE) was found to have a significant positive relationship with awareness of emotional impacts of triadic processes, which in turn had a significant positive relationship with triadic thinking and trauma. This could be because those children who are subjected to familial conflict (Table 12.4) and trauma are more practised and aware of these triadic conflicts and their emotional impacts, and perhaps have spoken to their parents about their traumas; therefore they exhibit more PAE:

Children frequently reported feeling 'invisible' during a conflict situation. Supporting Ringer and Crittenden (2007), it was found that children felt

Table 12.4 Invisible children

Interview	Extract
Rick	Just feel a bit annoyed that they have not thought about me, they have just been a bit selfish.
	I2: *That your parents have been a bit selfish?* P: Yes. I1: *How do you deal with situations like that...* P: I would just be really angry and annoyed, and feel a bit left out.
Dean	*What do you think the parents think the child is thinking and feeling?*
	P: I don't think they will be thinking about him. *What do you think that the parents think that he's feeling?* P: They aren't really caring. *Okay. What about if they were your parents?* *What would they be thinking and feeling?* P: They wouldn't know that I was feeling.

Table 12.4 (Continued)

Interview	Extract
John	But I wouldn't really think they would be taking notice of the boy.
Jack	They are probably not even thinking about him...They probably wouldn't think about me at the moment, they are on about the paper bit [school report]...They probably don't even know he's there.
Kate	They'll probably be a bit carried away, with all the arguing at each other, and just forget about the little girl...Like I said earlier, they probably wouldn't be focused on me. They'd be focusing on each other, and they'd forget about me...They'd be arguing with each other, so they would – yes, they'd be focusing on their argument, not me...No, they wouldn't know the right way, but they'd have an idea.

their parents were preoccupied with marital problems, leaving the child to feel as though the parents were not even aware of their existence in the conflict situation, and particularly that they were not being thought about.

We have conducted several further studies in differing contexts which produce broadly similar findings. For example, in a fostering service we similarly found that the children demonstrated more severe emotional reactions, such as anxiety, anger, and distress to the triadic scenarios (Dallos et al., 2014). Similarly this was also a finding in a study that looked at young people who were suffering with an eating disorder (Smalley and Dallos, 2014).

Discussion

From clinical work with families and these research studies, some consistent findings emerge. Overall it seems clear that triadic conflict situations appear to generate greater attachment-related anxiety responses than dyadic situations for children in their families. In the research studies all of the children displayed features of insecure attachment, and as discussed earlier for these children the triadic context of being with their parents does not indicate safety and comfort. An interesting and surprising finding has been that generally the children displayed significant awareness of their parents' feelings and also were confident that generally the parents were aware of their own thoughts and feelings. We have also observed this in a previous study of disadvantaged children in foster care (Dallos et al., 2014). It seems that children have not abandoned the idea that their parents understand their needs; however, they displayed less confidence that they would act upon their understanding. In fact, in this present study many of the children felt that they had to take the initiative to mediate and try to resolve the conflicts in the triadic scenarios. We do not have comparative data on how children with secure attachment experiences and strategies respond to the triadic pictures. However, it was apparent that children who are relatively more secure did show greater reflective awareness and more of an expectation that their parents would respond to offer some comfort. In a recent study on children in a mentoring scheme, we are finding that some do see the parents as being able to respond constructively; for example that the mother who is leaving to start another relationship will call them and eventually organize for the child to be able to live with her. A further point is that the triadic scenarios may help to unravel the puzzle of the 'transmission gap' in attachment theory; namely that the primary attachment figures attachment pattern does not simply predict the child's attachment styles (van Ijzendoorn, 1995; Crittenden, 2006). Crittenden refers to meshing and matching, for example that the child of a parent who uses avoidant strategies may develop an anxious ambivalent orientation in an attempt to 'wake her up' to gain an attachment response. Likewise, a child of a highly anxious and ambivalent parent may adopt an avoidant stance in order to gain some emotional independence (Crittenden, 2006; Dallos, 2014). An alternative triadic explanation is that children adopt different strategies in relation to the triadic processes between their parents. Furthermore, these may shift developmentally, so that a young child might cry and become involved, but later 'give up' and attempt to withdraw. In addition this will be influenced by the role that other siblings play. It is a frequent observation in family therapy that the child who is seen as the symptomatic, problematic one is also the one who is most entangled in the parental dynamics.

Clinical implications

Triangulation has been one of the cornerstone concepts in systemic family therapy. Most work in child clinical contexts has made the assumption that frequently problems displayed by children were more broadly influenced by their relationship between their parents. However, there has been surprisingly little empirical exploration of how children experience conflicts. The exception has been studies of children's responses to domestic violence, but less so on more enduring and less dramatic conflictual situations in families.

For family therapists and other clinicians working with children and families our findings may come as no surprise, but can be seen to support established formulations regarding the links between children's presenting problems and triadic dynamics. One core clinical issue, however, is how to intervene. One potential problem is that a triadic formulation may appear to blame the parents for the child's problems. This is further aggravated by the pervasiveness of medical models, for example diagnostic labels, such as ADHD, conduct disorder, Autistic Spectrum Disorder, eating disorder, and so on, which clearly locate the problems as residing within the child. These medical discourses can mean that triadic processes can become invisible and unrecognized (Dallos & Vetere, 2010). Parents who are involved in conflicts or tensions with each other can be seen to be in a heightened state of attachment anxiety, and this is not conducive to a recognition of the effects their distress is having on the child. As our children report at these times, they feel invisible. It is important therefore that therapy offers a secure base so that the parents do not feel blamed for upsetting their children, which could in turn aggravate their mutual recriminations. A number of strategies can be helpful to both address the triadic process and also to avoid the potential sense of blame for the parents which can lead, for example, to their withdrawing from therapy or becoming more rigidly insistent that a medical label is required for the child's problems:

1. It can be helpful to convene sessions with the parents which may initially be framed as giving them the opportunity to speak calmly about the child's problems, the effects they have had on them, and also how changes in their lives may have impacted on the children. The pacing of this needs to be sensitive in order not to suggest blame for the child's problems. Sometimes it can be useful to start by discussing how the problems have influenced their own emotional states, exhaustion, feelings of hopelessness, and that it may have made it difficult for them to find time to consider and nurture their own marital relationship. There is a fine balance here between not blaming them as parents nor simply attributing the cause of all their problems on the child.

2. Positive intentions and corrective scripts. Generally parents can be seen to be well intentioned and wanting to avoid the worst features of their own childhood experience. An exploration, for example using genograms, can be helpful in starting to examine what their own experiences have been. But it is important to frame this in terms of what they have learnt from their own childhoods and how they themselves attempted to deal with conflicts between their parents. This may reveal that they initially consider that they had been able to ignore the conflicts or that they had not substantially influenced them. However, a gentle exploration of this can reveal that in fact there were substantial impacts on them, and this can be discussed in relation to how they have tried to protect their own children from repeating this.

3. This is an extremely important and delicate process of exploration. Many parents want to do things differently (semantic intentions) but have not actually experienced their own parents taking account of their needs, offering reassurance and comfort in the context of conflicts between them. This may mean that they do not have an embodied sense of how family tensions can be resolved, and their somatic and sensory memories of escalating and uncontained conflict may be triggered in their own conflicts, a sense of

helplessness thereby ensuing in how they attempt to reassure and comfort their own children. In fact, what they may remember is that one or other parent pulled them in to side against the other, or that they felt blamed for the problems.

4. A sculpting exercise, for example using buttons or coins, can be employed to examine family dynamics, changes that have occurred over time in their relationship, and the positions that the children have adopted. This can reveal that different children have adopted different positions, for example that one child has become more entangled in their conflicts and difficulties.

5. Triangulation needs to be understood as a mutually maintaining process. So, for example, a child can be seen as not simply conscripted to become involved between the parents but that the child's involvement and problems in turn serve to maintain problems between the parents. It can also bestow a sense of importance and power to the involved child which they might find difficult to relinquish.

6. Time lines and time lags. In some cases the parents have had an awareness that their conflicts might impact on their child and have made attempts to resolve the problems. However, the children may not be aware that their parents have made changes in their relationship. In effect there can be a time lag, such that a child is still anxious about their parents' relationship because they are not aware that things have changed. Discussing changes over time can help to reassure a child, especially if this is being publicly 'witnessed' in the process of family therapy.

7. Discussion of triadic process. This can be the most potentially anxiety-provoking area to consider explicitly, and becomes more possible when the family has established a sense of security and safety in the therapeutic process. This is facilitated by the earlier framing of the parents' intentions as positive and a consideration of their corrective scripts; how they have attempted to improve on their own childhood experiences.

These are a few suggestions, but above all this research and the clinical experiences reported in this chapter point to the importance of placing triangulation as one of the central points of focus for work with children and 'their' problems. As the children have told us, without this they may continue to feel invisible, responsible, blamed, and propelled into medicalization of their problems. This amounts to a double assault on them: the impact of the triadic processes that shape their distress and subsequently becoming seen as the cause of the problems. Perhaps this is one of the reasons why, for example, many children prescribed Ritalin start to refuse to take their medication.

References

Ainsworth, N.D., Blehar, M.C., Waters, E., & Wall, S. (1978). *Patterns of Attachment: Assessed in the Strange Situation & At Home*. Hillside, NJ: Lawrence Erlbaum.
Amato, P.R., & Afifi, T.D. (2006). Feeling caught between parents: adult children's relations with parents and subjective well-being. *Journal of Marriage and Family, 68*, 222 235.
Bowen, M. (1978). *Family Therapy in Clinical Practice*. New York: Jason-Aronson.
Bowlby, J. (1969). *Attachment and loss (1), Attachment*. New York: Penguin Books.
Bowlby, J. (1982). Attachment and loss: retrospect and prospect. *American Journal of Orthopsychiatry, 52(4)*, 664–678.
Bowlby, J. (1988). *A Secure Base: Parent-Child Attachment and Healthy Human Development*. New York: Basic Books.
Buchanan, C.M., Maccoby, E.E., & Dornbusch, S.M. (1991). Caught between parents: adolescents' experience in divorced homes. *Child Development, 62*, 1008–1029.
Buehler, C., & Welsh, D.P. (2009). A process model of adolescents' triangulation into Parents' Marital Conflict: the role of emotional Reactivity. *Journal of Family Psychology 23(2)*, 167–180.
Byng-Hall, J. (1995). Creating a secure family base: some implications of attachment theory for family therapy. *Family Process, 34*, 45–58.
Crittenden, P.M. (2006). A dynamic-maturational model of attachment. *Australian and New Zealand Journal of Family Therapy, 27*, 105–115.
Dallos, R. (2014) Assessing attachment in families: beyond the Dyads. In: P. Holmes & S. Farnfield (eds.), *The Routledge Handbook of Attachment: Assessment*. London: Routledge.
Dallos, R. (2003). Using narrative and attachment theory in systemic family therapy with eating disorders'. *Clinical Child Psychology and Psychiatry, 8(4)*, 521–537.
Dallos, R., & Denford, S. (2008). A qualitative exploration of relationship and attachment themes in families with an eating disorder. *Clinical Child Psychology & Psychiatry*, 13(2), 305–322.
Dallos, R., & Draper, R. (2009). *An Introduction to Family Therapy: Systemic Theory and Practice*. England: Open University Press.
Dallos, R., & Vetere, A. (2010). Emotions, attachments and systems. *Context, 107*, 8–10.
Davies, P.T., & Cummings, E.M. (1994). Marital conflict and child adjustment: an emotional security hypothesis. *Psychological Bulletin, 116*, 387–411.
Davies, P.T., & Cummings, E.M. (1998). Exploring children's emotional security as a mediator of the link between marital relations and child adjustment. *Child Development, 69*, 124–139.
Davies, P.T., & Forman, E.M. (2002). Children's patters of preserving emotional security in the inter-parental subsystem. *Child Development, 73*, 544–562.
Dozier, M., & Kobak, R. (1992). Psychophysiology in adolescent attachment interviews: converging evidence for deactivating strategies. *Child Development, 63*, 1473–1480.
Dubois-Comtois, K., & Moss, E. (2008). Beyond the dyad: do family interactions influence children's attachment representations in middle childhood?' *Attachment & Human Development, 10*(4): 415–431.
Gerard, J.M., Krishnakumar, A., & Buehler, C. (2006). Marital conflict, parent-child relations, and youth maladjustment: a longitudinal Investigation of Spillover Effects. *Journal of Family Issues, 27*, 951–975.

Grych, J.H. (1988). Children's appraisals of interparental conflict: situational and contextual influences. *Journal of Family Psychology, 12,* 437–453.
Harold, G.T. & Conger, R.D. (1997). Marital conflict and adolescent distress: the role of adolescent awareness. *Child Development, 68,* 333–350.
Harold, G.T., Shelton, K.H., Geoke-Money, M.C., & Cummings, E.M. (2004). Marital conflict, child emotional security about family relationships and child adjustment. *Social Development, 13,* 350–376.
Heinrichs, N., Bertram, H., Kuschel, A. & Hahlweg, K. (2005). Parent recruitment and retention in a universal prevention program for child behavior and emotional problems: barriers to research and program participation. *Prevention Science, 6,* 275–286.
Ingoldsby, E.M. (2010). Review of interventions to improve family engagement and retention in parent and child mental health programs. *Journal of Child Family Studies,* 19(5): 629–645.
Johnston, J.R., Gonzalez, R. and Campbell, L.E.G. (1987) Ongoing Post divorce Conflict and Child Disturbance, J. of Abnormal Psychology, 15(4): 493–509.
Klagsbrun, M., & Bowlby, J. (1976). Responses to separation from parents: A clinical test for young children. *British Journal of Projective Psychology, 21,* 217–221.
Marvin, B. (2009). Defiant and disruptive child behaviour problems: A view from the 'Circle of Security' translated & published. In: K.H. Brisch & T. Hellbrugge (eds), Wege zu sicheren Bindungen in Familie und Gesellschaft. Pravention, Begleitung, Beratung und Psychotherapie, pp. 187–212. Stuttgart: Klett-Cotta.
Minuchin, S. (1974). *Families and Family Therapy.* Cambridge, MA: Harvard University Press.
Nicolotti, L., El-Sheikh, M., & Whitson, S.M. (2003). Children's coping with marital conflict and their adjustment and physical health: vulnerability and protective function. *Journal of Family Psychology, 17,* 315–326.
Palazzoli, M.S., Cecchin, G., Prata, G., & Boscolo, L. (1978). *Paradox and Counter Paradox.* New York: Jason Aronson.
Resnick, G. (1993). *Measuring Attachment in Early Adolescence: A Manual for the Administration, Coding, and Interpretation of the Separation Anxiety Test for 11–14 year-olds.* Unpublished manuscript.
Ringer, F., & Crittenden, P.M. (2007). Eating disorders and attachment: the effects of hidden family processes on eating disorders. *European Eating Disorders Review, 15,* 119–130.
Schindler, A., Thomasius, R., Sack, P.M., Gemeinhardt, B., & Kustner, U. (2007). Insecure family bases and adolescent drug abuse: a new approach to family patterns of attachment. *Attachment & Human Development,* 9(2), 111–126.
Shelton, K.H., & Harold, G.T. (2008). Pathways between interparental conflict and adolescent psychological adjustment: bridging links through children's cognitive appraisals and coping strategies. *The Journal of Early Adolescence, 28,* 555–582.
Smalley, V., & Dallos, R. (pending publication). With permission from Prof. Rudi Dallos.
van Ijzendoorn, M.H. (1995). Adult attachment representations, parental responsiveness, and infant attachment: a meta-analysis on the predictive validity of the Adult Attachment Interview. *Psychological Bulletin, 117,* 387–403.
Wright, J.C., Binney, V., & Smith, P.K. (1995). Security of attachment in 8–12 year olds: a revised version of the separation anxiety test, its psychometric properties and clinical interpretation. *J. Child Psychology and Psychiatry,* 36(5), 757–774.

13
Special Education in the Complex Institutional Environment of Health Care and Social Work – Structural Frame and Empirical Reality

Peter Nenniger and Mathias Mejeh

Special Education has become a much-discussed topic, in particular in issues concerning Inclusive Education. Too often, disputes are characterized by vague ideas and poorly reflected characteristics of systems in both General and Remedial Education (cf. e.g., Brown & Smith, 1992; Thomas & Loxley, 2001; Hinz, 2013). There is increased societal interest in facilitating the integration of children and adolescents with 'disabilities' in all areas of living including schools, by concerted efforts to support and offer empowerment for families and communities. Such efforts are claimed to enhance communication and social skills, augment favourable peer group interactions, facilitate individualized educational target programmes, post-school adjustment, and so on. Moreover, inclusion encourages more positive attitudes and deepens social connection with persons with disabilities as well as increasing their perceived social status through affiliation with non-disabled peers (Wikipedia, 2014).

Systematic overview and history of special education including controversies

One focus of discussion is the controversial understanding of 'disability' (e.g., Iezzoni & Freedman, 2008). The International Classification of Impairments, Disabilities and Handicaps may be helpful in this case (cf. Susser, 1990): 'Impairment' refers to a physical or mental defect at the level of a body system or organ, whereas 'disability' refers to person-level limitations in physical and psychocognitive activities, and 'handicap' to difficulties in social abilities or relations between the individual and society. However, the above perspective appears limited, in so far as the definitions draw insufficient attention to the dynamic character of 'impairment', 'disability', and 'handicap', and the interdependence inherent between them. During their lifetime, persons are submitted to permanent change, so that the above reference systems (defects in body systems, personal-level limitations, and relations to society) are interwoven, and this can 'cause' a changing construct of 'disability'. For instance, handicaps may elicit disabilities, but also appease them, at certain moments and in given circumstances.

A similar situation pertains to tensions between the medical and the social model of understanding disabilities (e.g., Engel, 1977). When comparing the social to the medical model, some argue that in the latter:

1. Disability is considered as a physiological, biological, or intellectual pathology, whereas in the social model the person is valued in her/his actual state and her/his strengths and needs are identified.
2. The disabled person is perceived as 'faulty' and impairment is diagnosed and labelled as the incentive for cure or treatment. In the social model, barriers are identified, solutions for overcoming barriers developed, and resources made available.
3. Disabled people are often segregated and brought to special or alternative services with the aim of reintegration (if the default is restored) or kept in separation. In contrast, within a social model, diversity is welcomed and there is also a place for these persons within this diversity.
4. Society is affected in specific (e.g., organizational or financial) aspects, whereas social conceptualizations consider that society is concerned with its own understanding and must evolve under social change.

The difference in the medical and social perspectives regards the interaction between societal conditions or expectations and the conditions of the individual: to what extent should disabled persons have to 'fit in' to a societal framework versus how far society itself should adapt to them. However, a closer look reveals that in some important areas the two views can be complementary rather than disjunctive, and the models can be distinguished by the emphasis they give to their perspective.

A better understanding evolves from a view on the historical development of special education and its position within the health system (cf. e.g., Betz, 2004; Krahn & Drumm, 2007; in Europe: European Agency, 2014; in the US: Institute of Medicine, 2007; Georgia Department of Public Health, 2014; in Asia: Lynch, 1994; and in Oceania: Mace, Shani, Caleb, & Sarah, 2014).

For this review, focusing on analyses over the last 300 years, four periods of special needs education can be distinguished (e.g., Blackhurst & Berdine, 1993) as follows:

1. **First Period:** At school, children with sensory disabilities are recognized and adapted instruction is introduced, but other disabled children remain

excluded from school. L'Epeé founded the first public school for people with disabilities in France in 1760. In 1784 Haüy founded the 'Institution Nationale des Jeunes Aveugles' and in the same period Itard developed different methods of education for disabled children. In the US, Gallaudet implemented the American Asylum for the Education of the Deaf and Dumb in 1817. From 1851, different schools opened for 'feebleminded' children and for 'retarded' children (c.f. historical background: Safford, 1996).

2. **Second Period:** Care is installed for the impaired children, mostly as medical care and rehabilitation. For this purpose, depending on disabilities, children are segregated into homogeneous groups.

A sign of the growing importance of special education in the US was the foundation of the Association of Medical Officers of American Institutions for Idiotic and Feebleminded Persons in 1876 and the creation of the Department of Special Education in 1897 by the National Education Association. At the onset of the 20th century, laws and decrees assuring that people with disabilities had their own right to education were enacted. In 1903 Binet (cf. Binet & Simon, 1905) created a test for 'mentally retarded' children. From 1930 to 1950 various associations for children with mental disabilities were founded. Depending on the disabilities, special education systems, organized in parallel to regular systems, were introduced after the Second World War.

3. **Third Period:** The principle of integration and normalization becomes common to special education.

The principle of normalization was mainly developed in Scandinavia (cf. Bank-Mikkelson, 1980; Nirje, 1970, 1985) and in Canada at the National Institute on Mental retardation (Wolfensberger, 1972, 1983). The central principle involves the acceptance of persons with disabilities by offering them conditions matching others, and it accepts associated risks rather than focusing on protection (details in Emerson, 1992). However, ideas of integration were in fact developed earlier. For example, Séguin's (1866) programme for independence and self-reliance in disabled students included a combination of physical and intellectual tasks. From 1901, after founding his school for children with mild disabilities, Décroly (1914/1978) elaborated a pedagogy focused on methods fostering independent learning. Later on Montessori (1909) designed the concept of the prepared environment, facilitating a maximum of independent learning and exploration by the child. In recent decades in Great Britain and Europe, there have been significant and fierce discussions in this area (cf. Mesibov, 1976; Perrin & Nirje, 1985; Brown & Smith, 1992; Chappell, 1992; Rapley & Baldwin, 1995; Culham,

2000), including debates about the consequences in practice (O'Brien & Tyne, 1981; Atkinson et al., 1985).

4. **Fourth Period:** Educational equality and equal educational services (e.g., inclusion) are introduced.

Special regulations for specific handicapped children were substituted by public laws (e.g., in Italy or in the US) that guaranteed the individual the right to free and appropriate public education in a least restrictive – environment (Details e.g., for Italy: Legge n. 328 08/11/2000 [Legge – quadro per la realizzazione del sistema integrato di interventie servizi sociali)]; Legge n. 17 28/01/1999 [Integrazione emodifica della legge – quadro 5 febbraio 1992, n. 104, per l'assistenza, l'integrazione sociale e i diritti delle persone handicappate]; Legge n. 104 05/02/1992 [Legg – quadro per l'assistenza, l'integrazione sociale e i diritti delle persone handicappate]); for the US: Disabilities Education Act of 1990, rev. 2004).

Globally, as an outcome of discussions in the UN, ideas about integration increasingly became a worldwide concern (e.g., UN, 1948, 1990, 1993; UNESCO, 1990, 1994a, 1994b, 2000; OECD: Hegarty, 1995) giving rise to several national initiatives and influencing the respective legislation in many countries (overviews: O'Hanlon, 1995 [Europe]; Booth & Ainscow, 1998, Booth, 2000 [UK]; European Agency, 2003; Biewer, 2006 [Austria, Germany]; Beaucher, 2014 [France]; Australian Research Alliance for Children and Youth, 2013 [Australia]).

Based on the Universal Declaration of Human Rights (UN, 1948), the right to a more inclusive education was part of several significant international declarations, such as:

- Convention on the Rights of the Child (UN, 1989)
- World Declaration for Education for All (UNESCO, 1990)
- Standard Rules on the Equalization of Opportunities for Persons with Disability (United Nations, 1993)
- Salamanca Statement and Framework for Action (UNESCO, 1994a, 1994b)
- Dakar Framework for Action (UNESCO, 2000).

Inclusion or integration as reflected in empirical reality

Despite the number of fundamental and ideological debates (e.g., Ballard, 1995; Murdoch, 1997; Riddell, 2000; Hinz, 2002), and several discussions concerning the consequences of inclusive schooling (e.g., Ainscow, 1999; Demmer-Dieckmann & Textor, 2007; Dorrance & Dannenbeck, 2013), more or less data-based general evaluations of the status of integration or inclusion-oriented approaches have been published (e.g., Specht, 1993; Allan, 1999; Salend, 1999; Klemm, 2009; Preuss-Lausitz, 2009, 2010;

Walter-Klose, 2012). In this context, diverse scientific programs and pilot projects have been initiated in the last few decades (e.g., Köbberling & Schley, 2000; Kreis, Lügstenmann, & Staub, 2008; Ontario Ministry of Education, 2009; UNICEF, 2010) which have resulted in significant opportunities for, and gains in additional knowledge in this domain (Hollenbach & Tillmann, 2009), although explicit and applicable knowledge is still lacking in many areas (e.g., Mejeh, 2014).

The most important general outcome worth highlighting is that successful implementation of inclusion depends on various factors relating to both teachers and students. In addition, the availability of personal, professional, and structural resources influences attitudes towards inclusion, both positively and negatively. This is in line with reviews of relevant publications about the effects of inclusive schooling (e.g., Ruijs & Peetsma, 2009) mainly impacting positively on students' cognitive achievement, but with negligible effects on emotional functioning.

Sermier Dessemontet (2012) and Sermier Dessemontet, Bless, and Morin (2012) researched the impact of inclusion on academic achievement and adaptive behaviour of children with intellectual disabilities, and concluded that differential effects of inclusive or separative settings in schools depend on the *subject* concerned: for example, significant differences in literacy, but no significant differences in mathematics and in global adaptive behaviour were reported. Comparing at-risk pupils' development in special and in regular education, Peetsma, Vergeer, Roeleveld, and Karsten (2001) reported better cognitive functioning in inclusive education than in special education; conversely, no clear differences were observed in socio-emotional functioning. No significant research has been carried out to investigate the potential impact of inclusion depending on the combination of types of special needs students included in a class.

In a study about the social experience of pupils with special needs in inclusive classes, Klicpera and Gasteiger-Klicpera (2003), and Krull, Wilbert, and Hennemann (2014) concluded that despite the support regarding cognitive functioning, students with special needs simultaneously require assistance in social integration, partly because of segregating tendencies emerging from the start of primary school.

Regarding the number of special needs students in inclusive classes (cf. Feyerer, 1997), Ruijs, Peetsma, and Van der Veen (2010) could not find any difference in cognitive achievement and in addition, no differential effects were observed within single types of special needs students. Disregarding possible confounding effects of intelligence, they found that the number of pupils with special needs in the inclusive class had no effect on achievement for both regular and special needs students. Consistent with other studies, no observable difference emerged in terms of socio-emotional development.

From research on professional education, Orthmann (2001), Kobi (2002), and Ginnold (2008) (sociological perspective: Stauber & Walter, 2004) report on problems in rehabilitation and the transition from school to work. They highlight that although students coming from integrative settings have easier access to the labour market, this setting is not necessarily a guarantee for success.

Several contexts suggest a challenge to reliable assessment concerning the availability of appropriate measures (Kuhl et al., 2012; Liebers & Seifert, 2012). The above discussions highlight that despite the existence of a sufficient number of assessment concepts and procedures, new calibrations and adaptations are imperative for inclusive contexts. Adaptation is required for the different levels and subjects.

Regarding carers' attitudes towards children with special needs, Kuhl and Walter (2008) found a tendency of more positive attitudes towards them than towards other groups of children and concluded that contact to disabled persons helps to foster a more favourable perspective. Regarding teachers' attitudes towards inclusive education and to their relations with parents of special needs students, Nind (2000), Peetsma and Blok (2007), Kuhl, Steiner, and Probst (2012) and Kuhl, Moser, Schäfer, and Redlich (2013) revealed that attitudes and beliefs about inclusion as well as patterns of interaction with disabled students play a crucial role. However, it is not clear what types of beliefs enable a teacher to deliver successful inclusive instruction. Furthermore it is unclear to what extent this may be associated with other variables (e.g., being a regular class teacher or assisting special needs teacher), the type of school (type of regular school [comprehensive school, grammar school, Gymnasium, etc.], special school), and the level of education (primary, secondary).

A systemic view of special education within health care and social work

Doing true justice to the complex frame of Special Education also requires viewing it within the wider and structured horizon of health care and social work.

According to the World Health Organization (World Health Organization, 2007), health systems comprise 'all organizations, people and actions whose primary intent is to promote, restore or maintain health. This includes efforts to influence determinants of health as well as more direct health-improving activities.' A health system is therefore more than the pyramid of publicly owned facilities that deliver personal health services. A wide variety of social work and health systems exist within various organizational structures (e.g., Lanfranchi, 2002). These have evolved from different national histories and depend on the services targeted for the specific population: from frames for market participants (e.g., Saltman & Von Otter, 1995) to public institutions resulting from coordinated efforts of governments, trade unions, charities, religious organizations, and other bodies. They are funded by a combination of public taxation, social or private health insurance, out-of-pocket payments, and donations (cf. Mossialos, Dixon, Figueras, & Kutzi, 2002).

In recent times, 'social work' has widened its perspective. According to the most recent global definition, adopted by the International Federation of Social Workers and International Association of Schools of Social Work, it embraces traditional social work activities and social development, and addresses social work knowledge, values, and practice (cf. Hare, 2004). With respect to special education, social work is concerned with supporting the family system. It is perceived as a social pedagogical intervention, with a broad scope, which is prevention-oriented and delimited in time. The focus is upon the concrete, actual situation of a family, and intervention aims to assist the family to help itself in its own recovery and subsequent independence. In this context it is intended that the family use different avenues of support (e.g., within specific support groups or self-helping communities) to cope with its problems and to strengthen the competence needed. The aims are then to support and enhance young people's established environments and/or proactively assist parents in their role as educators (e.g., Knorth, Kalverboer, & Knot-Dickscheit, 2010).

Within this frame, the place of special education can be construed as follows. Health services and social work are the closest neighbouring fields and contact areas for special education. Intersections with health care and/or social work may increase depending on the type and degree of impairment, disability, or handicap. Assessment and diagnosis require close cooperation: inclusion is often regarded as a matter mainly for schools, although this issue is controversial in some countries (e.g., Switzerland: Conférence intercantonale del' instruction publique, 2010; Jenni, 2011). Existing traditions and institutional structures have considerable impact in this context. Despite the diverse conceptions, any system of support available for children and young persons with special needs is complex, requiring coordination between teachers, health workers, and social workers.

Some central requirements in improving the service which children and their families receive (overview e.g., United States Administration for Children and Families, 2011) include:

- A coordinated and standardized assessment process to determine needs across education, health, and social care,
- An education, health, and care plan for each person with complex needs with an option for personal budgets that replaces separate statements from special needs and learning difficulty assessments,

- Verification that local commissioners' work is effective in the interest of the persons with special needs and that communication between the different services is functioning.

Measures supporting the above requirements regard:

- a support system that incorporates all public and free and other private nurseries, pre-schools and schools, colleges, academies, and similar institutions,
- an establishment of the required support in all institutions mentioned in the previous paragraph,
- opportunities and funding of appropriate specialist training for teachers and supporting staff,
- granting rights and protection in further education and professional training,
- preparing persons with special needs for adulthood and life outside the education system by ensuring that the support needed after school is available, and offering placement of supported internships, employer-based study programmes and other (or complementary) opportunities of specific qualification for the workplace.

Moreover, the conditions (institutional characteristics and properties of effective execution) indispensable for the respective actions play an important role, such as:

- traditional Special Education characteristics (e.g., problems due to specific handicaps),
- special children (e.g., categories of disabilities, categories of remedial strengths, grade of special needs),
- special teachers (e.g., type of education and training, experience, functions executed),
- specialists (e.g., doctor, therapist, social worker, guardian),
- 'novel' settings (e.g., type and purpose of segregation, type of school or class, resource facilities),
- special ratios in class or programme (class size, number of special needs students by class, number of teachers by class, ratio of special needs by regular students, number of teachers by class/school, number of special teachers by class/school),
- methods/facilities/tools available at school (e.g., Braille, sign language, rooms for one-to-one lessons, specialized teaching material, lifting ramps),

- involvement of schools in institutional and social environments (e.g., special services, diagnostic units, special programmes with associations, municipality, church, administration).

However, in a systemic view, communal and societal conditions cannot be neglected, as for example:

- Making people more acquainted with the real skills, values, attitudes, and behaviours of disabled persons (instead of arbitrary guesses or prejudice).
- Encouraging realistic expectations of parents, children, professionals, administrators, and scientists.
- Showing the common or overlapping characteristics of specialized and regular settings.
- Explaining the mental and social benefits resulting from the company with disabled persons.
- Providing interactions with diverse persons (in particular among children, however also children with adults).
- Minimizing conditions where disabled persons face placements outside normal and regular performances.
- Implementing links with the community and preparing for future life as early as possible.
- Estimating and planning amount and duration (sometimes lifetime) of routine costs realistically and accurately timed.

Moreover, the rights, wishes and needs of the individual should be considered (cf. Henry J. Kaiser Family Foundation, 2003).

Psychological, educational, and sociological perspectives on inclusion

Current concepts in psychology, education and related social sciences offer important cornerstones, which are decisive both in the success or failure of concepts and implementation of integrative or inclusive systems of education.

The first, psychological aspect, suggests the central view of deficits and remedial measures is too narrow. If in inclusion *all* relevant issues and *all* persons – not just the disabled – are considered, they have to be part of the respective considerations. For instance, dealing with deficits in learning and motivation has to be enlarged to favourable conditions of learning and motivation; analogously, concerns about remedial measures in social behaviour now become part of the class climate, social interaction, etc. (e.g., Abrams, Hogg, & Marques, 2004; Quick, 2008).

The second cornerstone emphasises the educational aspect, including educational and didactic issues in a heterogeneous learning environment within unified conditions of learning organization: for instance, didactic arrangements for cooperative learning, classroom management on differential instruction levels, and marking learning results attained under different learning conditions (e.g., Feuser, 2011; Soler & Sarsa, 2012; Ziemen, 2014).

Thirdly, the sociological facet focuses on societal values of fairness in creating conditions of equal opportunity for diverse groups with different goals: for example, regarding the place and the meaning of certificates, the conceptualization and the consequences of assessments, handling failure, the place of competitiveness and cooperation (e.g., Levinson, Cookson, & Sadovnik, 2002; Holland, 2012). In addition, wider deliberations about the place and purpose of education in society have come to the fore, such as questioning which rights and tasks are reserved for the family, or in considering the responsibility that schools have if families cannot cope with the demands of society. Another complex issue concerns questions about which deficit is classified as illness and which as divergent or deviant behaviour.

When the psychological, educational, and sociological aspects are brought together, inclusive education takes on a more comprehensive framework. Features include:

- embraces *all* persons concerned,
- enlarges the focus on single deficits to a schematic view of the problem with its favourable and unfavourable conditions,
- places remedial measures as one part of the whole educational, social, and medical environment (e.g., all educational and didactical issues in a heterogeneous learning environment, family care, and medical therapies and cures), and
- encompasses all relevant societal aspects (including the purpose and place of school), pertaining to the conditions of equal opportunity for the diverse groups with their different goals.

Some suggestions for constructive practice

Overall the findings presented provide a basis for implications for professionals working in the field. Inclusive education has a long history and many debates concerning theory and practice have taken place, and integrative or inclusive education is accepted now as a common global goal. However, there is no consensus-concerning methods and measures nor about the modus operandi of its implementation in a complex field.

Thus the following general remarks seem worthy of consideration:

- It is important that all actors concerned know their role within the whole system. Otherwise, locally well-intentioned action may be unconsciously rendered ineffective owing to issues in the wider system.

- It is also essential that the actors are aware of the current situation within their own field, as in ongoing implementation specific demands within the whole system often have not reached the state as required. In such situations opportunity and open space for targeted temporally provisional arrangements are inevitable as well as on the level of organization and formation.
- Achieving targets under uncertain or unpredictable conditions requires flexibility to allow for modification to plans. Regarding a single model as exhaustive is misleading because important aspects may be ignored.
- As successful inclusion assumes a similar, though not identical, appreciation of disability and special needs by all actors, transparent standardized assessments are an indispensable prerequisite.
- Successful implementation of integrative or inclusive measures can be reached by collaborative work; otherwise standards and guidelines are rarely sustainable in the long term.
- As integration or inclusion at school cannot be focused on a few competent and committed actors, *transition* of competence and of information to all persons involved combined with communication and cooperation become equally important; furthermore opportunities for familiarization and direct contact with disabled persons seem to deepen insight and sympathy.
- As the actual state of research on inclusion is still characterized by fragmentary, incomplete, and inconsistent results and conclusions, implementations (preferably conducted on a small scale) are tentative and require a gradual introduction with continual evaluation.

Currently, the state of special education in the complex institutional environment of social work and health care can, on the one hand, be described as a structured frame with incomplete coherent islands within it (that emerge as promising areas for development), and as a more or less functioning empirical reality with considerable room for increased effectiveness and efficiency. A tighter and structured interconnectedness of the education (school) system with social work and health care is required to manage both ground-level work with children and their families, and develop the type of systematic evaluations needed to move forward and organize practice in this field. Moreover, at the heart of this complex area are a vulnerable group of young people and their families, who need those around them to work well together; not just for the sake of their education and learning, but more for the sake of their social, emotional, and mental development and personal well-being.

References

Abrams, D., Hogg, M., & Marques, J. (2004). *Social Psychology of Inclusion and Exclusion.* New York: Taylor & Francis.

Ainscow, M. (1999). *Understanding the Development of Inclusive Schools*. London: Falmer Press.
Allan, J. (1999). *Actively Seeking Inclusion: Pupils With Special Needs in Mainstream Schools*. London: Falmer Press.
Atkinson, D., McCarthy, M., Walmsley, J., Cooper, M., Rolph, S., Aspis, S., Barette, P., & Baldwin, S. (1985). Sheep in wolf's clothing: impact of normalisation teaching on human services and service providers. *International Journal of Rehabilitation Research, 8*, 131–142.
Australian Research Alliance for Children and Youth. (2013). Inclusive Education for Students with Disability. A review of the best evidence in relation to theory and practice. Braddon ACT: ARACY. http://www.aracy.org.au/publications-resources/command/download_file/id/246/filename/Inclusive_education_for_students_with_disability__A_review_of_the_best_evidence_in_relation_to_theory_and_practice.pdf(state: 09/2014).
Ballard, K. (1995). Inclusion, paradigms, power and participation. In: C. Clark, A. Dyson & A. Millward (eds), *Towards Inclusive Schools?* , pp. 1–14. London: David Fulton.
Bank-Mikkelson, N. (1980). Denmark. In: R.J. Flynn & K.E. Nitsch (eds), *Normalisation, Social Integration and Community Services* , pp. 51–70. Baltimore, MD: University Park Press.
Betz, C.L. (2004). Transition of adolescents with special health care needs: review and analysis of the literature. Issues. *Comprehensive Pediatric Nursing, 27(3)*, 179–241.
Beaucher, H. (2014). La scolarisation des élèves handicapés et l'éducation inclusive. *Revue internationale d'éducation de Sèvres, 59*, 10–14.
Biewer, G. (2006). Schulische Integration in Deutschland und Österreichim Vergleich. [Comparison of integration at schools in Germany and Austria.] *Erziehung und Unterricht, 1&2*, 1–28.
Binet, A., & Simon, T. (1905). Methode nouveau pour la diagnostic nouveau des anormeaux. [New method for the new diagnostics of non-normals.] *Année psychologique, 11*, 191–244.
Blackhurst, A.E., & Berdine, W.H. (eds.) (1993). *An Introduction to Special Education*. New York: HarperCollins.
Booth, T. (2000). Inclusion and exclusion policy in England: Who controls the agenda? In: F. Armstrong, D. Armstrong & L. Barton (eds), *Inclusive Education: Policy, Contexts and Comparative Perspectives*, pp. 78–98. London: David Fulton.
Booth, T., & Ainscow, M. (1998). *From Them to Us: An International Study of Inclusion in Education*. London: Routledge.
Brown, H., & Smith, H. (1992). *Normalization: A Reader for the Nineties*. London: Routledge.
Chappell, A.L. (1992). Towards a sociological critique of the normalisation principle. *Disability, Handicap and Society, 7*, 35–51.
Conférence intercantonale del' instruction publique. (2010). Ecole et santé. Politiques de l'éducation et innovations. [School and health. Educational policy and innovations.] *Bulletin CIIP, 24*.
Culham, A. (2000). *Inclusion vs. Normalisation: Are They Compatible in Ethos?* MA Dissertation, Oxford Brookes University (unpublished).
Décroly, J.-O. (1914/1978). *Initiation à l'activité motrice et intellectuelle par les jeux éducatifs [Initiation of Motor and Intellectual Activity by Educational Games.]*, (réédit Delachaux et Niestlé, 1978: Initiation à l'activité motrice et intellectuelle par les jeux éducatifs), Neuchâtel: Delachaux et Niestlé.

Demmer-Dieckmann, I., & Textor, A. (Hrsg.) (2007). *Integrations forschung und Bildungspolitik im Dialog.* [Research on integration and education policy in dialogue.] Klinkhardt: Bad Heilbrunn.
Dorrance, C., & Dannenbeck, C. (Hrsg.) (2013). *Doing Inclusion. Inklusion in einer nicht inklusiven Gesellschaft.* [Doing inclusion. Inclusion in a non-inclusive society.] Klinkhardt: Bad Heilbrunn.
Emerson, E. (1992). What is normalisation? In: H. Brown & H. Smith (eds), *Normalisation: A Reader for the Nineties,* pp. 1–18. London: Routledge.
Engel, G. (1977). 'The need for a new medical model: a challenge for biomedicine'. *Science, 196* (4286), 129–136.
European Agency for Special Needs and Inclusive Education. (ed.) (2003). *Sonderpädagogische Förderung in Europa.* Thematische Publikation. [*Promotion of Special Education in Europe.* Thematic publication.] Brussels: European Agency for Development in Special Needs Education.
European Agency for Special Needs and Inclusive Education. (2014). Brussels: www.european_agency.org (state: 09.2014).
Feuser, G. (2011). Entwicklungslogische Didaktik. [Development oriented Didactics.] In: Kaiser, A. Schmetz, D. Wachtel, & P. Werner, B. (Hrsg.), *Didaktik und Unterricht,* pp. 86–100. Stuttgart: Kohlhammer.
Feyerer, E. (1997). *Behindern Behinderte? Auswirkungen integrativen Unterrichts auf nichtbehinderte Kinder in der Sekundarstufe I* [Are disabled persons disabling? Effects of inclusive instruction on children without disability at lower secondary level.] (Dissertation). Linz: Universität Linz.
Georgia Department of Public Health (2014). *Children & Youth With Special Healthcare Needs.* Atlanta (state: 09/2014).
Ginnold, A. (2008). *Der ÜbergangSchule-Beruf von Jugendlichen mit Lernbehinderung. Einstieg – Ausstieg –* Warteschleife. [Transition from school to job for young people with disability. Access – escape – waiting loop.] Bad Heilbrunn: Klinkhardt.
Hare, I. (2004). Defining social work for the 21st century. The international federation of social workers' revised definition of social work. *International Social Work, 47*(3), 407–424.
Hegarty, S. (1995). Resources. In: OECD (ed.), *Integrated Students With Special Needs Into Main-Streaming Schools,* pp. 77–81. OECD: Paris.
Henry J. Kaiser Family Foundation (2003). Understanding the Health Care Needs and Experiences of People with Disabilities: Findings from a 2003 Survey. http://dph.georgia.gov (state: 07/2009).
Hinz, A. (2002). Von der Integration zur Inklusion – terminologisches Spiel oder konzeptionelle Weiterentwicklung? [From Integration to Inclusion – terminological game or conceptual development?] *Zeitschrift für Heilpädagogik,* 53, 354–361.
Hinz, A. (2013). Inklusion – von der Unkenntnis zur Unkenntlichkeit? Kritische Anmerkungen zu einem Jahrzehnt Diskurs über schulische Inklusion in Deutschland. [Inclusion – from the ignored to the unrecognisable issue. Critical annotations to a decade of discourse about inclusion in Germany.] *Zeitschrift für Inklusion,* 1, 1, http://www.inklusion-online.net/index.php/inklusion-online/article/view/26/26 (accessed March, 2015).
Holland, M. (2012). Only here for the day: the social integration of minority students at a majority white high school. *Sociology of Education,* 2, 101–120.
Hollenbach, N., & Tillmann, K.-J. (Hrsg.) (2009). Die Schule forschend verändern. Praxis forschung aus nationale rund internationaler Perspektive. [Transforming

school by research. Research on practice from a national and an international perspective.] Klinkhardt: Bad Heilbrunn.

Henderson, B. (1996). Inclusion: educating students with and without disabilities. *New England Journal of Public Policy, 5*, 99–105.

Iezzoni, L.I., & Freedman, V.A. (2008). Turning the disability tide: the importance of definitions. *Journal of the American Medical Association, 299*(3), 332–334.

Individuals with Disabilities Education Act [IDEA]. (1990: Pub. L. No. 101–476, 104 Stat. 1142). Washington, DC. http://www.gpo.gov/fdsys/pkg/PLAW-108publ446/html/PLAW-108publ446.htm (accessed March, 2015).

Institute of Medicine. (2007). *The Future of Disability in America*. Washington, DC: The National Academies Press.

Jenni, O. (2011). Die neuen Sonderpädagogikkonzepteund das standardisierte Abklärungsverfahren: einekritische Betrachtungausärztlicher Sicht. [New concepts of special education and the standardized assessment procedure: a critical review from the medical perspective.] *Schweizerische Zeitschriftfür Heilpädagogik, 17*, 33–38.

Klemm, K. (2009). *Inklusion in Deutschland – eine bildungsstatische Analyse.* [Inclusion in Germany – a statistic-based analysis on education.] Bertelsmann Stiftung: Gütersloh.

Klicpera, C., & Gasteiger-Klicpera, B. (2003). Soziale Erfahrungenvon Grundschülern mit sonderpädagogischem Förderbedarf in Integrationsklassen – betrachtetim Kontext der Maßnahmenzur Förderung der sozialen Integration. [Social experience of primary-school pupils with special needs in inclusive classes – considered in context of measures fostering social integration.] *Heilpädagogische Forschung, 2*, 61–71.

Knorth, E.J., Kalverboer, M.E., & Knot-Dickscheit, J. (eds.) (2010). *Inside Out. How Interventions in Child and Family Care Work.* Antwerp: Garant.

Kobi, E.E. (2002). Personen kreismerkmale lernbehinderter Menschen und (berufs-)pädagogische Konsequenzen. [Characteristics of groups of persons with learning disabilities and consequences regarding {vocational} education.] *Berufliche Rehabilitation, 16*(3), 108–112.

Köbberling, A., & Schley, W. (2000): *Sozialisation und Entwicklung in Integrationsklassen. Untersuchungen zur Evaluation eines Schulversuchs in der Sekundarstufe.* [Socialisation and development in inclusive classes. Evaluative studies of a pilot project at the secondary level.] Weinheim: Juventa.

Krahn, G.L., & Drumm, C.E. (2007). Translating policy principles into practice to improve health care access for adults with intellectual disabilities: a research review of the past decade. *Mental Retardation and Developmental Disabilities Research Reviews, 13*, 160–168.

Kreis, A., Lügstenmann, F., & Staub, F. (2008). *Kollegiales Unterrichtscoaching als Ansatz zur Schulentwicklung.* [Co-Operative Coaching of Instruction as an Approach for the Development of Schools.] Kreuzlingen: Pädagogische Hochschule Thurgau.

Krull, J., Wilbert, J., & Hennemann, T. (2014). Soziale Ausgrenzung von Erstklässlerinnen und Erstklässlern mit sonderpädagogischem Förderbedarf im Gemeinsamen Unterricht. [Social exclusion of first class primary school pupils with special needs in inclusive tuition.] *Empirische Sonderpädagogik, 6 (1)*, 59–75.

Kuhl, J., & Walter, J. (2008). Die Einstellung von Studentenunterschiedlicher Studiengänge zu Menschen mitgeistiger Behinderung. [Attitudes of students in various study programmes towards mentally disabled persons.] *Heilpädagogische Forschung, 34(4)*, 206–219.

Kuhl, J., Krizan, A., Sinner, D., Probst, H., Hofmann, C., & Ennemoser, M. (2012). Von der sonderpädagogischen Diagnostik zurpädagogisch-psychologischen Diagnostik im Dienstschulischer Prävention. [From diagnostics of special needs to pedagogical-psychological diagnostic at the service of prevention at school.] In: V. Moser (Hrsg.), *Enzyklopädie Erziehungswissenschaft Online. Behinderten- und Integrationspädagogik: Institutionelle Felder.* Weinheim: Beltz. http://www.erzwissonline.de (state: 09/2014).

Kuhl, J., Steiner, K., & Probst, H. (2012). Die Arbeit Sonderpädagogischer Förderzentren aus der Sicht der Grundschule – Lehrerurteile zur Arbeit hessischer Beratungs- und Förderzentren. [The task of centres for special needs education from the perspective of the primary school – Judgements of teachers about the activity of the consulting and promotion service of the federal state of Hesse.] *Zeitschrift für Heilpädagogik, 63(3),* 120–128.

Kuhl, J., Moser, V., Schäfer, L., & Redlich, H. (2013). Zurempirischen Erfassung von Beliefs von Förderschullehrerinnenund – lehrern. [On the empirical acquisition of beliefs of special education teachers.] *Empirische Sonderpädagogik, 5 (1),* 3–24.

Lanfranchi, A. (2002). Schulerfolg von Migrationskindern. Die Bedeutung familienergänzender Betreuung im Vorschulalter. [School achievement of migrants. The importance of complementary family care for pre-schoolers.] Wiesbaden: VS Verlag für Sozialwissenschaften.

Legge n. 328 08/11/2000 'Legge quadro per la realizzazione del sistema integrato di interventi e servizi sociali'.

Legge n. 17 28/01/1999 'Integrazione e modifica della legge-quadro 5 febbraio 1992, n. 104, per l'assistenza, l'integrazione sociale e i diritti delle persone handicappate'.

Legge n. 104 05/02/1992 'Legge quadro per l'assistenza, l'integrazione sociale e i diritti delle persone handicappate'.

Levinson, D., Cookson, P., & Sadovnik, A. (2002). *Education and Sociology.* New York: Routledge.

Liebers, K., & Seifert, Chr. (2012). Assessment konzepte für die inclusive Schule – eine Bestandsaufnahme. [Assessment concepts for the inclusive school – a survey.] *Z. f. Inklusion, 3.* www.inklusion-online.net (accessed March, 2015).

Lynch, J. (1994). *Provision for Children with Special Educational Needs in the Asia Region.* Washington, DC: World Bank. http://www.inclusive-education.org/system/files/publications-documents/Lynch%20Provision%20SEN%20Asia.pdf (state: 09/2014).

Mace, A.O., Shani, M., Caleb, J., & Sarah, C. (2014). Educational, developmental and psychological outcomes of resettled refugee children in Western Australia: a review of school of special educational needs. *Journal of Paediatrics and Child Health, 10,* 1111f.

Mejeh, M. (2014). Möglichkeiten und Grenzen eines systemischen Ansatzes für die Integration von Menschen mit besonderem Förderbedarf. [Possibilities and limitations of a systemic approach regarding the integration of persons with special educational needs.] Dissertation. University of Koblenz-Landau. Landau: Faculty of Education.

Mesibov, G. (1976). Alternatives to the principle of normalisation. *Mental Retardation, 16,* 30–32.

Montessori, M. (1909). *Il Metodo della Pedagogia Scientifica applicato all'educazione infantile nelle Case dei Bambini* (revised in 1913, 1926, and 1935); revised and reissued in 1950 as *La scoperta del bambino*; (1912) English edition: *The Montessori Method: Scientific Pedagogy as Applied to Child Education in the Children's Houses.* New York: Frederick A. Stokes Company; (1948) Revised and expanded English edition issued as *The Discovery of the Child* (1950) Revised and reissued in Italian as *La scoperta del bambino.*

Montessori, M. (1967). *The Absorbent Mind*. New York: Delta.
Mossialos, E., Dixon, A., Figueras, J., & Kutzi, J. (2002). *Funding Health Care: Options for Europe*. Buckingham: Open University Press.
Murdoch, H. (1997). Stereotyped behaviours: how should we think about them? *British Journal of Special Education, 24,* 71–75.
Nind, M. (2000). Teachers' understanding of interactive approaches in special education. *Intern. Journal of Disability, Development and Education, 47,* 183–199.
Nirje, B. (1970). The normalisation principle – implications and comments. *Journal of Mental Subnormality, 16,* 62–70.
Nirje, B. (1985). The basis and logic of the normalization principle. *Australia & New Zealand Journal of Developmental Disabilities, 11,* 65–68.
O'Brien, J., & Tyne, A. (1981). *The Principle of Normalization: A Foundation for Effective Services*. London: Campaign for Mentally Handicapped People.
O'Hanlon, C. (1995). *Inclusive Education in Europe*. London: David Fulton.
Ontario Ministry of Education. (2009). *Realizing the Promise of Diversity: Ontario's Equity and Inclusive Education Strategy*. Toronto: Ministry of Education.
Orthmann, D. (2001). Berufliche Eingliederungsprozessebei Jugendlichen mit Lernbehinderung. Ergebnisseeiner Erkundungsstudie. [Processes of integration of young people with disabilities. Results of a pilot-study.] *Zeitschrift für Heilpädagogik, 52,* 398–404.
Peetsma, T., Vergeer, M., Roeleveld, J., & Karsten, S. (2001). Inclusion in education; comparing at-risk pupils' development in special and regular education. *Educational Review, 53*(2), 125–135.
Peetsma, T., & Blok, H. (Red.) (2007). *Onderwijs op maat en ouderbetrokkenheid; het integraleeindrapport*. [Fitting education and parents' engagement.] Amsterdam: SCO-KohnstammInstituut van de Universiteit van Amsterdam.
Perrin, B., & Nirje, B. (1985). Setting the record straight: a critique of some frequent misconceptions of the normalization principle. *Australia & New Zealand Journal of Developmental Disabilities, 11,* 69–74.
Preuss-Lausitz, U. (2009). Integrationsforschung. Ansätze, Ergebnisse und Perspektiven. [Research on integration, concepts, results and perspectives.] In: H. Eberwein, & S. Knauer (Hrsg.), *Integrationspädagogik*, S. 459–470. Weinheim: Beltz.
Preuss-Lausitz, U. (2010). Separation oder Inklusion. Zur Entwicklung der sonderpädagogischen Förderung im Kontext derallgemeinen Schulentwicklung. [Separation or inclusion. On the development of special needs facilitation in context of general school improvement.] In: Berkemeyer, N., Bos, W., Holtappels, H.G., McElvany, N., & Schulz-Zander, R. (Hrsg.), *Jahrbuch der Schulentwicklung*, Bd. 16, pp. 153–180. München: Juventa.
Quicke, J. (2008). *Inclusion and Psychological Intervention in Schools: A Critical Autoethnography*. Dordrecht: Springer.
Rapley, M., & Baldwin, S. (1995). Normalisation – metatheory or metaphysics? A conceptual critique. *Australia & New Zealand Journal of Developmental Disabilities, 20,* 141–157.
Riddell, S. (2000). Inclusion and choice: mutually exclusive principles in special educational needs? In: F. Armstrong, D., Armstrong & L. Barton (eds), *Inclusive Education: Policy, Contexts and Comparative Perspectives*, pp. 99–116. London: David Fulton.
Ruijs, N.M., & Peetsma, T.T.D. (2009). The effects of inclusion on students with and without special educational needs reviewed. *Educational Research Review, 4* (2), 67–79.

Ruijs, N., Peetsma, T., & Van der Veen, I. (2010). The presence of several students with special educational needs in inclusive education and the functioning of students with special educational needs. *Educational Review, 62* (1), 1–37.

Ruijs, N.N., Van der Veen, I., & Peetsma, T.T.D. (2010). Inclusive education and students without special educational needs. *Educational Research, 52* (4), 351–390.

Safford, P.A. (1996). *History of Childhood and Disability*. New York: Teacher's College Press.

Salend, S.J. (1999). The consequences on inclusion for students with and without handicaps and their teachers. *Remedial and Special Education, 20,*114–126.

Saltman, R.B. & Von Otter C. (1995). *Implementing Planned Markets in Health Care: Balancing Social and Economic Responsibility*. Buckingham: Open U.P.

Séguin, É. (1866). *Idiocy: Its Treatment by the Physiological Method*. New York: W. Wood & Co.

Sermier Dessemontet, R., Bless, G., & Morin, D. (2012). Effects of inclusion on the academic achievement and adaptive behavior of children with intellectual disabilities. *Journal of Intellectual Disability Research, 56*(6), 579–587.

Sermier Dessemontet, R. (2012). *Les effets de l'intégration scolaire sur les apprentissages d'enfants ayant une déficience intellectuelle. Une étude comparative*. Thèse de doctorat en Lettres. Fribourg: Université de Fribourg.

Specht, W. (1993). *Evaluation der Schulversuche zum gemeinsamen Unterricht behinderter und nichtbehinderter Kinder. Ergebnisse einer bundesweiten. Befragung von Lehrerinnen und Lehrern im Schulversuch. Forschungsbericht*. [Evaluation on school test phases of inclusive instruction of disabled and non-disabled children. Results of a national survey of teachers.] Graz: Zentrumfür Schulversuche und Schulentwicklung.

Soler, R., & Sarsa, J. (2012). Integration of the information and communication technologies in the teaching-learning processes: the inclusive school. *International Journal of Information and Education Technology, 5,* 564–570.

Stauber, B., & Walther, A. (2004). Übergangsforschung aus soziologischer Perspektive: Entstandardisierung von Übergängenim Leben junger Erwachsener. [Research on transitions from a sociological perspective: De-standardisation of transitions during the lifetime of young adults.] In: E. Schumacher (Hrsg.), *Übergänge in Bildung und Ausbildung*, pp. 47–67. Bad Heilbrunn: Klinkhardt.

Susser, M. (1990). Disease, illness, sickness: impairment, disability, and handicap. *Psychological Medicine, 20,* 471–473.

Thomas, G., & Loxley, A. (2001). *Deconstructing Special Education and Constructing Inclusion*. Buckingham: Open University.

UNESCO (1990). *World Declaration on Education for All*. Paris: UNESCO. http://www.unesco.org/education/wef/en-conf/Jomtien%20Declaration%20eng.shtm, accessed March, 2015).

UNESCO (1994a). *The Salamanca Statement and Framework for Action*. Paris: UNESCO. http://www.unesco.org/education/pdf/SALAMA_E.pdf (state: 09/2014).

UNESCO. (1994b). *World Conference on Special Needs Education: Access and Quality*. Paris: UNESCO. http://unesdoc.unesco.org/images/0009/000984/098427eo.pdf (state: 09/2014).

UNESCO (2000). *Dakar Framework for Action*. Paris: UNESCO. http://unesdoc.unesco.org/images/0012/001211/121147e.pdf (state: 09/2014).

UNICEF (2010). *Equity and Inclusion in Education*. Paris: UNESCO. http://www.unicef.org/education/files/Equity_and_Inclusion_Guide.pdf (state: 09/2014).

United Nations (1948). *Universal Declaration of Human Rights*. New York: United Nations New York. http://www.un.org/en/documents/udhr/ (state: 09/2014).

United Nations (1989). *Convention on the Rights of the Child.* New York: United Nations New York. http://www.ohchr.org/en/professionalinterest/pages/crc.aspx (state: 09/2014).

United Nations (1993). *The Standard Rules on the Equalization of Opportunities for Persons With Disabilities.* New York: United Nations New York. http://www.un.org/esa/socdev/enable/dissre00.htm (state: 09/2014).

United States Administration for Children and Families (2011). Child and Family Services Improvement and Innovation Act. United States Department of Health and Human Services. Washington, DC.

Walter-Klose, Chr. (2012). *Kinder und Jugendliche mit Körperbehinderung im gemeinsamen Unterricht. Befunde aus nationaler und internationaler Bildungsforschung und ihre Bedeutung für Inklusion und Schulentwicklung.* [Children and young people with physical handicap in inclusive classes. Outcomes from national and international research on education and their importance for inclusion and school advancement.] Oberhausen: ATHENA.

Wikipedia (2014). *Inclusion (Education),* http://en.wikipedia.org/wiki/Inclusion_%28education%29 (December, 2014).

Wolfensberger, W. (1972). *The Principle of Normalisation.* Toronto: National Institute on Mental Retardation.

Wolfensberger, W. (1983). Social role valorization: a proposed new term for the principle of normalization. *Mental Retardation, 21,* 234–239.

World Health Organization (WHO). (2007). *Everybody Business: Strengthening Health Systems to Improve Health Outcomes: WHO's Framework for Action.* Geneva: WHO.

Ziemen, K. (2014). Inklusion und Didaktik. [Inclusion and didactics.] *Schulpädagogik heute, 10,* 1–9.

14
Parental Acceptance and Children's Psychological Adjustment

Abdul Khaleque

This chapter contains a brief description of parental acceptance-rejection theory (PARTheory), definitions of the major concepts used in PARTheory, and its basic assumptions, especially the assumptions of the theory's personality sub-theory. It presents an overview of the attachment theory along with a brief comparison of these two theories. Discussion of conceptual frameworks of these two theories seems to be useful for a better understanding of the theoretical relationships among parental acceptance-rejection, attachment relationships, and psychological adjustment of children. The main focus is on the effects of parental acceptance and rejection on children's psychological adjustment and healthy lifespan development, with supportive cross-cultural research evidence and its implications for health professionals, practitioners, clinicians, social workers, educators, and counsellors globally.

Parental acceptance and rejection theory

Major concepts

PARTheory is an evidence-based theory of socialization and lifespan development of children and adults universally that aims to predict and explain major causes, consequences, and other correlates of parental acceptance and rejection worldwide (Rohner, 1980, 1986; Rohner, Khaleque, & Cournoyer, 2013). In PARTheory, *parental acceptance-rejection* refers to a bipolar dimension of parental warmth, with parental acceptance at the positive end of the continuum and parental rejection at the negative end. *Parental acceptance* refers to warmth, affection, love, care, comfort, support, or nurture that parents can feel or express towards their children. *Parental rejection* refers to the absence or withdrawal of warmth, affection, or love, and by the presence of a variety of physically and psychologically hurtful behaviours of parents towards their children. Parents can express their acceptance or love through physical, verbal, and symbolic behaviours indicating their feelings of warmth and affection towards their children. On the other hand, parents can express their rejection or lack of love by being cold and unaffectionate, hostile and aggressive, or indifferent and neglectful towards their children. In addition, parental rejection can be subjectively experienced by children in the form of undifferentiated rejection. In PARTheory, *undifferentiated rejection* refers to children's feeling that their parents do not really love them, which may or may not be objectively true.

Psychological adjustment refers in PARTheory to an individual's position on the constellation of seven personality dispositions central to PARTheory's personality sub-theory. These dispositions include: hostility, aggression, passive aggression, and problems with the management of hostility and aggression; emotional unresponsiveness; dependence or defensive independence depending on the form, frequency, durations, and severity of perceived rejection; impaired self-esteem; impaired self-adequacy; emotional instability; and negative worldview. Additionally, the theory predicts that the experience of rejection by an attachment figure is likely to induce feelings of anxiety and insecurity as well as becoming associated with cognitive distortions. Perceived parental warmth and acceptance, on the other hand, has been found to be associated worldwide with psychological adjustment, with positive personality and behavioural development (Khaleque & Rohner, 2002, 2011, 2012; Khaleque, 2013b, 2014a).

The basic assumptions of parental acceptance-rejection theory

PARTheory assumes that parental acceptance has consistent positive effects, and that parental rejection has consistent negative effects on the psychological adjustment and behavioural functioning of both children and adults worldwide (Rohner, 1980, 1986; Rohner & Khaleque, 2005). The theory attempts to answer five classes of questions concerning parental acceptance and rejection. These are:

1. What happens to children who perceive themselves to be loved (accepted) or unloved (rejected) by their parents?
2. To what extent do the effects of childhood rejection extend into adulthood and old age?
3. Why are some parents warm, loving, and accepting, and others cold, aggressive, neglectful, and rejecting?
4. How is the total fabric of a society, as well as the behaviour and beliefs of people within a society, affected by the fact that most parents in that society tend to either accept or reject their children?
5. Why do some children and adults cope more effectively than others with the experiences of childhood rejection?

Sub-theories of PARTheory

PARTheory is divided into three distinguishable sub-theories:

Personality Sub-Theory. This sub-theory postulates that parental acceptance-rejection has profound influence in shaping children's personality development over the lifespan. The sub-theory assumes that humans have developed an enduring, biologically based emotional need for positive response from the people who are most important to them. The need for positive response includes an emotional wish, desire, or yearning (whether consciously recognized or not) for comfort, support, care, concern, nurturance, and the like. Parents are typically the people who can best satisfy this need for infants and children. But sources of support and acceptance for adolescents and adults expand to include peers, teachers, intimate partners, and other attachment figures (Rohner, 1999).

PARTheory's personality sub-theory assumes that the emotional need for positive response from significant others (parents or other attachment figures) is a powerful motivator in children. When this need is not met by parents, children are predisposed emotionally and behaviourally to respond in specific ways (Rohner, 1986, 1999). The sub-theory predicts that parental acceptance is likely to lead to the development of psychological adjustment and positive personality dispositions, and parental rejection is likely to lead to the development of psychological maladjustment and negative personality dispositions in children. In particular, the sub-theory postulates that children who perceive themselves to be accepted by their parents are likely to develop: (1) low hostility and aggression, (2) independence, (3) positive self-esteem, (4) positive self-adequacy, (5) emotional stability, (6) emotional responsiveness, and (7) positive worldview. On the other hand, the personality sub-theory postulates that children who perceive themselves to be rejected by their parents are likely to develop: (1) hostility and aggression, (2) dependence or defensive independence, (3) negative self-esteem, 4) negative self-adequacy, (5) emotional instability, (6) emotional unresponsiveness, and (7) negative worldview.

Sociocultural systems sub-theory

This sub-theory attempts to predict and explain major causes and sociocultural correlates of parental acceptance and rejection worldwide. The sub-theory predicts, for example, that children are likely to develop cultural beliefs about the supernatural world (God and spiritual beings) as being malevolent (i.e., hostile, treacherous, destructive, or negative in some way) in societies where they tend to be rejected. Contrarily, the supernatural world is expected to be perceived as benevolent (i.e., warm, generous, protective, or positive in some other way) in societies where most children are raised with warmth and acceptance. Substantial cross-cultural evidence confirms these predictions (Rohner, 1999; Batool & Najam, 2009). PARTheory's sociocultural sub-theory also predicts, and cross-cultural evidence confirms, that parental acceptance and rejection tend to be associated worldwide with many other sociocultural correlates such as family structure, artistic preferences, and job choices of individuals (Rohner, 1986, 1999; Rohner, Khaleque, & Cournoyer, 2005).

Coping Sub-Theory. Not all rejected individuals develop serious adjustment problems. Some are able to cope with the impact of rejection more effectively than others. This issue is addressed in PARTheory's coping sub-theory. Studies in the US and across the world confirm PARTheory's assumption that nearly 80% of children and adults, irrespective of geographic location, race, and ethnicity, tend to be negatively affected by parental rejection (Khaleque, 2001; Khaleque & Rohner, 2002, 2011, 2012; Khaleque, 2013b, 2014a). A small fraction of the remaining 20% is termed 'copers' in PARTheory. They are the people who experienced significant parental rejection in childhood but who, nonetheless, continue to be psychologically well adjusted as defined in PARTheory's personality sub-theory. According to PARTheory's coping sub-theory, copers are of two types: 'affective copers' and 'instrumental copers' (Rohner, 1999). Affective copers are those individuals who develop overall positive mental health despite parental rejection. Instrumental copers are those individuals who do well in their professional, occupational, or task-oriented lives despite psychological impairment due to parental rejection in early life (Rohner, 1999).

Paradigm shift in PARTheory

PARTheory research, until 2000, focused mainly on parent–child relations (specifically, parental acceptance-rejection). But research only on parental acceptance-rejection could not provide a comprehensive answer to the following question: why do some accepted people show the same constellation of personality dispositions as rejected individuals? This question led Rohner (2006) to make a major paradigm shift in PARTheory's personality sub-theory.

Original PARTheory Postulate. Parental rejection is associated with the specific cluster of personality dispositions noted in personality sub-theory.

Reformulated Postulate. Perceived rejection by an *attachment figure at any point in life* is associated with the same cluster of personality dispositions found among children and adults rejected by parents in childhood.

The first empirical study to test the above reformulated postulate of PARTheory was conducted in 2001 (Khaleque, 2001). This study examined the impact of perceived acceptance-rejection by intimate male partners on the psychological adjustment of adult females in the US. Results showed that partner acceptance had significant impact on women's psychological adjustment. Additionally, results showed that both partners' acceptance and paternal acceptance had a significantly greater impact on women's psychological adjustment than did maternal acceptance (Rohner & Khaleque, 2008). Thus PARTheory has gradually expanded beyond its initial concerns with *parental* acceptance-rejection, and started focusing on all aspects of *interpersonal* acceptance and rejection (Khaleque, 2007).

Attachment theory

Basic concepts

Attachment is an important theoretical approach to study and understand intimate relationships (Bowlby, 1982; Ainsworth & Bowlby, 1991; Colin, 1996; Cassidy & Shaver, 1999). Attachment theory provides important theoretical constructs for explaining intimate relationships in childhood and adulthood. Bowlby constructed the basic tenets of attachment theory, drawing from the concepts of Darwinian theory, ethology, developmental psychology, and psychoanalysis. Ainsworth expanded the theory with empirical support (Bretherton, 1995). Although infant research was the original basis of attachment theory, it was later formulated as a lifespan theory (Bowlby, 1980; Ainsworth, 1989). In recent years, it has been applied to the study of intimate adult relationships (Shaver & Clark, 1994; Feeney, 1999). Attachment theory has attracted enormous interest during the last quarter of the 20th century (Cassidy & Shaver, 1999). According to Bowlby (1969) and Ainsworth (1973), attachment is as an enduring affective bond characterized by a tendency to seek and maintain proximity to a significant attachment figure, particularly under stress. As an emotional bond, Ainsworth (1989) defined attachment as 'a relatively long-enduring tie in which the partner is important as a unique individual and is interchangeable with none other'. According to Ainsworth (1989), attachment like all other affectional bonds includes the following elements: (1) an emotional bond; (2) an enduring relationship; (3) the need to maintain proximity; (4) feeling of distress upon separation; (5) pleasure in reunion; and (6) grief at loss.

Assumptions of attachment theory

A brief description of attachment theory's major assumptions is given below:

Biological Evolutionary Basis. One of the fundamental assumptions of attachment theory is its evolutionary perspective focusing on the psychobiological base of attachment behaviour (Bowlby, 1958, 1982). Accordingly, attachment theory assumes that humans have a biologically based propensity to develop enduring emotional bonds with attachment figures. Human attachment bonds are subject to adaptive changes over the lifespan.

Behavioural system. In attachment theory, a behavioural system refers to a set of discrete behaviours that function in an organized way to help the individual achieve attachment. The theory proposes that attachment behaviour is a goal-corrected behavioural system. The goal is to attain attachment, and the person goes on trying whatever will work to achieve the goal. For example, if crying does not help bring the attachment figure to the child, the child may try some alternative ways (crawl, walk, or run) to draw the attention of the attachment figure. Attachment theory also assumes that the behavioural system-controlling attachment tends to be active from the cradle to the grave (Bowlby, 1982). Attachment behaviour tends to be activated in an individual either by external threatening conditions (frightening stimuli or events) or internal threatening conditions (illness and pain). The intensity of activation of attachment behaviour tends to vary with the intensity of the threat (Colin, 1996).

Secure-Base Concept. The secure-base concept is one of the most important assumptions of attachment theory. Ainsworth provided empirical evidence to support the concept of attachment figure as a secure base from which an infant can explore the world (Ainsworth & Bowlby, 1991). Ainsworth (1989) indicated that being near the attachment figure tends to support exploration, and being away from the attachment figure tends to activate attachment behaviour. According to attachment theorists, differences in the quality of attachment relationships depend on the specific nature of early social exchanges between the caregiver and the child (Ainsworth et al., 1978; Thompson, 2008). In other studies in a laboratory playroom in the US, Rheingold and Eckerman (1970) and many others showed that infants explore contentedly if mothers are present, but become distressed when separated from their mothers.

Internal Working Model. Another important concept developed by Bowlby (1969) in attachment theory is the notion of an internal working model or representational model. According to Bowlby (1994), each individual perceives events, forecasts the future, and constructs his or her plans with the help of working models of the world which he/she builds for himself/herself. A key feature of an individual's working model is his/her notion of *who* his/her attachment figures are, *where* they may be found, and *how* they may be expected to respond. Attachment theory assumes that internal working models of oneself and others are formed during the course of attachment-eliciting events. According to attachment theorists, internal working models begin to form during the early months of life, and continue to develop and reshape in later life. Children develop certain expectations regarding their interactions with attachment figures on the basis of repeated experience. These expectations are integrated and embodied in the mental representation models or internal working models that may influence the formation and development of later models.

Continuity and change

Attachment theory assumes continuity and change in attachment bonds and behaviours across the lifespan. A set of well-integrated assumptions has been proposed regarding the development of attachment bonds and intimate relationships throughout the lifespan. Many of the theory's assumptions about infancy and childhood have been well supported by research (Bretherton & Munholland, 2008). However, propositions about adult attachment and intimate relationships need more research for empirical support (Colin, 1996).

Comparison between PARTheory and attachment theory

Agreement between the two theories

PARTheory and the attachment theory agree on at least five basic assumptions, which are briefly described below:

Evolutionary Perspective. A common feature of both theories is an evolutionary perspective. Attachment theory assumes that human beings have a biologically based and phylogenetically acquired propensity to develop enduring emotional bonds of attachment with non-interchangeable attachment figures. Attachment theory emphasizes the evolutionary adaptiveness of these attachment bonds. PARTheory, on the other hand, assumes that human beings have a phylogenetically acquired biological need for positive response (i.e., need for care, comfort, support, nurturance, love, affection, etc.) from parents, significant others, or attachment figures. In addition, PARTheory assumes that humans have acquired over the course of hominid evolution the propensity to respond in specific ways when this need is not fulfilled. Attachment theory implicitly recognizes PARTheory's postulates that human beings have a phylogenetically acquired need for positive response (1990).

Universal Propensities. Both PARTheory and attachment theory argue that the propensities cited above are universal because they are thought to be rooted in human biology.

Representational Model. Both theories draw heavily from the common concept of representational model, called 'mental representations' in PARTheory and 'internal working models' in attachment theory.

Resistance to Loss of Significant Relationships. According to both PARTheory and attachment theory, children and adults tend to resist the disruption or loss of affectional bonds of attachment with parents or significant others.

Importance of Affectional Bonds. Both PARTheory and attachment theory make a distinction between general affectional bonds and specific attachment bonds. As noted earlier, person with whom the individual has an affectional bond is called in PARTheory a 'significant other'. A significant other is any person with whom an individual has a relatively long-lasting emotional bond, who is uniquely important to the individual, and who is interchangeable with no one else. An attachment figure has all these characteristics, but has one additional *essential* characteristic. Specifically, to be an attachment figure, as defined in PARTheory, one's sense of emotional security, happiness, and well-being must be dependent to some degree on the quality of relationship with the other person (Rohner & Khaleque, 2005). According to PARTheory, parents are generally the most significant of others for children because they are typically children's attachment figures (Rohner, 1999). The concept of affectional bonds in attachment theory is amplified earlier in the beginning of the subsection on basic concepts.

Differences between the two theories

Despite strong similarities between the two theories, they also diverge in important respects. These differences, however, do not necessarily mean disagreements. According to Rohner (1999), major differences include:

- **Major Focus.** PARTheory traditionally focuses on the quality of parenting, especially characterized by parental acceptance-rejection (i.e., warmth/affection, hostility/aggression, indifference/neglect, and undifferentiated rejection). Attachment theory traditionally focuses on the attachment behaviour of children, especially infants and toddlers, towards the parent, especially the mother, although recent attention to 'caregiving' patterns in attachment relationships is evident (e.g., George & Solomon, 1996).
- **Age Differences.** Originally, PARTheory concentrated on school-aged children, adolescents, and adults, whereas attachment theory concentrated primarily on infants and toddlers. Now, however, both theories are trying to take a lifespan perspective, focusing on infancy through old age.
- **Differences in Measurement Approaches.** PARTheory tends to rely heavily (but not exclusively) on individuals' self-reports of parental treatment as revealed by questionnaires and interviews. Attachment theory, on the other hand, tends to rely heavily on behaviour observations by researchers, focusing on infancy and early childhood.
- **Differences in Approach of Personality Outcomes of Parenting.** In PARTheory personality outcomes of parenting behaviours are viewed as dimensions or continua, which range from positive to negative. On the other hand, in attachment theory, personality outcomes are viewed as types or categories, such as secure attachment or insecure attachment.
- **Focus on a Single Primary Personality Outcomes Versus a Constellation of Personality Outcomes of Different Parenting Styles.** PARTheory focuses on personality as a constellation of interrelated characteristics influenced by different parenting styles. Attachment theory emphasizes different types or categories of attachment behaviours as the primary personality outcomes of different parenting styles.

Despite these differences, both PARTheory and attachment theory have made significant contributions to the understanding of the nature, characteristics, and dynamics of attachment relationships and their developmental consequences for children and adults cross-culturally (Carrillo & Ripoll-Nunez, 2014).

Cross-cultural effects of parental acceptance-rejection

Since 1930s, a large number of studies have been conducted on the antecedents and the consequences of perceived parental acceptance-rejection for cognitive, emotional, and behavioural development of children, and for personality functioning of adults within the US and worldwide (Rohner, 1986, 1990; Khaleque & Rohner, 2002). Research on parent–child relations consistently indicates that perceived parental rejection typically has serious consequences for the psychological development and personality functioning of children and adults (Rohner, 1991). In a review of available cross-cultural and intracultural studies, for example, Rohner and Britner (2002) provided evidence of worldwide correlations between parental acceptance-rejection and other mental health issues including: (1) depression and depressed affect; (2) behaviour problems–conduct disorders, externalizing behaviours, and delinquency; (3) substance abuse; and, (4) psychological maladjustment.

Depression. Parental rejection has been found to be linked consistently with both clinical and non-clinical depression within almost all major ethnic groups in America, including African-Americans (Crook, Raskin, & Eliot, 1981), Asian-Americans (Greenberger & Chen, 1996), European-Americans (Whitbeck, Conger, & Kao, 1993), and Mexican-Americans (Dumka, Roosa, & Jackson, 1997). Moreover, parental rejection has been shown to be associated with depression in many countries internationally, including Australia (Parker, Kiloh, & Hayward, 1987), China (Chen, Rubin, & Li, 1995), Egypt (Fattah, 1996), Germany (Richter, 1994), Hungary (Richter, 1994), Italy (Richter, 1994), Sweden (Richter, 1994), and Turkey (Erkman, 1992). It is also interesting to note that a number of longitudinal studies show that perceived parental rejection in childhood tends to be associated with the development of depressive symptoms in adolescence and adulthood (Chen, Rubin, & Li, 1995).

Behaviour Problems. According to Rohner and Britner (2002), parental rejection appears to be a major predictor in almost all forms of behaviour problems, including conduct disorder, externalizing behaviour, and delinquency. Cross-cultural findings supporting this suggestion come from many countries across the world, including Bahrain (Al-Falaij, 1991), China (Chen, Rubin, & Li, 1997), Croatia (Ajdukovic, 1990), Egypt (Ahmed, 2008), England (Maughan, Pickles, & Quinton, 1995), India (Saxena, 1992), and Norway (Pedersen, 1994). As with depression, a number of longitudinal studies in the US (Ge, Best, Conger, & Simon, 1996), and internationally (Chen, Rubin, & Li, 1997), show that parental rejection also tends to precede the development of behaviour problems.

Substance Abuse. Possible support for the worldwide correlation between parental acceptance-rejection and substance abuse comes from substantial research evidence in Australia (Rosenberg, 1971), Canada (Hundleby & Mercer, 1987), England (Merry, 1972), the Netherlands (Emmelkamp & Heeres, 1988), and Sweden (Vrasti et al., 1990). These studies clearly indicate that parental rejection is a etiologically connected with both drug abuse and alcohol abuse. Besides these cross-national studies, parental rejection has also been found to be linked with substance abuse in most ethnic groups in the US, including African-Americans (Myers, Newcomb, Richardson, & Alvy, 1997), Asian-Americans (Shedler & Block, 1990), and Hispanics (Coombs, Paulson, & Richardson, 1991). In addition, Rohner and Britner (2002) cited a large number of studies thoroughly documenting the relation between parental rejection and substance abuse among European-American middle-class and working-class Americans.

Neuropsychological Effects of Rejection. Recent studies have shown that perceived rejection is related to developmental trauma disorder (Van Der Kolk, 2010) and to post-traumatic stress disorder (Courtois, 2004). Moreover, emotional neglect in childhood may be a significant risk factor for cerebral infarction in old age (Wilson et al., 2012). Perceived rejection and other forms of long-term emotional trauma are often implicated in the alteration of brain chemistry (Ford & Russo, 2006). Several brain imaging (fMRI) studies reveal that specific parts of the brain (i.e., the anterior cingulate cortex and the right ventral prefrontal cortex) are activated when people feel rejected (Eisenberger, 2012). Moreover, Fisher, Aron, and Brown (2006) found that different regions of the brain were activated among adults who were accepted versus those who were rejected by their partners.

Psychological Adjustment and Maladjustment. Numerous studies conducted across the world support the postulate of a significant transcultural association between perceived parental acceptance-rejection and psychological adjustments. For example, Rohner (1975) found supportive evidence for this postulate in a holocultural study of 101 societies worldwide. Moreover, Cournoyer (2000) reported a partial list of the sociocultural groups in different countries, where this finding has been replicated and reconfirmed. This list includes: the US with African-Americans, European-Americans, and Hispanic-Americans (Rohner, 1986); Bahrain (Al-Falaj, 1991); Bangladesh (Rohner, Khaleque, Elias, & Sultana, 2010); Egypt (Ahmed, 2008); India (Parmer & Rohner, 2010); Japan (Rohner, Uddin, Shamsunnaher, & Khaleque, 2008); Korea (Chyung & Lee, 2008); Czechoslovakia (Matejeck & Kaducova, 1984); Pakistan (Malik & Rohner, 2012); Peru (Gavilano, 1988); Mexico (Rohner, Roll, & Rohner, 1980); Nigeria (Haque, 1988); St. Kitts, West Indies (Rohner, Kean, & Cournoyer, 1991); and Turkey (Erkman & Rohner, 2006). In addition, a meta-analysis of 43 studies drawing from 7,563 respondents worldwide showed that the predicted relations between perceived parental acceptance-rejection and psychological adjustment emerged almost invariably in all studies (Khaleque & Rohner, 2002).

Meta-analytic studies on interpersonal acceptance-rejection and its effects

The strongest body of evidence about the worldwide relations between psychological adjustment-maladjustment and parental acceptance-rejection comes from a number of cross-cultural and intracultural meta-analyses conducted to test the basic assumptions of PARTheory's personality sub-theory. So far nine meta-analyses have been conducted to test the central postulates of the PARTheory (Khaleque, 2013a). These meta-analyses were based on a total of 322 studies on PARTheory. These studies were conducted over period of 37 years (1975–2012). The studies represented an aggregated sample of 89,934 respondents. The respondents were taken from 25 countries in five continents. The overall results of these meta-analyses confirmed that the central postulates of the PARTheory's personality sub-theory are true for children and adults regardless of differences in races, ethnicities, cultures, gender, and geographical boundaries.

Results of one meta-analytic review have shown that significant pan-cultural associations exist between perceived maternal and parental acceptance and the overall psychological adjustment of both children and adults (Khaleque & Rohner, 2002). Another meta-analytic review, based on 30 studies from 16 countries in five continents involving 12,087 children, has shown that both paternal and maternal acceptance-rejection often make independent or unique contributions to the psychological adjustment and personality development of children (Khaleque, 2013b). In addition, the experience of parental acceptance tends worldwide to be associated with the development of children's prosocial behaviour (such as generosity, helpfulness, and empathy), and in adults with a sense of overall well-being and positive psychological and physical health (Rohner & Khaleque, 2014). Results of two other meta-analyses (Khaleque, 2014a, 2014b) showed that perceived maternal and paternal rejections in the forms of indifference/neglect, and hostility/aggression have significant effect on the overall psychological maladjustment of children across ethnicities, cultures, gender, and geographical boundaries.

Personality Dispositions. As noted earlier, PARTheory's personality sub-theory assumes that children and adults universally – irrespective of culture, race, ethnicity, gender, and socioeconomic status – are phylogenetically predisposed to develop a specific constellation of personality dispositions as a consequence of varying degrees of perceived parental acceptance or rejection (Rohner, 1986, 1990, 1999). Results of a meta-analysis have shown that both children's and adults' perceptions of paternal and maternal acceptance are transculturally associated with their positive personality dispositions, including low hostility and aggression, independence, positive self-esteem, positive self-adequacy, emotional responsiveness, emotional stability, and positive worldview (Khaleque & Rohner, 2011). Results of two other meta-analyses (Khaleque, 2014a, 2014b) have shown that both maternal and paternal indifference and neglect, and hostility and aggression correlated significantly with seven negative personality dispositions, including (1) hostility and aggression, (2) dependence or defensive independence, (3) negative self-esteem, (4) negative self-adequacy, (5) emotional instability, (6) emotional unresponsiveness, and (7) negative worldview of children across ethnicities, cultures, and geographical boundaries as postulated in PARTheory.

Significance of *Paternal* acceptance-rejection

The majority of studies that assess the relation between parental rejection and psychological maladjustment tend to focus predominantly on the influence of mothers' behaviour even though fathers' are often as strongly implicated as mothers in many developmental outcomes. An increasing number of studies show that perceived *paternal* acceptance often has as strong or even stronger implications than perceived maternal acceptance for children's positive developmental outcomes, including psychological adjustment (Rohner & Veneziano, 2001). Results of a recent meta-analytic review have shown that father love tends to have a significantly stronger relationship with children's psychological adjustment than does the relationship between mother love and children's psychological adjustment cross-culturally (Khaleque & Rohner, 2012). Moreover, in a review of a large number of cross-cultural studies, Rohner & Britner (2002) have found that perceived paternal rejection tends to have stronger negative implications than perceived maternal rejection for the development of depression, conduct disorder, and substance abuse.

Studies drawing a conclusion that paternal love often predicts specific child and adult outcomes better than maternal love tend to deal with the following six issues among children, adolescents, and adults (Rohner & Veneziano, 2001): (1) personality and psychological adjustment problems, (2) mental illness, (3) psychological health and well-being, (4) conduct disorder, (5) substance abuse, and (6) delinquency. The literature on paternal love shows that paternal acceptance-rejection tends to be deeply implicated in a wide variety of outcomes including cognitive, emotional, and behavioural problems, and psychological well-being of children and adult offspring. This literature further indicates that paternal love seems to affect offspring development at all ages from infancy through adulthood (Rohner & Veneziano, 2001). Several studies assessing the influence of variations in paternal love show that fathers sometimes have a different influence on sons versus daughters from the influence that mothers have (Ali, Khaleque, & Rohner, 2014).

Conclusion

Global research evidence provided in this article and elsewhere lends credibility to PARTheory's contention that perceived parental rejection is one of the major causes of social, emotional, cognitive, and behavioural problems of children, adolescents, and adults everywhere – regardless of race, ethnicity, culture, gender, and geographical boundary, or other such defining conditions. Having said this, however, it should also be noted that perceived acceptance-rejection appears to account universally for an average of about 26% of the variance in the psychological adjustment, personality development, and behavioural functioning of children and adults, leaving approximately 74% of the variance to be accounted for by other factors (Khaleque & Rohner, 2002, 2011). Nonetheless, results of well over 500 studies completed so far on the central tenets of PARTheory – especially PARTheory's personality sub-theory – are so robust and stable cross-culturally that professionals and practitioners should feel confident in using them for developing policies, practices, and intervention strategies to deal with the problems of psychological adjustment, personality dispositions, and behavioural functioning of children and adults globally.

Take home lessons for practitioners

Nearly 4,000 worldwide studies on PARTheory suggest the following important messages for professionals and practitioners globally:

1. Children's feelings of being loved (accepted), cared, and appreciated probably have greater developmental outcomes than any other single parental influence.
2. Every cultural and ethnic group has its own ways of communicating love and affection. Parents should find culturally appropriate ways to communicate love, warmth, and affection. Moreover, parents should avoid behaviours that indicate coldness, hostility/aggression, and indifference/neglect that induce a feeling of rejection in children.
3. Compared to children who feel loved, children who feel rejected are likely to develop a pattern of psychological maladjustment, and personality dispositions including hostility/aggression, dependence, low self-esteem, low self-adequacy, emotional unresponsiveness, emotional instability, negative worldview, anxiety, and insecurity.
4. Children who perceive themselves to be rejected are also likely to develop behavioural problems, conduct disorders, delinquency, substance abuse, and depression.

5. Father's love-related behaviours often have as strong or even stronger implications for children's psychological adjustment, personality and socio-emotional development than do mother's love.

References

Ahmed, R.A. (2008). Review of Arab research on parental acceptance-rejection. In: F. Erkman (ed.), *Acceptance: The Essence of Peace. Selected Papers From the First International Congress on Interpersonal Acceptance and Rejection*, pp. 201–224. Istanbul: Turkish Psychology Association.
Ainsworth, M.D.S. (1989). Attachment beyond infancy. *American Psychologist, 44*, 709–716.
Ainsworth, M.D.S. (1990). Some considerations regarding theory and assessment relevant to attachment and beyond. In: M.T. Greenberg, D. Ciechetti & E.M. Cummings (eds), *Attachment in the Preschool Years*, pp. 463–489. Chicago, IL: University of Chicago Press.
Ainsworth, M.D.S., & Bowlby, J. (1991). An ethological approach to personality development. *American Psychologist, 46*, 331–341.
Ainsworth, M.S., Blehar, M.C., Waters, E., & Wall, S. (1978). *Patterns of Attachment: Assessed in the Strange Situation and at Home*. Hillsdale, NJ: Erlbaum.
Ajdukovic, M. (1990). Differences in parent's rearing style between female and male predelinquent and delinquent youth (abstract). *Psychologische Beitrage, 32*(1–2), 7–15.
Al-Falaij, A. (1991). Family conditions, ego development and socio-moral development in juvenile delinquency: a study of Bahraini adolescents. Unpublished doctoral dissertation, University of Pittsburgh, PA.
Ali, S., Khaleque, A., & Rohner, R.P. (2014). Gender differences in the relation between perceived parental acceptance and psychological adjustment of children and adult offspring: a multi-cultural meta-analysis. Unpublished manuscript.
Batool, S., & Najam, N. (2009). *Relationship Between Perceived Parenting Style, Perceived Parental Acceptance-Rejection (Par) and Perception of God Among Young Adults*. Quaideazam University, Islamabad, Pakistan.
Bowlby, J. (1958). The nature of the child's tie to his mother. *Journal of Psychoanalysis, 39*, 350–373.
Bowlby, J. (1980). *Attachment and Loss*, Vol. 3: Loss. New York: Basic Books.
Bowlby, J. (1969/1982). *Attachment and Loss*, Vol. 1, 2nd Edition. New York: Basic Books.
Bowlby, J. (1994). *The Making and Breaking of Affectional Bonds*. New York: Routledge.
Bretherton, I. (1995). The origin of attachment theory: John Bowlby and Mary Ainsworth. In: S. Goldberg, J. Kerr & R. Muir (eds), *Attachment Theory: Social, Developmental, and Clinical Perspectives*, pp. 45–84. Hillsdale, NJ: Analytic Press.
Bretherton, I., & Munholland, K.A. (2008). Internal working models in attachment relationships: Elaborating a central construct in attachment theory. In: J. Cassidy & P. Shaver (eds), *Handbook of Adult Attachment: Theory, Research and Clinical Applications*, 2nd edition, pp. 102–127. New York: The Guilford Press.
Carrillo, S., & Ripool-Nunez, K.J. (2014). Adult intimate relationships: linkages between parental acceptance rejection theory and adult attachment theory. Unpublished manuscript.

Cassidy, J., & Shaver, P.R. (eds). (1999). *Handbook of Attachment: Theory, Research, and Clinical Applications*. New York: The Guilford Press.

Chen, X., Rubin, K.H., & Li, B. (1995). Depressed mood in Chinese children: relations with school performance and family environment. *Journal of Consulting and Clinical Psychology, 63*(6), 938–947.

Chen, X., Rubin, K.H., & Li, B. (1997). Maternal acceptance and social and school adjustment in Chinese children: a four-year longitudinal study. *Merrill-Palmer Quarterly, 43*, 663–681.

Chyung, Y.J., & Lee, J. (2008). Intimate partner acceptance, remembered parental acceptance in childhood, and psychological adjustment among Korean college students in ongoing intimate relationships. In: R.P. Rohner & T. Melendez (eds), *Parental Acceptance-Rejection Theory Studies of Intimate Adult Relationships. Cross-Cultural Research, 42*(1), 77–86.

Colin, V.L. (1996). *Human Attachment*. New York: McGraw-Hill Companies, Inc.

Coombs, R.H., Paulson, M.J., & Richardson, M.A. (1991). Peer vs. parental influence in substance use among Hispanic and Anglo children and adolescents. *Journal of Youth and Adolescence, 20*(1), 73–88.

Cournoyer, D.E. (2000). Universalist research: Examples drawing from the methods and findings of parental acceptance-rejection theory. In: A.L. Comunian & U. Gielen (eds), *International Perspective on Human Development*, pp. 213–232. Berlin, Germany: Pabst Science Publishers.

Courtois, C.A. (2004). Complex trauma, complex reactions: Assessment and treatment. *Psychotherapy, 41*, 412–425.

Dumka, L.E., Roosa, M.W., & Jackson, K.M. (1997). Risk, conflict, mothers' parenting, and children's adjustment in low-income, Mexican immigrant, and Mexican American families. *Journal of Marriage and the Family, 59*(2), 309–323.

Eisenberger, N.L. (2012). Broken hearts and broken bones: a neural perspective on the similarities between social and physical pain. *Association for Psychological Science, 21*(1), 42–47.

Emmelkamp, P.M.G., & Heeres, H. (1988). Drug addiction and parental rearing style: a controlled study. *The International Journal of the Addictions, 23*(2), 207–216.

Erkman, F., & Rohner, R.P. (2006). Youth's perceptions of corporal punishment, parental acceptance, and psychological adjustment in a Turkish metropolis. In: R.P. Rohner (ed.), *Corporal Punishment, Parental Acceptance-Rejection, and Youth's Psychological Adjustment. Cross-Cultural Research, 40*, 250–267.

Fattah, F.A. El. (1996). *Symptoms of Depression and Perception of Parental Acceptance and Control*. Paper presented on symposium on PARTheory, Zagazig University, Egypt.

Feeny, J.A. (1999). Adult romantic attachment and couple relationships. In: J. Cassidy & P.R. Shaver (eds), *Handbook of Attachment: Theory Research, and Clinical Applications*, pp. 355–377. New York: Guilford Press.

Fisher, H.E., Aron, A., & Brown, L.L. (2006). Romantic love: a mammalian brain system for mate choice. *Philosophical Transactions of the Royal Society, B, 361*, 2173–2186.

Ford, J.D., & Russo, E. (2006). Trauma-focused, present-centered, emotional self-regulation approach to integrated treatment for posttraumatic stress and addiction: trauma adaptive recover group education and therapy (TARGET). *American Journal of Psychotherapy, 60*, 335–355.

Gavilano, G. (1988). *Maternal Acceptance-Rejection and Personality Characteristics Among Adolescents in Different Socio-Economic Sectors*. Thesis for completion of Bachelor's Degree, Catholic University of Peru, Lima, Peru.

Ge, X., Best, K.M., Conger, R.D., & Simon, R.L. (1996). Parenting behaviors and the occurrence and co-occurrence of adolescent depressive symptoms and conduct problems. *Developmental Psychology, 32*(4), 717–731.

George, C., & Solomon, J. (1996). Representation of relationships: links between caregiving and attachment. *Infant Mental Health Journal, 17*, 198–216.

Greenberger, E., & Chen, C. (1996). Perceived family relationship and depressed mood in early and late adolescence: a comparison of European and Asian Americans. *Developmental Psychology, 32*, 707–716.

Haque, A. (1988). Relationship between perceived maternal acceptance-rejection and self-esteem among young adults in Nigeria. *Journal of African Psychology, 1*, 15–24.

Hundleby, J.D., & Mercer, G.W. (1987). Family and friends as social environments and their relationship to adolescents' use of alcohol, tobacco, and marijuana. *Journal of Marriage and the Family, 49*, 151–164.

Khaleque, A. (2001). Parental acceptance-rejection, psychological adjustment, and intimate adult relationships. Unpublished Master's thesis, University of Connecticut, Storrs, CT.

Khaleque, A. (2007). Parental acceptance-rejection theory: beyond parent-child relationships. *Interpersonal Acceptance, 1*(1), 2–4.

Khaleque, A. (2013a). Testing the central postulates of parental acceptance-rejection theory: an overview of meta-analyses. *Interpersonal Acceptance, 7*(1), 1–3.

Khaleque, A. (2013b). Perceived parental warmth and affection, and children's psychological adjustment, and personality dispositions: a meta-analysis. *Journal of Child and Family Studies, 22*, 297–30611.

Khaleque, A. (2014b). Perceived parental aggression, and children's psychological maladjustment, and negative personality dispositions: a meta-analysis of multicultural studies. Unpublished manuscript.

Khaleque, A. (2014a). Perceived parental neglect, and children's psychological maladjustment, and negative personality dispositions: a meta-analytic review. *Journal of Child and Family Studies.* doi: 10.1007/s10826-014-9948.

Khaleque, A., & Rohner, R.P. (2002). Perceived parental acceptance-rejection and psychological adjustment: a meta- analysis of cross- cultural and intracultural studies. *Journal of Marriage and Family, 64*, 54–64.

Khaleque, A., & Rohner, R.P. (2011). Transcultural relations between perceived parental acceptance and personality dispositions of children and adults: a meta-analytic review. *Personality and Social Psychology Review, 15*, 1–13.

Khaleque, A., & Rohner, R.P. (2012). Pancultural associations between perceived parental acceptance and psychological adjustment of children and adults: a metal analytic review of worldwide research. *Journal of Cross-Cultural Psychology, 43*, 784–800.

Malik, F., & Rohner, R.P. (2012). Spousal rejection as a risk factor for parental rejection of children. *Journal of Family Violence, 27*(4), 295–301.

Matejcek, Z., & Kadubcova, B. (1984). Self-conception in Czech children from the point of view of Rohner's Parental Acceptance-Rejection Theory. *Ceskoslovenska Psychologie, 28*(2), 87–96.

Maughan, B., Pickles, A., & Quinton, D. (1995). Parental hostility, childhood behavior, and adult social functioning. In: J. McCord (ed.), *Coercion and Punishment in Long-Term Perspectives*. Cambridge: Cambridge University Press.

Merry, J. (1972). Social characteristics of addiction to heroin. *British Journal of Addiction, 67*, 322–325.

Myers, H.F., Newcomb, M.D., Richardson, M.A., & Alvy, K.T. (1997). Parental and family risk factors for substance use among inner-city African American children and adolescents. *Journal of Psychopathology and Behavioral Assessment, 19*, 109–131.

Parmar, P., & Rohner, R.P. (2010). Perceived teacher and parental acceptance and behavioral control, school conduct, and psychological adjustment among school-going adolescents in India. *Cross-Cultural Research, 44*(3), 253–265.

Parker, G., Kiloh, L., & Hayward, L. (1987). Parental representations of neurotic and endogenous depressives. *Journal of Affective Disorders, 13*, 75–82.

Rheingold, H., & Eckerman, C. (1970). The infant separates himself from his mother. *Science, 168*, 78–83.

Richter, J. (1994). Parental rearing and aspects of psychopathology with special reference to depression. In: C. Perris, W.A. Arrindell & M. Eisemann (eds), *Parenting and Psychopathology*, pp. 235–251. Chichester, England: John Wiley & Sons Ltd.

Rohner, R.P. (1975). *They Love Me, They Love Me Not: A Worldwide Study of the Effects of Parental Acceptance and Rejection*. New Haven, CT: HRAF Press.

Rohner, R.P. (1980). Worldwide tests of parental acceptance-rejection theory: an overview. *Behavior Science Research, 15*, 1–21.

Rohner, R.P. (1986). *The Warmth Dimension: Foundations of Parental Acceptance-Rejection Theory*. Beverly Hills, CA: Sage Publications, Inc.

Rohner, R.P. (1990). *Handbook for the Study of Parental Acceptance and Rejection*. Storrs, CT: Rohner Research.

Rohner, R.P. (1999). Acceptance and rejection. In: D. Levinson, J. Ponzetti & P. Jorgensen (eds), *Encyclopedia of Human Emotions*, Vol. 1, pp. 6–14. New York: Macmillan. Southern community. *Journal of Marriage and the Family, 58*, 842–852.

Rohner, R.P. (2006). Introduction to PARTheory studies of intimate partner relationships. Paper presented at the 1st International Congress on Interpersonal Acceptance and Rejection, Istanbul, Turkey.

Rohner, R.P., & Britner, P.A. (2002). Worldwide mental health correlates of parental acceptance-rejection: review of cross-cultural and intracultural evidence. *Cross-Cultural Research, 36*, 16–47.

Rohner, R.P., Kean, K.J., & Cournoyer, D.E. (1991). Effects of corporal punishment, perceived caretaker warmth, and cultural beliefs on the psychological adjustment of children in St. Kitts, West Indies. *Journal of Marriage and the Family, 53*, 681–693.

Rohner, R.P., & Khaleque, A. (2005). *Handbook for the Study of Parental Acceptance and Rejection*. Storrs, CT: Rohner Research.

Rohner, R.P., & Khaleque, A. (2008). Relations between perceived partner and parental acceptance, behavioral control, and psychological adjustment among heterosexual adult women in the U.S. In: J.K. Quinn & I.G. Zambini (eds), *Family Relations: 21st Century Issues and Challenges*, pp. 187–197. New York: Nova Science Publishers Inc.

Rohner, R.P., & Khaleque, A. (2014). Essentials of parenting: Parental warmth, behavioral control, and discipline. In: K.D. Keith (General Editor), *The Encyclopedia of Cross-Cultural Psychology*. Malden, MA: Wiley-Blackwell.

Rohner, R.P., Khaleque, A., & Cournoyer, D.E. (2005). Parental acceptance-rejection theory, methods, evidence, and implications. *Ethos, 33*, 299–334.

Rohner, R.P., Khaleque, A, & Cournoyer, D.E. (2013). *Introduction to Parental Acceptance-Rejection Theory, Methods, Evidence, and Implications*. Retrieved 7 May 2013, from http://www.cspar.uconn.edu.

Rohner, R.P., Khaleque, A., Shamsuddin, E., & Sabina, S. (2010). Relationship between perceived teacher and parental acceptance, school conduct, and the psychological adjustment of Bangladeshi adolescents. *Cross-Cultural Research, 44*, 239–252.

Rohner, R.P., Roll, S., & Rohner, E.C. (1980). Perceived parental acceptance-rejection and personality organization among Mexican and American elementary school children. *Behavior Science Research, 15*, 23–39.

Rohner, R.P., Uddin, M.K., Shamsunnaher, M., & Khaleque, A. (2008). Intimate partner acceptance, parental acceptance in childhood, and psychological adjustment among Japanese adults. *Cross-Cultural Research, 42*, 87–97.

Rohner, R.P., & Veneziano, R A. (2001). The importance of father love: history and contemporary evidence. *Review of General Psychology, 5*, 382–405.

Rosenberg, C.M. (1971). The young addict and his family. *British Journal of Psychiatry, 118*, 469–470.

Saxena, V. (1992). Perceived maternal rejection as related to negative attention-seeking classroom behavior among primary school children. *Journal of Personality and Clinical Studies, 8*(1–2), 129–135.

Shaver, P.R., & Clark, C.L. (1994). The psychodynamics of adult romantic attachment. In: J.M. Masling & R.F. Bornslein (eds), *Empirical Perspectives on Object Relations Theory*, Vol. 5, pp. 105–156. Washington, DC: American Psychological Association.

Shedler, J., & Block, J. (1990). Adolescent drug use and psychological health: a longitudinal inquiry. *American Psychologist, 45*(5), 612–630.

van der Kolk, B.A. (2010). Developmental trauma disorder: towards a relational diagnosis for children with complex trauma histories. Unpublished manuscript.

Vrasti, R., Eisemann, M., Podea, D., Olteanu, I., Scherppler, D., & Peleneagra, R. (1990). Parental rearing practices and personality in alcoholics classified according to family history. In: C.N. Stefanis, C.R. Soldatos & A.D. Rabavilas (eds), *Psychiatry: A World Perspective*, Vol. 4, pp. 359–364. Amsterdam: Elsevier Science Publishers.

Whitbeck, L.B., Conger, R.D., & Kao, M.Y. (1993). The influence of parental support, depressed affect, and peers on the sexual behavior of adolescent girls. *Journal of Family Issues, 14*(2), 261–278.

Wilson, R.S., Boyle, P.A., Levine, S.R., Yu, L., Anagnos, S.E., Buchman, A.S., Schneider, J.A., & Bennett, D.A. (2012). Emotional neglect in childhood and cerebral infarction in older age. *Neurology, 79*(15), 1534–1539.

15
Rehearsals! for Growth: Enhancing Family Well-Being Through Dramatic Play

Daniel J. Wiener

> Improv[isation] does not constitute an escape from reality but rather permission to create and explore new realities, to experience imagined truth as present truth.
>
> (Daniel J. Wiener, 2009, p. 358)

Introduction

Rehearsals! for Growth (RfG) is an application of theatre improvisation (improv) techniques to psychotherapy of relationships, principally families. RfG provides therapists with a powerful resource to address three broad tasks in the successful therapy of families: (1) altering the affective climate during therapy sessions to inject playfulness and instil hope; (2) broadening the range of displayed social identities and expressive behaviours that members present to other; and (3) changing recurrent yet dysfunctional transactional patterns among its members. RfG is not in itself a comprehensive method of therapy but rather an approach that can be *combined* with other modalities, providing tools for enhancing the effectiveness of family therapy.

The key insight that led to the creation of RfG is that competent stage-improvisation shares a number of characteristics with good interpersonal relationship functioning. These include: (1) *attentiveness* to others' words and actions; (2) *flexibility* in both initiating and accepting others' directions and suggestions; and (3) *validation* of others' reality. Improvisation thus permits therapists both to assess family functioning and to develop these desirable characteristics through practice during sessions.

In RfG practice, family members episodically are offered the opportunity to enact brief tasks and scenes with one another. Such enactments may both involve unusual conditions or rules (termed 'exercises') and the playing of characters different from those that family members ordinarily identify with as themselves (termed 'games'). Such offers, made in the spirit of invitations to play or experiment, serve as therapeutic tools for both assessment and intervention. Numerous theatre games have been adapted, modified, or invented to serve these therapeutic ends (Wiener, 1994).

RfG therapy is a praxis that relies on establishing an atmosphere of non-literalness and non-seriousness in order to alter the prevailing 'stuckness' of families in the problem-saturated mentality they most often present in therapy.

> Although an oversimplification, it is helpful to think of humans as operating in two distinct mental modes – 'survival mind' and 'adventure mind.' *Survival mind* focuses our attention purposefully toward the future in order to get desired results, scan for dangers, and promote the feeling of being in control of that future. By contrast, *Adventure mind* activity is present-centered and absorbed in living fully for the moment. As adults, we experience Survival mind as the properly dominant mode and view Adventure mind as an infrequent (and risky) lapse into childishness. Improvisation has the power to re-acquaint adults with the joy and absorption of Adventure mind that they often left behind in childhood. It utilizes improvisation to reclaim the power, vividness and enjoyment of 'child's mind' thereby exploring alternatives to the sensible, functional and routine patterns that keep us stuck as adults.
>
> (Wiener, 2014, home page)

Conceptual foundations of rehearsals for growth

Family Systems Thinking. Though possessing a lengthy intellectual history, Systemic Family Therapy emerged in the 1970s out of an epistemological paradigm shift that has resulted in the formation of an independent mental health profession, Marriage and Family Therapy. This conceptual shift, entailing the interactivity and inseparability of observer/observed and of actor/acted upon, profoundly challenges both the theory and practice of healing inherent within the classical medical model (Hoffman, 1981).

Social Constructivism. The philosophical foundation of RfG is rooted in the stance that social reality is constructed and invented, rather than discovered. As individual identities are situated in a social-relational context, interpersonal relationships are co-created via an ongoing process. Rather than viewing therapy as a procedure for finding out 'who I am', RfG therapy aims to encourage exploration and invention of *'who else I can be'* in the context of one's relationships. Relationship harmony results from mutual validation, an act of meaning-creation broadly defined as occurring when family members mutually and actively contribute to co-creating their mutual reality, collaboratively interpreting their unfolding experiences and co-creating their own shared view of themselves-in-relationship.[1]

There is support in the marriage and family therapy (MFT) literature for the importance of reality-creation in marital commitment and satisfaction (Stephen, 1984; Levine & Busby, 1993; Dufore, 1999), though the study of mutual validation in family units has not been researched. RfG therapy shares the goals and rationale of Systemic-constructivist couple therapy (SCCT) which is designed to increase a couple's sense of we-ness, where we-ness is defined as 'the identity that each partner establishes in relationship to the other' (Reid, Dalton, Laderoute, Doell, & Nguyen, 2006).

Embodied Psychotherapy. Because of its roots in theatre, RfG may be classified as a drama therapy of relationships. Drama Therapy, which emerged as a profession in the United States 35 years ago, utilizes a diversity of theatrical forms for therapeutic ends. One central concept common to all forms of drama therapy is *concrete embodiment*, which allows the abstract to become concrete through the client's body. Most psychotherapy mediates experience exclusively through verbal representation. Not only is this practice limiting to adult clients but it marginalizes children's participation in therapy. When clients of any age act out an idea or an experience rather than merely talk about it, therapy becomes more vivid and concrete.

Dramatic Enactment. In psychotherapy, *enactments* refer to activities performed by clients at the direction of therapists. Enactments are instigated by therapists chiefly for the clinical purposes of assessment, client self-discovery, emotional catharsis, and/or skills-training. A subclass of enactments is Dramatic Enactments (DEs), which are therapeutic activities that involve some element of acknowledged pretended identity. That is, DEs are understood by all present as performances by actors assuming dramatic roles in contrast to persons' performances as 'themselves,' i.e., in their conventional social identities.[2] Roles offered clients in DEs may vary in *Distancing*, which allows the therapist to change the degree to which the role being played is 'like one symbolically' or 'like one actually.'

The therapeutic advantages of encouraging and structuring client DE performances within therapy are twofold: (1) DEs potentiate client exploration of non-habitual behaviours; and (2) clients experience a greatly reduced sense of accountability for the 'on-stage' behaviours of the characters they portray when in a dramatic role. Core to the use of DE is our previously noted capacity to pretend – that is to behave deliberately in the moment in a manner at variance with how we behave 'as ourselves'.

Yet within psychotherapy pretence has often been viewed in a negative, even pathological light. Within the psychodynamic paradigm it is associated with unconsciously driven defence mechanisms and conscious self-deception; interpersonally, it is a synonym for one sort of ethically unacceptable conduct. Further, pretence stands in opposition to the Rogerian ethos of transparency and authenticity for the conduct of therapists, and by extension to their clients. It may thus be necessary to address directly this prejudicial attitude when it arises in offering clients dramatic roles.

Conducting family therapy using RfG: Objectives

Accessing Spontaneity Through Improvisation. J.L. Moreno, the founder of psychodrama, regarded spontaneity as an essential component of mental health, describing it as follows: 'Spontaneity operates in the present, now and here; it propels an individual toward an adequate response to a new situation or a new response to an old situation' (Moreno, 1953, p. 42). The essence of improvisation is action undertaken without planning in the present moment, effectively the embodiment of Morenean spontaneity.

In the RfG method, improv is not intended only for clients but also as an integral part of the therapist's ongoing praxis. Viewed more broadly, psychotherapy can be viewed as an improvisational art in which the therapist continually adjusts in the moment to unanticipated client responses. While improvising with clients, therapists' creativity is activated; a therapist who devises, shapes, or modifies, in the moment, a previously known technique (including a previously used improv game) to suit a case is improvising. Conversely, while an improv game may be novel to clients (the enactment of which draws on their spontaneity) a therapist who uses such a game 'off the shelf' is clearly *not* improvising. Moreno would call the described form of an improv game, including any of those described in the case example below, a 'conserve', in contrast to one that is formed spontaneously or is fitted to present circumstance (Kipper, 2000).

Improvisation as a Tool for Discovery. Improvisational enactment not only inducts clients into unfamiliar functioning in the present moment as a growth-enhancing experience, but is itself a 'middle way' to discover the consequences of non-habitual choices, particularly in the social realm. At one end of the experiential spectrum, we try out new actions in thought, which has the advantage of being safe from real-life consequences but also has the possible disadvantage of not being in complete accord with reality (as we don't fully know the validity of what we assume or what we are unaware of). At the other end of the spectrum we can take action in the real world, which surely gives us valuable experience, but often leaves us at risk of having to live with the consequences of these actions. Improv, as a middle way, allows us to try out behaviours that have some unforeseen consequences, but with the safety of immunity from such consequences. Hence the word 'rehearsals' in RfG, differentiating it from some consequential performance.

Promoting Attentiveness and Mutual Validation Among Family Members. 'The Blocking/Accepting distinction is fundamental to all of improvisation... An offer is any communication that signifies, indicates, or assures some aspect of social, historical, psychological or physical reality' (Wiener, 1994, p. 59). Blocking, which can be total or partial, is the invalidation of an offer, while accepting validates that offer. Blocking is regularly encountered in family therapy, being at once a symptom and cause of interpersonal conflict. RfG games and exercises require players to be attentive to one another and explicitly instruct players to accept the offers of the other players. The successful outcome of RfG games and exercises hinges on the mutual acceptance of offers by all players; when these outcomes are not attained, the cause is most often readily traceable to the blocking of offers. Both the proclivity to block offers generally and in specific contexts arising in a game or scene are central data used in the RfG therapist's assessment of relationship dynamics. Active coaching by the therapist/director both teaches clients to shift from blocking to accepting each other's offers.

Format of RfG family therapy sessions

The distinctive format of RfG therapy sessions typically consists of the following phases:

(1) Verbal therapy, leading up to the therapist proposing an enactment.
(2) If accepted, some of the clients and the therapist move to another area of the office (the 'stage') and are directed by the therapist in the enactment. Clients are referred to as 'players' when engaged in enactment.
(3) At the enactment's conclusion, clients and therapist return to their original seating. The therapist de-roles the clients from their player characters when necessary and leads a discussion, called the *Post-Enactment Processing* (PEP). The PEP includes current reactions, observations regarding the recently performed enactment and insights linking the performance to previous experiences.
(4) These insights may lead the therapist back to (1) or directly to (2), when a repeated or different enactment is offered.

Case example: The 'R' family

[In the case example that follows I intersperse *italicized commentary* with narrative to inform the reader of both features of RfG methods and the rationale for selected choices made by myself as the therapist. Following a presentation of necessary information to orient the reader to the case, the focus will be on the distinctive RfG interventions central to treatment, leaving out much of the verbal therapy that took place.]

The R family consisted of Gladys and Willy, both 41; their two children, Jason, age 9 and Bethany, age 7; and, age 14, Gladys's son Franklyn from a previous relationship. Gladys and Willy had been married for 11 years. Franklyn lived in the R household except when staying with his bio-dad every other weekend. Willy had been unemployed for the past 11 months while Gladys worked full time.

The presenting problems included: the long-standing, episodic fighting between Jason and Bethany; long-standing underlying disagreements between the parents over handling discipline for both younger children; and Franklyn's recently discovered, unaccounted-for absences from school.

The precipitating incident leading to Gladys seeking family therapy had occurred the week before our first session. An administrator at Franklyn's school had notified Gladys that Franklyn had been truant five days during the previous month, coinciding with his coming home after midnight on a number of school nights. Getting only evasive and untruthful answers from Franklyn, Gladys had tried to discuss the problem with Willy, who counselled waiting for Franklyn to explain himself when he was ready, and admonishing Gladys for being too confrontational with Franklyn. Feeling unsupported and blamed by Willy, Gladys had then confronted Willy on what she characterized as his 'ostrich-like denial'. The fight that ensued escalated to the point that Willy walked out on Gladys, only returning home a few hours later. Threatening divorce if matters didn't improve, Gladys got Willy to agree to couples therapy.

By the time of their first couple's session the crisis had eased slightly, although the atmosphere was still palpably tense. Outwardly, the problem of Franklyn's truancy had been handled solely by Gladys; enlisting support from Franklyn's bio-dad, she had arranged for Franklyn to enter group counselling at the school; Franklyn was compliant and is now attending classes regularly there. The crisis in the marriage had been one of demoralizing fear that they didn't love one another sufficiently to make the changes needed to cope with their differences.

I began couples therapy with Gladys and Willy in a fairly low-key manner, explaining that the first session would be devoted to my learning about their family rather than attempting to change anything from the outset. I constructed a genogram (a kinship diagram widely used in family therapy) from information they supplied during the initial interview, establishing an atmosphere of collaboration and respect. *Doing so was not difficult to accomplish but, in my experience, is necessary preparation for successfully eliciting more challenging self-disclosures, promoting interactions requiring higher emotional intensity, and offering therapist-designed interventions.* I mentioned in passing that at some later point in therapy I might invite them to try some activities that would involve some physical movement and play-acting on their part. *I usually 'plant the seed' for RfG enactments in such an off-hand way: until 'Survival Mind' is first relaxed somewhat by demonstrated trustworthiness and familiarity, it is usually not possible to coax out 'Adventure Mind.'*

Of the two, Gladys was more consistent as a disciplinary parent; she was the eldest daughter in her Family of Origin and had a fairly strict parenting style which contrasted with Willy's less-consistent permissiveness. Willy had been raised by elderly parents, in effect as an only child; his two siblings were more than 18 years older than he. Willy's relationship with Franklyn was civil but not warm; other than a shared common interest in watching televised sports games, they kept their distance from one another except in Gladys's presence.

Five sessions of supportive, mostly verbal therapy sufficed to stabilize the couple; both partners became reassured that they still loved one another and felt heartened that: (1) they could constructively engage verbally with their spouse over those personal differences that had been seen recently as insurmountable obstacles to their happiness; and (2) their marriage could endure persistent differences between the spouses.

During the fourth session I introduced Gladys and Willy to their first RfG exercise. In *Mirrors* (Wiener, 1994, p. 69) Gladys and Willy faced each other, standing 5 feet apart. Assigning Gladys the temporary role of Leader and Willy the role of Follower, I had Gladys initiate slow, continuous physical movement from the waist up that was to be mirrored/imitated simultaneously by Willy. I called 'Switch!' every 20 seconds or so, indicating that they were to exchange roles. After four such switches I called, 'Mutual!' indicating that Gladys and Willy were to continue simultaneous movement without a designated leader or follower. *When Mirrors is done with eye contact throughout and without words, players often experience intimate connection to each other. Additionally, comfort with taking reciprocal roles is developed and tested as each player alternates as Leader and Follower. Attentiveness and intimacy are heightened while players engage in mutuality of movement without an assigned leader or follower.*

As she later confirmed, Gladys seemed more at ease with the Leader role, though she competently imitated Willy when following. Willy kept smiling when leading, occasionally grinning and playfully placing his body in extreme positions, obliging Gladys to imitate him. Mutual movement, which is usually only truly mutual for brief moments, eluded the couple completely; Gladys was visibly leading throughout. After the enactment Willy reported that the game had allowed him to experience the enjoyment of taking the initiative in their relationship, something he described as 'not happening much any more.' Gladys appeared surprised to hear him say this, but conceded that she was used to 'calling the shots' at home. I suggested a homework assignment to the couple that they schedule a few two-hour periods at a weekend when both were at home, during which one of them would be the designated Leader and the other the Follower for one hour, after which they were to switch roles for another hour. They reported at the next session that they had tried this and that it had been a satisfactory experience for both of them. *In-session enactments serve to help the therapist assess relationship patterns, to heighten client awareness of habitual, recurrent features operant in their relationships, and to explore less familiar alternatives to these habitual patterns. Homework offers clients selective opportunities to put into practice desirable or promising alternative behaviours or roles in situ.*

During the fifth session I had the couple enact *One Word at a Time* (Wiener, 1994, p. 65), in which Gladys and Willy, standing alongside one another with their arms around their partner's waist, narrated a made-up story as though being one person, each alternating in adding only one word to the emerging story. The only rule governing their choice of words was to keep the sentences that were being formed grammatically correct.

As the mind of Partner A will often anticipate completion of the entire sentence following the addition of his next word, Partner B's addition of her next word, even when grammatically correct, usually disconfirms the anticipated next word of A's mentally constructed sentence. Consequently, successful performance of this exercise requires blocking one's own idea to allow oneself to go along with/validating the idea of one's partner. Becoming stymied at how to continue the sentence in the new direction or upset at one's partner indicates difficulty in sharing control with one's partner.

Gladys and Willy performed this exercise fairly well, only twice getting stuck: once, Gladys added a word that did not fit grammatically, necessitating starting the sentence again; another time, Willy paused for over five seconds before adding his word. Both reported the exercise to be challenging and fun; the story they co-created was original though a bit hard to follow. Gladys *and Willy's performance demonstrated their sufficient capacity to co-construct a narrative cooperatively.*

At the end of the fifth session both Gladys and Willy appeared to be greatly relieved that their marriage had survived the crisis of two months earlier and were inclined to end therapy at that time. I pointed out that, though they had indeed pulled back from the brink, they had not worked on resolving their differences in handling co-parenting decisions and suggested that they try a few sessions of family therapy in which it would be possible for me to view a fuller interplay of family dynamics. Gladys and Willy agreed to bring in their family for at least three more sessions.

The mood of the first R family therapy session was restrained: both parents overtalked for the children, who all appeared less than enthusiastic about participating. In order to enliven the session and shift the atmosphere, I produced three inflated balloons that I instructed the family to keep in the air throughout the session. Immediately the affective climate shifted as all family members, particularly Jason and Bethany, began to move to keep the balloons from dropping to the carpet amidst laughter and, at times, athletic feats worthy of favourable commentary. Only Franklyn seemed aloof, interacting merely by swatting away any balloons that came his way. *Play brackets prior experience so that it is socially permissible to explore alternatives to conventional behaviour without the consequences that ordinarily ensue from 'real life' conduct. In family therapy, members who are often highly reactive to one another's behaviours are able to become more relaxed and tolerant of the same or similar behaviours from others when performed in a play context.*

Seeking to learn more about the R family's interaction around the recurrent conflict between the two younger children, I proposed the RfG game *Excuses* (Wiener, 1994, p. 97) to be played with Jason and Bethany cast as two naughty-yet-imaginative young siblings, 'Sam' and 'Susan', having to convince their angry parents that they both should be let off without punishment when mud had appeared on a white carpet. In this game, the players of the children's roles are coached to accept all of one another's offers fully, co-creating a story which, no matter how absurd or fanciful, they would jointly stick to, and which would even make their parents proud of them. *While Jason's and Bethany's roles as Sam and Susan were minimally distanced from their actual life roles, the premise of the game required their characters to cooperate loyally, as blame of one another or disagreement on their story would result in the punishment of both.* In a variation of this RfG game tailored to this family, I had Gladys and Willy play Sam and Susan's parents, but with Gladys playing the inclined-to believe the kids' parent and Willy the sceptical, punitive one. *Again, the parental roles were minimally distanced from actual life roles, but with their attitudes reversed.*

Jason and Bethany took to their roles effortlessly; wide-eyed, they explained that the neighbour's dog, 'Frisbee', had been scratching at the front door and had tracked in the mud that soiled the carpet when they let her in. 'And,' Bethany as 'Susan' went on, 'Frisbee led us out to the neighbour's house, where...' 'a...a...burglar was just leaving by the back door!' Jason finished (both children made frequent eye contact with each other, nodding vigorously at each other's words). 'We didn't chase the burglar 'cause you always told us to stay out of danger and call the police instead, so Sam dialled 911 and we brought in Frisbee for her safety and gave her water until it was safe to let her out...'

At this point I cued the parents to respond to what had happened. Following their scripted attitude, Gladys praised the kids' bravery, honesty, and prudence, while Willy protested that the kids had probably made up their story just to avoid punishment. Without allowing the parents to engage in an argument with one another, I ended the scene and moved all four players back to their original seats and began a post-enactment processing. When I invited all players in turn to report on what their character had experienced during the game, Bethany said, 'It was fun getting to make stuff up!' while Jason offered, 'I wasn't nervous at all!' Gladys reported that she felt both proud that her children were so imaginative yet also dismayed that they were so capable of inventing stories. (Upon questioning she reflected that this was her own, not her character's experience.) Nodding in agreement with his wife, Willy stated, 'For a while I've suspected that this family would run differently, probably better, if our kids agreed to present us parents with a common front.' Gladys looked at Willy incredulously. 'You want them to gang up on us?' She asked him. 'Well, look what happens when they fight with each other – we wind up fighting over *their* fighting!' Willy shot back (both Jason and Bethany seemed absorbed in witnessing this discussion). 'But,' said Gladys after a short pause, 'we're the parents, and we should agree on what the rules are, regardless.' I asked Gladys and Willy if they had

had similar conversations in front of Jason and Bethany at home; both of them nodded. 'And what usually happens when you do?' I asked. 'Oh, we get into it and they go quiet for a while,' Willy answered. 'Would you be happier if your parents agreed on how to deal with your fighting?' I asked the children, alternately looking at each one. 'Yeah,' Bethany answered in a subdued voice. Jason nodded, his eyes downcast. 'OK, so here's a suggestion,' I offered. 'The next time you two have a fight, and when your parents find out about it, remind them that you want both of them to come up with a decision they both agree upon. That doesn't mean,' I said, turning to the parents, 'that the parent who is around can't make a decision on the spot, only that you later discuss with one another, out of earshot of the kids, what happened and what you now agree the right decision is. Then you both announce to them what you've agreed your policy or decision is. Even if you have to flip a coin to decide, I want you to present Jason and Bethany with a unanimous decision. Try this for a week; let's see what happens.' Gladys and Willy slowly nodded. *In most family therapy approaches, getting the parental partnership to function as a unified front improves family functioning. Here, the enactment of the Excuses game gave me a pretext for giving the R family a directive that the children had a stake in seeing carried out.*

The next week, I inquired about the results of my directive. The family reported that on two occasions the parents had announced to the children their joint decision following squabbles between Jason and Bethany. All reported satisfaction with this result; I encouraged them to continue this practice for another two weeks.

In the next session, seeking ways to have the children, including Franklyn, witness further parental cooperation, I offered the game *Poet's Corner* (Wiener, 1994, p. 84), in which two players improvise to co-create a scene which simulates a staged reading of a poem. One player takes the role of a foreign Poet who recites a poem 'in his/her native tongue' by using gibberish (nonsense syllables that are treated as intelligible speech), all the while making broad, frequent gestures and varying his/her vocal inflection. The Poet pauses at intervals to allow the other player, the Translator, to 'translate' that line of the poem into English. This 'translation' is an invention which is suggested by the Poet's gestures and vocal inflections. Correspondingly, the Poet shapes his/her own gestures and vocal inflections on his next turn to match the Translator's emerging verbal narration of the 'poem.' I assigned the Poet role to Gladys and the Translator role to Willy.

Willy began by addressing me and the three children as the audience to a poetry reading of 'Klabashi,' a famed Japanese poet, indicating Gladys, standing off to one side. Grinning and bowing, Gladys exchanged a few gibberish words with Willy, then proceeded to utter a long line of gibberish, accompanied by waving her arms about. Willy 'translated': 'The seagulls swooped down from the rooftops, skimming the waves...' Alternating gibberish 'poetry' and English 'translation' for six lines, Gladys/Klabashi and

Willy performed the poem together. The audience clapped enthusiastically at the poem's end, and again after Gladys/Klabashi had taken a deep bow. Both performers were grinning, evidently quite pleased with themselves. *Of course, in addition to offering the children an opportunity to witness their parents' solidarity, the game gave the parents an occasion to experience that solidarity themselves. As is the case when performing other RfG games and exercises, there is risk in allowing oneself to venture into the unknown. The trust developed among players sharing this risk creates a sense of solidarity between them.*

Though the Poet's Corner game works best when the players attend closely to one another, it is fairly robust in co-creating the illusion of a translated poem even with a modest degree of shared attention. *While something is learned whenever an enactment is attempted, a performance that works well aesthetically is more likely to be experienced as a memorable and transformative event for players and audience alike.*

Immediately following this enactment, Jason and Bethany insisted on a chance to play *Poet's Corner* themselves, though there was a brief squabble about which would get the coveted 'Poet' role. We ended with two more enactments of this game, so that both children could have a turn at playing the Poet role. Though the novelty of the game had worn off, all seemed satisfied; even Franklyn seemed entertained, though he had been a passive spectator throughout the entire series of enactments.

As noted earlier, Franklyn was a reluctant participant in our family sessions, avoiding eye contact and responded verbally with minimal and vague answers to questions. He had actively participated only in the non-verbal exercise Mirrors I had had him perform with Jason at an earlier session. Motioning Franklyn to sit alongside me as Gladys and Willy were preparing to start *Poet's Corner*, I told him I'd appreciate his help after the enactment ended in describing what had taken place. *By asking Franklyn to describe the Poet's Corner enactment by Gladys and Willy I was warming him up to the roles of observer and commentator to become further involved in family sessions.* At the conclusion of *Poet's Corner*, when I asked Franklyn what he had seen happening, he astonished all present by reciting a lengthy and accurate list of reactions that included those of other family members as spectators to the enactment, though omitting any of his own.

Immediately building upon Franklyn's performance as commentator to *Poet's Corner*, I proposed a scene in which Bethany was to perform the role of an athlete at a new Olympic sport – ultra-slow 'Olympic Chair-Sitting.' This event would be televised, I continued, with play-by-play commentary by the team of… (here I nodded to Willy and Franklyn). 'Let's have a run-through over here.' (I gestured to the far end of the office, moving one armless chair to the centre of the far wall, while turning two other chairs, side by side, to face the armless chair from the family seating area.) *This game, Slo-Mo Commentator (Wiener, 2003), was previously created specifically for inducting adolescents into family therapy participation. The commentator role is a performing role that appears to be outside the focus of the spectators, which is visually directed toward the athlete. Given their previous connection as sports fans, I thought Willy a fitting partner to Franklyn in the commentator role.*

I explained to Bethany that she was to start at the office doorway, walking extremely slowly to that chair, and then, still moving very, very slowly, sit down on it. 'Remember,' I told her, 'the whole action should take you at least a full minute.' Giggling, Bethany stood by the doorway, eager to begin. Turning to Franklyn and Willy, now seated in the other two chairs, I said: 'I'll get you guys started by sitting in with you at the beginning. You're playing a couple of sportscasters. The only rule for both of you players is that you accept whatever is done or said by all other players as true, even if that changes an idea you already had for the scene. Now, what are your names?' 'Sam,' replied Willy immediately. Franklyn hesitated. 'You can give your character any name you want,' I said to Franklyn. 'Drew,' Franklyn said, finally. 'OK, Sam and Drew, you're working for International Sports Network and you're here to cover the Olympic Women's Chair Sitting Qualifiers, here in...' 'Brunswick,' Franklyn offered. 'Right, Brunswick, and who's this next competitor?' 'Ana Petralova, from Latvia,' Willy supplied. 'Yes, and Ana had a problem last spring, didn't she?' I asked. 'What was that, anyway?... Oh, we're about to go live – take it away, Drew and Sam!' (I stood behind their chairs, ready to jump in if needed). Glancing at one another, Franklyn/Drew and Willy/Sam began their 'broadcast':

SAM: OK, folks, coming to you live from Brunswick, we're Sam and Drew from the....

DREW: .... International Sports Network, to bring you the Chair-sitting Olympic competition...

SAM: 'yes, the women's competition – nex' up is Ana Petrova (Sam evidently forgot that he had named her 'Petralova' earlier, though no one seemed to notice), who made an impressive showing at last year's event in... say, where was that, Drew?

DREW: Palm City, I think – yeah, she placed fourth there, would done better if her coach hadn't gotten busted...

(I signalled to Bethany to begin her 'warm-up exercises,' which consisted of arm swings and deep knee bends – I pantomimed doing these very slowly)

DREW: Look, Sam, I think Ana's about ready to begin her second attempt – she wiped out the first time and trails Wilma Miller, who's been having a terrific day, so far...

SAM: Yeah, she'll need at least a 9.3 to stay close to the leaders... OK, there she goes!

(I had signalled Bethany to begin her ultra-slow approach to the chair)

SAM: A good start! She's in the zone now! (B, in extreme slow motion, pumped her arms and moved forward with a high-knee stride).

> DREW: Look, she's about to position herself for the Sit – this is what separates the great competitors from the sorta-OK's... (B, leaning to one side, began to sit on the chair)... too short, too short, she's gonna miss the centre of the seat...
>
> (B came down on the right edge of the chair seat, waving her arms slowly to the left)
>
> SAM: A tough break for Anna – she'll lose points for both form and accuracy...
>
> (B, raising both arms, stood up from her seated position)
>
> DREW: Yeah, too bad, the scores are: 6, 6, and 5 – I'm afraid she's out of contention for a medal this time... (I signalled for them to 'wrap up')... this has been Sam and Drew from the Interzonal chair competition for women...

Joining in the loud applause from Gladys and Jason, I waved Bethany back to the family seating and had Willy and Franklyn turn their chairs around to face the family group. Bethany was laughing uncontrollably, while Willy and Franklyn both had smirks on their faces. It appeared that everyone had had a good time with this enactment.

Along with congratulating Bethany, Willy and Franklyn, I asked Franklyn how he had experienced playing Drew during the scene. He replied that it was fun to pretend being a sportscaster and that he had enjoyed having Willy as a partner (*this was the first time Franklyn had made a self-referential comment; thereafter, Franklyn was frequently responsive to questions about his thoughts and feelings*). When asked, Bethany, whose participation in the verbal therapy had up until this point been infrequent, stated that she had liked having everyone watch her and wanted to play more games like this.

Family therapy continued for a total of seven sessions, not including the initial five sessions of couple's therapy. By its conclusion, Gladys and Willy had strengthened their parental partnership, backing up each other's decisions consistently. Jason and Bethany's at-home fighting with one another had diminished in both frequency and intensity. Franklyn had chosen to share with Willy the reason for his previous school absences (he had been hanging out at the home of another truant classmate); Willy had made it clear he would not keep this disclosure secret from Gladys and that Franklyn would need to face his mother with that news, but offered to be present when Franklyn told his mother, which offer Franklyn had accepted.

Lessons for the clinician

There are several advantages of incorporating RfG in family therapy relative to exclusively verbal psychotherapy: (1) heightened emotional impact of dramatic enactment compared with verbal interventions; (2) full inclusion of children in therapy sessions, who are frequently marginalized or excluded in talk-only sessions; and (3) embodied rehearsal of alternatives to habitual interactions, which are discovered through in-session enactments and reinforced through homework between sessions.

The playful exploration that RfG facilitates occurs when the therapist establishes a context for safe adventuring. Therapists cannot successfully induce clients to playfulness and a spirit of adventure if they are not themselves receptive to that same attitude at the time of the therapeutic encounter. 'Of course, this does not mean that RfG therapists need always be lighthearted and planless, only that they are not so anxious or burdened as to contribute to an atmosphere of anxiety that may cause rigidity and lack of creative exploration in the session' (Wiener, 2012, p. 3). In RfG therapy, a therapist who finds him/herself thus burdened cannot offer improv technique successfully at that time, so it is important for therapists to 'check in' with themselves (Wiener, 1994, p. 144) continually. It is also necessary that therapists using improv techniques have had personal experience playing some of these games, for it is axiomatic in therapy that you cannot lead others effectively where you have not been yourself. In sum, the playfulness of therapist simultaneously sets a constructive mood for clients and renders the therapist receptive to his/her own spontaneity and creativity.

Notes

1. Note that this definition of mutual validation differs sharply from the operational definition used by cognitive-behavioural therapists, when each partner (1) demonstrates an accurate perception of the other's intended meaning and (2) conveys non-judgemental acceptance of the other (Gottman, 1993).
2. For a more nuanced analysis of the distinctions between non-DEs and DEs, see Wiener (2000).

References

Dufore, D.S. (1999). *Marital similarity, marital interaction, and couples' shared view of their marriage* (Doctoral dissertation). Syracuse University.

Gottman, J.M. (1993). The roles of conflict engagement, escalation, and avoidance in martial interaction: a longitudinal view of five types of couples. *Journal of Consulting and Clinical Psychology, 61*, 6–15.

Hoffman, L. (1981). *Foundations of family therapy.* New York: Basic Books.

Kipper, D.A. (2000). Spontaneity: does the experience match the theory? *International Journal of Action Methods: Psychodrama, Skill Training and Role Playing, 53*, 33–47.

Levine, L.B., & Busby, D.M. (1993). Co-creating shared reality with couples. *Contemporary family Therapy, 15*, 405–421.

Moreno, J.L. (1953). *Who Shall Survive? A New Approach to the Problem of Human Interrelations.* Washington, DC: Nervous & Mental Disease Publishing.

Reid, D.W., Dalton, E.J., Laderoute, K., Doell, F.K., & Nguyen, T. (2006). Therapeutically induced changes in couple identity: the role of we-ness and interpersonal processing in relationship satisfaction. *Genetic, Social, and General Psychology Monographs, 132,* 241–284.

Stephen, T.D. (1984). A symbolic exchange framework for the development of intimate relationships. *Human Relations, 37,* 393–408.

Wiener, D.J. (2014). Rehearsals! for Growth website (retrieved from http://www.rehearsalsforgrowth.com/).

Wiener, D.J. (2012). Improvisation and innovation in psychotherapy: variations of the *presents* action exercise. *International Journal of Social Science Tomorrow, 1*(1), 1–12.

Wiener, D.J. (2009). Rehearsals for Growth: Drama therapy with couples. In: D.R. Johnson & R. Emunah (eds), *Current Approaches in Drama Therapy in North America,* 2nd edition, 355–373. Springfield, IL: Charles C. Thomas.

Wiener, D.J. (2003). Creating a participating role for adolescents in family therapy. In: C. Sori & L. Hecker (eds), *The Therapist's Notebook for Children and Adolescents,* Ch. 40. New York: Haworth.

Wiener, D.J. (2000). Struggling to grow: using dramatic enactments in family therapy. *Journal of Family Psychotherapy, 11*(2), 9–21.

Wiener, D.J. (1994). *Rehearsals for Growth: Theater Improvisation for Psychotherapists.* New York: W.W. Norton.

16
Trauma and Development: Holistic/Systems-Developmental Theory and Practice

Jack Demick

Introduction

Post-traumatic growth (PTG) – defined by Tedeschi and Calhoun (1995) as an individual's experience of positive change resulting from the struggle with a traumatic event – has become a flagship issue for the positive psychology movement of the 21st century (Seligman & Csikszentmihalyi, 2000). While the literature of the last 50 years has widely documented the negative impact of adversity on human beings (e.g., often leading to Post-Traumatic Stress Disorder and concomitant changes in neuroendocrinology and neuroanatomy on the biological level of organization), the newer construct of PTG provided a framework to document distinct types of positive change following adversity. Five specific types of positive change have been shown to occur, in contrast, at the psychological (changed sense of self evidenced by perceptions of *greater psychological strength* and *a larger number of new opportunities*) and sociocultural (changed sense of other characterized by *improved relationships* and changed philosophy of life as embodied in *spiritual development* and *greater life appreciation*) levels of organization.

Although Tedeschi and Calhoun (2004) greatly elaborated the PTG construct, that some individuals change for the better following trauma can be traced to the ancient writings of all religions and cultures. Through the present, the singer Kelly Clarkson's (2011) recent reworking of Nietzsche's (1889) well-known quote, 'What does not kill me makes me stronger', has become the mantra of relationship empowerment for adolescent girls worldwide. In between these extremes, 20th-century scholars had also proposed the possibility of positive change not only following a *trauma* (an experience-producing injury or pain) but also a *crisis* (a dramatic upheaval in a person's life that may develop into a trauma over time), a *transition* (a passage from one position, state, or stage to another), or *stress* more generally (responses occurring when environmental demands exceed individuals' capabilities), all of which have been used synonymously in the literature.

Twentieth-century psychiatrists and psychologists were included among this latter group of scholars as follows. The psychiatrist Frankl (1958) developed a form of *existential therapy*, logotherapy, whose main tenet was that human beings are motivated by 'a will to meaning', an inner pull to find meaning in life under all circumstances even the most miserable. This was based on his Nazi concentration camp experiences as a physician and prisoner from which he developed personal insight that 'the salvation of man is through love and in love' (p. 57). Yalom's (1980) variant of existential therapy, in its individual and group forms, focused on how individuals negotiate the four 'givens' of the human condition, namely, isolation, meaninglessness, mortality, and freedom. Research from this perspective (Yalom & Lieberman, 1981) documented that terminally ill patients and bereaved spouses often experience positive changes (e.g., rearranging life's priorities to become less preoccupied with trivialities, living life more immediately rather than delaying gratification, communicating more openly with family and friends). In a different vein, the psychiatrist Caplan (1964) – in response to the 1942 Boston Coconut Grove nightclub fire claiming 493 lives – developed *crisis theory* (characterized by individual differences in adaptation related to personal and interpersonal resources) and preventive psychiatry (crisis intervention in non-normative crises and early intervention in normative developmental transitions).

More in research than in practice, 20th-century psychologists also broached positive changes following suffering. For example, Maslow (1968) posited that successfully negotiating a *hierarchy of needs* (physiological, safety, belongingness, esteem, cognitive, aesthetic) leads some to experience *self-actualization* whereby they rejoice in the experience of living (peak experiences). He acknowledged, however, exceptions to this rule (e.g., accomplished artists who starve rather than give up their painting or poetry). Dohrenwend's (1978) model on the relations between social stress and psychopathology proposed that natural stress reactions to life events (e.g., anxiety, depression) lead – depending on individuals' material supports, social supports, and psychological characteristics – to one of three outcomes: (a) psychopathology (stress reactions persist and become self-sustaining); (b) status quo (persons return to pre-stress psychological states); and (c) growth (individuals use the event to develop psychologically). Finally, Loevinger (1966) and her followers demonstrated that traumatic events (e.g., divorce) lead some individuals to more advanced stages of ego development.

This work, which also addresses the possibility of development following traumatic events, is not based on a new theoretical movement (e.g., positive psychology) but rather, in line with previous discussion, on a grand developmental theory with a distinguished history within the field of psychology, namely, Werner's (1957) organismic-developmental theory. Although this theory underwent numerous iterations, several are briefly described and compared to PTG theory. This is followed by an overview of recent empirical work on adaptation to life transitions. The chapter then concludes with a discussion of treatment recommendations for those experiencing difficult life events, including trauma, based on identification of research-derived conditions facilitating developmental advance.

Theoretical considerations

Heinz Werner's (1957) Organismic-Developmental Theory. Werner's original theory was 'organismic' insofar as psychological part-processes (cognition, affect, valuation, action) are considered in relation to the total context of human activity. Organismic theories in psychology are a family of holistic theories, stressing the organization, unity, and integration of human beings manifest in individual development. The idea of an implicitly 'organismic theory' dates back to Goldstein's (1939) *The Organism: A Holistic Approach to Biology Derived from Pathological Data in Man*. Organismic theories in psychology were thus inspired by organismic approaches in biology. However, the most direct influence from inside psychology came from Gestalt psychology.

Following completion of his doctoral dissertation on the psychology of aesthetic enjoyment at the University of Vienna, Werner moved to the Psychological Institute at Hamburg in 1917 where he participated in discussions about a new psychological movement, Gestalt psychology, epitomized in aphorisms such as *the whole is greater than the sum of its parts* and *one can perceive the glass as half full or half empty*. However, rather than identifying with the Berlin School of Gestalt psychology (Wertheimer, Koffka, Kohler), best known for its principles of perceptual organization (in perceiving objects, we perceive forms, gestalts, which cannot be analyzed in terms of their separate elements) including the laws of similarity (objects are perceptually grouped together if they are similar), closure (our perception fills in the visual gap when parts of a whole picture are missing), and proximity (objects close to each other are perceived as a group), he became more closely aligned with the Leipzig School, proponents of which (Krueger, Sander) criticized the former for not being genuinely holistic in its narrow focus on perception instead of on the acting, feeling, thinking organism.

Werner (1957) summarized his holistic position as follows: '...The totality is not a super-ordinated unity built up of elements and something more than their sum. It has an entirely different origin: it is prior to any division into elements whatsoever...The elements are not precedent to the whole but the whole, as a basic entity, is the precursor of its basic parts' (pp. 8–9). Thus, an organismic orientation conceptualizes a problem from the viewpoint of the whole organism and not of a disembodied process: for example, studying olfaction as related to human beings versus wolves represents an organismic orientation, whereas studying olfaction by itself does not. In line with this organismic focus, he made the methodological distinction between process and achievement, advocating the use of both holistic (idiographic, qualitative) and quantitative methodologies. 'If we restrict our efforts to the calculation of average age scores and developmental curves of achievement, the essential goal of genetic psychology, viz., the understanding of the process of growth, can never be achieved' (p. 497). The classic example of the process-achievement distinction is that, although two individuals may obtain the same Full Scale IQ score on a standardized intelligence test, they most likely show differential cognitive assets and liabilities evident only from qualitative analyses of processes underlying individual subtest performance.

The original theory was 'developmental' in that it assumes that 'wherever there is life, there is growth and systematic orderly sequence' (Werner, 1957, p. 125) and provides a systematic principle governing developmental progression and regression. This *orthogenetic principle* states that, whenever development occurs, it involves moving '... from a state of relative globality and undifferentiatedness towards states of increasing differentiation and hierarchic integration' (Werner & Kaplan, 1963, p. 7). Werner elaborated this view of development by specifying polarities characterizing lesser versus more advanced developmental status, that is, development ranging from the *interfused to subordinated* (individuals' goals are not sharply differentiated versus drives and momentary states are subordinated to long-term goals), *syncretic to discrete* (lack of differentiation between inner and outer experience versus accurately distinguishing between internal feelings and those of others out-there), *diffuse to articulate* (experience in which the part has the quality of the whole versus experience comprised of distinguishable parts), *rigid to flexible* (perseverative or compulsive behaviour versus the capacity to change behaviour depending on situational demands), and *labile to stable* (fluid stimulus-bounded behaviour versus unambiguous, precise behaviour).

As a general mode of analysis applicable to the organizational features (relationships of parts to each other and to the whole) of the development of any phenomenon (rather than simply age differences), Werner employed the orthogenetic principle to analyse development in the physical (e.g., motor skills), cognitive (e.g., perception), and psychosocial (e.g., emotions) domains. For example, in the development of the motor skill of grasping, he demonstrated that initially a child's legs, hands, mouth, and feet are all used in the movements of grasping. However, directed manual grasping subsequently proceeds from the use of global body movements to differentiated body movements, which involve the integration of articulated grasping constituents (refinement in relevant finger manipulation) in relation to objects.

The principle and the polarities figured into Werner's comparative focus as he argued that general laws of 'mental life as a whole' should account for *microgenesis* (development of a thought), *ontogenesis* (development of an individual), *pathogenesis* (development of pathology), *phylogenesis* (development of a species), and *ethnogenesis* (development of a culture). He thus developmentally ordered paired groups with respect to degree of differentiation and hierarchic integration (e.g., child-adult, person with schizophrenia-normal adult). In contrast to the normal adult who, on the Rorschach, provides integrated whole responses (in which the parts are organizationally differentiated from one another and some highlighted while others subordinated to form an overarching perception; for example, 'two people cooking meat over pots as a butterfly flies in between them' on Card II), both children and those with schizophrenia provide vague organizational responses to the cards ('looks like a blob') or responses in which the parts are organizationally separated but non-integrated (e.g., 'this is a person, a person, a pot, a butterfly'). Although originally termed the comparative-developmental approach (both of which applied to Werner's unique developmental emphasis), the approach quickly became known as *organismic-developmental theory* to emphasize primarily its holistic and developmental aspects.

Wapner and Demick's (1998) holistic, developmental, systems-oriented approach

Wapner and Demick's (1998) elaboration of Werner's organismic-developmental theory first appeared in Damon's *Handbook of Child Psychology* (5th ed.). This elaboration was similar to Werner in that it was *holistic* (assuming that human functioning is an integrated system whose parts may be considered in relation to the functioning whole) and *developmental* (assuming that progression and regression may be assessed against the ideal of development embodied in the orthogenetic principle, a mode of analysis applicable to developing organizational features of any phenomenon). The elaboration placed equal emphasis on a third dimension, namely, the *systems-oriented* nature of human functioning.

The introduction of this dimension led Wapner and Demick to posit that the appropriate unit of analysis for human functioning is the *person-in-environment system*. This assumed that the person-in-environment system consists of three aspects of person (*biological*, e.g., health; *intrapersonal*, e.g., stress; *sociocultural*, e.g., role) and three analogous aspects of environment (*physical*, e.g., natural; *interpersonal*, e.g., family members; *sociocultural*, e.g., laws). Aspects of person and of environment are viewed as inseparable and mutually defining of one another (*transactionalism*) so that the person-in-environment system is a holistic entity with environmental setting built into every analysis (*contextualism*). This conceptualization came to figure prominently within the field of environmental psychology for both its unit of analysis and focus on context broadly defined (Wapner & Demick, 2002).

As a paradigmatic problem, the elaboration chose *critical person-in-environment transitions across the life span*, noting some transitions so critical that they are universal in a given sociocultural context (e.g., transitions from home to nursery school, from unmarried to married person status in middle-class America), others non-normative (e.g., transitions following forced migration, accidents, natural disasters), and others leading to self-transformation without social expectancy (e.g., transitions following nightmares, visions, strange encounters). Thus, what is considered a critical transition is experientially defined. The elaboration also demonstrated the ways in which a perturbation at one level of the system (physical, intrapersonal, or sociocultural aspect of person; physical, interpersonal, or sociocultural aspect of the environment) impacts all other aspects of the system and the unified system as a whole. *Structural (part-whole)* and *dynamic (means-ends)* analyses were employed to describe and explain how systems attempt to restore dynamic equilibrium following critical transitions (endorsing the complementarity of qualitative and quantitative methods with flexible drawing from both depending on the problem) with adaptation (optimal relations between persons and their environments) considered the endpoint or telos of development.

A need to specify the interrelations between experience (cognition, affect, valuation) and action over the course of critical transitions also became apparent. Drawing on Wapner (1969) on relations among cognitive processes and Demick and Wapner (1990) on relations between individuals and societies, psychological part-processes were structurally conceptualized as *supportive* (simultaneously occurring cognitive operations facilitate one another making for greater efficiency in achievement of ends), *antagonistic* (the operation of one function lessens the operation of another), or *substitutive/vicarious* (one level of functioning parallels another).

The importance of individual differences in person-in-environment functioning also became paramount. Thus, the orthogenetic principle was employed to characterize individual differences in self-world relationships surrounding critical transitions. With the orthogenetic principle as the ideal, four self-world relationships (and accompanying modes of coping) from lesser to more developmentally advanced status were proposed (with b and c below assumed at the same developmental level). These were: (a) a *dedifferentiated person-in-environment system state* (characterized by *accommodation*, passively waiting for things to be different); (b) a *differentiated and isolated person-in-environment system state* (evidenced by *disengagement*, distancing oneself from the situation); (c) a *differentiated and conflicted person-in-environment system state* (using *non-constructive ventilation*, aggressive acts without constructive ways of remedying uncertain situations); and (d) a *differentiated and hierarchically integrated person-in-environment system state* (employing *constructive assertion*, planned creative action for goal attainment not dominated by emotion).

Demick's (2006) Holistic/Systems-Developmental Theory (HSDT). More recently, a series of changes was incorporated into the previous approach. These changes (Demick, 2006) included the following:

- The approach was renamed holistic/systems-developmental theory (HSDT) to *parallel Werner's original organismic-developmental theory*, and highlight that our collective assumptions constitute *not only a multi-method approach but also a grand theory of human experience and action*, and *broaden even further the multi-systemic nature of human functioning* (not only does the individual operate as a unified system at the biological, psychological, and sociocultural levels of organization but this system is embedded in a larger person-in-environment system).
- The interpersonal aspect of the person-in-environment system was re-construed as the *inter-organismic aspect of the environment* allowing for consideration of the crucial role of animals in human functioning (cf. Lu, Melicharek, Trent, Sobieraj, & Demick, 2014).
- The *differentiated and in conflict self-world relationship* was re-conceptualized as having more developmentally advanced status than the *differentiated and isolated self-world relationship* on the reasoning that, in the latter, the self regressively experiences 'anger turned inward' as depression (Freud, 1917) rather than maintaining directedness toward the world out-there, literally less self-destructive.
- The paradigmatic problem of critical transitions was expanded to include the study of those who experienced behavioural misadventures (Lipsitt, 1989), defined as injuries not the result of illness (e.g., accidents, suicide attempts, drug/alcohol consumption), and persons with psychopathology because, similar to those undergoing transitions, these individuals' personal capabilities are exceeded by environmental conditions leading to *disequilibrated person-in-environment system states*.
- The construct of cognitive style, individual differences in individuals' characteristic modes of processing information, was integrated within the theory. Witkin et al.'s (1954) *field dependence-independence (FDI) cognitive style* was employed for several reasons. FDI research was placed within a differentiation framework, a variant of Werner's theory. Researchers also uncovered numerous correlates of these styles in disparate areas, leading FDI theory and HSDT to focus on all levels of human functioning (Demick, 2014). Further, FDI theory and individual differences in self-world relationships are complementary in terms of a multi-method approach. Whereas FDI theory is amenable to quantitative research towards predicting human functioning, self-world relationships are useful towards describing qualitatively human experience and action. This addition affirmed our commitment to a differential developmental psychology complementary to a general developmental psychology.

- An alternative telos of development, namely, flexibility and resilience, was proposed to advance a transactional and contextual conceptualization of positive adjustment cutting across persons and the broadly defined contexts that they inhabit.

Relevant HSDT research

Against this backdrop, HSDT generated empirical research on person-in-environment transitions relevant to the problem of trauma and development. Research on maternal loss, transition to parenthood, adaptation to infant and child adoption, and transitions of older adulthood is now presented.

Early Maternal Loss. Certainly no one will deny that the early loss of a parent constitutes a trauma for those experiencing it. However, most research on this problem has treated early parent loss in childhood and/or effects of this loss on individuals' subsequent mental health. In contrast, Frackman (2000) under my supervision conducted a mixed-methods study on positive sequelae of early maternal loss, focusing holistically on intelligence, including both cognitive and emotional intelligence.

Women experiencing maternal loss prior to the age of 18 years completed standardized tasks of cognitive intelligence, emotional intelligence, and PTG, and participated in Giorgi's (2012) phenomenological interviews ('Please tell me about your experience of losing your mother'). In line with expectation, there was a positive correlation between overall PTG and emotional intelligence. Contrary to expectation, while participants did not surpass normative samples on emotional intelligence, they scored higher than normative samples on cognitive intelligence. Finally, the majority spontaneously identified *development of empathy* and *psychological independence* as the major positive benefits of this loss.

Transition to Parenthood. In a recent *New York Times* op-ed piece, Finkel (2014) discussed 'the trauma of parenthood' and concluded that new parenthood is jarring, isolating, and under-supported. He cited findings that parenthood leads men and women to be less satisfied with their lives and, in some, to exhibit clinical depression for up to five years. These effects are particularly pronounced for fathers and for those in the lower socioeconomic class because they are more environmentally than biologically (e.g., post-partum depression, sleeplessness) based.

In contrast, HSDT work has presented a more balanced view, conceptualizing parenthood as a disequilibrating experience affecting all levels of parent-in-environment system functioning. For example, this transition has been shown to impact: (a) *physical aspect of parent* (e.g., foetus leads mother to gain weight and to experience fatigue, anxiety, or stress); (b) *intrapersonal aspect of parent* (e.g., parenthood may lead to higher levels of cognitive development); (c) *sociocultural aspect of parent* (e.g., egalitarian parents resort to more traditional gender roles); (d) *physical aspect of environment* (e.g., parents alter their homes by child-proofing); (e) *inter-organismic aspect of environment* (e.g., parents lose touch with friends because of time pressure and give away pets for child safety); and (f) *sociocultural aspect of environment* (e.g., parents consider family developmental tasks and develop family history/themes). Similarly, holistic research also documented that the transition to parenthood shapes not only the experience and action of individual parents but also of marital dyads (e.g., less marital satisfaction) and of family systems (e.g., shifts in family members' alliances).

While at first glance most of these changes appear unfavourable, HSDT research has complemented quantitative and qualitative analyses, qualifying that many changes have both positive and negative consequences. For example, changes to mothers' physical functioning encompass 'pregnancy glow', positive maternal approach behaviour to newborns, and increased wayfinding ability in child care settings; changes to traditional gender roles often lead to more efficient couples functioning; changes to physical environments lead to less cluttered homes; changes to the inter-organismic aspects of environment lead to more effective management of family support network members including friends; and shifts in family alliances allow disconnected family members (older children) to re-establish once-connected relationships with each other and with parents.

Based on Werner's assertion that 'wherever there is life there is growth and systematic orderly sequence', HSDT's developmental assumptions led to an alternative view of parent development (Demick, 2002). Whenever there is a perturbation to the parent-in-environment system (e.g., cognitive disequilibrium in response to a child's behaviour), parents must reorganize their self-world relationships to restore equilibrium. In this way, positive developmental processes occur with great frequency in daily transactions with children. Qualitative accounts indicate that parents are constantly faced with restoring cognitive equilibrium or more general equilibrium to the parent-in-environment system in a dialectical process that may feel equivalent every time they are faced with a novel, or not so novel, stimulus from their children. Thus, parents are continually faced with attempting to return differentiated and conflicted parent-in-environment system states to more differentiated and integrated ones. However, the process becomes easier over time, particularly for parents who come to prioritize the inter-organismic aspect of environment of which their children are a part over the psychological aspect of their own functioning. This leads to greater self-development, involving a decrease in narcissism through realization that another individual's (child's) wellbeing is necessarily more important than one's own.

Family Adaptation to Infant/Child Adoption. A recent guide by the American Academy of Pediatrics (2013) cautioned families and practitioners to 'assume that all children who have been adopted or fostered have experienced trauma' (p. 7). Although this work is less negative than earlier academic writing, an HSDT research programme on family adaptation to infant/child adoption has taken a more comprehensive stance using developmentally ordered and other individual differences.

An early study (Demick, 1993) assessed the effects of open versus closed adoption (communication versus no communication between biological and adoptive parents) on children and families. Speculating that open adoption represents a differentiated and integrated self-world relationship and traditional closed adoption either a dedifferentiated, a differentiated and isolated, or a differentiated and conflicted one, no differences in life satisfaction, stress, and control in parents practising open versus closed adoption were found, although those practising open adoption worried less about attachment to their children and felt confident about the 'story' they would have to tell their children. Further, relative to all groups, adoptive mothers in open adoptions reported lower self-esteem, although this appeared related to heightened empathy from meeting their children's birth mothers. There was also a clear-cut selection effect with those with cultural/political family orientations opting for open adoption while those with traditional/moral/religious family orientations chose closed adoption.

Likewise and Demick (2014) conducted a study on the adaptation of children and parents to infant adoption. They administered a variety of standard tasks of socio-emotional development to children between the ages of 8 and 10 years who were adopted prior to 1 year of age and to their parents who fell into one of three categories of couples: gay, heterosexual, and lesbian. On measures of socio-emotional development, children of lesbians exhibited the most optimal development followed by those of heterosexuals followed by those of gays. There was also more congruence in parents' perceptions of their children in the lesbian couples relative to the other groups and, from interview data, gays reported more prejudice and discrimination than other parents, which they worried might impact their children. In another study, Storey and Demick (2014) refuted the typical monolithic view of infant adoption. Using phenomenological interviews with a sample of college students adopted in infancy, three distinct structures of adoption experience were identified, *dedifferentiated: insecure, differentiated and non-integrated: secure,* and *differentiated and integrated: secure,* roughly corresponding to Ainsworth's (1973) types of attachment relationships in infants and children.

Finally, based on the contextual notion that societal attitudes impact the person-in-environment systems of those adopted, Sclafani, Lawrence, and Demick (2014) conducted a community survey on 2,000+ individuals in the northeastern US. They assessed the extent to which participants agreed with 25 adoption myths (e.g., *being taken away from one's birth mother in infancy is traumatic leading to a 'primal wound,' there exists an 'adopted child syndrome' characterized by delinquency and violence*) and found the following.

Those with some connection to adoption (nuclear family member, extended family member, friend, acquaintance) rated adoption myths as less true than those without adoption contact. Further, the overall attitudes of this sample were more favourable than those described in earlier cohorts of adults (Miall, 1987). However, the findings indicated that, in contrast to the generally favourable attitudes of the entire sample, adoption attitudes varied strongly related to numerous individual differences (sex, age, race/ethnicity, sexual orientation, political party affiliation, birthplace) with certain groups espousing less positive attitudes. Those in lower socio-economic classes expressed less favourable attitudes towards adoption possibly related to the elitist (resource-consuming) nature of the institution (Demick, 2012). Relative to young and middle-aged adults, older adults held more positive attitudes towards adoption perhaps in light of an increasing realization of the obligatory (versus chosen) nature of kin relationships.

Transitions of older adulthood

Retirement. Several studies (cf. Wapner, Demick, & Damrad, 1988; Wapner & Demick, 2003) were conducted on older adults' transition to retirement, which for some may be construed as traumatic. One mixed-methods study assessed the experience and action of individuals undergoing retirement and the role of planning with their social network members in adapting to this new status. Four types of retirement experience were delineated: (a) *transition to old age* (experienced as a transition to the last phase of life characterized by a need to put things in order); (b) *new beginning* (perceived as a time in life to do what one wants); (c) *continuation* (perceived not as an event of importance since valued work activities are continued); and (d) *imposed disruption* (experienced as the devastating loss of a highly valued sphere of activity). Retirees with social network members highly involved in pre-retirement planning and whose lives were only moderately changed by the retirees' retirement exhibited the most optimal adaptation.

A follow-up study eight years later with these participants revealed that retirees moved to person-in-environment system states in which their lives were extremely busy, filled with working activities including employment. Although not occurring immediately following retirement, subsequent post-retirement experience was most often characterized as *continuation* (with retirement perceived in hindsight as a non-event since valued activities are continued). Another study uncovered sex differences in retirement experience (e.g., relative to men, women retired at younger ages and reported more pre-retirement planning, financial worries, and positive attitudes towards work and old age).

Nursing Home Adaptation. Older adults recently admitted to nursing homes responded to questionnaires on cherished possessions and on adaptation to the nursing home (Wapner, Demick, & Redondo, 1990). The presence of cherished possessions was positively related to residents' adaptation to nursing homes. Cherished possessions of those entering nursing homes largely functioned to provide historical continuity, comfort, and a sense of belonging. In contrast to other studies (e.g., Csikszentmihalyi & Rochberg-Halton, 1981) demonstrating a shift with age from objects of action to objects of contemplation, here there was a reversion to objects of action, a problem worthy of further empirical inquiry. The study also uncovered sex differences in cherished possessions: relative to men, women had more cherished possessions, attributed less utilitarian meaning to them, and associated them more with comfort and a greater number of self-other relationships. These findings led to strong practical recommendations (e.g., encouraging men entering nursing homes to bring their cherished possessions with them).

Summary

This review of HSDT research suggested that future studies on trauma and development may benefit from broader views of *holism, development, persons, environments, systems, individual differences, structural (integration of old and new environments) and dynamic (planning) analyses*, and *methodological flexibility* – all to capture the complexity of human functioning in ecologically valid contexts and to demonstrate the mutual value of using conceptualization and methodology from one subfield of psychology (developmental) to advance the conceptualization and methodology of another (clinical).

For example, to understand the central roles of schema reconstruction in Tedeschi and Calhoun's model of PTG, Janoff-Bulman (2004) delineated three models differentiating the five positive changes. A *strength through suffering* model (with *no pain, no gain*, survivors' new self-perceptions are understandable in the light of their painful losses) captures the changes of personal strength and new possibilities without evoking survivors' assumptive worlds. A *psychological preparedness* model (because of successful coping with trauma, survivors become better prepared for and less likely to be traumatized by subsequent tragedies) implicates survivors rebuilding viable assumptive worlds but does not implicate any of the five positive changes since psychological preparedness represents survivors' status and not their perceptions. An *existential re-evaluation* model (survivors experience existential struggles in the process of rebuilding their inner worlds, engaging in explicit meaning-making in the face of loss) involves three of the five changes, namely, appreciation of life, relating to others, and spiritual development.

However, Tedeschi and Calhoun's model of PTG, as interpreted by Janoff-Bulman, appears to be concerned with the isolated variable of post-traumatic coping. From the perspective of HSDT, the problem of PTG could be significantly advanced by introducing *holistic/systems considerations* (e.g., how are post-traumatic growth and other positive constructs such as hardiness, resilience, and mindfulness related? How does post-traumatic growth impact individuals internally at all levels of organization and externally with respect to other environmental systems?), *developmental considerations* (e.g., how does post-traumatic growth first appear and then manifest itself over time? Do these effects last indefinitely or do they change during ontogenesis? Are there structural relationships among the five positive changes at different intervals following trauma?), and *contextual considerations* (e.g., are there similarities and/or differences in post-traumatic growth related to the age, sex, race/ethnicity, physical status, personality, intelligence, pre- and post-trauma psychopathological status of survivors? Are there cross-cultural similarities and/or differences in the manifestation of post-traumatic growth?).

Lessons to take home for practitioners

Calhoun and Tedeschi (2013) delineated treatment recommendations for fostering PTG. They recommended that therapists: (a) initially provide support for survivors to manage high levels of emotional distress, allowing survivors to regain a deliberate ability to engage cognitively in the trauma's aftermath; (b) listen to rather than try to resolve issues, permitting survivors to process their own experience (with therapists assuming the role of *expert companions*); (c) respect and be willing to engage in existential and spiritual matters that patients have developed or are trying to rebuild; (d) relate to survivors' stories in a personal manner allowing them to feel respected and encouraged to see the value in their stories; (e) exhibit sensitivity to the psychological needs of survivors, never offhandedly introducing didactic information or comments (e.g., *from pain comes suffering*); and (e) allow survivors enough time to adapt to the aftermath of the trauma before introducing growth issues. Following from this, Kilmer et al. (2014) adapted these clinical recommendations for children/adolescents, beginning with initial efforts to build on children's resources (including family support members using psychoeducation), to develop and support their active coping (e.g., employing cognitive-behavioural techniques), and to help them develop or rebuild viable inner narratives, all the time sharing the essential ingredient of PTG treatment, namely, allowing time for adaptation before exploring growth and without conveying a sense of deficit if none is evidenced.

Similar to PTG treatment recommendations growing out of empirical research, HDST clinical interventions were also based on empirical research. They have taken the form of recommendations *promoting conditions that facilitate developmental advance* as follows.

Holism and Multi-Method Complementarity. Based on the assumptions of holism and multi-method complementarity, an HSDT clinical approach is informed by the integration of psychoanalytic and cognitive-behavioural techniques, applied here to the context of individual outpatient therapy. As individuals enter my office for the first time, they are faced with a small wooden sign reading *Your Story Matters* with what seem to be butterfly wings coming out of its sides. Many of them, including children and adolescents, are struck by the message, commenting that they have never felt as if their story has mattered to anyone; the wing-like features often communicate to adults the potential transformative nature of having someone listen to and respect their life narratives. In the process of recounting these stories, patients often experience catharsis or the purging of the emotions, develop insights into current behaviours related to the past, and rebuild their personal narratives into more adaptive ones.

Although this sounds similar to psychoanalytic psychotherapy, the goal is not to foster insight, assumed to lead to behaviour change. Unfortunately Freud was incorrect in this assumption, for insight begets insight rather than behaviour change. Once patients have developed some degree of understanding, experienced emotional discharge if necessary, and reworked their personal narratives, they may be more ready to change their behaviours (with less possibility of symptom substitution); that is, to go out into the world and act differently. The results of these real-life interventions can in their therapists' offices be discussed and refined for future use. This general approach, referred to as *holistic-developmental-pragmatic psychotherapy*, has met with considerable successful with patients of different ages and diagnoses.

Anchor Point. The establishment of anchor points (bearing resemblance to Winnicott's, 1958, *transitional objects* construct) has been shown in HSDT research to play a positive role in adaptation to new environments (through spatial organization and social network development). Thus, patients experiencing difficult life events including trauma have been encouraged to develop anchor points to aid in their adaptation. Initial anchor points have included the safe confines of therapists' offices, which are then generalized to other safe places in patients' environments (e.g., various rooms in homes, being in the presence of additional confidants) in which patients feel comfortable enough to deal with the aftermath of these difficult events and then to begin to rebuild their stories.

Cognitive Restructuring. Currently the term 'cognitive restructuring' is most associated, in cognitive-behavioural therapies, with the psychotherapeutic process of learning to identify and dispute maladaptive or irrational thoughts known as *cognitive distortions* (e.g., all-or-nothing thinking, magnification, magical thinking) associated with numerous psychopathologies. On a more general level, cognitive restructuring refers to any method that helps people think differently about thoughts, feelings, situations, and/or events. Other psychotherapeutic approaches promoting cognitive restructuring have included behavioural experiments to test beliefs that may be unhelpful and Socratic questions to explore patients' beliefs. It is this last usage that has figured prominently in HSDT recommendations for clinical intervention.

Certain aphorisms associated with Gestalt psychology have served as guiding principles for patients who are asked to examine past and present phenomena through new lenses. Some of these principles (adages) have included: *the whole is greater than the sum of its parts* (e.g., helping to explain to patients the complexity of individual, family, or societal functioning); *one can see the glass as half full rather than half empty* (to foster optimism rather than pessimism); and *one must take one step back in order to take two steps forward* (to help patients understand Werner's construct of spiral rather than linear development related to needed periods of consolidation).

The use of cognitive restructuring in psychotherapy was also strengthened by the introduction of *field dependence-independence cognitive style* into HSDT. Most simply, on the basis of two experimental perceptual tasks (Rod-and-Frame Test, Group Embedded Figures Test) (Witkin et al., 1954), individuals were identified who were influenced by field (visual) cues and cannot easily disembed objects from surrounding fields as *field dependent* (FD) and those who rely on bodily cues and can easily differentiate objects from fields as *field independent* (FI). They also found constellations of personality characteristics correlated with these styles such that FD individuals typically exhibit a global body concept, limited sense of separate identity, and *unusual sensitivity to the social surround*, while FI persons demonstrate an articulated body concept, sense of separate identity, and *greater ability in analytic tasks*.

This has led me to consider cognitive style differences in both research subjects and patients such that FD individuals may make better use of social support networks in adaptation to difficult life events, while FI individuals might find cognitive restructuring techniques to constitute more helpful interventions. Further, HSDT research (cf. Lipsitt & Demick, 2012) demonstrated a third group of individuals, *FDI-mobile*, with the capacity to shift flexibly between FD and FI depending on situational demands. Resilient individuals were subsequently identified as those with a combination of FDI mobility and character perseverance. Thus, holistic-developmental-pragmatic psychotherapy aims to assess and remediate FDI cognitive style, flexibility, perseverance, and resilience towards more optimal person-in-environment adaptation following difficult life events.

Planning. In line with attempts to foster individuals' cognitive restructuring ability, numerous HSDT studies provided evidence that simple requests for individuals to verbalize plans about future actions to be taken to advance to more ideal person-in-environment system states may bring those states into effect. As noted, retirees with greater degrees of pre-retirement planning with support network members (spouses) experienced more ideal post-retirement person-in-environment system states than those with lesser degrees of planning. Thus, planning is a useful cognitive process that should be nurtured in all patients (e.g., children, adolescents, adults, families) but especially in those experiencing difficult life events including trauma. Since planning is associated with goal-directed behaviour, planning interventions have the potential to foster motivation and a future orientation in those whose motivation and future orientation have been interrupted.

Self-World Distancing. HSDT research has generally indicated that a decrease in self-world distancing between individuals and the consequences of their negative actions may lead to safer, more optimal person-in-environment functioning. Applied to the clinical context, patients encouraged to allow themselves the opportunity to distance themselves from recent traumatic events (e.g., instead discussing other difficult but less stressful and potent events that were handled successfully) may identify adaptive strategies and coping mechanisms that allow them to work through problematic thoughts, feelings, and behaviours associated with more recent trauma.

Triggers to Action. HSDT research has suggested that making people aware of the precipitating events or triggers to their own or others' actions leads to heightened awareness, which in turn leads to appropriate action and more optimal person-in-environment functioning. Over the course of treatment, as patients become better able to deal with recent stressful events, it is important for them to begin to identify triggers associated with the stressful event that lead them to less developmentally advanced action towards replacing these behaviours with more developmentally advanced action. For example, the childhood trauma of losing a mother to obesity and poor lifestyle habits may lead some when faced with maternal memories to overeat non-adaptively (e.g., perhaps as identification or engaging in self-destructive behaviour related to unresolved grief), which should ultimately lead to attempts to replace non-adaptive actions with more adaptive ones (e.g., maternal memories leading to engaging in simple health-conscious behaviours, and paving the way for the larger action of initiating a diet regime).

Reculer Pour Mieux Sauter (Draw Back in order to make a better jump). In line with previous points, HSDT research indicated that negative experiences (e.g., loss of self-esteem) serve the function of fostering greater self-insight and providing the formal condition of dissolution of a prior organization of the self. Thus, allowing and/or encouraging patients to work through all stressful life events, including daily hassles faced by all (e.g., minor inner, financial, time pressure, work-related, environmental, family, health concerns), may lead to developmental advances in self-experience. These advances in self-experience may ultimately serve a patient well in working through the sequelae of larger, more difficult events.

Individual Differences. Many HSDT studies suggested that consideration of individual differences is a route to foster developmental progression. As reported, families with cultural/intellectual orientations show optimal person-in-environment system adaptation following open adoptions while those with religious/moral emphases show optimal adaptation following closed adoptions. Thus, consideration of individual differences most broadly defined has the potential to suggest differential clinical interventions to foster the optimal adaptation of children, adolescents, adults, couples, and/or families who have recently experienced difficult life events. Extending the adoption example, the former may find cognitive, intellectual, and/or political (e.g., grassroots) interventions and the latter, religious and/or spiritual interventions, differentially efficacious towards restoring optimal person-in-environment system functioning following a transition, crisis, or trauma. Developmentally oriented interventions tailored to children versus adults and to children versus adolescents in both types of families also appear indicated.

Summary and conclusions

There are similarities between Tedeschi and Calhoun's clinical suggestions for the fostering of PTG and HSDT recommendations for psychological interventions aimed at restoring equilibrium following disequilibrating changes in person-in-environment systems. Both consider that changes in patients following difficult life events are not merely cognitive but also affective and experiential in nature so that practitioners, particularly in the early stages of treatment, must maintain empathic neutrality to facilitate patients' expressing emotional aspects, and therapists' understanding, of clinical issues. Both acknowledge the need for treatment to be conducted in phases (e.g., PTG researchers suggest that the negative aftermaths of trauma be worked through prior to introduction of PTG constructs while holistic-developmental-pragmatic therapists address emotion sharing and understanding prior to the initiation of encouraging patients to act differently in the world). Both share a focus on fostering patients' cognitive engagement towards developing new life narratives following difficult life events. However, there are basic differences between the two with HSDT advocating broader views of persons, environments, holism, development, individual differences, cognitive restructuring, and conditions facilitating developmental advance.

As regards comparison to other approaches, HSDT clinical interventions are *not* identical with *Gestalt therapy* (Perls, Hefferline, & Goodman, 1951), although both were influenced by the larger movement of Gestalt psychology. The core of Gestalt therapy process includes: patients' enhanced awareness of present-moment sensation, perception, bodily feelings, emotion, and behaviour; emphasis on the therapist–patient relationship; and patients' need to develop self-regulating adjustments to the interrelations among self, therapist, and the physical and social aspects of their real-life environments. Thus, both approaches share holistic notions of persons, environments, and person-environment systems.

However, most striking from this and other approaches, HSDT and its clinical implications underscore Werner's generalization that 'whenever there is life, there is growth and systematic orderly sequence.' In line with his holistic, comparative emphasis (general laws of mental life as a whole) and developmental conception (development as a mode of analysis for the study of any phenomenon with equal applicability to processes ranging from microgenesis, development of a thought, to pathogenesis, development of pathology), chances for developmental advance are much more frequent in HSDT interventions given the dynamic nature of the everyday interrelations among developing aspects of persons, environments, and person-in-environment systems.

References

Ainsworth, M.S. (1973). The development of infant-mother attachment. In: B.M. Caldwell & H.N. Ricciuti (eds), *Review of Child Development Research*, Vol.3, pp. 1–94. Chicago: University of Chicago Press.

American Academy of Pediatrics. (2013). *Helping Foster and Adoptive Families Cope With Trauma.* Washington, DC: American Academy of Pediatrics Press.

Calhoun, L.G., &Tedeschi, R.G. (2013). *Posttraumatic Growth in Clinical Practice.* New York: Routledge.

Caplan, G. (1964). *Principles of Preventive Psychiatry.* New York: Basic.

Clarkson, K. (2011). Stronger (What doesn't kill you). *On Stronger* [CD]. New York: RCA Records.

Csikszentmihalyi, M., & Rochberg-Halton, E. (1981). *The Meaning of Things: Domestic Symbols of the Self.* New York: Cambridge.

Demick, J. (2014). *Group Embedded Figures Test (GEFT) Manual* (Rev. ed., including computerized test). Menlo Park, CA: Mind Garden.

Demick, J. (2012). Review of C.W. Gailey's blue-ribbon babies and labors of love: race, class, and gender in U.S. adoption practice. *Adoption Quarterly, 15*(1), 67–69.

Demick, J. (2006). Effects of children on adults: Parenthood and beyond. In: C. Hoare (ed.), *The Oxford Handbook of Adult Development and Learning*, pp. 329–343.New York: Oxford.

Demick, J. (2002). Stages of parental development. In: M.H. Bornstein (ed.), *Handbook of Parenting. Being and Becoming a Parent*, Vol. 3, 2nd edition, pp. 389–413. Mahwah, NJ: Erlbaum.

Demick, J. (1993). Adaptation of marital couples to open versus closed adoption: A preliminary investigation. In: J. Demick, K. Bursik & R. Dibiase (eds), *Parental Development*, pp. 175–201. Hillsdale, NJ: Erlbaum.

Demick, J., & Wapner, S. (1990). Role of psychological science in promoting environmental quality. *American Psychologist, 45*(5), 631–632.

Dohrenwend, B.S. (1978). Social stress and community psychology. *American Journal of Community Psychology, 6*, 1–15.

Finkel, E.J. (2014, June).The trauma of parenthood. *New York Times*, p. SR12.

Frackman, G. (2008). *Maternal Loss and Emotional Intelligence in Women: An Exploration Into the Potential Benefits of Childhood Trauma* (Unpublished senior thesis). Providence, RI: Brown University.

Frankl, V.E. (1959). *Man's Search for Meaning.* New York: Pocket Books.

Freud, S. (1917). Mourning and melancholia. In: *The Standard Edition of the Complete Psychological Works of Sigmund Freud*, Vol. XIV, pp. 237–258. London: Hogarth.
Giorgi, A. (2012). The descriptive phenomenological psychological method. *Journal of Phenomenological Psychology, 43*(1), 3–12.
Goldstein, K. (1939). *The Organism: A Holistic Approach to Biology Derived From Pathological Data in Man*. New York: American.
Janoff-Bulman, R. (2004). Posttraumatic growth: three explanatory models. *Psychological Inquiry, 15*(1), 30–34.
Kilmer, R.P., Gil-Rivas, V., Griese, B., Hardy, S.J., & Hafstad, G.S. (2014). Posttraumatic growth in children and youth: clinical implications of an emerging literature. *American Journal of Orthopsychiatry*. Advance online publication
Likewise, R., & Demick, J. (2014). *Child, Coparent, and Family Functioning in Gay, Lesbian, and Heterosexual Infant Adoptions*. Manuscript in preparation.
Lipsitt, L.P. (1989). Development of self-regulatory behavior in infants: Towards understanding the origins of behavioral misadventures. In: S. Doxiadis (ed.), *Early Influences Shaping the Individual*, pp. 207–215. New York: Plenum.
Lipsitt, L.P., & Demick, J. (2012). Theory and measurement of resilience: Views from development. In: M. Ungar (ed.), *The Social Ecology of Resilience: A Handbook of Theory and Practice*, pp. 43–51. New York: Springer.
Loevinger, J. (1966). The meaning and measurement of ego development. *American Psychologist, 21*, 195–206.
Lu, F., Melicharek, J., Trent, N., Sobieraj, A., & Demick, J. (2014). *Human Personality and Sex Differences in Physiological Effects of Human-Canine Play*. Manuscript in preparation.
Maslow, A.H. (1968). *Toward a Psychology of Being*, 2nd edition. New York: Harper.
Miall, C.E. (1987). The stigma of adoptive parent status: Perceptions of community attitudes toward adoption and the experience of informal social sanctioning. *Family Relations, 36*, 34–39.
Nietzsche, F. (1889). *Goetzen-Daemmerung, oder: Wie man mit dem Hammer philosophisiert*. Leipzig: Naumann.
Perls, F., Hefferline, R., & Goodman, P. (1951). *Gestalt Therapy: Excitement and Growth in the Human Personality*. New York: Julian.
Sclafani, D.C., Lawrence, K., & Demick, J. (2014). *Individual Differences in Community Attitudes Toward Infant/Child Adoption*. Manuscript in preparation.
Seligman, M.E. P., & Csikszentmihalyi, M. (2000). Positive psychology: an introduction. *American Psychologist, 55*(1), 5–14.
Storey, A., & Demick, J. (2014). *Toward Refuting a Monolithic View of Adoption: College Students' Phenomenological Narratives of Having Been Adopted*. Manuscript in preparation.
Tedeschi, R.G., & Calhoun, L.G. (2004). Posttraumatic growth: conceptual foundations and empirical evidence. *Psychological Inquiry, 15*(1), 1–18.
Tedeschi, R.G., & Calhoun, L.G. (1995). *Trauma and Transformation: Growing in the Aftermath of Suffering*. Thousand Oaks, CA: Sage.
Wapner, S. (1969).Organismic-developmental theory: Some applications to cognition. In: J. Langer, P. Mussen & N. Covington (eds), *Trends and Issues in Developmental Theory*, pp. 35–67. New York: Holt.
Wapner, S., & Demick, J. (2003). Adult development: The holistic, developmental, and systems-oriented perspective. In: J. Demick & C. Andreoletti (eds), *Handbook of Adult Development*, pp. 63–83. New York: Kluwer.

Wapner, S., & Demick, J. (2002). The increasing *contexts* of *context* in the study of environment-behavior relations. In: R.B. Bechtel & A. Churchman (eds), *Handbook of Environmental Psychology*, pp. 3–14. New York: Wiley.

Wapner, S., & Demick, J. (1998). Developmental analysis: A holistic, developmental, systems-oriented perspective. In: W. Damon (Series ed.) & R.M. Lerner (Vol. ed.), *Handbook of Child Psychology:* Vol. 1. *Theoretical Models of Human Development*, 5th edition, pp. 761–805. New York: Wiley.

Wapner, S., Demick, J., & Damrad, R. (1988, April). *Transition to Retirement: Eight Years After*. Paper presented at the annual meeting of the Eastern Psychological Association, Buffalo, NY.

Wapner, S., Demick, J., & Redondo, J.P. (1990). Cherished possessions and adaptation of older people to nursing homes. *International Journal on Aging and Human Development, 31*(3), 299–315.

Werner, H. (1957). *Comparative Psychology of Mental Development.* New York: International Universities Press.

Werner, H., & Kaplan, B. (1963). *Symbol Formation.* New York: Wiley.

Winnicott, D.W. (1958). *Through Pediatrics to Psychoanalysis.* New York: Basic.

Witkin, H.A., Lewis, H.B., Hertzman, M., Machover, K., Meissner, P.B., & Wapner, S. (1954). *Personality Through Perception: An Experimental and Clinical Study.* Oxford, England: Harper.

Yalom, I. (1980). *Existential Psychotherapy.* New York: Basic.

Yalom, I., & Lieberman, M.A. (1981). Bereavement and heightened existential awareness. *Psychiatry, 54*(4), 334–345.

17
Relationships Between Grandparents and Their Grandchildren: An Applied Dyadic Perspective

Bert Hayslip Jr., Robert J. Maiden, and Megan L. Dolbin-MacNab

Introduction: The nature of grandparenting and grandparent-grandchild relationships

That becoming a grandparent is a common experience for many adults is underscored by the fact that, as life expectancy has increased, the chances of becoming a grandparent have also increased (Hayslip & Page, 2012). Moreover, more children know their grandparents (and great-grandparents) than at any time in history (Dunifron, 2012). Reflecting the near universality of the experience of grandparenting, 75% of those born in 2000 can expect to have at least one grandparent still living when they reach age 30. Nearly 60% of older adults have at least one grandchild, and 80% of middle-aged and older adults are grandparents.

It is difficult, if not impossible, to understand the experiences of grandparents apart from their relationships with their grandchildren. Thus, the central theme of this chapter is that grandparents and grandchildren are best thought of in *dyadic* terms; their influence on one another is *dynamic* and *bidirectional*, reflecting a *developmental family systems* approach to understanding such relationships (Combrinck-Graham, 1985). Indeed, understanding grandparents and grandchildren at the level of their relationships with one another *as well as* in the context of their relationships to their adult children, spouses, age peers, and friends is key to not only understanding such relationships, but also to designing and carrying out clinical interventions targeting each member of the dyad. Significantly in this respect, Xu and Chi (2011) found that rural Chinese grandparents who reported the most life satisfaction saw their families as harmonious, their grandchildren as filial in nature, and received more instrumental support but *less* monetary support from them. Likewise, Sigurdardottir and Julursdottir (2013) have stressed the mutual, reciprocal nature of the support between grandparents and grandchildren to each generation's benefit.

While most people become a grandparent in their late 40s or early 50s, for others, it is non-normative; they do not become grandparents until their 60s or 70s. The essential non-normativeness of grandparenting is underscored by its *countertransitional* nature – it is a role persons assume that is based upon the actions of *others* (Hagestad, 1985). It follows that the experience of grandparenting, and consequently the nature of the influence grandparents have on their grandchildren *as well as* the grandchild's impact upon a grandparent, is largely *unique* to each grandparent-grandchild dyad, dependent upon (1) the *meaning* that grandparenting has for the individual, wherein there are advantages to middle-aged and older persons whose identities centralize the role of grandparent (Reitzes & Mutran, 2004a), (2) the particular behavioural *style* derived from this meaning that persons enact, affecting the nature and extent of contact with a grandchild, (3) *how* that grandparent is perceived by the grandchild, i.e. negatively or positively, subject to the gender of the grandchild (Shore, Hayslip, & Henderson, 2000), (4) the *nature and extent of their contact* with grandchildren (as mediated by one's children or son/daughter-in laws, see also Sims & Rofail, 2013), and (5) each person's particular place along a *developmental continuum of youth to later life*, where changing life circumstances and the salience of gender-specific roles alter the nature of this relationship, when family dynamics are altered by events such as death or illness, or when grandchildren become independent (Bangerter & Waldron, 2014). While the seeds of a continued close relationship with a grandparent in adulthood are often sown in childhood (Geurts, Van Tilburg, & Poortman, 2012), Villar et al. (2010) found that grandparents perceived greater changes in their relationships with their grandchildren as the latter grew older. (6) In addition, the unique family circumstances in which one assumes the role of grandparent impact the grandparent-grandchild dyad. In this respect, Stelle et al. (2010) found that grandparents' gender, sexual orientation, and extent of physical or mental decline accounted for the great diversity they observed in grandparent-grandchild relationships.

Grandparents are more likely to be men *and* women who are younger, employed, and who even still have adult children at home. This grandparent may also be caring for a mother or father who is quite old or this grandparent may be cared for by an adult child or a grandchild. In this latter respect, Boquet et al. (2011) found that grandchildren caring for a dying grandparent not only experience guilt, stress, and fatigue in doing so, but they also lose the role of 'grandchild'. Smith (2012) not only found that the dynamics of the grandparent-grandchild relationship were influential in affecting the experience of caregiving, but also that such dynamics were altered by the experience of caregiving, consistent with understanding such relationships in a dyadic, fluid manner. Ihara, Horio, and Tompkins (2012) have underscored the complexity of this caregiving in noting the salience of not only the grandchild's ability to provide care for a grandparent, but also his/her motivation for doing so, as influenced by the strength of the intergenerational bond, caregiver stress and financial hardship, the degree to which the grandchild has time to provide care, and the physical distance from the grandparent. Key, however, is that feelings of closeness and affection must *first* exist if grandchildren are to provide help and assistance to a frail grandparent (Even-Zohar, 2011).

Many persons enjoy their roles as grandparents and maintain happy and fulfilling relationships with their grandchildren and the parents of these children. Indeed, grandparents who can clearly and actively express their affection towards a grandchild positively influence that child's social-interpersonal development (Mansson, 2013). Complementarily, whether grandparents feel they are important in the lives of their grandchildren and consequently influence them in many ways influences and is influenced by how grandparents define their roles (as central or peripheral). This role definition lays the groundwork for their self-efficacy as grandparents: how (and if) they will aid in their grandchild's development as well as how they will influence the family as a whole. There is much variability in grandparenting, and consequently, the responsibility for child discipline, financial assistance, patterns of visitation, giving advice to the parents, sharing religious faith, and supporting the parents in decision-making are salient dimensions of the grandparent role for *some* persons but not others.

Ideally, a grandparent's role responsibilities and extent of involvement in a grandchild's life must be negotiated between grandparents, their adult children and their partners, and in some cases even older grandchildren themselves. Thus, issues of boundariness and communication transcend most grandparent-parent/grandparent-grandchild conflicts. In setting new boundaries and expectations, families can choose to either repeat patterns of involvement that they experienced earlier in life or actively work to create new parameters defining the grandparent-grandchild relationship (Hayslip, Maiden, Page, & Dolbin-MacNab, 2015).

As grandparenting is a *tenuous* role, one which can be objectively defined but is functionally ambiguous (see Rosow, 1985), some grandparents may have difficulty in constructing their roles in a meaningful and adaptive manner and may experience significant discrepancies in their expectations versus the reality of grandparenting. On the other hand, the tenuousness of the role may free up persons to define grandparenting in a manner which best fits them personally. Thus, a grandparent can play the roles of mentor, family historian, pseudo-parent, friend, or ally (in the case of a grandchild's difficulties with a parent). In addition, they may represent a living ancestor who teaches grandchildren ethnic traditions, experience, culture, and history (Reitzes & Mutran, 2004a), or advocate for/participate in school-related activities on behalf of their grandchildren (Watson, 2010).

Grandparenthood has many existential advantages: it can buffer one's fears about isolation, loneliness, dying, or not feeling valued as a person, wherein Friedman, Hechter, and Kreager (2008) found grandparents who invested themselves more fully into the grandparent role to be less uncertain about the end of life. Also, in transmitting values to a younger grandchild (Pratt, Norris, Hebblethwaite, & Arnold, 2008) and in serving as a support for that child and his/her family in times of crisis, grandparents can positively influence their grandchildren. As noted above, one must *first* be (and be perceived as being) emotionally close to a grandchild in order to influence them, though in some cases, the symbolic nature of a grandparent's role in a given family system may be an influence on a grandchild's educational or career goals, wherein emotional closeness to a grandparent predicts the goals that grandchildren set for themselves as well as such goal attainment (Wise, 2010). Moreover, grandparents who are more highly educated tend to positively impact their grandchildren's academic abilities (Ferguson & Ready, 2011), and both greater emotional and financial involvement by grandparents longitudinally predict their grandchildren's prosocial behaviour and school involvement (Yorgason, Padilla-Walker, & Jackson, 2011).

Just as some grandparents are emotionally distant regarding their grandchildren, not all grandchildren are close to their grandparents, wherein adolescent and young adult grandchildren's perceptions of their closeness to a grandparent *vary* with grandchild-grandparent frequency of contact, grandparent age, health, and level of education (see, e.g., Hokoyama & MaloneBeach, 2013), as well as the grandparent's particular personality attributes (Hokoyama & MaloneBeach, 2013). Interestingly, Seibert and Kerns (2009) found children to sometimes use their grandparents as attachment figures to provide stability and security in their lives. Indeed, we have found that meaningful frequent contact with a grandparent can mitigate the effect of a parent's divorce, mental illness, or death (Henderson, Hayslip, Sanders, & Louden, 2009).

Importantly, grandchild-grandparent contact is bidirectional. That is, it is likely that at least some grandchildren might help socialize their grandparents to matters of contemporary culture, such as using modern technology, violence in the schools, assistance in learning about aspects of culture particular to the child's world, such as music, new scientific discoveries, fashion, drug use, or sexuality. In this respect, despite the fact that what we know about grandparenting is mostly based upon grandmothers, it should be made clear that grandfathers and step-grandfathers can *also* be viable sources of wisdom and influence. Interestingly, male grandchildren's stories about their grandfathers emphasize the importance of work and recreation, with grandmothers playing supporting roles, while adult granddaughters' stories suggest that their grandmothers must make up for the deficiencies of their grandfathers (Goodsell, Bates, & Behnke, 2011).

It should be pointed out that grandparents can indeed foster maladaptive behaviour in their grandchildren (Bailey, Hill, Oesterle, & Hawkins,

2009). They can also contribute to marital discord or model pathological behaviours which grandchildren may internalize, reflecting the latter's response to underlying family conflict (Hayslip, Maiden, Page, & Dolbin-MacNab, 2015). Even investing oneself *too* heavily into a grandchild's life, i.e. spending more nights with a grandchild, can have counter-intuitive and negative effects on a grandparent's self-esteem (Won, 2010). Just as children value their independence, so too do grandparents!

Grandparents' contact with their grandchildren: A precursor of influence

The nature and extent of one's contact with a grandchild sets the tone for the extent to which one can be influential in that child's life, where most (68%) grandparents see their grandchildren every one or two weeks, and the vast majority (89%) feel that they play at least a somewhat important role in their grandchildren's lives (AARP, 2002; Lampkin, 2012). As geographic distance is the strongest predictor of grandparent-grandchild contact (Reitzes & Mutran, 2004b), grandparents who live far from their grandchildren may need education about options for electronic communication available to them (e.g., Skype, email, text messaging) or other means of staying in contact with their grandchildren. Herme, Westerback, and Quadello (2010) found that as the physical proximity between grandparents and grandchildren increases, there were fewer face-to-face contacts and phone calls, but more letters and cards. Even given the accessibility of text messaging, this form of contact from grandchildren lessened with greater physical proximity. Apparently and unfortunately, out of sight is out of mind! In such cases, grandparents may need to be especially proactive in maintaining meaningful contacts with their grandchildren, as in scheduling weekend visits, weekly dinners together, regular phone calls, taking advantage of opportunities to babysit, or taking vacations together.

It is important to note that the nature and extent of grandparents' contact with their grandchildren is primarily *mediated* by the quality of the grandparent's relationship to the grandchild's parent (see Connidis, 2010). This mediational role impacts the quality of the grandparent-adult child relationship, where the adult child serves as a *gatekeeper*. Consequently, how the adult child functions as a gatekeeper influences whether disagreements with adult children regarding the nature and extent of contact with grandchildren exist, and if they exist, how they are handled. The nature of such contact should ideally be discussed prior to the birth of the grandchildren, with an acknowledgement by all that a grandparent's needs may change and his/her involvement may need to be discussed again, as for example, when one of the parents dies or the couple divorces. As there may be intergenerational and intercultural differences in expectations about a grandparent's involvement or about issues relating to child care and discipline and/or values in raising a child, these differences can result in family conflicts, particularly when such expectations are unclear or not mutually agreed upon before the birth of a grandchild (Maiden & Zuckerman, 2008).

What lies ahead? It is likely that future cohorts of grandparents will be in the grandparent role for a longer period of time, be more highly educated, be in better health, have fewer grandchildren (decreasing the competition between grandchildren for a grandparent's time), and be more likely to be retired (Uhlenberg, 2009). Thus, future generations of grandparents may be able to make more meaningful investments into their grandchildren's lives owing to their greater longevity and the greater availability of programmes and services for older adults.

Grandparenthood and Development. We have noted above that grandparent-grandchild relationships are likely to be different when grandchildren are young and grandparents are in good health versus when grandchildren are adults and grandparents are older or frail (see Coali & Hertwig, 2011). Understanding grandparenting in the context of both the development of the grandparent and of the grandchild has been extensively discussed by Hayslip and Page (2012) and (Hayslip, Maiden, Page, & Dolbin-MacNab, 2015). Clearly, as children mature and age, the nature of a grandparent's involvement with them varies, where when grandchildren are young, grandparents may focus on play and childcare, while during adolescence, grandparents may be a sounding board, a cheerleader, or serve as the family's historian, transmitting family values developed over time in the process (Michels, Albert, & Ferring, 2011). As Connidis (2010) has observed, while their contact with grandparents lessens as grandchildren get older and become more independent, this does not necessarily translate into less meaningful contact. On the other hand, grandparents who are ill, impaired, retired, or widowed may be viewed differently by grandchildren who expect their grandparents to be physically active, mentally alert, or capable of travelling. In adulthood, grandchildren expect grandparents to buffer parental relationships and be a role model and a financial advisor.

From a helping perspective, an adult child's needs for instrumental and emotional support often elicit a grandparent's support in times of family stress; in this respect, maternal grandmothers are the most likely to be involved (Condon et al., 2013). While grandparents typically do not interfere in the rearing of their grandchildren (Connidis, 2010), this norm of non-interference may put some grandparents in a *double bind* (Thomas, 1990); they may be caught between the expectation that they be available to help and the limits set by their adult children regarding child-rearing. Interestingly, *remote or distant* grandparents (Cherlin & Furstenberg, 1986) may not be helpful and, indeed, may cause additional stress to parents by bringing up long-standing family conflicts or insisting on being involved in decision-making. In such cases, minimal involvement in a grandchild's life might be a better option for both the grandparent and parent.

As noted above, a grandparent's physical and/or cognitive health influence contact with and perceptions of them by grandchildren. In this respect, grandparents with dementia present many difficulties for grandchildren (Celdran, Tirado, & Villar, 2011), though demented grandparents and their grandchildren attribute no less symbolic and emotional salience to the grandparent role versus non-demented grandparents and their grandchildren (Werner & Lowenstein, 2001). It follows that grandchildren who interact with grandparents suffering from dementia may have to learn new ways of communicating and learn patience in doing so. They may also learn the value of being patient and gain insight about the meaning of life in caring for them (Celdran et al., 2011).

Special circumstances bearing on grandparent-grandchild relationships

The Death of a Grandchild. Although the death of a grandchild is unusual, its impact on grandparents is substantial. Grandparents' emotional needs when a grandchild dies are two-fold; they grieve for their adult child as well as for themselves (Reed, 2000). A grandchild's death can undermine relationships with surviving grandchildren or with an adult child, in that the grief that grandparents often experience is *disenfranchised* (Doka, 2002). Disenfranchised grief typically undermines the opportunities grandparents have to share their feelings with others and to get emotional support from them. Importantly, this grief, and the anger and sorrow that may accompany it, can interfere with relationships with an adult child, with one's friends, or even with one's spouse, wherein grandparents may resent the fact that their emotional needs were not met in the wake of a grandchild's death. Complicating matters is the fact that family customs and rituals may not meet a grandparent's needs. While grandparents are often put in the delicate position of supporting their adult child as well as meeting their own needs for support from others, grandparents respond to loss in a similar manner compared to the grandchild's own parents (see Hayslip & White, 2008).

The Divorce of an Adult Child. Grandparents also grieve when they lose contact with their grandchildren because of their adult child's divorce. While this can facilitate granddaughter-grandmother relationships (Holladay et al., 1998), especially when the mother has custody of the grandchildren and has moved away, both maternal grandmothers' and paternal grandparents' contacts with their grandchildren are diminished when a parent divorces (Ahrons, 2007). Importantly, the impact of divorce on the grandparent depends upon whether the grandparent is an *agent* in the life of a grandchild (in providing support and serving as a role model for a grandchild), or whether the grandparent is a *victim* (where persons view grandparenting as compensating for the lack of other sources of life satisfaction; Drew & Smith, 1999).

Raising a Grandchild. While the number of grandparents raising grandchildren has increased over the last few decades (Hayslip & Kaminiski, 2005), the number of caregiving grandparents has risen again in recent years as a result of the recession of 2008–2009 (Pew Foundation, 2010). Normatively, custodial grandparents tend to be younger, the mother's parents, in worse health, more socially isolated, poorer, less highly educated, and raising boys, all relative to non-custodial grandparents (Generations United, 2009). In some cases, grandparent caregiving exists in a *skipped generation* household, where the adult parent is absent. In contrast, *co-parenting* households are defined by the co-residence of the grandparent and adult child. Even in these situations, the grandparent may still have primary caregiving responsibility. Not surprisingly, grandparents in skipped generation households tend to fare worse physically and emotionally, owing to their diminished resources and greater comparative isolation from others compared to co-parenting grandfamily households (Generations United).

Grandparent caregiving is usually linked to the divorce, drug use, incarceration, job loss, teenage pregnancy, or death of the adult child, as well as to the abandonment or abuse of the grandchild. These circumstances often stigmatize and isolate grandparents from needed social and emotional support, making it difficult for them to be treated equitably by social service providers and fellow grandparents who are not raising a grandchild (see Hayslip & Glover, 2008; Hayslip, Glover, & Pollard, in press). Indeed, grandparent caregivers often experience health difficulties as a consequence of having neglected their health to the exclusion of their grandchildren's (Baker & Silverstein, 2008). They are also likely to be living on a fixed income and sometimes experience difficulties in parenting a grandchild (Hayslip & Kaminski, 2005). Indeed, the impact of grandmothers' distress on grandchildren's adjustment is mediated by dysfunctional parenting (Smith, Palmieri, Hancock, & Richardson, 2008), This distress may be exacerbated by the grandparent's negative attitudes towards child-rearing as well as being reflected in the tendency of some grandparents to rely on their grandchildren for emotional support (Kaminski, Hayslip, Wilson, & Casto, 2008).

Until recently, the impact of the adult child on the grandparent caregiver was underappreciated; we now know that such conflicts as well as disappointment in that adult child as a poor parent are experienced by many grandparent caregivers (Hayslip et al., 2009), and that grandparent caregivers grieve over the many losses they have experienced in taking on this responsibility (Backhouse & Graham, 2013), wherein their plans for the future, the quality of their relationship to the grandchild, and even their satisfaction with their marriages are all often undermined. While most grandparent caregivers are women, grandfathers raising grandchildren also sometimes report health concerns, depression, and feeling powerless in child rearing (McCallion & Kolomer, 2006). If the relationship with the adult child is ambivalent, conflictual, or poorly structured, the demands on the grandparent caregiver are more debilitating (Hayslip et al., 2009).

Mental health implications of the grandparent-grandchild dyad: General considerations

Clinicians working with grandparents and grandchildren benefit from educating themselves and seeking training about and thoroughly understanding the unique circumstances of grandparents in a given family system (see Hayslip, Maiden, Page, & Dolbin-MacNab, 2015). While few grandparents likely actually seek professional help for difficulties that they are experiencing in their roles as grandparents, there are many grandparents who could be considered *at risk* for the development of problems in their relationships with their adult children and/or their grandchildren (Hayslip, Maiden, Page, & Dolbin-MacNab, 2015). It is also likely that there are grandparents who are currently having problems related to their grandparenting roles, but who are reluctant to seek professional help.

As discussed by (Hayslip, Maiden, Page, & Dolbin-MacNab, 2015), persons at risk and/or who are already experiencing difficulties might be: grandparents who are in poor physical health, those who are involuntarily isolated from their grandchildren, those with a history of difficult relationships with their adult children, and those with a history of difficulty adjusting to major life events. Other grandparents at risk may have experienced unanticipated role changes for which they are unprepared such as a serious illness or a divorce, having to cope with the divorce of their adult children, the death of a grandchild, or having to assume full-time care of a grandchild. Still others must cope with the birth of a grandchild with a disability, teenage pregnancy, challenges in relationships with daughters or sons-in-law who discourage their involvement, unfulfilled expectations about the nature and degree of their involvement in a grandchild's life. Still others may have difficulty defining their roles as grandparent in the context of their roles as workers retirees, or as caregivers for an ill spouse or older parent (see Hayslip et al., in press). Indeed, even well-meaning and well-adjusted grandparents face numerous adjustments in dealing with the divorce/separation of an adult child (Doyle, O'Dywer, & Timonen, 2010), the serious illness of a grandchild (Wakefield et al., 2014), in discovering that a grandchild has been exposed to domestic violence (Semberg, 2013), or in dealing with the fact that a grandchild is GLBQ ('gay, lesbian, bisexual, and queer') (Scherrer, 2010).

What clinicians can do to help grandparents and their grandchildren

There are many things that practitioners can do to help grandparents, and in so doing, also strengthen relationships with their grandchildren.

As these have been discussed in depth elsewhere (see Hayslip, Maiden, Page, & Dolbin-MacNab, 2015), we address them only in brief here. Clearly, mental health professionals need to be aware of the above issues confronting most grandparents *as well as* to those connected to the unique circumstances of grandparents whose grandchild has died, whose adult children have divorced, or who have taken on the caregiving role in raising their grandchildren. For some grandparents, individual or family counselling might be necessary (see Hayslip, Maiden, Page, & Dolbin-MacNab, 2015), while for others, psychoeducational or support groups, or other community resources/programming designed specifically for grandparents are more appropriate.

As pointed out by Hayslip, Maiden, Page, & Dolbin-MacNab, 2015, at the minimum, clinicians should regularly explore the particular challenges a given middle-aged or older adult faces specifically related to grandparenting. Importantly, persons may expect and look forward to the role, but be denied access to their grandchildren. While these issues may not be central to grandparents' presenting concerns, they may nevertheless create some distress and relationship difficulties. Clinicians should realize that although there are many positives associated with the grandparenting role, it has the potential to disrupt one's life plans and create relational conflict. It is worth noting that for some older grandparents and/or those whose health is poor, they may fear that they may not live long enough or be in good enough health to enjoy their grandchildren.

For many grandparents, disappointment in what the grandparent role has turned out to be or confusion about how the role should be defined can be a serious and major threat to their relationships with their children and grandchildren as well as negatively impact their own mental health. Professionals can be helpful in assisting grandparents in identifying those aspects of grandparenting that are the most fulfilling to them. In reframing grandparenting in this manner, grandparents can view themselves as *resources* in their grandchildren's lives, and grandparents can learn to develop strategies for building close emotional connections with their grandchildren and providing them with ideas for activities they can do together, as discussed by Strom and Strom (2011).

In cases where conflict prevents contact with a grandchild, grandparents can also be assisted in developing coping strategies and in revising the meaning they have previously assigned to the role of grandparent (see Kivnick, 1983). For some grandparents, faced with situations that are beyond their control, that is being denied access to their grandchildren, redefining the salience of grandparenting for them in terms of its being a key component of their identity as middle-aged or older persons may be necessary. As this may be painful for some persons, clinicians can help support the grandparent in this process and aid in making choices, lessening unrealistic expectations, and relating to one's children and grandchildren in a manner that is consistent with this newly defined grandparent role.

In cases where relationship difficulties with an adult child are present regarding a grandparent's involvement, clinicians can help grandparents clarify what kinds of help are needed (e.g., cooking meals, grocery shopping) and what types of help might be less helpful (e.g., giving parenting advice, childcare for an infant), encouraging them to be open to feedback from their adult children in the process. Moreover, grandparents should discuss the extent to which they are willing and capable of providing the help they and an adult child have agreed upon.

In this respect, grandparents can be helped to understand and accept the boundaries as set by their adult children (e.g., scheduling visits to a grandchild). Importantly, understanding the perceptions of an adult child regarding their involvement in a grandchildren's upbringing (e.g., accepting a grandparent's love of the grandchild, recognizing a grandparent's desire to not be alone in later life, addressing a grandparent's concerns about the adequacy of adult child's parenting abilities) is a key component of such understanding, and grandparents and adult children should be assisted in finding ways to prevent their disagreements regarding the grandparent's role from negatively impacting the grandchildren (see Hayslip, Maiden, Page, & Dolbin-MacNab, 2015). In most cases, desired outcomes involve the addressing of conflicts and relational issues and the establishment of appropriate intergenerational boundaries. This spares the grandchildren of the consequences of problematic relationship dynamics.

Parents can also learn how to set boundaries with grandparents who cannot or do not wish to set healthy relational boundaries, as providing no help, the wrong kind of help, too much help, or help at the wrong time, for example insisting on being involved shortly after the birth of a grandchild, may be problematic. Likewise, grandparents can be too involved or not sufficiently involved in their grandchildren's lives. As pointed out by Hayslip et al. (in press), it is important to remember that these conflicts usually reflect larger issues of inclusion/exclusion, respect, and generativity. Ultimately, the clinician's role is to identify relational conflicts and help grandparents and their adult children (and in some cases their adult grandchildren) and find ways to resolve or manage those conflicts. Resolving such differences may be especially difficult and challenging when grandparents live far away from their grandchildren.

Unique Aspects of Grandparenting: Mental Health Considerations. In cases where a grandchild has died, grandparents must be encouraged not to neglect their own emotional needs in providing support to a grieving son or daughter. Additionally, as noted by Hayslip and White (2008), important for grandparents are continuing bonds with the grandchild who died, which can be achieved in many ways, for example participating in funerals/memorial services, sharing memories, developing holiday rituals, creating symbolic representations (e.g., photographs and objects representing the child). Being included by their adult children in these types of activities and being able to express their own feelings are important aspects of their relationship to a grieving child.

Clinicians can also help grandparents cope with their reactions to their adult children's divorce (see Hayslip, Maiden, Page, & Dolbin-MacNab, 2015). Grandparents can be taught how to best support their grandchildren (e.g., being available to listen, providing a place to stay, offering financial support), be alerted to the impact of being judgemental about the failure of an adult child's marriage, and be helped in how to encourage their adult children to make decisions in the grandchildren's best interests, as in not arguing in front of the children or allowing the children to maintain contact with both parents and grandparents (see Maiden & Zuckerman, 2008). Grandparents may also need help in expressing desires related to their future involvement with their grandchildren in a proactive but non-aggressive manner, with the hope that such proactive discussions may prevent future difficulties.

Regarding grandparents who are raising their grandchildren, as many grandparent caregivers display resilience in response to the many challenges they face (Hayslip et al., 2013), clinicians should emphasize grandparent resilience as a personal resource and assist such persons in coping with the challenges they face in raising a grandchild, to include gaining information and access to needed social, medical, or counselling-related services for them or their grandchildren. Importantly, to decrease grandparent caregivers' feelings of being stigmatized, clinicians can help reframe grandparent caregiving in terms of *choices* that one's children make *on their own*, versus seeing the adult child who has failed as a parent as someone whom *they* created and are, in effect, responsible for in raising someone who somehow was not up to the task of being a loving and effective parent. Reframing their situation in this manner allows them to feel less guilty about and less personally responsible for an adult child's parental and personal failings and enables them to work to find solutions to the challenges they now face as a full-time caregiver. They would also be more likely to attend to their own health difficulties, which either predated the raising of their grandchild or resulted from the stresses associated from the caregiving role.

An additional contribution that clinicians can make is in helping grandparent caregivers deal with the paradox of painful and pleasurable experiences in raising a grandchild which make defining oneself as a caregiver especially challenging (Backhouse & Graham, 2012), as well as coping with their anger, sadness, and disappointment regarding a parent's substance abuse (Templeton, 2011). In addition to support groups and assistance from friends and family, psychoeducational programmes are excellent options for increasing grandparent caregivers' social support as well as providing them with needed information about parenting, child development, and other relevant topics, as exemplified via the work of Strom and Strom (2011).

Though reliable data do not exist, it would not be unusual to observe that a small minority of grandparent caregivers may need more intensive psychotherapeutic help to help them address their distress and the complex, and often ambivalent feelings they may have about their caregiving responsibilities and their family relationships, especially to the extent that such feelings interfere with their everyday functioning and their ability to parent a grandchild. An important and common dimension of such feelings is clearly defining mutually agreed upon boundaries within the intergenerational family system (e.g., in having the grandparent set limits on an adult child's visits if that child is disruptive or dangerous).

Caregiving grandparents and grandchildren may also benefit from interventions designed to strengthen the emotional bond between the grandparent and the grandchild. It is important to note that strengthening this bond is an *equally important* therapeutic goal with grandparents who are *not* raising their grandchild.

In closing, we suggest that clinicians attend to any biases they may have regarding grandparent caregiving (e.g., that grandparent caregivers must have been poor parents), the death of a child (e.g., that the grandparent should support the adult child at all costs to himself/herself), or about an adult child's divorce (e.g., that grandparents' marriages serve as a model for the divorce and personal failure of their adult children). Recognizing and confronting such personal biases can enable the clinician to avoid being judgemental of grandparents in such situations. In this manner, they can be most effective in supporting *all* grandparents in the face of any distress they may be experiencing, and consequently strengthen the bonds with their grandchildren.

References

Ahrons, C.R. (2007). Family ties after divorce: long-term implications for children. *Family Process, 46,* 53–65.
American Association of Retired Persons (AARP). (2002). *The Grandparent Study.* Washington, DC.
Bailey, J., Hill, K., Oesterle, S., & Hawkins, D. (2009). Parenting practices and problem behavior across three generations: monitoring, harsh discipline, and drug use in the intergenerational transmission of externalizing behavior. *Developmental Psychology, 45,* 1214–1226.
Backhouse, J., & Graham, A. (2012). Grandparents raising grandchildren: negotiating the complexities of role identity conflict. *Child and Family Social Work, 17,* 305–315.
Backhouse, J., & Graham, A. (2013). Grandparents raising grandchildren: acknowledging the experience of grief. *Australian Social Work, 66,* 440–454.
Baker, L., & Silverstein, M. (2008). Preventative health behaviors among grandmothers raising grandchildren. *Journals of Gerontology: Social Sciences, 63B,* S304–S311.
Bangerter, L., & Waldron, V. (2014). Turning points in long distance grandparent-grandchild relationships. *Journal of Aging Studies, 29,* 88–97.
Boquet, J., Oliver, D., Wittenberg-Styles, E., Doorenbos, A., & Demiris, G. (2011). Taking care of a dying grandparent: case studies of grandchildren in the hospice caregiver role. *American Journal of Hospice and Palliative Medicine, 28,* 564–568.

Celdran, M., Tirado, C., & Villar, F. (2011). Learning from the disease: lessons drawn from adolescents having a grandparent suffering from dementia. *International Journal of Aging and Human Development, 68*, 243–259.

Cherlin, A., & Furstenberg, F. (1986). *The New American Grandparent.* New York: Basic Books.

Coali, D., & Hertwig, R. (2011). Grandparental investment: a relic of the past or reinvestment in the future? *Current Directions in Psychological Science, 20*, 93–98.

Combrinck-Graham, L. (1985). A developmental model for family systems. *Family Process, 24*, 139–150. doi: 10.1111/j.1545-5300.1985.00139.x.

Condon, J., Corkindale, C., Luszcz, M., & Gamble, E. (2013). The Australian first-time grandparents study: time spent with a grandchild and its predictors. *Australasian Journal on Ageing, 32*, 21–27.

Connidis, I.A. (2010). *Family Ties and Aging.* Thousand Oaks, CA: Pine Forge Press.

Doka, K.J. (ed.). (2002). *Disenfranchised Grief: New Directions, Challenges, and Strategies for Practice.* Champaign, IL: Research Press.

Doyle, M., O'Dywer, C., & Timonen, V. (2010). 'How can you just cut off a whole side of the family and say move on?' The reshaping of paternal grandparent-grandchild relationships following divorce or separation in the middle generation. *Family Relations, 59*, 587–598.

Drew, L., & Smith, P. (1999). The impact of parental separation/divorce on grandparent-grandchild relationships. *International Journal of Aging and Human Development, 48*, 191–216.

Dunifron, R. (2012). The influence of grandparents in the lives of children and adolescents. *Child Development Perspectives, 7*, 55–60.

Even-Zohar, A. (2011). Intergenerational solidarity between adult grandchildren and their grandparents with different levels of functional ability. *Journal of Intergenerational Relationships, 9*, 128–145.

Ferguson, J., & Ready, D. (2011). Expanding notions of social reproduction: grandparents' educational attainment and grandchildren's cognitive skills. *Early Childhood Research Quarterly, 26*, 216–226.

Friedman, D., Hechter, M., & Kreager, D. (2008). A theory of the value of grandchildren. *Rationality and Society, 20*, 31–63.

Generations United. (2009). *Grandfacts: Data, Interpretation, and Implications for Caregivers.* Washington, DC: Author.

Goodsell, T., Bates, J., & Behnke, A. (2011). Fatherhood stories: grandparents, grandchildren, and gender differences. *Journal of Social and Personal Relationships, 28*, 134–154.

Geurts, T., Tilburg, Van T., & Poortman, A. (2012). The grandparent-grandchild relationship in childhood and adulthood: a matter of continuation? *Personal Relationships, 19*, 267–278.

Hagestad, G.O. (1985). Continuity and connectedness. In: V.L. Bengtson & J.F. Robertson (eds), *Grandparenthood*, pp. 31–48. Beverly Hills, CA: Sage.

Hayslip, B., Davis, S., Neumann, C., Goodman, C., Smith, G., Maiden, R., & Carr, G. (2013). The role of resilience in mediating stressor-outcome relationships among grandparents raising their grandchildren. In: B. Hayslip & G. Smith (eds), *Resilient Grandparent Caregivers: A Strengths-Based Perspective*, pp. 48–69. New York: Routledge.

Hayslip, B., Maiden, R., Page, K., & Dolbin-MacNab, M. (2015). Grandparenting. In: P. Lichtenberg, B., Mast, B., Carpenter & J. Wetherell (eds), *APA Handbook*

of Clinical Geropsychology, pp. 497–511. Washington, DC: American Psychological Association.
Hayslip, B., & Glover, R. (2008). Traditional grandparents' views of their caregiving peers' parenting skills: Complimentary or critical? In: B. Hayslip & P. Kaminiski (eds), *Parenting the Custodial Grandchild: Implications for Clinical Practice*, pp. 149–164. New York: Springer.
Hayslip, B., Glover, R., Harris, B., Miltenberger, P., Baird, A., & Kaminski, P. (2009). Perceptions of custodial grandparents among young adults. *Journal of Intergenerational Relationships, 7,* 209–224.
Hayslip, B., Glover, R., & Pollard, S. (in press). Traditional grandparent peers' perceptions of custodial grandparents: Extent of life disruption and needs for social support, social, and mental health services. In: M.H. Meyer (ed.), *Grandparenting in the US*. Amityville, NY: Baywood.
Hayslip, B., Herrington, R., Glover, R., & Pollard, S. (2013). Assessing attitudes toward grandparents raising their grandchildren. *Journal of Intergenerational Relationships, 11,* 1–24.
Hayslip, B., & Kaminski, P. (2005). Grandparents raising their grandchildren: a review of the literature and suggestions for practice. *The Gerontologist, 45,* 262–269.
Hayslip, B., Maiden, R., Page, K., & Dolbin-MacNab, M. (in press). Grandparenting. In: P. Lichtenberg, B. Mast, B. Carpenter & J. Wetherell (eds), *APA Handbook of Clinical Geropsychology*. Washington, DC: American Psychological Association.
Hayslip, B., & Page, K. (2012). Grandparenthood: Grandchild and great-grandchild relationships. In: R. Blieszner & V. Bedford (eds), *Handbook of Families and Aging*, pp. 183–212. Santa Barbara, CA: Praeger.
Hayslip, B., & White, D. (2008). Grandparents as grievers. In: M.S. Stroebe, R.O. Hansson, W. Stroebe & H. Schut (eds), *Handbook of Bereavement Research*, 3rd edition, pp. 441–460. Washington, DC: American Psychological Association.
Henderson, C., Hayslip, B., Sanders, L., & Louden, L. (2009). Grandmother-grandchild relationship quality predicts psychological adjustment among youth from divorced families. *Journal of Family Issues, 30,* 1245–1264.
Hurme, H., Westerback, S., & Quadrello, T. (2010). (2010). Traditional and new forms of contact between grandparents and grandchildren. *Journal of Intergenerational Relationships, 8,* 264–280.
Hokoyama, M., & MaloneBeach, E. (2013). Predictors of grandparent-grandchild closeness: an ecological perspective. *Journal of Intergenerational Relationships, 11,* 32–49.
Holladay, S., Lackovich, R., Lee, M., Coleman, M., Harding, D., & Dento, D. (1998). (Re)constructing relationships with grandparents: a turning point analysis of granddaughters' relational development with maternal grandmothers. *International Journal of Aging and Human Development, 46,* 287–303.
Ihara, E., Horio, B., & Tompkins, C. (2012). Grandchildren caring for grandparents: modeling the complexity of family caregiving. *Journal of Social Service Research, 38,* 629–636.
Kaminski, P., Hayslip, B., Wilson, J., & Casto, L. (2008). Parenting attitudes and adjustment among custodial grandparents. *Journal of Intergenerational Relationships, 6,* 263–284. doi: 10.1080/1535077080215773.
Kivnick, H.Q. (1983). Dimensions of grandparental meaning: Deductive conceptualization and empirical derivation. *Journal of Personality and Social Psychology, 44,* 1056–1068. doi: 10.1037/0022-3514.44.5.1056.

Lampkin, C.L. (2012). *Insights and Spending Habits of Modern Grandparents*. Washington, DC: American Association of Retired Persons.

Maiden, R.J., & Zuckerman, C. (2008). Counseling grandparents parenting their children's children: Case studies. In: B. Hayslip, Jr. & P. Kaminski (eds), *Parenting the Custodial Grandchild: Implications for Clinical Practice*, pp. 197–214. New York, NY: Springer.

Mansson, D. (2013). Affectionate communication and relational characteristics in the grandparent-grandchild relationship. *Communication Reports, 26*, 47–60.

McCallion, P., & Kolomer, S. (2006). Depression and caregiver mastery in grandfathers caring for their grandchildren. In: B. Hayslip & J. Patrick (eds), *Custodial Grandparenting: Individual, Cultural, and Ethnic Diversity*, pp. 105–114. New York, NY: Springer.

Michels, T., Albert, I., & Ferring, D. (2011). Emotional relationships with grandparents: The adolescent view. *Journal of Intergenerational Relationships, 9*, 264–280.

Pew Foundation. (2010). *Since the Start of the Great Recession, More Children Raised by Grandparents.* http://pewresearch.org/pubs/1724.

Pratt, N., Norris, J.E., Hebblethwaite, S., & Arnold, M. (2008). Intergenerational transmission of values: family generativity and adolescents' narratives of parent and grandparent value teaching. *Journal of Personality, 76*, 171–198.

Reed, M.L. (2000). *Grandparents Cry Twice: Help for Bereaved Grandparents*. Amityville, NY: Baywood Publishing Company.

Reitzes, D.C., & Mutran, E.J. (2004a). Grandparent identity, intergenerational family identity, and well-being. *The Journal of Gerontology: Social Sciences, 59B*, S213–S219.

Reitzes, D.C., & Mutran, E.J. (2004b). Grandparenthood: factors influencing frequency of grandparent-grandchild contact and grandparent role satisfaction. *The Journal of Gerontology: Social Sciences, 59B*, S9–S16.

Rosow, I. (1985). Status role change through the life cycle. In: R. Binstock & E. Shanas (eds), *Handbook of Aging and the Social Sciences*, 2nd edition, pp. 62–93. New York, NY: Academic Press.

Scherrer, K. (2012). The intergenerational family relationships of grandparents of GLBQ grandchildren. *Dissertation Abstracts International: Humanities and Social Sciences, 72* (12-A), 4762 (abstract).

Seibert, A., & Kerns, K. (2009). Attachment figures in middle childhood. *International Journal of Behavioral Development, 33*, 347–355.

Semberg, L. (2013). Be there for my grandchild-grandparents' responses to their grandchildren's exposure to domestic violence. *Child and Family Social Work, 18*, 23–30.

Shore, R.J., Hayslip, B., & Henderson, C. (2000). Perceptions of grandparents' influence in the lives of their grandchildren. In: B. Hayslip & R. Goldberg-Glen (eds), *Grandparents Raising Grandchildren: Theoretical, Empirical and Clinical Perspectives*, pp. 35–46. New York: Springer.

Sigurdardottir, S., & Julursdottir, S. (2013). Reciprocity in relationships and support between grandparents and grandchildren: an Icelandic Example. *Journal of Intergenerational Relationships, 11*, 118–133.

Sims, M., & Rofail, M. (2013). The experience of grandparents who have limited or no contact with their grandchildren. *Journal of Aging Studies, 27*, 377–386.

Smith, T. (2012). Adult grandchildren providing care to frail elderly grandparents. *Dissertation Abstracts International: Section A: Humanities and Social Sciences, 72* (11-A), 4320 (abstract).

Smith, G.C., Palmieri, P., Hancock, G., & Richardson, R. (2008). Custodial grandmothers' psychological distress, dysfunctional parenting, and grandchildren's adjustment. *International Journal of Aging and Human Development, 67,* 327–358.
Stelle, C., Fruhauf, C., Orel, N., & Landry-Meyer, L. (2010). Grandparenting in the 21st Century: issues of diversity in grandparent-grandchild relationships. *Journal of Gerontological Social Work, 53,* 682–701.
Strom, P.S. & Strom, R.D. (2011). Grandparent education: raising grandchildren. *Educational Gerontology, 37,* 910–923.
Templeton, L. (2012). Dilemmas facing grandparents with grandchildren affected by parental substance abuse. *Drugs, Education, Prevention, and Policy, 19,* 11–18.
Thomas, J. (1990). The grandparent role: a double bind. *International Journal of Aging and Human Development, 31,* 169–177.
Uhlenberg, P. (2009). Children in an aging society. *Journal of Gerontology: Social Sciences, 64B,* S489–S496.
Villar, F., Triado, C., Piazo-Hernandis, S., Cedlran, M., & Sole, C. (2010). Grandparents and their adolescent grandchildren: generational stake or generational complaint? A study with dyads in Spain. *Journal of Intergenerational Relationships, 8,* 281–297.
Wakefield, C., Drew, D., Ellis, S., Doolan, E., McLoone, J., & Cohn, R. (2014). 'What they're not telling you': a new scale to measure grandparents' information needs when their grandchild has cancer. *Patient Care and Counseling, 94,* 351–355.
Watson, M. (2010). The facilitators and inhibitors for grandparents raising grandchildren in relation to parental involvement in school on behalf of their grandchildren. *Dissertation Abstracts International: Humanities and Social Sciences, 70*(7-A), 2839 (abstract).
Werner, P., & Lowenstein, A. (2001). Grandparenthood and dementia. *Clinical Gerontologist, 23,* 115–129.
Wise, R. (2010). Intergenerational relationship characteristics and grandchildren's perceptions of grandparent goal influence. *Journal of Intergenerational Relationships, 8,* 54–68.
Won, S. (2010). The closeness between grandparents and grandchildren and its impact on grandparents' well-being. *Dissertation Abstracts International Section A: Humanities and Social Sciences, 71* (2-A), 717 (abstract).
Xu, L., & Chi, I. (2011). Life satisfaction among rural Chinese grandparents: the roles of intergenerational family relationship and support exchange with grandchildren. *International Journal of Social Welfare, 20,* S148–S159.
Yorgason, J., Padilla-Walker, L., & Jackson, J. (2011). Nonresidential grandparents' emotional and financial involvement in relation to early adolescent grandchild outcomes. *Journal of Research on Adolescence, 21,* 552–558.

18
The Psychology of Possibilities: Extending the Limits of Human Functioning

Christelle Ngnoumen and Ellen Langer

Bad apples and the elderly: Ageing, health, and illness as problems of definition

In a study by Langer and Crum (2007), female room attendants who were primed to view their work as a form of exercise demonstrated decreases in BMI, waist-to-hip ratio, and weight. This study showed that – especially for individuals unaware that they are getting required amounts of physical exercise – priming the idea of exercise can result in benefits without actually changing daily habits. The results support a monistic model of human functioning, which sees the mind and body as ontologically indistinct components of a single system. The study suggests that female attendants could not previously experience the benefits of their work owing to the lack of its inclusion in common conceptions and national public health definitions of physical activity. This calls into question the extent to which national conceptions and labels of health and disease perpetuate the prevalence of these diseases. As researchers and medical professionals, we still don't fully know the extent to which the institutionalization of individuals with mental illness and with chronic disease is merely a direct result of the institutionalization of their labels and conceptions into the larger social system in the first place. In other words, it could be that we don't really become sick until the hand that feeds us apples decides to call them bad apples.

The issue concerning ageing, health, and disease as related to problems of definition is perhaps best expressed in McWhinney's (1987) characterization of illness as 'the subjective perception by a patient of an objectively defined disease'. In other words, the medical world designs labels, which are then mindlessly consumed by the general public, in turn dictating how individuals attend to themselves. By way of this process, labelled individuals' identities crystallize around the labels that they are given, leading to an adoption of stereotypical behaviours portrayed through the media.

Unfortunately, because the media serves in transmitting information and labels, increased globalization and westernization (which includes the transmission of the English language and of English labels) has contributed to what Ethan Watters coins the 'Americanization of Mental Illness', or the spreading of American definitions and conceptualizations of mental illness and abnormality across other cultures. This has further contributed to overmedicalization and to decreased responses to mind-body medicine. The prescribing and use of pharmaceutical interventions dichotomizes mind and body by fuelling an illusion of symptoms as stable and beyond individuals' control.

Old? Senior? Elder? Elderly? For some, the word 'elderly' still strikes a nerve despite its adoption as a less pejorative label for ageing individuals in contemporary language. Contrary to popular usage, the terms 'elder' and 'elderly' are not synonymous. The former is an adjective and is used relatively (e.g., My elder brother, Henry, is three years older than me) whereas the latter is a noun that describes a wise and respected individual of advanced age. The majority of the general population misuses the two terms, however. Unfortunately, the relative – and flexible – nature of the term 'elder' tends to be overlooked and is ascribed the same assumption of stability as labels of illness. Relatedly, the venerable qualities originally subsumed in the term 'elderly' are also overlooked, and people focus solely on the seemingly stable aspect of advanced age.

In a discussion of ageism, Palmore (2010) describes how prejudice and discrimination against older people reduces longevity. Both positive and negative forms of ageism pervade most social structures. Elders are employed less and are residentially segregated. Age-dependent federal and state benefit programmes such as Supplemental Security Income (SSI) and Medicare reinforce shame among elders. Within the family, norms against older women marrying younger men and norms against widows and divorced elders remarrying all fuel the same stereotypes about ageing that leave elders undermined, neglected, and in worst cases abused (Palmore, 2010). Similar to labels of illness, our society's labels for ageing individuals have managed to foster implicit negative attitudes about the elderly as being inflexible, incompetent, low in personal control, and susceptible to ill-health.

From acute diseases to chronic illness: Changes in conceptions of ageing and health

Over the past century, improved medical care and prevention efforts have resulted in a dramatic increase in life expectancy, from 47 years for Americans born in 1900 to 79 years for those born in 2009 (Centers for Disease Control and Prevention [CDC], 2014). This drastic shift in life expectancy coincides with a major shift in the leading causes of death in the US, moving away from infectious and acute diseases (e.g., pneumonia, tuberculosis, diphtheria) towards more chronic and degenerative illnesses (e.g., heart disease, cancer, diabetes). In 2010, the top three causes of death for US adults aged 65 or older were heart disease (27%), cancer (22%), and respiratory disease (7%) (CDC, 2014). Many researchers have concluded from such statistics that ageing and chronic illness are inextricably linked.

A diagnosis of a chronic disorder can be psychologically devastating (Phillips & Pagnini, 2014). Chronic illnesses are often preventable, however, and while it is typically assumed that susceptibility to these illnesses and disabilities increases with age, poor health is not an inevitable consequence of ageing. Moreover, ageing is not an inevitable consequence of an innate and time-activated genetic programme as biologists assumed 50 years ago. To date, there is no direct evidence that age changes are governed by a genetic programme (Hayflick, 2010). In fact, there is more direct evidence that shows that ageing is accelerated – and more importantly impeded – by psychological, behavioural, and environmental factors within the individual's control. To prevent the onset of chronic illness, for example, CDC recommends that people adopt healthier behaviours (e.g., regular physical activity, a healthy diet, a tobacco-free lifestyle), and claims that getting regular health screenings (i.e., mammograms, colonoscopies) can reduce a person's risk for most chronic diseases, including the leading causes of death (Blackman, Kamimoto, & Smith, 1999). While numerous national efforts have been placed on educating the public about the behavioural and environmental factors associated with health, less of an emphasis has been placed on educating the public about the impact of mental processes on health and well-being.

A vast literature provides strong evidence for the potentially powerful influence of mental processes on health and well-being (e.g., Langer, Janis, & Wolfer, 1975; Miller & Seligman, 1975; Langer & Rodin, 1976; Schultz, 1976; Rodin & Langer, 1977; Langer, Rodin, Beck, Weinman, & Spitzer, 1979; Langer, Beck, Janoff-Bulman, & Timko, 1984; Kamen & Seligman, 1987; Langer, Perlmuter, Chanowitz, & Rubin, 1988; Peterson, Seligman, & Vaillant, 1988; Scheier, Matthews, & Owens, 1989; Kamen-Siegel, Rodin, Seligman, & Dwyer, 1991; Scheier & Carver, 1992; Levy & Langer, 1994; Maier & Smith, 1999; Levy, Hausdorff, Hencke, & Wei, 2000; Levy, 1996, 2003; Levy, Slade, Kunkel, & Kasl, 2002; Cohen, Doyle, Turner, Alper, & Skoner, 2003; Levy, Slade, & Gill, 2006; Levy & Leifheit-Limson, 2009; Levy, Zonderman, Slade, & Ferrucci, 2009). For example, Langer and Rodin (1976) found that institutionalized elderly adults who were encouraged to assume a more engaged role in their lives (i.e., by making more decisions) became more alert, more active, happier, and healthier. Follow-up data 18 months later revealed that the experimental group also lived longer than comparison groups. Furthermore, 15% of the experimental group had died versus 30% of the comparison group (Rodin & Langer, 1977). Other studies have demonstrated that cognitive reappraisals may provide relief from the pains of major surgery (Langer, Janis, & Wolfer, 1975). Studies have also found that perceived health was a better predictor of mortality than actual health (Kaplan & Camacho, 1983; Idler & Kasl, 1991; Levy, Slade, Kunkel, & Kasl, 2002). Perhaps some of the strongest evidence in support of the powerful influence of mindsets on health and well-being comes from within the medical world itself and its observation of placebo effects. Langer (2009) observes that subjects exposed to fake poison ivy developed real rashes. Similarly, people given placebo caffeine have been shown to experience increased motor performance and heart rate (and other effects congruent with the subjects' beliefs about the effects of caffeine and not with its pharmacological effects).

Mind-body monism: Evidence for the powerful influence of mindsets on aging and health

Research rooted in mindfulness theory, such as Ellen Langer's work on mindlessness and choice, involves an approach to improving physical and psychological health that is based on an assumption that the mind and body comprise a single system. According to mind-body monism, both mental processes and bodily processes are essentially part of one substance, and of one underlying reality. According to this view, every change in the human being is simultaneously a change at the level of the 'mind' (e.g., cognitive and attitudinal changes) as well as the 'body' (e.g., cellular, hormonal, and neural changes). The influence of people's interpretations on the ways their bodies respond was confirmed by research which found that people can achieve better health through reorienting their attitudes towards themselves and their environments (Feltz & Landers, 1983; Fansler, Poff, & Shephard, 1985; Lee, 1990; Page, Levine, & Leonard, 2005; Langer & Crum, 2007).

Levy and Langer (1994) explored the role of cultural beliefs about ageing on memory loss among elderly American and Chinese participants. They wanted to determine whether negative stereotypes about ageing contribute to memory loss in old age. This study compared the memory performance of younger and older participants from mainland Chinese, American deaf, and hearing American cultures. The study revealed an interaction in which younger participants from the three groups performed similarly on the memory tasks, whereas the older deaf and older Chinese participants outperformed the older American hearing group. The authors found a positive correlation between views about ageing and memory performance among the older participants. The results suggest that cultural beliefs about ageing play a role in determining the degree of memory loss people experience in old age.

Langer, Chanowitz, Palmerino, Jacobs, Rhodes, and Thayer (1990) demonstrated that humans have the capacity to shift discontinuously to an 'earlier' context or mindset. Specifically, elderly men between 70 and 75 years of age were taken to a retreat to live for a week as if it were 20 years earlier. The experimental group had participants attempt to be psychologically where they were 20 years ago (e.g., participants were instructed to hold all discussions about the past in the present tense). The control group had participants reminisce about the past of 20 years previously and implicitly included the recognition that they were now here, 20 years later (e.g., participants were instructed to hold all discussions about the past in the past tense). Results indicated that this reverse temporal shift in participant's mindsets was followed by a reverse temporal shift in participant's physical and cognitive functioning. Based on ratings of facial photographs by judges blind to the hypothesis, both groups looked younger after the intervention compared to before the intervention. Compared to the control group, participants in the experimental group showed a greater improvement on finger length – an index of joint flexibility – and manual dexterity. Finger length increased for 37.5% of the experimental group and remained the same for the rest of the group, whereas 33.3% of the comparison group actually got worse on this measure. Only 1% in this latter group improved. There was also an increase in sitting height for the experimental group when compared with the sitting height of the control group. Those in the experimental group were able to sit taller, and they also had gained more weight, as revealed in measures of body weight, tricep skinfold, and bideltoid breadth. On the Digit Symbol subtest of the Wechsler Adult Intelligence Scale (WAIS) – a measure of attention, perceptual speed, motor speed, visual scanning, and memory – 63% of the experimental group improved their scores, compared to only 44% of the control group.

Langer et al. (2010) demonstrated improved vision in young adults as a result of simple mindset manipulations. To test the malleability of visual acuity – measured using the Snellen eye chart – participants were presented with several mindset-primes such as pilots have excellent vision, one is bound to see less as one reads down the eye chart, and one should be able to read the first few lines of an eye chart. In all experiments, comparison groups did not differ significantly in their baseline visual performance. After the mindset intervention, however, significant differences in visual acuity manifested. For individuals who were primed with the pilot mindset, vision improved by 40%. In reversing the order of the Snellen chart (which thereby primed individuals with the mindset that the letters would soon become readable), participants accurately saw a significantly greater proportion of letters from the smallest line of the reversed Snellen chart. Lastly, in presenting a shifted Snellen chart (e.g., a chart that began with letters equivalent to those of medium-size letters on the normal chart, thereby exploiting individuals' pre-existing mindset that they should be able to read the first few lines of the chart), participants read significantly more letters accurately when the letters were presented at the top of the chart compared to when they were presented at the bottom third of the chart. By using a range of mindset manipulations, the researchers extended the priming literature to vision and were able to explore visual acuity in mundane circumstances, allowing for greater generalization.

Hsu, Ching, and Langer (2010) found that cues that directly and indirectly signal ageing prime diminished capacity. Moreover, the absence of age cues primes improved health and longevity. Across a series of experiments, they found that women who think they look younger after having their hair coloured or cut show a decrease in blood pressure and appear younger in controlled photographs; clothing is an age-related cue that influences longevity; baldness cues old age and influences the speed of ageing; women who bear children later in life are positively influenced by the surrounding presence of younger age-related cues; and large spousal age differences result in age-incongruent cues that differentially affect longevity.

Taken together, the aforementioned studies suggest that mindsets – implicit beliefs and expectations that people hold about actions, behaviours, activities, and about members of specific social groups – have both indirect and direct effects on health. It is such emphasis on psychosocial influences on health that triggered the development of the biopsychosocial model of health (Engel, 1977), which argues that health and illness are the products of interactions among biological (e.g., genetic predispositions such as sex), psychological (e.g., personalities and construals), and social factors (e.g., cultural beliefs; poverty). The biopsychosocial model of health stands in contrast to the biomedical model of health. The biomedical model of health is the traditional view of Western medicine, and it conceptualizes health as the absence of deviations from a norm of measurable somatic variables (Engel, 1977; Papas, Belar, & Rozensky, 2004). A critical assumption of the biomedical model of health is that social, psychological, and behavioural factors play little or no role in health. As such, the biomedical model subscribes to reductionism (e.g., the view that complex phenomena are ultimately derived from a single primary principle) and mind-body dualism (e.g., the view that mental processes and the body are fundamentally different and separate entities).

The implications of the aforementioned findings that positive mindsets can have positive effects on one's health have been largely obscured as researchers have devoted their energies to finding mediating – as opposed to direct – links between such 'psychological' interventions and 'physical' consequences. Such focus on mediating links is based on the assumption of a split between the mind and the body, the mind-body dualism that is inherent in the biomedical model of health. Much research attention has been sidetracked from accepting the fact that the mind has direct and indirect influences on the body, which subsequently deterred further investigations from exploring how such influences can be beneficially maximized. As such, there may be vast areas of human potential, ordinarily latent, that have remained outside our conscious influence. Mindfulness theory research, such as the work by Langer and Crum (2007), has successfully delineated the actual full potential of the mind-body whole, and has demonstrated how a more mindful attitude can lead to the achievement of much richer levels of human development. At the core of this view is the psychology of possibility, wherein previously presumed 'limits' to human functioning are questioned.

Extending human functioning and health through mindful re-labelling

Mindlessness holds things still and creates an illusion of stability (Langer, 2009). In reality, however, nothing stays still. A narrow understanding of illness promotes a limited understanding of cure, which consequently closes us off to the benefits of alternative therapeutic interventions. The large prevalence of chronic illness among the elderly population seems to have unfortunately led to an implicit association between chronic illness and old age such that old age is commonly viewed as a period of inevitable cognitive and physical decline and has been used as an inaccurate predictor of performance and ability (Langer, 1982). Furthermore, the language commonly used to describe illness, such as chronic and in remission, constrains individuals' experiences by priming expectations of ill-health and dictating attention and behaviour. This language also creates the illusion that symptoms are stable and unmanageable. Individuals quickly adopt stereotypical responses and behaviours that are in line with particular illnesses. It is in this manner that labels corresponding to chronic conditions rob individuals of personal control and potentially prevent the achievement of optimal health and well-being.

Scientific investigations are what generate the profiles of various diseases, including their commonly experienced symptoms, prognoses, and successful forms of therapeutic interventions. Generally, profiles of diseases are based on mere associations and averages and therefore do not provide information about the moment-to-moment experiences of those conditions. Despite the fact that the majority of health information is obtained through correlational research, Langer (2009) found that there is a tendency among researchers to transform probabilities into absolutes. This health information is mindlessly consumed by the general public, and the pre-formed symptom categories it provides encourage individuals to overlook their idiosyncratic experiences which, for the most part, are never wholly in line with the normative data gathered across different individuals.

The crystallization of mindsets, either resulting from mindset inertia (i.e., the tendency for a mindset to remain stable because it was previously successful) or from the absence of relevant environmental triggers, is likely to be accompanied by a corresponding crystallization of physical functioning. Changing individuals' stereotypical mindsets about health (e.g., that physical functioning necessarily deteriorates with age) to more positive mindsets about health (e.g., that the order typically assumed to exist between the stages in any developmental process is not inevitable) can potentially give rise to corresponding changes in physical functioning (Langer, 1989, 2006, 2008; Langer et al., 1990). Stereotypes about how we 'should' age and what our 'limits' are prevent us from considering alternative possibilities and prevent us from uncovering our true potential. Once we shake loose from the negative clichés that dominate our thinking about health, we can mindfully open ourselves to possibilities for more productive lives no matter what our age (Langer et al., 2010). Importantly, mindfulness-based studies underscore the significance of exploring the as-yet-untapped potential of the mind-body whole. Most of the research in the field is concerned primarily with the extinct (e.g., 'what has been') and the extant (e.g., 'what actually is'). Most of us live sealed in unlived lives, constrained by stereotypes we've adopted as truths.

Langer and Abelson (1974) were the first to note the overwhelming power of labels in dictating consequent decisions and behaviour. Following research rooted in labelling theory has demonstrated that people who are labelled ill experience a decline in their general functioning and self-esteem that is more pronounced compared with individuals suffering from the same symptoms who are not labelled (Lai, Hong, & Chee, 2000). In a preliminary study, Langer and colleagues assessed the effects of the labels cured and in remission on breast cancer survivors' general health and well-being. Specifically, cured primed the idea of health while in remission primed illness. Results revealed that participants who saw their cancer as cured reported higher scores on measures of general health and emotional well-being compared to participants who considered themselves in remission. These results suggest an inextricable relationship between psychological processes (e.g., how participants perceived their illness) and health outcomes (e.g., subjective and evaluative well-being). These results suggest that patients' general health may improve upon calling those in remission cured and upon instructing them to focus on moments during which they do not experience any symptoms.

Given the increasing rates in chronic illness as well as the increasing associated healthcare costs observed over the last century, it is puzzling that there remains a reluctance to inform the public of the ways in which health definitions can become self-fulfilling by shaping individuals' conceptions and experiences of illness. On the one hand, one could argue – as many have – that such silence from the medical world first occurred when the hand that feeds us noticed that it profited from selling bad apples. Such arguments are built upon the observations that, contrary to the belief that disease spreads as a function of people, patients – and thus revenue – seem to grow as a function of disease. To date, about 75% of the wealth in America comes from the wallets of people over 50 years of age (Bouchez, 2010), which coincidentally also happens to be the same group of people who are the targets of ageism and of healthcare burdens (Palmore, 2010). On the other hand, some have also argued that the increased revenue model only holds until a certain point, after which too many people made sick from bad apples presents an overall cost to the medical world, in which case more urgent measures would need to be taken to undo the damage that has been done. Perhaps alerting the public of the constraining and self-fulfilling power of normative data and of mindless labelling is where we now need to be.

How many apples a day? Reclaiming control through mindfulness

How we feel at any moment in time requires a careful inspection of the hands that feed us, when they fed us, what they fed us, and why it is that they – as opposed to ourselves – are doing the feeding. It is sometimes the case that relying on the hands of others does us more harm than good. How can I be sure that this person feeding me is paying attention to my individual needs and allergies? How can I be sure that s/he is not simply mindlessly approaching me with a generalized diet that is applied to all hungers that seem similar to mine? And most importantly, what if I am not hungry?

It is important that we attend to our deviations from normative data about disease – to our idiosyncrasies. It is important that we do so without at the same time succumbing to the negative connotations that are often attributed to the term 'idiosyncracy' itself. By paying attention to particulars about ourselves and our bodies, we may come to find that our symptoms are less severe or less pervasive than the definitions of the particular illness we think we have had led us to think. This is to say, most clinical diagnoses consist of lists of symptoms that have been found to appear across a majority of individuals. Rarely does an individual experience all of the symptoms from that general list. It is therefore important for the individual to recognize the extent to which s/he diverges from – as opposed to converges with – that general list when evaluating functioning.

Our experiences of the diseases we think we have therefore necessitate frequent reality testing, for it may be that mood, and general well-being, can be significantly uplifted upon merely recognizing that one actually suffers from only two of five normatively reported symptoms as opposed to all five. Given the amount of significance and reality that we attach to numbers, as a culture, it would not be surprising to find that the actual exercise of counting down symptoms would yield improved mood and/or well-being. It is also important that people recognize the appearance of positive symptoms, or of markers of healing and improvement, throughout the course of their conditions. Individuals must also come to recognize that our culture is shaped by an aversion to pain such that medical concepts and labels are only framed in the negative. In the same way, only negatively framed deviations from normal are addressed. Because positively framed deviations from normal are rare, it is a lot harder for us to attend to and appreciate such moments, and they instead become lumped with neutrality. As a result of the health model's negative orientation, normative data about diseases and their symptoms become the norm and individual instances of neutrality or positivity become idiosyncrasies. An ironic reversal occurs here wherein the focus of negative symptoms becomes 'normative' while more healthy deviations from that [diseased] norm now gain the term 'idiosyncracies', which carries problematic negative connotations when in reality it shouldn't. This shift in our understanding of 'idiosyncracies' is a result of mindless adherence to outdated models of illness.

Mindlessness involves a tendency to operate automatically according to outdated principles and without paying attention to context and perspective. Mindfulness, its counterpart, is a process whereby one becomes aware and receptive to present moment experiences. It is marked by openness to novelty, alertness to distinctions, sensitivity to different contexts, and awareness of multiple perspectives. Whereas mindless views of ageing, health, and illness increase suffering, more mindful attitudes towards ageing and illness increase quality of life (Langer, 2009). More mindful and active engagement with our surroundings, such as by paying closer attention to variations in our individual experiences, allows us to create labels that fit those experiences more appropriately. Mindfully redefining our experiences by using our own labels redirects choice and the control of our care into our own hands.

Lessons for clinical practice

According to Greenbaum (2010), each generation has the potential to control and reinvent the final stage of life. Mindfulness-based research seeks to identify domains in which previously presumed 'limits' of human functioning could be controlled and extended, with the hope of uncovering a more enriched model of health. Mindfulness research seeks to demonstrate the powerful control that the mind has over physiological processes as well as to elucidate the extent of growth that is possible throughout all stages of the lifespan.

Psychological conditions such as depression and chronic pain mark the leading causes of disability in the United States, with an estimated 26% of the population afflicted each year, and accounting for 75% of medical expenses. More clinical interventions should consider exploring the ways in which better health can be attained through reorienting people's attitudes towards themselves and their environments. This has the greatest implication for people who cannot afford expensive therapeutic and pharmaceutical forms of treatment.

The language of illness primes expectations and dictates attention and behaviour. Patients' identities tend to crystallize around the diagnostic labels that they are given, leading to an adoption of stereotypical behaviours that support their clinical diagnoses. Keeping this in mind, greater efforts should be placed into encouraging people to overcome passive acceptance of labels, to consider both normative data about illness as well as their own personal idiosyncrasies, and to use – and importantly, to trust – this knowledge to guide their behaviours in a manner that benefits their health. Increasing people's self-awareness and curiosity through mindfulness techniques (e.g., viewing symptoms in novel ways; questioning assumptions about medical conditions) will introduce control over their symptoms. More perceived control over health and well-being increases health and happiness, and decreases dependence on more formal systems of health care.

References

Blackman, D.K., Kamimoto, L.A., & Smith, S.M. (1999). Overview: surveillance for selected public health indicators affecting older adults – United States. *Morbidity and Mortality Weekly Report CDC Surveillance Summaries, 48*, 1–6.

Bouchez, B. (2010). Marketing: Age is more than just a number. In: S. Greenbaum (ed.), *Longevity Rules: How to Age Well Into the Future*. Carmichael, CA: Eskaton.

Cohen, S., Doyle, W.J., Turner, R.B., Alper, C.M., & Skoner, D.P. (2003). Emotional style and susceptibility to the common cold. *Psychosomatic Medicine, 65*, 652 –657.

Crum, A.J., & Langer, E.J. (2007). Mind-set matters: exercise and the placebo effect. *Psychological Science 18*, 2, 165–171.

Engel, G.L. (1977). The need for a new medical model: a challenge for biomedicine. *Science, 196*, 129–136.

Fansler, C.L., Poff, C.L., & Shepard, K.F. (1985). Effects of mental practice on balance in elderly women. *Physical Therapy, 65*, 1332–1337.

Feltz, D.L., & Landers, D.M. (1983). The effects of mental practice on motor skill learning and performance: a meta-analysis. *Journal of Sport Psychology, 5*, 25–57.

Greenbaum, S. (ed.) (2010). *Longevity Rules: How to Age Well Into the Future*. Carmichael, CA: Eskaton.

Hayflick, L. (2010). The $1 billion misunderstanding. In: S. Greenbaum (ed.), *Longevity Rules: How to Age Well Into the Future*. Carmichael, CA: Eskaton.

Hsu, L.M., Chung, J., & Langer, E.J. (2010). The influence of age-related cues on health and longevity. *Perspectives in Psychological Science, 5*, 632–648.

Idler, E.L., & Kasl, S. (1991). Health perceptions and survival: do global evaluations of health status really predict mortality? *Journal of Gerontology, 46*, S55–S65.

Kamen, L. & Seligman, M.E. (1987). Explanatory style and health. In: M. Johnston & T. Marteau (eds), *Current Psychological Research and Reviews: Special Issue on Health Psychology, 6*, 207– 218.

Kamen-Siegel, L., Rodin, J., Seligman, M.E., & Dwyer, J. (1991). Explanatory style and cell-mediated immunity in elderly men and women. *Health Psychology, 10*, 229–235.

Lai, Y.M., Hong, C.P., & Chee, C.Y. (2000). Stigma of mental illness. *Singapore Medical Journal, 42*(3), 111–114.

Langer, E. (1982). Old age: An artifact? In: S. Kiesler & J. McGaugh (eds), *Aging: Biology and Behavior*. New York: Academic Press.

Langer, E. (1989). *Mindfulness*. Reading, MA: Addison-Wesley.

Langer, E. (2006). *On Becoming an Artist: Reinventing Yourself Through Mindful Creativity.* New York, NY: Ballentine.
Langer, E. (2008). Mindfulness/Mindlessness. In: S. Lopez (ed.), *Encyclopedia of Positive Psychology.* London, England: Blackwell Publishing.
Langer, E.J. (2009). *Counter Clockwise: Mindful Health and the Power of Possibility.* New York, NY: Ballantine Books.
Langer, E.J., & Abelson, R.F. (1974). A patient by any other name…: clinician group difference in labeling bias. *Journal of Consulting and Clinical Psychology, 42,* 4–9.
Langer, E., Beck, P., Janoff-Bulman, R., & Timko, C. (1984). The relationship between cognitive deprivation and longevity in senile and non-senile elderly populations. *Academic Psychology Bulletin, 6,* 211–226.
Langer, E., Chanowitz, B., Palmerino, M., Jacobs, S., Rhodes, M., & Thayer, P. (1990). Nonsequential development and aging. In: C. Alexander & E. Langer (eds), *Higher stages of Human Development: Perspectives on Adult Growth.* New York, NY: Oxford University Press.
Langer, E., Djikic, M., Pirson, M., Madenci, A., & Donohue, R. (2010). Believing is seeing: Using mindlessness (mindfully) to improve visual acuity. *Psychological Science, 21*(5), 661–666.
Langer, E.J., Janis, I.L., & Wolfer, J.A. (1975) Reduction of psychological stress in surgical patients. *Journal of Experimental Social Psychology, 11,* 155–165.
Langer, E., Perlmuter, L., Chanowitz, B., & Rubin, R. (1988). Two new applications of mindlessness theory: aging and alcoholism. *Journal of Aging Studies, 2,* 289–299.
Langer, E. & Rodin, J. (1976). Effects of choice and enhanced personal responsibility for the aged: a field experiment in an institutional setting. *Journal of Personality and Social Psychology, 34*(2), 191–199.
Langer, E., Rodin, J., Beck, P., Weinman, C., & Spitzer, L. (1979). Environmental determinants of memory improvement in late adulthood. *Journal of Personality and Social Psychology, 37*(11), 2003–2013.
Lee, J.R. (1990). Osteoporosis reversal: the role of progesterone. *International Journal of Clinical Nutrition, 10,* 384–391.
Levy, B. (1996). Improving memory in old age through implicit self-stereotyping. *Journal of Personality and Social Psychology, 71,* 1092–1107.
Levy, B.R. (2003). Mind matters: cognitive and physical effects of aging self-stereotypes. *Journal of Gerontology: Psychological Science, 58,* 203–211.
Levy, B., Hausdorff, J., Hencke, R., & Wei, J. (2000). Reducing cardiovascular stress with positive self-stereotypes of aging. *Journal of Gerontology: Psychological Sciences, 55,* 1–9.
Levy, B., & Langer, E. (1994). Aging free from negative stereotypes: successful memory in China and among the American deaf. *Journal of Personality and Social Psychology, 66,* 989–997.
Levy, B.R., & Leifheit-Limson, E. (2009). The stereotype-matching effect: greater influence on functioning when age stereotypes correspond to outcomes. *Psychology and Aging, 24,* 230–233.
Levy, B.R., Slade, M.D., & Gill, T. (2006). Hearing decline predicted by elders' age stereotypes. *Journal of Gerontology: Psychological Sciences, 61,* 82–87.
Levy, B.R., Slade, M., Kunkel, S., & Kasl, S. (2002). Longevity increased by positive self-perceptions of aging. *Journal of Personality and Social Psychology, 83,* 261–270.
Levy, B.R., Zonderman, A., Slade, M.D., & Ferrucci, L. (2009). Negative age stereotypes held earlier in life predict cardiovascular events in later life. *Psychological Science, 20,* 296–298.

Maier, H., & Smith, J. (1999). Psychological predictors of mortality in old age. *Journals of Gerontology: Psychological Sciences, 54B,* 44–54.
McWhinney, I.R. (1987). Health and disease: problems of definition. *Canadian Medical Association Journal, 136*(8), 815.
Miller, W.R. & Seligman, M.E. (1975). Depression and learned helplessness in man. *Journal of Abnormal Psychology, 84,* 228–238.
Page, S., Levine, P., & Leonard, A. (2005). Effects of mental practice on affected limb use and function in chronic stroke. *Archives of Physical Medicine and Rehabilitation, 86:* 399–402.
Palmore, E. (2010). How to reduce ageism. In: S. Greenbaum (ed.), *Longevity Rules: How to Age Well Into the Future.* Carmichael, CA: Eskaton.
Papas, R.K., Belar, C.D., & Rozensky, R.H. (2004). The practice of clinical health psychology: Professional issues. In T. Boll, R.G. Frank, E. Baum & J.L. Wallander (eds), *Handbook of Clinical Health Psychology: Volume 3. Models and Perspectives in Health Psychology.* Washington, DC: American Psychological Association.
Peterson, C., Seligman, M.E.P., & Vaillant, G.E. (1988). Pessimistic explanatory style is a risk factor for physical illness: a thirty-five year longitudinal study. *Journal of Personality and Social Psychology, 55,* 23–27.
Phillips, D. & Pagnini, F. (2014). A mindful approach to chronic illness. In: Ie, A., Ngnoumen, C. & Langer, E. (eds), *Handbook of Mindfulness.* New York, NY: Wiley-Blackwell.
Rodin, J., & Langer, E. (1977). Long-term effects of a control-relevant intervention with the institutionalized aged. *Journal of Personality and Social Psychology, 35*(12), 897–902.
Scheier, M.F., & Carver, C.S. (1992). Effects of optimism on psychological and physical well-being: the influence of generalized outcome expectancies. *Health Psychology, 16,* 201–228.
Scheier, M.F., Matthews, K.A., Owens, J.F., Magovern, G., Sr., Lefebvre, R.C., Abbott, R.A., & Carver, C.S. (1989). Dispositional optimism and recovery from coronary artery bypass surgery: the beneficial effects on physical and psychological well-being. *Journal of Personality and Social Psychology, 57,* 1024–1040.
Schulz, R. (1976). Effects of control and predictability on the physical and psychological well-being of the institutionalized aged. *Journal of Personality and Social Psychology, 33,* 563–573.
Watter, E. (2010, January 8). The Americanization of mental illness. *The New York Times.*

Index

Acceptance and Commitment Therapy (ACT), 2, 6, 102, 106, 109
  empirical evidence, 102, 109
adjustment problems, 118, 192, 229, 237
adolescence, 1, 6, 8, 10; 7, 33, 52, 92, 107, 124, 136, 138, 139, 141, 142, 149, 155, 158, 191, 234, 284
adoption, 11, 85, 177, 266, 267–9, 274, 275, 296, 297
adult child as gatekeeper, 165, 283
adventure mind, 245–9
adversary, 147
advisor, 111–19, 284
aetiology, 15, 18, 22, 27, 47
affectional bonds, 230, 232–3
ageism, 297, 304
aggression, 71, 92, 136, 140, 227–8, 233, 236–8
  see also violence
aging, 11–12, 296–9, 301, 305
alternative medicine, 14–27
American Psychiatric Association, 2, 47, 69
anger, 15, 59, 70, 72–4, 82, 107, 115, 146, 190, 192, 197–99, 202, 265, 285, 290
anorexia, 20, 190
anxiety, 1, 2, 5, 6, 8, 9, 14, 20, 23, 45, 52, 59–60, 68–79, 90–1, 109, 115, 147–8, 158, 160, 162, 172, 176–7, 187–9, 192–3, 197–202, 204–5, 227, 238, 257, 260, 266
anxious ambivalent patterns, 196
at-risk behaviour, 8
attachment, 8, 9, 104, 123, 142, 156, 187, 189–94, 196–204, 268, 282
attachment theory, 226, 230–3
attention, 1, 2, 15, 245, 254, 300–2, 304
autobiographical narratives, 36–8, 48
avoidance, 105, 106–7, 188, 193, 199

behavioral disinhibition, 136
behaviour, 4, 21, 25, 38, 42, 48, 52, 56, 69, 75, 84, 90, 92, 102–18, 239, 244, 246–47, 250, 262
behaviour-in-context, 103–4, 106
biochemical imbalances, 68
biological evolution, 5, 70, 73–4, 79, 230
biomedical model, 3, 16, 301
biopsychosocial, 3, 14, 52, 301
blame, 69–70, 72, 113, 164, 188, 190, 197, 199, 203, 252
borderline personality, 7, 109, 157

cancer, 41, 109, 298, 303
career success, 82–3
caring, 4, 8, 47, 58, 76–7, 111, 128–31, 280, 285
CBT (cognitive behavior therapy), 8, 110, 172
child behavior, 8, 172, 174–6
children, 14, 26, 33, 46, 52–63, 71–6, 81–94, 108, 111, 124–33, 135, 139, 143, 145, 147–50, 156, 165–6, 172–8, 182–3, 187–205, 209–18, 226–39, 246, 248, 249, 251, 252–4, 257, 263, 267–8, 271–3, 275, 279, 280, 289–91, 301
chronic illness, 297–8, 302–3
chronic stress, 7, 161
classroom climate, 58, 62
clinical case, 8, 193
clinical implications, 9, 27, 94, 173, 203–5, 276
cognitive
  functioning, 82, 85, 212, 300
  restructuring, 272, 273, 275
  style, 145, 265, 273
committed action, 106
communal trauma, 146
communication, 11, 23, 47, 76–7, 126, 138, 166, 174–5, 177, 181, 192, 208, 215, 218, 247, 268, 281, 283

community, 7, 12, 20, 33, 46, 52–3, 56, 58, 61, 91, 93–4, 102, 104, 112, 118, 123, 126, 128–9, 138, 143–4, 147–9, 166, 172–3, 181, 216, 268, 288
  violence, 1, 5, 7, 70–4, 91, 93, 136, 138–40, 142, 143, 146, 148, 154, 159, 161, 166, 203, 268, 282, 287
competence, 6, 54–7, 60, 90, 126, 128–31, 214, 218
conduct disorders, 1, 21, 90, 234, 238
confidence, 6, 57, 59, 128–31, 202
conflict management, 188
connection, 6, 70, 85, 86, 93, 103, 113, 119, 128–31, 137, 141, 150, 176, 208, 250, 255, 269, 288
context, 3, 4, 6, 33, 44, 47, 52–4, 58–60, 62, 92, 102, 110, 112, 114, 118–19, 123–4, 128, 130, 131, 143, 166, 189, 191, 194–5, 202–4, 212, 214, 245, 248, 251, 257, 261, 264, 266, 270, 272, 274, 279, 284, 287, 299, 305
contextual behavioural, 6, 102–8
contextualism, 103, 119, 128, 263
control, 12, 37, 41, 49, 72, 75, 113, 117, 128, 142, 144, 190, 192, 231, 245, 251, 268, 288, 297–8, 300, 302, 304–5
co-parenting, 192, 251, 286
coping, 136, 146, 155, 160, 177, 179, 188, 192, 198, 201, 229, 264, 270, 274, 288, 290
coping efficacy, 192
coping responses, 188
criminality, 7, 138–9, 148
crisis, 2, 43, 181, 249, 251, 259–60, 275, 282
cultural beliefs, 228, 299, 301
cultural bereavement, 44
cultural factors, 3, 7, 44
cultural psychiatry, 34, 39, 46–7
culture, 3, 5, 6, 14, 34, 43–8
  conflict, 45
  shock, 45
cure, 15, 16, 19–20, 24, 26, 209, 217, 302, 303
custodial grandparents, 286

day care, 123
death of a grandchild, 285, 287
defusion, 106, 107

delinquency, 129, 137, 139, 143, 146, 234, 237–8, 268
dependence, 1, 227, 265, 273, 306
depression, 1, 6, 8, 14–5, 17, 19–23, 25, 35–6, 41, 44, 52, 59, 69, 76, 83, 89, 109, 129, 137, 147, 156–60, 162, 176, 188, 192, 234, 237–8, 260, 265–6, 286, 305
development, 4, 6, 7, 9–11, 52–4, 59–62, 75, 92, 104, 107, 110, 119, 123–4, 126–33, 136–7, 140–2, 145, 149, 155, 166, 172–3, 176, 187–9, 192, 212, 214, 218, 226–30, 234, 236, 238, 259–76, 281, 284–5, 290, 302
developmental family system, 279
diagnosis, 2, 4, 14, 23, 34, 140, 214, 298
differentiation, 11, 262, 263, 265
discoverer, 111–19
disease, 1, 3–4, 15, 16, 23–5, 27, 34–5, 44, 47–8, 75, 135, 138, 178, 296, 297–8, 302–5
disenfranchised grief, 285
disruptive behaviours, 188
distress, 7, 8–9, 19, 25, 48, 55, 86–7, 146, 172, 187–90, 192, 202, 204–5, 230, 271, 286, 288, 291
divorce, 87, 125, 147, 191, 198, 249, 260, 282, 285–8, 290–1, 297
DNA-v model, 102–3, 106–14, 117–9
double bind, 284
drama therapy, 246
dyadic nature, 11
  relationships, 193

early intervention, 7, 43, 52, 109, 148–50, 195, 260
early years, 59
education, 4, 6, 9, 22, 25, 39, 41, 42, 49, 53, 54–8, 60–1, 78, 81, 83, 91–3, 106, 125, 129, 132, 138, 148, 208–18, 282–3
educational systems, 9
emotional
  freedom, 69, 74, 76, 79
  instability, 227–8, 237–8
  security, 192, 232
  trauma, 235
emotional expressiveness, 10

emotions, 5, 14, 55, 59, 68–79, 82, 85, 88, 90, 112–15, 119, 123, 129, 138, 142, 181, 191, 262, 272
empirical reality, 208, 211–3, 218
enactment, 10, 244, 246–50, 252–7
environmental variable, 8
epidemiology, 2
equilibrium, 264, 267, 275
equivalence, 7, 127, 132–3
ethics, 5, 35, 58, 74, 78
evaluation, 57, 84, 93, 123–4, 126, 142, 149, 181, 211, 218
evidence-based, 53, 56, 92, 163, 173, 180, 226
evolution, 5, 70–4, 79, 103, 119, 230, 232
evolutionary perspective, 230, 232
evolution science, 110, 119
expectations, 19, 26, 45, 86, 129–30, 147, 182, 209, 216, 231, 281, 283–4, 287, 301–2, 305
exploration, 77, 107, 113, 140, 189, 196, 203–4, 210, 231, 245–6, 257

family, 118, 124–6, 128, 132, 137–9, 143, 147–8, 150, 155–6, 158, 160, 163, 166, 172, 176, 178–80
  dynamics, 143, 155, 193, 205, 251, 280
  systems, 10, 245, 267, 279
  therapy, 8, 190, 195, 203, 205, 244–9, 251, 253–4, 256
field dependence-independence, 265, 273
film, 37, 40–1
friendships, 84, 113, 116, 124, 132
fun, 55, 251–3, 256
functional contextualism, 103, 119
fusion, 106–7

games, 92, 175, 245, 248, 250, 254, 256–7
genetic causes of emotional disorders, 68
genetic vulnerability, 7
Gestalt psychology, 10, 261, 273, 275
globalization, 34, 48, 297
goodness-of-fit, 132
grandchildren, 11–12, 279–91
grandparent, 8, 11–12, 26, 279–91
  caregiving, 280, 286, 288, 290, 291
  as resources, 286, 288

grandparent-grandchild contact, 279, 283
grandparent-grandchild dyads, 280, 287
grandparenting styles, 11, 284, 285
gratitude, 77–8, 81–2, 88–91
grief, 230, 274, 285
guidelines for empathic therapy, 77–8
guilt, 5, 15, 68–77, 190, 280, 290

habit, 6, 117, 257, 274, 296
happiness, 6, 14, 79, 81–2, 94, 130, 157, 181, 232, 250, 306
health, 1–6, 9, 12, 14–16, 21, 23–7, 34, 37, 40–1, 47–8, 52–63, 81–3, 88, 90, 109, 123, 125–7, 131, 132, 135–8, 143, 148, 154, 156, 161, 163, 172–3, 181, 187, 209, 213–4, 218, 229, 234, 236, 247, 263, 274, 282, 284, 286–7, 288, 290, 296–9, 301, 302–6
  ageing, 12, 296–9, 301, 305
  care, 9, 14, 23–4, 34–6, 38, 39, 41–3, 47–8, 123, 183, 208, 213–4, 218, 303
  economics, 2
  humanities, 34, 35–6, 40, 48
  promotion, 3, 4, 16, 52–62, 163
helplessness, 60, 69, 70, 72, 75–9, 198, 204
history, 1, 5, 10, 22, 24, 26–7, 35–6, 70, 83, 104, 105, 107–8, 110, 112–13, 115, 117, 137, 156–7, 166, 208, 217, 245, 260, 267, 279, 281, 287
history of special education, 208
holism, 270–1, 275
holistic/systems-developmental theory, 10, 259, 265
homeless youth, 7, 157
hope, 6, 59, 81–2, 84, 86, 88–91, 164, 244
household income, 87, 125, 129, 132
HSDT (holistic/systems developmental theory), 10–11, 265–8, 270–76
human nature, 69, 70–1, 79)
hunting, 71

idiosyncrasy, 304
illness, 1, 3–5, 12, 14–22, 24–7, 33–49, 54, 70, 76, 81, 135–6, 146, 147, 164, 217, 231, 237, 265, 280, 282, 287, 296–8, 302–6

immigrants, 46–8
implementation, 9, 47, 59, 61, 92, 93, 142, 180, 212, 216, 218
improvisation, 10, 244–5, 247
inclusion, 208, 211–14, 216, 218, 289
inclusive education, 9, 208, 211–13, 217
indicator, 6–7, 22, 55, 123–7, 129–33, 137
individual differences, 23, 88, 94, 260, 264–5, 268, 269–70, 274–5
influence model, 138
integration, 11, 42, 93, 208–12, 218, 261–3, 270–1
interdependence, 128, 130, 165, 209
international declarations, 211
Internet, 8, 24, 159, 172–4
  interventions, 172, 173, 176
  psychotherapy, 172
  therapy, 10
  treatment, 173–80
interventions, 3–12, 17, 19, 42–4, 53, 56–7, 60–3, 81–2, 88–94, 104, 108, 110, 119, 126, 148–50, 160, 164, 172–80, 182–83, 248, 256, 271–76, 279, 291, 297, 301–2, 305

labels, 12, 23, 77, 108, 203, 296–7, 302–6
language, 6, 7, 38, 46, 105, 114, 118, 124, 126–7, 131, 187–88, 215, 297, 302, 305
lay person, 14, 22
lessons, 26, 62, 149, 164, 215, 238, 256, 271, 305
life event, 7, 10, 11, 163, 165, 260–1, 272–5, 287
life satisfaction, 6, 81–4, 87, 90–1, 93, 158, 268, 279, 285
longevity, 11, 82–3, 284, 297, 301
love, 5, 10, 37, 74–9, 113, 138, 157, 226–27, 232, 237–9, 249, 260, 289

maladjustment, 10, 147, 188, 192, 228, 234, 235–6, 237–8
marital-distance regulators, 190
masking, 192
measurement model, 7, 129, 132
medical model, 3, 4, 20, 22, 68, 69, 203, 209, 245
medicine, 3, 5, 16, 17, 33–8, 43, 48–9, 81, 297, 301

memory, 15, 23–4, 299–300
mental health, 1–8, 14, 19, 36–43, 46–9, 52–62, 135–50, 172–6, 187, 229, 234, 245, 247, 266, 287–8
  illness, 1, 2, 15, 17–8, 20, 24–5, 36–45, 47–8, 54, 70, 76, 146–7, 164, 173, 237, 282, 296–7
  literacy, 15–16, 21–6
methodology, 25, 270
microsystems, 144
migration, 34, 44–6
mind, 3, 36–7, 41, 69, 78, 83, 139, 245, 249, 296, 299, 301
mind-body, 3, 83, 297
  dualism, 301
  monism, 299–302
mindfulness, 2, 12, 102, 108–9, 117, 271, 299, 301, 303, 304–6
mindsets, 12, 299–303
mis-matched patterns, 190
mood, 1, 38, 40, 85, 90, 93, 148, 177, 251, 257, 304
multiple models, 190
mutual validation, 10, 245–7, 257

natural selection, 5, 71–4
nature, 14, 69–70, 72, 75, 93, 111, 275, 280
  nurture, 59, 226
negative
  experiences, 7, 274
  legacy emotions, 5, 68, 72–9
neuroscience, 47, 70
normality (definitions of), 6
normalization, 108, 210
noticer, 111–19
nurturance, 10, 228, 232

online
  community, 181
  therapy, 8, 10, 159, 172, 173–5, 180
operant behavior, 104
optimism, 59, 84, 86, 88, 90–1, 273

paradigm shift, 2, 3, 33–49, 229, 245
parental
  acceptance, 9–10, 226
  acceptance-rejection, 226–36
  anxiety, 8
  conflict, 139, 191

depression, 176
  monitoring, 129, 137–8, 143, 149
  rejection, 10, 226–9, 234–5, 237–8
parenthood, 124, 266–7, 276
parenting, 8, 11, 60, 68, 129, 138–9, 148, 150, 172, 233, 249, 251, 286, 289–90
  interventions, 8, 172–80, 183
parent training, 104
patient, 3, 4, 7, 15–16, 20, 23, 25–7, 34–5, 38–9, 43–4, 48, 68–9, 79, 109, 156, 181, 260, 271–5, 296, 303, 305
peacemaker, 188
peer contagion, 142
periods of special needs education, 209
personality, 4, 7, 10, 17, 21, 27–8, 41, 52, 85–7, 92, 94, 109, 129, 130, 137, 140, 145, 149, 157, 162, 226–9, 233–4, 236–9, 271, 273, 282
person-in-environment, 11, 263–5, 268–9, 273–6
perspective, 3, 12, 14, 16–20, 27, 35, 38, 47, 77, 113, 118–9, 123–4, 128, 137, 141, 187, 193, 196, 208, 213–4, 216–7, 230, 232–3, 260, 270, 279, 284, 305
phenomenological interviews, 266, 268
physical
  abuse, 158, 162
  health, 14, 88, 126, 236, 287
  illness, 14–26, 38, 44
physiological responses, 191
place of special education (within health system), 214
planning, 61, 154, 155, 162, 247, 269, 270, 273–4
playfulness, 244, 257
positive psychology, 5, 10, 12, 14, 53, 68–9, 81–2, 88–9, 91–3, 259–60
  self-esteem, 10, 228, 237
post-partum
  depression, 266
pragmatic psychotherapy, 272–3
prehistoric emotions, *see* negative legacy emotions
prevention, 1, 4, 21, 52–3, 56, 135, 138, 165–6, 172–3, 214, 297
priming, 12, 296, 301–2

primitive emotions, *see* negative legacy emotions
problem-solving, 7, 53–4, 116, 141, 160–1, 175
prosocial gaming, 92
  relationships, 147, 149, 164–6
protective factors, 147, 149, 165–6
psychiatric diagnosis, 2, 14, 23, 27
psychiatry, 33, 34, 37–41, 43, 46–8
psychodrama, 247
psychological
  adjustment, 226–30, 232, 235–9
  flexibility, 106, 112, 117
  health, 1, 9, 156, 237, 299
  maladjustment, 10, 147, 188, 228, 234, 236–7
  vulnerability, 160
psychological abuse, 8
psychopharmacology, 20
psychotherapy, 2, 10, 17, 19, 38, 48, 90, 244, 246–7, 256, 272–3
PTSD, 7, 147, 160, 162
public attitudes, 15

rehearsal, 10, 244–57
relational frame theory, 103–5, 110, 118, 119
relationships, 3, 5, 7, 8, 10, 12, 15, 22, 47, 58, 60, 62, 70–9, 84–6, 88–90, 102, 112–14, 116, 119, 123–4, 129, 136, 138, 147–8, 157–8, 166, 187, 189, 191–3, 226, 230–4, 244–6, 250, 264–5, 267–71, 279–82, 284–5, 287–91
relative deprivation, 144
representations, 191–2, 232, 289
resilience, 4, 6, 11, 53–4, 59, 62, 148, 150, 165, 266, 271, 273, 290
resiliency, 7, 90, 147–9
resources, 4, 25, 43, 53–6, 59–61, 79, 125–6, 132, 144, 148, 163, 166, 172–3, 176–7, 181, 209, 212, 260, 271, 286, 288
respond empathetically, 189
retirement, 269, 273
risk, 4, 21, 26, 44, 53, 60, 71, 92, 116, 128, 181, 191, 210, 247, 254, 287, 298
  behavior, 7–8, 135, 156–66, 190
  development, 9

risk-taking, 107, 114–5, 117, 135
risky behaviours, 12, 123, 126, 129, 135–50

SAFE approach, 59
school-based, 6, 52–3, 56–7, 61–2, 109
selection model, 138
self awareness, 53, 59, 306
self-esteem, 10, 22, 146, 148–9, 157, 160, 162, 166, 176, 179, 227–8, 237–8, 268, 274, 283
self-harm, 1, 7, 44, 109, 135, 155–6, 162
self-healing, 3
self-world distancing, 274–5
sensation seeking, 107, 117, 137, 141, 145, 149
separation anxiety, 193
sexual risk, 7, 137–40, 143, 146, 149
sexual trauma, 146, 158
shame, 15, 68–79
  and anxiety, 5, 69, 71, 73–9
single parent, 124, 128, 132, 143, 156, 177, 179, 198, 238
social
  awareness, 59
  constructivism, 10, 15, 245–6
  control, 144
  relationships, 15, 47, 82, 84–6, 88–9, 112, 136, 138, 147
social and emotional development, 52–3, 61–2
  emotional education, 54, 58
  emotional learning, 4, 52, 54, 55–8
social skills training, 3
social support, 46, 84, 108, 158, 165, 178–80, 182–3, 260, 273, 290
social work, 9, 25, 208, 213–6, 218, 226
sociocultural, 3, 11, 59, 228–9, 235, 259, 263–7
somatic states, 187
special education, 9, 208–10, 212–5, 218
spirituality, 6, 78, 81, 88–9, 128
spontaneity, 247, 257
stereotypes, 18
stigma, 15, 36, 39, 41–2, 43, 48, 54, 62, 109, 156, 286, 289
strategic thinking, 188
strengths, 5, 8, 10, 53–4, 58, 61, 69, 81–2, 88–92, 111, 113, 118, 128, 209, 215

subjective models, 14, 16–7, 26
subjective well-being, 81–3, 85–8, 126–7, 191
substance abuse, 109, 146, 234–8, 290
suicidal, 7–8, 44–6, 72, 146, 148
  attempt, 160, 164
  behaviour, 148, 154–66
  ideation, 7–8, 45, 155–6, 158, 160–1
survival mind, 245, 249
symptoms, 1, 4, 12, 20, 22, 24, 26, 34, 48, 90–1, 131, 136, 140, 147, 157, 161, 165, 178, 188, 190–1, 234, 297, 302–6
systemic therapy, 187

take sides, 188–9, 200
targeted intervention, 4–5, 53, 56–7, 60–2
teacher education, 57
temperament, 86, 94, 131, 136, 145
therapy, 2, 6, 8–10, 17, 19, 27, 36, 38, 44, 48, 69–70, 72–3, 77–9, 90–1, 94, 102, 106–10, 119, 164, 172–3, 187, 190, 195–6, 203–5, 244–57, 260, 272
thinking, 11, 43, 69–70, 104–5, 107, 139, 142, 154, 155, 159, 165, 187–8, 196, 201–2, 245–6, 261, 272, 303
transgenerational, 11
transitions, 11, 260–1, 264–6, 269
trauma, 7, 10–11, 18, 69, 76, 146–7, 158, 160, 197–99, 201, 235, 259–76
treatment, 2, 3, 14–15, 17, 19–20, 22–7, 38, 47–8, 91–2, 104, 106, 108–10, 150, 163–5, 172–5, 178, 180, 209, 233, 248, 261, 271, 274–5, 305
triangulation, 187–205

universal intervention, 4, 53, 60–2

values, 43, 45, 74, 77–9, 82, 103, 106–7, 110–11, 113, 117–8, 138, 166, 214, 216–7, 282–4
video gaming, 92–3
violence, 1, 5, 7, 70–4, 91, 93, 136, 138–9, 142–3, 146, 148, 154, 159, 161, 166, 203, 268, 282, 287
virtues, 82, 88
vision, 264, 300–1

vulnerable, 4, 40, 54–5, 78, 155, 160
vulnerable group, 7, 46, 156, 164, 218

warmth, 9–10, 83, 139, 176, 226–8, 233, 238
well-being, 52–60, 62–3, 81–94, 108–9, 123–33, 147, 172, 176–8, 179, 183, 187, 191, 218, 232, 237, 244, 298–9, 302–4, 306
western medicine, 33, 301
whole school approach, 53, 56, 58–61
willfulness, *see* violence
wounded healer, 38

Printed and bound by CPI Group (UK) Ltd, Croydon, CR0 4YY